PassExam

EA Review: Part 3 (Representation, Practice and Procedures)

The IRS Enrolled Agent Exam: 2010-2011 (New Edition)

Edward Mulwa. E.A., MST.

Copyright © 2010 SRH Media (All Rights Reserved)

This publication is designed to provide accurate and authoritative information in regard to the subject matter covered. It should not be used as a source for tax advice. No claim is made to original government works. However, within this publication, the following are subject to SRH Media copyright: (a) the gathering, compilation, and arrangement of such government materials, (b) the historical, statutory, and other notes/references, and (c) the commentary, and other materials.

Printed in the United States of America

TABLE OF CONTENTS

		Page
	INTRODUCTION	5

Unit 1 Contents:

1.01	AUTHORITY TO PRACTICE	12
1.02	ENROLLMENT TO PRACTICE BEFORE THE IRS	16
1.03	RULES OF PRACTICE	17
1.04	SANCTIONS FOR VIOLATION	25
1.05	DISCIPLINARY PROCEEDINGS	26
1.06	RENEWAL FOR ENROLLMENT TO PRACTICE	32
1.07	UNIT 1: QUESTIONS	38
1.08	UNIT 1: ANSWERS	68

Unit 2 Contents:

2.01	TAX RETURN PREPARER	96
2.02	PREPARER PENALTIES	100
2.03	TAXPAYER PENALTIES	113
2.04	EARNED INCOME TAX CREDIT (EITC)	132
2.05	UNIT 2: QUESTIONS	139
2.06	UNIT 2: ANSWERS	166

Unit 3 Contents:

3.01	UNIT DEFINITIONS	197
3.02	THIRD-PARTY AUTHORIZATION	198
3.03	POWER-OF-ATTORNEY (POA)	199
3.04	THE CENTRALIZED AUTHORIZATION FILE (CAF)	206
3.05	UNIT 3: QUESTIONS	209
3.06	UNIT 3: ANSWERS	226

Unit 4 Contents:

4.01	NOTICE OF UNDERREPORTED INCOME — CP-2000	243
4.02	THE COLLECTION PROCESS	243
4.03	AUTOMATED COLLECTION SYSTEM (ACS):	244
4.04	THE FEDERAL TAX LIEN	244
4.05	LEVY	246
4.06	BANKRUPTCY	249
4.07	INNOCENT SPOUSE RELIEF (INJURED SPOUSE)	250
4.08	INSTALLMENT AGREEMENT	252
4.09	OFFERS IN COMPROMISE	254
4.1	PERIOD FOR COLLECTION AFTER ASSESSMENT	256
4.11	TAXPAYER ADVOCATE SERVICE (TAS)	257
4.12	UNIT 4: QUESTIONS	259
4.13	UNIT 4: ANSWERS	271

Unit 5 Contents:

5.01	EXAMINATION OF RETURNS	284
5.02	APPEALS PROCESS	290
5.03	REFUNDS AND CREDIT	296
5.04	UNIT 5: QUESTIONS	300
5.05	UNIT 5: ANSWERS	315

Unit 6 Contents:

6.01	SOURCES OF TAX LAW	331
6.02	STATUTORY SOURCES	332
6.03	ADMINISTRATIVE SOURCES	333

6.04	JUDICIAL SOURCES	338
6.05	UNIT 6: QUESTIONS	341
6.06	UNIT 6: ANSWERS	351

Unit 7 Contents:

7.01	AUTHORIZED IRS E-FILE PROVIDER	351
7.02	E-FILE APPLICATION AND PARTICIPATION	360
7.03	SUITABILITY CHECK	361
7.04	RALS AND FEE RESTRICTIONS	364
7.05	RESPONSIBILITIES OF E-FILE PROVIDERS	365
7.06	ADVERTISING STANDARDS	368
7.07	SANCTIONS	368
7.08	E-FILE PROVIDER PENALTIES	371
7.09	RECORD-KEEPING	372
7.10	BASIC RECORDS	372
7.11	SPECIFIC RECORDS	374
7.12	HOW LONG TO KEEP RECORDS	376
7.13	BOOKKEEPING SYSTEM	377
7.14	UNIT 7: QUESTIONS	378
7.15	UNIT 7: ANSWERS	390

INTRODUCTION

ABOUT THE ENROLLED AGENT EXAMINATION

Special Enrollment Examination (SEE)

Generally, passing the Special Enrollment Examination (SEE) enables an individual to become an enrolled agent through demonstrating special competence in tax matters. Those who pass the SEE also undergo an additional background check before enrollment.

An <u>Enrolled Agent</u> (E.A.) is a person who has earned the privilege of practicing before the IRS. Enrolled agents, like attorneys and certified public accountants (CPAs), can represent taxpayers in both examinations and collection matters. There are currently about 40,000 active Enrolled Agents.

In 2006, Thomson Prometric was selected to develop and administer the new computer-based version of the Special Enrollment Examination (SEE) on behalf of the IRS. Initially, the exam used to be administered in four parts.

The examination now contains <u>three</u> parts. The length of each part is 3.5 hours (not including the pre-examination tutorial and post-examination survey). The parts of the examination are:
- **SEE Part 1** – Individuals
- **SEE Part 2** – Businesses (Sole Proprietorships, Partnerships, C and S Corporations, Fiduciaries, Estate and Gift Tax, and Trusts)
- **SEE Part 3** – Representation, Practices and Procedures (Ethics, Recordkeeping Procedures, Appeal Procedures, etc.)

Testing Window

The current testing window for the Enrolled Agent examination is from May 1, 2010 through February 28, 2011. Information to be tested on will be based on the 2009 tax laws. This new **PassExam EA Review 2010 – 2011 (New Edition)** is designed for the current testing window of May 1, 2010 through February 28, 2011.

Registration Process

Candidates who wish to register for the examination must first have a Preparer Tax Identification Number (PTIN) which can be applied through <u>www.irs.gov</u> for a fee of $64.25, beginning on September 2010.

To register for an examination, you must complete Form 2587 by using one of the three following options:
1. Online
   Completing Form 2587 online is considered an "express registration." This is the only way to register and schedule an examination in the same day.
   To register and schedule an examination online, follow these steps:
   - Access **www.prometric.com/irs** and click **Register for your test**.
   - If it's your first time, click **Create Account** to set up your user ID and password.
   - Complete the registration process by clicking on **Scheduling**.

2. By fax to 800.347.9242
   - Fax your completed Form 2587 to Prometric at 800.347.9242.
   - Wait one full calendar day before scheduling an examination appointment.

3. By mail
   - Mail your completed Form 2587 to:
     Prometric
     Attn: IRS Special Enrollment Examination
     1260 Energy Lane
     St. Paul, MN 55108
   - Wait six to 10 calendar days for delivery and processing before scheduling an examination appointment.

Scheduling Your Examination

Candidates may take each part of the examination at their convenience. Consequently, parts do not have to be taken on the same day, or on consecutive days.

Candidates may take examination parts:
- Up to four times each during May 1, 2010 to February 28, 2011.
- Up to four times each during May 1, 2011 to February 29, 2012.

Once your registration has been processed, you can schedule an examination appointment at any time online at **www.prometric.com/irs** or by calling 800.306.3926 between 8 a.m. and 8 p.m. (Eastern time), Monday through Friday.

You will be provided a number confirming your appointment. Record and keep this confirmation number for your records—you will need it to reschedule, cancel or change your appointment in any way.

You must schedule your exam within **one year** from the date your registration form has been processed by Prometric. Testing is not available in the months of March and April.

Examination Locations

The Examinations are administered by computer at Prometric testing centers. Currently, the Special Enrollment Examination is given at nearly 300 Prometric testing centers located across the United States and internationally. Test centers are located in most major metropolitan areas.

A complete list of these testing centers, addresses and driving directions is located at **www.prometric.com/irs.** In the box titled **Do More**, click on "Continue" and select your preferred test location. Most locations are open on Saturdays and some locations are open on Sundays and evenings.

Testing Fees

The testing fee is **$101** for each part of the examination. This fee is paid at the time you schedule your examination. Accepted forms of payment include: MasterCard, Visa, American Express, Discover, Diner's Club cards bearing the MasterCard symbol and JCB. Electronic checks are also accepted when scheduling by phone. Money orders, paper checks and cash are <u>not</u> accepted. Examination testing fees are <u>not</u> refundable or transferable.

Rescheduling Your Testing Appointment

If you need to reschedule an examination for another date, time or location, you must contact Prometric. Rescheduling fees will apply as follows:
- **No fee** if you reschedule at least **30 calendar days** prior to your appointment date.
- **$35 fee** if you reschedule **five to 29 calendar days** before your appointment date.
- **Another $101 full examination fee** if you reschedule **less than five calendar days** before your appointment date.

Rescheduling an exam must be done online at **www.prometric.com/irs** or by calling 800.306.3926. You cannot reschedule an examination by fax, e-mail or voicemail. If you miss your appointment or arrive late and are not allowed to test, your entire examination fee will be forfeited and you must pay $101 to schedule a new appointment.

Testing Center Procedures

Your examination will be given by computer at a Prometric testing center. You do not need any computer experience or typing skill to take your examination. Before you start the examination, you will receive a personalized introduction to the testing system. You can also take a pre-examination tutorial if you wish.

You should arrive at the testing center at least **30 minutes before** your scheduled examination appointment. When you arrive, you will be required to sign a signature log and have your photo taken electronically. You will also be asked to place a finger on a scanner that will generate a temporary digital representation of your fingerprint.

The date and time you enter and exit the exam room will be recorded and the signature log will be verified against your electronic photo and the digital fingerprint.
The fingerprint template is permanently erased within 48 hours after your test is completed.

Identification Required

You must present a valid, non-expired form of identification before you can test. That identification document **must**:
- Be government-issued (e.g., driver's license, passport, state-issued identification card or military identification card)
- Contain **both** a current photo and your signature (if it does not, you must present two identification cards: one with your photo and one with your signature)
- Have a name that exactly matches the name used to register for the examination (including designations such as "Jr." and "III")

Testing Regulations

To ensure that all candidates are tested under equally favorable conditions, the following regulations and procedures will be observed at each testing center. Failure to follow any of these security procedures may result in the disqualification of your examination and forfeiture of testing fees.

References - No reference materials, papers or study materials are allowed at the test center.
If you are found with these or any other aids, you will not be allowed to continue the examination and your answers will not be scored. Candidates will not be able to leave the testing room with a copy of any

notes taken during the exam. Some examination questions may contain excerpts from the Internal Revenue Code or Income Tax Regulations.

Calculators - Candidates will be able to use an onscreen calculator during the exam. Prometric will furnish each candidate with a handheld calculator that is silent, solar or battery-operated and nonprogrammable (without paper tape-printing capabilities or alphabetic keypads). Candidates **are not allowed** to bring their own calculators.

Personal Items - Prometric is not responsible for items left in the reception area of the testing center. While lockers are provided, it is recommended that personal items not be brought into the testing center. Note the following:
- Electronic equipment—cameras, tape recorders, cell phones, PDAs, pagers, etc.—is not permitted in the testing room and must be powered off while stored in a locker.
- Pocket items—keys, wallet, etc.—must remain in your pocket or be stored in a locker during testing.
- Other personal items—watches, outerwear that is not being worn while testing (sweater, jacket, etc.), briefcases, purses, etc.—are not permitted in the testing room.
- Food and drink, including water, are not allowed in the testing room.

Breaks - If you leave the testing room while an examination is in progress, you must sign out/in on the roster and you will lose examination time. You are not allowed to use any electronic devices or phones during breaks.

Visitors - No guests, visitors or family members are allowed at the testing center.

Misconduct or disruptive behavior - Candidates who engage in any kind of misconduct or disruptive or offensive behavior may be dismissed from the examination. Examples are: giving or receiving help, taking part in an act of impersonation, removing test materials or notes from the testing room, using rude or offensive language and behavior that delays or interrupts testing.

Weapons - Weapons are not allowed at the testing center. Test center administrators are not allowed to answer any questions pertaining to the examination content. If you do not understand a question on the examination, you should answer the question to the best of your ability.

Question Types
The questions on the Enrolled Agent examination are multiple-choice questions. Each provides four options (A through D) from which you choose your answer. Three different multiple-choice formats are used. Each format is shown in the following examples.

Format 1—Direct Question
Which of the following entities are required to file Form 709, United States Gift Tax Return?
   A. An individual
   B. An estate or trust
   C. A corporation
   D. All of the above

Format 2— Incomplete Sentence

Supplemental wages are compensation paid in addition to an employee's regular wages. They **do not** include payments for:
- A. A. Accumulated sick leave
- B. B. Nondeductible moving expenses
- C. C. Vacation pay
- D. D. Travel reimbursements paid at the Federal Government per diem rate

Format 3—All of the Following Except

There are five tests which must be met for you to claim an exemption for a dependent. Which of the following is **not** a requirement?
- A. A. Citizen or Resident Test
- B. B. Member of Household or Relationship Test
- C. C. Disability Test
- D. D. Joint Return Test

Experimental Questions – The Enrolled Agent examination may include some experimental questions that will not be scored. If present, they are distributed throughout the examination and will not be identified as such. These are used to gather statistical information on the questions before they are added to the examination as scored items. These experimental questions will not be counted for or against you in your final examination score.

Examination Results

Scores will be shown on screen at the end of your examination and you will receive a printed score report. Examination scores are confidential and will be revealed only to you and the IRS.

Scaled scores are determined by calculating the number of questions answered correctly from the total number of questions in the examination and converting to a scale that ranges from **40** to **130**. The IRS has set the scaled passing score at **105**, which corresponds to a minimum level of knowledge deemed acceptable by those persons who will be practicing before the IRS.

Fail - If you fail, your score report will show a scaled score between **40** and **104**. You will also receive diagnostic information to assist you with future examination preparation. Diagnostic information will show an indicator of 1, 2, or 3 meaning:

(1) Considerably below the minimally acceptable score. It is important for you to approach how you study this topic as you prepare to take the test again. You may want to consider taking a course or participating actively in a study group on this topic.

(2) Marginally below the minimally acceptable score. You should study this topic in detail as you prepare to take the test again.

(3) At or above the minimally acceptable score. Be sure to review this topic as you prepare to take the test again.

You must reschedule and pass any parts of the examination you failed prior to applying for enrollment.

Pass - If you pass, the score report will only show a passing designation. It will not show a score. All score values above passing indicate that a candidate *is* qualified - not *how* qualified. When you pass all three parts of the examination, you should file Form 23, Application for Enrollment to Practice Before the Internal Revenue Service.

Sample Test Score Report

> Score Report for, John Doe.
>
> **Special Enrollment Examination - PART 3: Representation, Practices and Procedures**
>
> Scaled
>
> Topic Area   Marginally below the minimally acceptably score
>
> Grade: **Fail**
> (A total score of 105 is required to pass)

Rescheduling Failed Examination Parts

Candidates do not need to take more than one part of the examination (SEE 1, SEE 2 or SEE 3) on the same day or consecutive days. Between the May 1 and February 28 test window, candidates may take each part of the examination up to four times. If a candidate fails any part of the examination, he or she must re-register with Prometric online at **www.prometric.com/irs** or by calling 800.306.3926.

Candidates who do not pass a part of the examination after four attempts during the May 1 to February 28 test window must wait until the next test window before attempting to retake any failed part of the examination again.

Carryover of Scores

Candidates who pass a part of the examination under the new format can carryover passing scores up to two years from the date the candidate took the examination. For example, let's assume a candidate takes and passes part 1 on November 15, 2010. Subsequently the candidate takes and passes part 2 on February 15, 2011. That individual has until November 14, 2012 to pass, the remaining part otherwise he/she loses credit for part 1. On February 14, 2013, if that individual still has not passed all other parts of the examination, he/she loses credit for part 2.

Feedback

Candidates will be surveyed at the conclusion of the examination, which will allow an opportunity to provide both Prometric and the IRS with feedback on the examination questions or the testing experience. While your comments are considered, you will not receive a response to your survey comments. Alternatively, candidates who wish to receive a written response can make an official written request. The request must include your name, PTIN number, the examination title, the date you tested and the details of your concern, including all relevant facts. Be sure to include your return address. Mail your letter to:

> Prometric
> ATTN: SEE Feedback
> 1260 Energy Lane
> St. Paul, MN 55108

Applying for enrollment

After passing all 3 parts of the examination, you must file Form 23, Application for Enrollment to

Practice Before the Internal Revenue Service, within one year of the date you passed all parts of the examination. Form 23 is available online at **www.irs.gov**, click on "tax professionals" and then click on "enrolled agents." Copies of the score report do not need to be submitted to the IRS when submitting your application for enrollment (Form 23). The IRS's Office of Professional Responsibility will process, review and act on your application for enrollment.

As part of the evaluation of your enrollment application, the Office of Professional Responsibility will conduct a background check that will include a review of any tax compliance issues you may have, including failure to timely file and pay, penalties, etc.

UNIT 1: PRACTICE BEFORE THE IRS

Unit 1 Contents:
1.01 AUTHORITY TO PRACTICE
1.02 ENROLLMENT TO PRACTICE BEFORE THE IRS
1.03 RULES OF PRACTICE
1.04 SANCTIONS FOR VIOLATION
1.05 DISCIPLINARY PROCEEDINGS
1.06 RENEWAL FOR ENROLLMENT TO PRACTICE
1.07 UNIT 1: QUESTIONS
1.08 UNIT 1: ANSWERS

1.01 AUTHORITY TO PRACTICE

Practice before the IRS encompasses all matters connected with presentation to the IRS (IRS) or any of its personnel relating to a taxpayer's rights, privileges, or liabilities under laws or regulations administered by the IRS. Such presentations include:
   (a) The preparation and filing of necessary documents.
   (b) Correspondence with and communications to the IRS.
   (c) The representation of a taxpayer at conferences, hearings, and meetings.

Circular No. 230 is a Treasury Department Circular that sets forth the regulations governing practice before the IRS. These regulations in Circular 230 governing the practice of attorneys, certified public accountants, enrolled agents, enrolled actuaries and appraisers before the IRS are found under *Title 31 Code of Federal Regulations, Subtitle A, Part 10.* The circular also contains rules regarding eligibility to become an enrolled agent and renewal of enrollment.

What Is Practice Before the IRS?

Practice before the IRS covers all matters relating to any of the following:
   (1) Communicating with the IRS for a taxpayer regarding the taxpayer's rights, privileges, or liabilities under laws and regulations administered by the IRS.
   (2) Representing a taxpayer at conferences, hearings, or meetings with the IRS.
   (3) Preparing and filing documents with the IRS for a taxpayer.
   (4) Corresponding and communicating with the IRS

Just preparing a tax return, furnishing information at the request of the IRS, or appearing as a witness for the taxpayer is not practice before the IRS. These acts can be performed by anyone.

An income tax return preparer is defined as person (including a partnership or corporation) who prepares for *compensation* all or a substantial portion of a tax return or claim for refund under the income tax provisions of the Code.

Recognized Representatives

A recognized representative is an individual that meets the following three criteria:
1) Is appointed as an *attorney-in-fact* under a power of attorney.
2) Files a declaration of representative
3) Is one of the following:
    (a) Attorney, Certified public accountant (CPA), Enrolled agent, Enrolled actuary, Any individual who is granted temporary recognition by the Director of Practice
    (b) Any individual authorized to represent a taxpayer with whom a special relationship exists
    (c) Unenrolled return preparer actuary who prepares and signs a taxpayer's return as the preparer, or who prepares a return but is not required (by the instructions to the return or regulations) to sign the return.

A. **Attorneys and CPAs** - Any attorney or CPA who is not currently under suspension or disbarment from practice may practice before the IRS by filing a written declaration that the attorney or CPA is currently qualified and is authorized to represent the party or parties. An attorney or a CPA means any person who is duly qualified to practice as an attorney or CPA in any state, territory, or possession of the United States, including a Commonwealth, or the District of Columbia.

B. **Enrolled Agents** - An Enrolled agent is any individual, other that an attorney or CPA, that is enrolled to practice before the IRS and is in good standing i.e. not currently under suspension or disbarment from practice before the IRS. Enrolled agents, like attorneys and CPAs, are not restricted as to which taxpayers they can represent, what types of tax matters they can handle, and which IRS offices they can practice before.

C. **Unenrolled Return Preparers.** An unenrolled return preparer is an individual other than an attorney, CPA, enrolled agent, or enrolled actuary who prepares and signs a taxpayer's return as the preparer, or who prepares a return but is not required (by the instructions to the return or regulations) to sign the return.

An unenrolled return preparer is permitted to appear as a representative only before customer service representatives, revenue agents, and examination officers, with respect to an examination regarding the return he or she prepared.

An unenrolled return preparer **cannot:**
   a) Represent a taxpayer before other offices of the IRS, such as Collection or Appeals. This includes the Automated Collection System (ACS) unit.
   b) Execute closing agreements.
   c) Extend the statutory period for tax assessments or collection of tax.
   d) Execute waivers.

e) Execute claims for refund.
   f) Receive refund checks.
   g) Take any acknowledgements, oaths, or certification as a Notary Public relating to any tax return, protest, or other document that the preparer has prepared or that the preparer has assisted in preparing.
D. **Enrolled Actuaries** – Must be enrolled as an actuary by the Joint Board for the Enrollment of Actuaries and must not currently be under suspension or disbarment from practice before the IRS. Practice as an enrolled actuary is limited to issues involving the following categories:
   (a) employee plans
   (b) annuity plans
   (c) deductibility of employer contributions
   (d) qualification of bond purchase plans
   (e) collectively bargained plans
   (f) treatment of funded welfare benefits
   (g) qualified asset accounts
   (h) transfers of excess pension assets to retiree health accounts
   (i) excise taxes payable as a result of an accumulated funding deficiency
   (j) deferred compensation
   (k) pension plans
   (l) nonqualified plans

Unenrolled Agents

The IRS may authorize an individual to represent a taxpayer with whom a special relationship exists. The following unenrolled people may be authorized to represent an individual or entity before the IRS:
A. **Employee** - An employee. A regular full-time employee can represent his or her employer. An employer can be, but is not limited to, an individual, partnership, corporation (including a parent, subsidiary, or other affiliated corporation), association, trust, receivership, guardianship, estate, organized group, governmental unit, agency, or authority.
B. **Family** - An individual can represent members of his or her immediate family. Immediate family means a spouse, child, parent, brother, or sister of the individual.
C. **Corporation** – A bona fide officer of a corporation (including a parent, subsidiary, or other affiliated corporation), association, or organized group can represent the corporation, association, or organized group. An officer of a governmental unit, agency, or authority, in the course of his or her official duties, can represent the organization before the IRS.
D. **Unenrolled Return Preparers** - Unenrolled return preparers are limited to representation of a taxpayer before revenue agents and examining officers of the Examination Division in the offices of District Director with respect to the tax liability of the taxpayer for the taxable year or period covered by a return prepared by the unenrolled return preparer.
E. **Partnership** – A general partner may represent a partnership.

F. **Fiduciary** – A trustee, receiver, guardian, administrator, executor stands in the position of a taxpayer and acts as the taxpayer, NOT as a representative.
G. **Others** – In general an individual who is granted temporary recognition by the Director of Practice may represent a taxpayer on specific matters even if the taxpayer is not present, provided the individual presents satisfactory identification and proof of his or her authority to represent the taxpayer.
H. **Representing one-self** - Individuals may appear on their own behalf before the IRS provided they present satisfactory identification. The individual does not have to file a written declaration of qualification and authority.

Persons Ineligible to Practice before the IRS

Generally, the following individuals are not permitted to practice before the IRS under circular 230 and publication 470:

(a) Government officers and employees of the executive, legislative, or judicial branch of the United States Government.
(b) An officer or employee of the District of Columbia.
(c) A Member of Congress.
(d) A Resident Commissioner.
(e) State officers and employees whose duties require them to pass upon, investigate, or deal with tax matters for such State or subdivision, may not practice before the IRS, if such employment may disclose facts or information applicable to Federal tax matters.
(f) Former Government employee who personally and substantially participated in a particular matter involving specific parties may not represent or knowingly assist such parties in that particular tax matter, after being separated from government employment.
(g) Any individual who has been convicted of any criminal offense under the Revenue Laws of the United States or any offense involving dishonesty or breach of trust.
(h) Any individual who is under disbarment or suspension from practice as an attorney, CPA, PA, or actuary.
(i) Any individual who is disbarred or suspended from practice before the IRS.
(j) Corporations, associations, partnerships, or other business entities are ineligible to practice.
(k) Any individual whose application for enrollment to practice before the IRS has been denied.

Assistance from Disbarred or Suspended Persons

According to circular 230, a practitioner may not, knowingly and directly or indirectly accept assistance from or assist any person who is under disbarment or suspension from practice before the IRS or from any former government employee where the provisions in circular 230 or any federal law would be violated.

1.02 ENROLLMENT TO PRACTICE BEFORE THE IRS

The Director of the Office of Professional Responsibility will issue an enrollment card to each individual whose application for enrollment to practice before the IRS is approved. An enrolled agent must send notification of any change of address to the address specified by the Director of the Office of Professional Responsibility. This notification must include the enrolled agent's:

(1) Name
(2) Prior address
(3) New address
(4) Social security number or tax identification number
(5) Date

There are two way of becoming an enrolled agent:
1) Written examination
2) IRS experience

- **Form 2587** - Applicants can apply to take the special enrollment examination (SEE) by filing Form 2587.
- **Form 23** - Individuals who have passed the examination or are applying on the basis of past service and technical experience with the IRS can apply for enrollment by filing Form 23 (*Application for Enrollment to Practice before the IRS*)
- **Form 8554** - Applicants for renewal of enrollment must file Form 8554 (*Application for Renewal of Enrollment to Practice before the IRS*). To qualify for renewal, applicants must complete the necessary hours of continuing professional education during each 3-year enrollment cycle.

Appeal for Denial of Application - The Director of the Office of Professional Responsibility must inform the applicant as to the reason(s) for any denial of an application for enrollment. The applicant may, within 30 days after receipt of the notice of denial of enrollment, file a written appeal of the denial of enrollment with the Secretary of the Treasury or his or her delegate.

Temporary Recognition - On receipt of a properly executed application, the Director of the Office of Professional Responsibility may grant the applicant temporary recognition to practice pending a determination as to whether enrollment to practice should be granted.

Fee - A reasonable nonrefundable fee will be charged for each application for enrollment as an enrolled agent filed with the Director of the Office of Professional Responsibility.

1.03 RULES OF PRACTICE

An attorney, CPA, enrolled agent, or enrolled actuary authorized to practice before the IRS has the duty to perform certain acts and is restricted from performing other acts. These practitioners cannot engage in disreputable conduct, otherwise they would be subject to disciplinary action.

Duties

Practitioners must promptly submit records or information requested by officers or employees of the IRS. When the Office of Professional Responsibility requests information concerning possible violations of the regulations by other parties, the practitioner must provide the information and be prepared to testify in disbarment or suspension proceedings. A practitioner can be exempted from these rules if he or she believes in good faith and on reasonable grounds that the information requested is privileged or that the request is of doubtful legality.

Confidentiality Privilege

The confidentiality protection for certain communications between a taxpayer and an attorney (also known as privileged communications) applies to similar communications between a taxpayer and any federally authorized tax practitioner. Federally authorized tax practitioners include attorneys, certified public accountants, enrolled agents, enrolled actuaries, and certain other individuals allowed to practice before the IRS. This confidentiality privilege cannot be used in any administrative proceeding with an agency other than the IRS.

Communications Protected Under the Confidentiality Protection

The confidentiality protection applies to communications that would be considered privileged if they were between the taxpayer and an attorney and that relate to:
a) Noncriminal tax matters before the IRS, or
b) Noncriminal tax proceedings brought in federal court by or against the United States.

Protection of tax advice communications does not apply to any written communications between a federally authorized tax practitioner and a director, shareholder, officer, employee, agent, or representative of a corporation. It also does not apply if the communication involves the promotion of the direct or indirect participation of the corporation in any tax shelter.

Knowledge of Client's Omission

A practitioner who knows that his or her client has not complied with the revenue laws or has made an error or omission in any return, document, affidavit, or other required paper, has the responsibility to advise the client promptly of the noncompliance, error, or omission, and the consequences of the noncompliance, error, or omission.

Due diligence
A practitioner must exercise due diligence when performing the following duties:
1. Preparing or assisting in the preparing, approving, and filing of returns, documents, affidavits, and other papers relating to IRS matters.
2. Determining the correctness of oral or written representations made by him or her to the Department of the Treasury.
3. Determining the correctness of oral or written representations made by him or her to clients with reference to any matter administered by the IRS.

Reliance on Others - a practitioner will be presumed to have exercised due if the practitioner relies on the work product of another person and the practitioner used reasonable care in engaging, supervising, training, and evaluating the person, taking proper account of the nature of the relationship between the practitioner and the person.

Performance as a Notary
A practitioner who is a notary public and is employed as counsel, attorney, or agent in a matter before the IRS, or has a material interest in any tax matters, cannot engage in any notary activities related to that matter.

Negotiations of Taxpayer Refund Checks
Practitioners who are income tax return preparers may not endorse or otherwise negotiate (cash) any refund check issued to the taxpayer.

Fees
In general, a practitioner may not charge an unconscionable (excessive) fee in connection with any matter before the IRS.

Contingent Fees - A contingent fee includes a fee that is based on a percentage of the refund reported on a return, or on a percentage of the taxes saved, or fee that depends on specific result being attained. A contingent fee also includes any fee arrangement in which the practitioner will reimburse the client for all or a portion of the client's fee in the event that a position taken on a tax return or other filing is challenged by the IRS or is not sustained.

A practitioner may not charge a contingent fee for preparing an original tax return or for any advice rendered in connection with a position taken or to be taken on an original tax return.

A contingent fee may be charged for preparation of or advice in connection with an amended tax return or a claim for refund (other than a claim for refund made on an original tax return), but only if the practitioner reasonably anticipates at the time the fee arrangement is entered into that the amended tax return or refund claim will receive substantive review by the IRS.

Circular 230 permits charge of contingent fee in the following situations:
1) A practitioner may charge a contingent fee for services rendered in connection with the Service's examination of, or challenge to
   a) An original tax return, or
   b) An amended return or claim for refund or credit where the amended return or claim for refund or credit was filed within 120 days of the taxpayer receiving a written notice of the examination of, or a written challenge to the original tax return.
2) A practitioner may charge a contingent fee for services rendered in connection with a claim for credit or refund filed solely in connection with the determination of statutory interest or penalties assessed by the IRS.
3) A practitioner may charge a contingent fee for services rendered in connection with any judicial proceeding arising under the IRS.

Fee Information - Practitioners are allowed to publish the availability of a written schedule of fees and disseminate the following fee information:
   (a) Fixed fees for specific routine services.
   (b) Hourly rates.
   (c) Range of fees for particular services.
   (d) Fee charged for an initial consultation.

Any statement of fee information in which costs may be incurred must include a statement disclosing whether clients will be responsible for such costs. A practitioner may not charge more than the published rates within 30 calendar days from date the written schedule of fees was published. Fee information may be communicated in professional lists, telephone directories, print media, mailings, and electronic mail, facsimile, hand delivered flyers, radio, television, and any other method.

Records of the Client

A practitioner must (at the request of a client) promptly return any and all records of the client that are necessary for the client to comply with his or her Federal tax obligations, even if there is a dispute over fees between the practitioner and the client. However, the practitioner may retain copies of the records returned to a client.

Records of the client' is defined as:
   (1) All written or electronic material that was provided to the practitioner in the course of the practitioner's representation of the client
   (2) All Materials that were prepared by the client or a third party (not to include an employee or agent of the practitioner) at any time and provided to the practitioner with respect to the subject matter of the representation.

(3) Any return, claim for refund, schedule, affidavit, appraisal or any other document prepared by the practitioner, or his or her employee or agent, that was presented to the client with respect to a prior representation if such document is necessary for the taxpayer to comply with his or her current Federal tax obligations.

Conflict of Interests

A practitioner is not allowed to represent a client before the IRS if the representation involves a conflict of interest. A conflict of interest exists if:
- (a) The representation of one client will be directly adverse to another client, or
- (b) There is a significant risk that the representation of one or more clients will be materially limited by the practitioner's responsibilities to another client, a former client or a third person, or by a personal interest of the practitioner.

However, the practitioner may represent a client if the following conditions are met:
1. The practitioner reasonably believes that the practitioner will be able to provide competent and diligent representation to each affected client.
2. The representation is not prohibited by law.
3. Each affected client waives the conflict of interest and gives informed consent, confirmed in writing by each affected client, at the time the existence of the conflict of interest is known by the practitioner. The confirmation may be made within a reasonable period of time after the informed consent, but not later than 30 days.

Copies of the written consents must be retained by the practitioner for at least 36 months from the date of the conclusion of the representation of the affected clients, and the written consents must be provided to any officer or employee of the IRS upon request.

Advertising and Solicitation

Advertising and solicitation by practitioners is permitted by circular 230, however, several restrictions exist:
1) A practitioner may not use solicitation containing a false, fraudulent, or coercive statement or claim.
2) Enrolled agents are not allowed to use the term *'certified'* or imply an employer/employee relationship with the IRS when describing their professional designation. However, the following descriptions are acceptable for enrolled agents:
   - a) Enrolled to represent taxpayers before the IRS
   - b) Enrolled to practice before the IRS
   - c) Admitted to practice before IRS

Solicitation Rules - A practitioner may not persist in attempting to contact a prospective client if the prospective client has made it known to the practitioner that he or she does not desire to be solicited.

Radio and television broadcasts must be recorded and the practitioner must retain a recording of the actual transmission. In the case of direct mail and e-commerce communications, the practitioner must retain a copy of the actual communication, along with a list of persons to whom the communication was mailed or distributed. The copy must be retained by the practitioner for a period of at least 36 months (3 years) from the date of the last transmission or use.

Targeted direct mail solicitation is direct mail campaign targeted to *non-clients* whose unique situation would be the main reason for the solicitation.

Documents, Affidavits and Other Papers
The following are restrictions imposed on practitioners in regard to tax returns, documents, affidavits and other papers:
1. A practitioner may not advise a client to take a position on a document, affidavit or other paper submitted to the IRS unless the position is not frivolous.
2. A practitioner may not advise a client to submit a document, affidavit or other paper to the IRS that:
    a) The purpose of which is to delay or impede the administration of the Federal tax laws
    b) That is frivolous
    c) That contains or omits information in a manner that demonstrates an intentional disregard of a rule or regulation unless the practitioner also advises the client to submit a document that evidences a good faith challenge to the rule or regulation.

Advising Clients on Potential Penalties
A practitioner is required to inform a client of any penalties that may apply to the client with respect to the following situations:
   a) A position taken on a tax return if the practitioner advised the client with respect to the position taken
   b) The practitioner prepared or signed the tax return
   c) Any document, affidavit or other paper submitted to the IRS

Covered Opinions
A covered opinion is written advice (including electronic communications) by a practitioner concerning one or more Federal tax issues arising from:
1. A transaction that is similar to a transaction that, at the time the advice is rendered, the IRS has determined to be a tax avoidance transaction and identified by published guidance.

2. Any partnership or other entity, any investment plan or arrangement, or any other plan or arrangement, the principal purpose of which is the avoidance or evasion of any tax imposed by the Internal Revenue Code.
3. Any partnership or other entity, any investment plan or arrangement, or any other plan or arrangement, *a significant purpose* of which is the avoidance or evasion of any tax imposed by the Internal Revenue Code if the written advice:
    a) Is a reliance opinion.
    b) Is a marketed opinion.
    c) Is subject to conditions of confidentiality.
    d) Is subject to contractual protection.

4. Written advice provided to an employer by a practitioner in that practitioner's capacity as an employee of that employer solely for purposes of determining the tax liability of the employer.
5. Written advice that does not resolve a Federal tax issue in the taxpayer's favor, unless the advice reaches a favorable conclusion to the taxpayer at any confidence level (e.g., not frivolous, realistic possibility of success, reasonable basis or substantial authority) with respect to that issue.

1. **A Reliance Opinion** – Written advice is a *reliance opinion* if the advice has more than 50 % likelihood that one or more significant Federal tax issues would be resolved in the taxpayer's favor. Written advice is not treated as a *reliance opinion* if the practitioner discloses in the written advice that it was not intended or written by the practitioner to be used, and that it cannot be used by the taxpayer, for the purpose of avoiding penalties that may be imposed on the taxpayer.

2. **A Marketed Opinion** – Written advice is a *marketed opinion* if the practitioner knows or has reason to know that the written advice will be used by a person other than the practitioner, in promoting, marketing or recommending a partnership or other entity, investment plan or arrangement to one or more taxpayers. Written advice is not treated as a *marketed opinion* if the practitioner discloses in the written advice that it was not intended or written by the practitioner to be used, and that it cannot be used by the taxpayer, for the purpose of avoiding penalties that may be imposed on the taxpayer.

3. **Conditions of Confidentiality** – Written advice is subject to *conditions of confidentiality* if the practitioner imposes a limitation on disclosure of the tax treatment or tax structure of the transaction on one or more recipients of the written advice, and the limitation on disclosure protects the confidentiality of that practitioner's tax strategies, regardless of whether the limitation on disclosure is legally binding.

4. **Contractual Protection** – Written advice is subject to contractual protection if the taxpayer has the right to a full or partial refund of fees paid to the practitioner if all

or a part of the intended tax consequences from the matters addressed in the written advice are not sustained, or if the fees paid to the practitioner are contingent on the taxpayer's realization of tax benefits from the transaction.

Federal tax issue – A Federal tax issue is a question concerning the Federal tax treatment of an item of income, gain, loss, deduction, or credit, the existence or absence of a taxable transfer of property, or the value of property for Federal tax purposes.

Requirements for Covered Opinions
A practitioner providing a covered opinion must comply with each of the following requirements:
1) Use reasonable efforts to identify and ascertain the facts. The practitioner must not base the opinion on any unreasonable factual assumptions.
2) The opinion must relate the applicable law.
3) The practitioner must not assume a favorable resolution of any significant Federal tax issue.
4) The opinion must not contain internally inconsistent legal analyses or conclusions.
5) The opinion must consider *all* significant Federal tax issues.
6) The opinion must provide the practitioner's conclusion as to the likelihood that the taxpayer will prevail on the merits with respect to each significant Federal tax issue considered in the opinion. If the practitioner is unable to reach a conclusion with respect to one or more of those issues, the opinion must state that the practitioner is unable to reach a conclusion with respect to those issues. The opinion must describe the reasons for the conclusions, including the facts and analysis supporting the conclusions, or describe the reasons that the practitioner is unable to reach a conclusion as to one or more issues.
7) The opinion must provide the practitioner's overall conclusion as to the likelihood that the Federal tax treatment of the transaction or matter that is the subject of the opinion is the proper treatment and the reasons for that conclusion. If the practitioner is unable to reach an overall conclusion, the opinion must state that the practitioner is unable to reach and overall conclusion and describe the reasons for the practitioner's inability to reach a conclusion.
8) An opinion must disclose the existence of any compensation arrangement, such as a referral fee or a fee-sharing arrangement, between the practitioner and any person with respect to promotions, marketing, or recommendations of the entity, plan, or arrangement that is the subject of the opinion.

Tax Return Positions
- A practitioner may not sign a tax return as a preparer or advise a client to take a position on a tax return if the practitioner determines that the tax return or the position on a tax return co a position that does not have a realistic possibility of

being sustained on its merits (the realistic possibility standard) <u>unless</u> the position is not frivolous and is adequately disclosed to the IRS.
- A practitioner advising a client to take a position on a tax return, or preparing or signing a tax return as a preparer, generally may rely in good faith without verification upon information furnished by the client. The practitioner may not, however, ignore the implications of information furnished to, or actually known by the practitioner, and must make reasonable inquiries if the information as furnished appears to be incorrect, inconsistent with an important fact or another factual assumption, or incomplete.
- A practitioner advising a client to take a position on a tax return, or preparing or signing a tax return as a preparer, generally may rely in good faith without verification upon information furnished by the client. The practitioner may not, however, ignore the implications of information furnished to, or actually known by, the practitioner, and must make reasonable inquiries if the information as furnished appears to be incorrect, inconsistent with an important fact or another factual assumption, or incomplete.

Realistic Possibility Standard
A position has a realistic possibility of being sustained if a reasonable and well-informed analysis by a person knowledgeable in tax law would lead such a person to conclude that the position has approximately a one-in-three, or greater, likelihood of being sustained on its merits.

For signing preparers, the relevant date for determining realistic possibility is generally the date the preparer signs and dates the return. The relevant date for non-signing preparers is generally the date, based on all the facts and circumstances, that the preparer provides the advice.

For positions contrary to a revenue ruling or a notice but which satisfy the realistic possibility standard, a preparer will not be considered to have recklessly or intentionally disregarded a revenue ruling or a notice if the position contrary to the revenue ruling or notice satisfies the realistic possibility standard. This rule also does not apply to a position contrary to a regulation.

Section 7525
Section 7525 provides a privilege of confidentiality for communications between a taxpayer and a *federally authorized tax practitioner* that has essentially the same scope as the federal attorney-client privilege. The privilege applies only to communications related to *tax advice*. Tax Advice is defined as advice given by a federally authorized tax practitioner with respect to a matter that is within the scope of the practitioner's authority to practice before the IRS. The taxpayer must assert the confidentiality privilege because it is not automatic.

Section 7525 confidentiality privilege does **not** protect the following situations:

1) Information disclosed to a tax practitioner for the purpose of preparing a return.
2) Criminal tax matters before the IRS or in federal court.
3) Written communications made in connection with the promotion of direct or indirect participation in a tax shelter.
4) Information that is also available from non-privileged sources.
5) Communication between the taxpayer's tax practitioner and a third-party who provides information about the taxpayer to the practitioner

Furnishing Information

A practitioner must promptly submit records or information in any matter before the IRS, *unless* the practitioner believes in good faith and on reasonable grounds that the records or information are privileged.

1.04 SANCTIONS FOR VIOLATION

Censure, Disbarment, and Suspension

The Secretary of the Treasury, or delegate, after notice and an opportunity for a proceeding, may censure (public reprimand), suspend, or disbar any practitioner from practice before the IRS if the practitioner:
   a) Is shown to be incompetent or disreputable.
   b) Fails to comply with any IRS regulation.
   c) Willfully and knowingly misleads or threatens a client or prospective client with intend to defraud.

Disreputable Conduct

Any practitioner or unenrolled return preparer may be disbarred or suspended from practice before the IRS, or censured, for disreputable conduct. The following list contains examples of conduct that is considered disreputable:
1. Being convicted of any criminal offense under the revenue laws or of any offense involving dishonesty or breach of trust.
2. Knowingly giving false or misleading information in connection with federal tax matters, or participating in such activity.
3. Soliciting employment by prohibited means as discussed in section 10.30 of Treasury Department Circular No. 230.
4. Willfully failing to file a tax return, evading or attempting to evade any federal tax or payment, or participating in such actions.
5. Misappropriating, or failing to properly and promptly remit, funds received from clients for payment of taxes or other obligations due the United States.
6. Directly or indirectly attempting to influence the official action of IRS employees by the use of threats, false accusations, duress, or coercion, or by offering gifts, favors, or any special inducements.
7. Being disbarred or suspended from practice as an attorney, CPA, public accountant, or actuary, by the District of Columbia or any state, possession,

territory, commonwealth, or any federal court, or any body or board of any federal agency.
8. Knowingly aiding and abetting another person to practice before the IRS during a period of suspension, disbarment, or ineligibility.
9. Using abusive language, making false accusations and statements knowing them to be false, circulating or publishing malicious or libelous matter, or engaging in any contemptuous conduct in connection with practice before the IRS.
10. Giving a false opinion knowingly, recklessly, or through gross incompetence; or following a pattern of providing incompetent opinions in questions arising under the federal tax laws.

1.05 DISCIPLINARY PROCEEDINGS

Institution of Proceeding
Whenever the Director of the Office of Professional Responsibility determines that a practitioner violated any laws governing practice before IRS, the Director may do one of the following:
1) Reprimand the practitioner, or
2) Institute a proceeding for a sanction of disbarment or suspension (a proceeding is instituted by the filing of a complaint).

Usually, a proceeding for disbarment or suspension will not be instituted unless the practitioner has been *notified in writing* about the law, facts, and conduct warranting such action and has been accorded an opportunity to dispute the facts, assert additional facts, and make arguments.

Conferences
Director of the Office of Professional Responsibility may confer with a practitioner on issues concerning allegations of misconduct irrespective of whether a proceeding has been instituted. A practitioner may voluntarily *consent* to be sanctioned instead of going through the proceedings. The Director may either accept or decline the *offer of consent*, or may request that some revisions to be made to the offer of consent.

Contents of a Complaint
The following must be contained in a complaint made against a practitioner:
1) Charges
2) Specification of sanction
3) Demand for answer

1. **Charges** - A complaint must:
    a) Name the respondent
    b) Inform the respondent of the charges brought against him/her

    c) Provide description of the facts and law that constitute the basis for the proceeding.
    d) Be signed by the Director of Office of Professional Responsibility or a person representing the Director.

2. **Specification of Sanction** - The complaint must specify the sanction sought by the Director of the Office of Professional Responsibility against the practitioner. If the sanction sought is a suspension, the time duration of the suspension must be specified.

3. **Demand for answer** - The Director of the Office of Professional Responsibility must do the following within the complaint:
    (i) Notify the respondent (practitioner) of the time for answering the complaint, which may not be less than 30 days from the date of *service of the complaint*.
    (ii) Include the name and address of the Administrative Law Judge with whom the answer must be filed.
    (iii) Include the name and address of the person representing the Director to whom a copy of the answer must be served.
    (iv) Note that a decision by default may be rendered against the respondent (practitioner) in the event an answer is not filed as required.

Service of Complaint

In general, the complaint must be served on the respondent or his agent by one of the following ways:
1) Certified or first class mail to the last known address
2) In person - Proof of service in person must:
3) Be a written statement, sworn or affirmed by the person who served the complaint and:
    (i) Identify the manner of service
    (ii) Include the name of recipient,
    (iii) Identify the relationship of the recipient to the respondent (practitioner).
    (iv) Include the Place, date and time of service.
    (v) Other means agreed to by the respondent (practitioner).

Within 10 days of serving the complaint, copies of the *evidence* in support of the complaint must be served on the respondent.

Filing an Answer

The respondent (practitioner) must file an answer with the Administrative Law Judge and have the same answer served to the Director of the Office of Professional Responsibility within the time specified in the complaint.

Contents of the Answer - The answer must be written and contain a statement of facts that constitute the respondent's grounds of defense. General denials are not permitted. The respondent must *specifically admit or deny* each allegation set forth in the complaint. Otherwise, the respondent may state that he or she is without sufficient information to admit or deny a specific allegation.

The respondent may not deny a material allegation in the complaint that he or she knows to be true, or state that the respondent is without sufficient information to form a belief, when he or she possesses the required information. The respondent also must state affirmatively any special matters of defense on which he or she relies.

Failure to Deny or Answer Allegations - Every allegation in the complaint that is not denied in the answer is considered as an admission and will be considered proved, thus no further evidence in respect of such allegation will need to be cited as proof at a hearing.

Failure to File An Answer - Failure to file an answer within the time prescribed constitutes an admission of the allegations of the complaint and a waiver of hearing, therefore the Administrative Law Judge may make the decision by default without a hearing or further procedure.

Signature - The answer must be signed by the respondent or his/her agent and must include a statement directly above the signature acknowledging that the statements made in the answer are true and correct and that knowing and willful false statements may be punishable under law.

Motions
At any time after the filing of a complaint against a practitioner, any party may file a motion with the Administrative Law Judge. Motions must be in writing and must be served on the opposing party. A motion must concisely specify its grounds and the relief sought, and, if appropriate, must contain a memorandum of facts and law in support.

Representation
During the proceedings before the Administrative Law Judge, a respondent (practitioner) may appear in person, be represented by a practitioner, or be represented by an attorney who has not filed a declaration with the IRS.

Administrative Law Judge (ALJ)
Proceedings on complaints for the sanction of a practitioner are conducted by an Administrative Law Judge. The Administrative Law Judge has the authority to:
    (1)   Administer oaths and affirmations.
    (2)   Make rulings on motions and requests.

(3) Determine the time and place of hearing and regulate its course and conduct.
(4) Adopt rules of procedure and modify them from time to time for the orderly disposition of the proceedings.
(5) Rule on offers of proof, receive relevant evidence, and examine witnesses.
(6) Take or authorize the taking of depositions or answers to requests for admission.
(7) Receive and consider oral or written argument on facts or law.
(8) Hold or provide for the holding of conferences for the settlement or simplification of the issues with the consent of the parties.
(9) Act and take measures that are necessary or appropriate to the efficient conduct of any proceeding.
(10) Make decisions.

Discovery

Discovery may be permitted, at the discretion of the Administrative Law Judge, only upon written motion demonstrating the relevance, materiality, and reasonableness of the requested discovery. Within 10 days of receipt of the answer, the Administrative Law Judge will notify the parties of the right to request discovery and the time-frame for filing a request.

In response to a request for discovery, the Administrative Law Judge may order one of the following:
   a) Depositions upon oral examination, or
   b) Answers to requests for admission.

Discovery shall not be authorized if:
   (a) It will unduly delay the proceeding.
   (b) It will place an undue burden on the party required to produce the discovery sought.
   (c) It is frivolous or abusive.
   (d) It is cumulative or duplicative.
   (e) The material sought is privileged or otherwise protected from disclosure by law.
   (f) The material sought relates to mental impressions, conclusions, of legal theories of any party, attorney, or other representative or a party prepared in the anticipation of a proceeding.
   (g) The material sought is available generally to the public, equally to the parties, or to the party seeking the discovery through another source.

Hearings

An Administrative Law Judge will preside at the hearing on a complaint filed for the sanction of a practitioner. The hearing should not occur later than 180 days after the time for filing the answer.

Procedural Requirements for Hearing:
1. Hearings must be steno-graphically recorded and transcribed
2. Testimony of witnesses must be taken under oath or affirmation.
3. An evidentiary hearing must be held in all proceedings prior to the issuance of a decision by the Administrative Law Judge

Cross-Examination

A party is entitled to present his or her case or defense by:
 (a) Oral or documentary evidence
 (b) Submitting rebuttal evidence
 (c) Conducting cross-examination in the presence of the Administrative Law Judge

The parties are not limited from presenting evidence contained within a deposition when the Administrative Law Judge determines that the deposition has been obtained in compliance with the rules.

Each party must file and serve the opposing party prior to any hearing a pre-hearing memorandum containing the following:
1) A list of all proposed exhibits to be used in the party's case in chief.
2) A list of proposed witnesses, including a synopsis of their expected testimony, or a statement that no witnesses will be called.
3) Identification of any proposed expert witnesses, including a synopsis of their expected testimony and a copy of any report prepared by the expert or at his or her direction.
4) A list of undisputed facts.

Appealing the Administrative Law Judge Decision
 (i) Appeal of the Administrative Law Judge decision is made with the Secretary of the Treasury or his/her delegate.
 (ii) The appeal must include a brief that states exceptions to the decision of the Administrative Law Judge and supporting reasons for such exceptions.
 (iii) The appeal and brief must be filed (in duplicate) with the Director of the Office of Professional Responsibility within 30 days of the date that the decision of the Administrative Law Judge is made. Then the Director will immediately furnish a copy of the appeal to the Secretary of the Treasury or delegate who decides appeals.
 (iv) A copy of the appeal for review must be sent to any non-appealing party.

Effect of Disbarment, Suspension, or Censure

When the final decision in a case is against the respondent (practitioner), the effects may be as follows:
1. **Disbarment** - When the final decision in a case is against the practitioner (and such decision is for disbarment, the respondent will **not** be permitted to practice before

the IRS unless and until authorized to do so by the Director of the Office of Professional Responsibility

2. **Suspension** - When the final decision in a case is against the practitioner and such decision is for suspension, the respondent will **not** be permitted to practice before the IRS during the period of suspension. For periods after the suspension, the practitioner's future representations may be subject to conditions.

3. **Censure** - When the final decision in the case is against the practitioner and such decision is for censure, the respondent **will** be permitted to practice before the IRS, but the respondent's future representations may be subject to conditions.

Note: A practitioner may be subject to the sanction of either suspension or censure for failure to advise his or her clients about a potential conflict of interest or for failure to obtain the clients' written consents.

Notice of Disbarment, Suspension, Censure, or Disqualification
Upon the issuance of a final order censuring, suspending, or disbarring a practitioner or a final order disqualifying an appraiser, the Director of the Office of Professional Responsibility may give notice of the censure, suspension, disbarment, or disqualification to appropriate officers and employees of the IRS and to interested departments and agencies of the Federal government, including state authorities.

Petition for Reinstatement
The Director of the Office of Professional Responsibility may allow a petition for reinstatement from any person disbarred from practice before the IRS after 5 years have expired from the date of the disbarment or disqualification.

Roster
The Director of the Office of Professional Responsibility will maintain *rosters* of the following people, and may make available for public inspection:
1. Enrolled agents, including individuals:
    (i) People who have been granted active enrollment to practice.
    (ii) People have their enrollment placed in inactive status for failure to meet the requirements for renewal for enrollment.
    (iii) People who have their enrollment placed in inactive retirement status.
    (iv) Whose offer of consent to resign from enrollment has been accepted by the Director of the Office of Professional Responsibility
2. Individuals who have been censured, suspended or disbarred from practice before the IRS or upon whom a monetary penalty was imposed.

1.06 RENEWAL FOR ENROLLMENT TO PRACTICE

To maintain active enrollment to practice before the IRS, each individual is required to have his or her enrollment renewed. Failure to receive notification from the Director of the Office of Professional Responsibility of the renewal requirement will not be justification for the individual's failure to satisfy this requirement.

Form 8554 is the application form used Application for Renewal of Enrollment to Practice before the IRS.

A reasonable nonrefundable fee will be charged for each application for renewal of enrollment as an enrolled agent filed with the Director of the Office of Professional Responsibility.

Renewal Cycles

Renewal cycles are determined by the last digit of the Social Security Number. If SSN ends in:
- 0, 1, 2, or 3 – The renewal cycle is between November 1, 2009 and January 31, 2010
- 4, 5, or 6 – The renewal cycle is between November 1, 2010 and January 31, 2011
- 7, 8, or 9 – The renewal cycle is between November 1, 2008 and January 31, 2009
- If one does not have an SSN, he or she is required to renew as if the last digit were 7, 8, or 9

In order to qualify for renewal of enrollment, an individual enrolled to practice before the IRS must complete 72 hours of Continuing Professional Education (CPE) over the 3-year enrollment cycle to remain active. This must include at least 2 hours of Ethics CPE each year.

A minimum of 16 hours of continuing education credit, including 2 hours of ethics or professional conduct, must be completed during each enrollment year of an enrollment cycle.

An individual who receives initial enrollment during an enrollment cycle must complete 2 hours of qualifying continuing education credit for each month enrolled during the enrollment cycle. Enrollment for any part of a month is considered enrollment for the entire month.
- An Enrollment year is a calendar year (January 1 to December 31).
- An Enrollment cycle means 3 successive enrollment years preceding the effective date of renewal.
- The effective date of renewal is the 1st day of the 4th month following the close of the period for renewal

Qualifying CPE Courses

To qualify for CPE credit for an enrolled agent, a course of learning must:
1. Be a *qualifying program* designed to enhance professional knowledge in any of the following:
    a) Federal taxation or Federal tax related matters
    b) Accounting
    c) Tax preparation software
    d) Taxation
    e) Ethics
2. Be a qualifying program consistent with the Internal Revenue Code and effective tax administration.
3. Be sponsored by a qualifying sponsor.

Qualifying Programs

Qualifying programs for CPE credits include:
a) Formal programs.
b) Correspondence or individual study programs (including taped programs).
c) Serving as an instructor, discussion leader, or speaker.
d) Credit for published articles and books.

A. Formal Program:

A formal program qualifies as continuing education programs if:
(i) It requires attendance. The program sponsor must provide each attendee with a certificate of attendance.
(ii) It Requires that the program be conducted by a qualified instructor, discussion leader, or speaker, i.e., a person whose background, training, education and experience is appropriate for instructing or leading a discussion on the subject matter of the particular program
(iii) It Provides or requires a written outline, textbook, or suitable electronic educational materials.

B. Correspondence or individual study programs:

Programs must be conducted by qualifying sponsors and completed by the enrolled individual on an individual basis. The allowable credit hours for such programs will be measured on a basis comparable to the measurement of a seminar or course for credit in an accredited educational institution. These types of programs qualify as continuing education programs if they:
1) Require registration of the participants by the sponsor.
2) Provide a means for measuring completion by the participants (e.g., a written examination), including the issuance of a certificate of completion by the sponsor.
3) Provide a written outline, textbook, or suitable electronic educational materials.

C. **Serving as an instructor, discussion leader, or speaker:**
   1) One hour of continuing education credit will be awarded for each contact hour completed as an instructor, discussion leader, or speaker at an educational program that meets the continuing education requirements.
   2) Two hours of continuing education credit will be awarded for actual subject preparation time for each contact hour completed as an instructor, discussion leader, or speaker at such programs. It is the responsibility of the individual claiming such credit to maintain records to verify preparation time.
   3) The maximum credit for instruction and preparation may not exceed 50% of the continuing education requirement for an enrollment cycle.
   4) An instructor, discussion leader, or speaker who makes more than one presentation on the same subject matter during an enrollment cycle, will receive continuing education credit for only one such presentation for the enrollment cycle.

D. **Credit for published articles and books:**
   1) For enrolled agents, CPE credits will be awarded for publications on Federal taxation or Federal tax related matters, including accounting, tax preparation software, and taxation or ethics, provided the content of such publications is current and designed for the enhancement of the professional knowledge of an individual enrolled to practice before the IRS. The publication must be consistent with the Internal Revenue Code and effective tax administration.
   2) The credits allowed will be on the basis of one hour credit for each hour of preparation time for the material. It is the responsibility of the person claiming the credit to maintain records to verify preparation time.
   3) The maximum credits for publications may not exceed 25% of the CPE requirement of any enrollment cycle.

Sponsors

Sponsors are individuals or institutions responsible for presenting CPE qualifying programs. To qualify as a sponsor, a program presenter must:
   a) Be an accredited educational institution.
   b) Be recognized for CPE purposes by the licensing body of any State, territory, or possession of the United States, including a Commonwealth, or the District of Columbia.
   c) Be recognized by the Director of the Office of Professional Responsibility as a professional organization or society whose programs include offering CPE opportunities in the area of federal taxation.
   d) File a sponsor agreement with the Director of the Office of Professional Responsibility and obtain approval of the program as a qualified CPE.

A qualifying sponsor must ensure the program complies with the following requirements:

(i) Programs must be developed by individual(s) qualified in the area of federal taxation
(ii) Program subject matter must be current
(iii) Instructors, discussion leaders, and speakers must be qualified with respect to program content
(iv) Programs must include some means for evaluation of technical content and presentation
(v) Certificates of completion must be provided to the participants who successfully complete the program
(vi) Records must be maintained by the sponsor to verify the participants who attended and completed the program for a period of 3 years following completion of the program. In the case of continuous conferences, conventions, and the like, records must be maintained to verify completion of the program and attendance by each participant at each segment of the program.

Measuring CPE Coursework

1. All CPE programs will be measured in terms of contact hours. The shortest recognized program will be one contact hour.
2. A contact hour is 50 minutes of continuous participation in a program. Credit is granted only for a full contact hour, i.e., 50 minutes or multiples thereof. For example, a program lasting more than 50 minutes but less than 100 minutes will count as one contact hour.
3. Individual segments at continuous conferences, conventions and the like will be considered one total program. For example, two 90-minute segments (180 minutes) at a continuous conference will count as three contact hours.
4. For university or college courses, each semester credit hour will equal 15 contact hours and a ¼ semester credit hour will equal 10 contact hours.

Recordkeeping Requirements for CPE

Each individual applying for renewal for enrollment must retain the following information with regard to qualifying CPE credit hours for a period of 3 years, following the date of renewal of enrollment:

(i) The name of the sponsoring organization.
(ii) The location of the program.
(iii) The title of the program and description of its content.
(iv) Written outlines, course syllabi, textbook, and/or electronic materials provided or required for the course;
(v) The dates attended.
(vi) The credit hours claimed.
(vii) The name(s) of the instructor(s), discussion leader(s), or speaker(s), if appropriate.

(viii) The certificate of completion and/or signed statement of the hours of attendance obtained from the sponsor.

To receive CPE credit for service completed as an instructor, discussion leader, or speaker, the same records listed above will need to be maintained for 3 years following the date of renewal of enrollment.

To receive CPE credit for publications, the following information must be maintained for a period of 3 years following the date of renewal of enrollment:
      a) The publisher.
      b) The title of the publication.
      c) A copy of the publication.
      d) The date of publication.
      e) Records that substantiate the hours worked on the publication.

Waivers for CPE Requirements

1) A waiver from the CPE requirements for a given period may be granted by the Director of the Office of Professional Responsibility for the following reasons:
2) Health issues that prevented compliance with the CPE requirements.
3) Extended active military duty.
4) Absence from the United States for an extended period of time due to employment or other reasons, so long as the individual does not practice before the IRS during such absence.
5) Other compelling reasons, which will be considered on a case-by-case basis.
6) A request for waiver must be accompanied by appropriate documentation like a medical certificate or military orders.
7) A request for waiver must be filed no later than the last day of the renewal application period.
8) If a request for waiver is not approved, the individual will be placed in inactive status and placed on a roster of inactive enrolled individuals.
9) If a request for waiver is approved, the individual will be notified and issued a card evidencing renewal.

Failure to Meet the Renewal Requirements

1. An individual who fails to meet the requirements of eligibility for renewal of enrollment will be notified by the Director of the Office of Professional Responsibility at his or her enrollment address by first class mail. The notice will state the basis for the determination of noncompliance and will provide the individual an opportunity to furnish information in writing relating to the matter within 60 days of the date of the notice.
2. An individual who has not satisfied the requirements of eligibility for renewal will be placed on a roster of inactive enrolled individuals.

3. Individuals placed in inactive enrollment status and individuals ineligible to practice before the IRS may not state or imply that they are enrolled to practice before the IRS or use the terms enrolled agent the designations "EA" or other form of reference to eligibility to practice before the IRS.
4. An individual placed in an inactive status must file an application for renewal of enrollment and satisfy the requirements for renewal within 3 years of being placed in an inactive status.
5. Inactive enrollment status is not available to an individual who is the subject of a disciplinary matter in the Office of Professional Responsibility.

1.07 UNIT 1: QUESTIONS

TRUE/FALSE
Please select either (A) for True or (B) for False

1. Preparing a tax return, furnishing information at the request of the IRS, or appearing as a witness for the taxpayer is considered practice before the IRS.
    A. TRUE
    B. FALSE

2. Michael Smith is an Enrolled Agent with an office that 4 other Enrolled Agents. Kimberly Wilson is a CPA who was suspended from practice for 1 year by the Office of Professional Responsibility. Kimberly knows Michael and asks him for employment for the one-year period of suspension. Michael employs Kimberly for the sole purpose of corresponding and communicating with the IRS on issues arising for Michael's clients. Michael is allowed to employ Kimberly because the suspension is for less than 2 years, Kimberly is limited to corresponding and communicating with the IRS and the clients are really Michael's not Kimberly's.
    A. TRUE
    B. FALSE

3. Mary Pecan, a CPA, prepared a tax return for a client. The return contained a frivolous position that could not be defended under any circumstances. The examiner who conducted the examination made a referral to the Office of Professional Responsibility. After all procedural requirements have been met; the Office of Professional Responsibility will make a final, binding decision as to the appropriate sanction for Mary.
    A. TRUE
    B. FALSE

4. A representative qualified to practice before the IRS **cannot** prepare or sign a formal written protest on behalf of a client to request an appeals conference.
    A. TRUE
    B. FALSE

5. A paid preparer must give the taxpayer a copy of his or her tax return in addition to the copy filed with the IRS.
    A. TRUE
    B. FALSE

6. The Office of Professional Responsibility will make available for public inspection at the Office of Professional Responsibility the roster of all persons enrolled to practice,

the roster of all persons censured, suspended, or disbarred from practice before the IRS, and the roster of all disqualified appraisers.
   A. TRUE
   B. FALSE

7. Nancy had e-mail correspondence in 2003 with her longtime tax return preparer, an enrolled agent. The correspondence related to tax advice on the depreciation of rental property Nancy had acquired in 2003. Nancy never filed the 2003 or subsequent returns. Nancy was notified by the IRS that she is the subject of a criminal investigation for the failure to file her returns. The IRS has issued a subpoena to obtain the e-mails as part of its investigation. The e-mails with her preparer are confidential communications between Nancy and her federally authorized practitioner and are therefore protected under Internal Revenue Code Section 7525.
   A. TRUE
   B. FALSE

8. After April 1, 2007, an individual who received initial enrollment during an enrollment cycle must complete two (2) hours of qualifying continuing education credit for each month enrolled during the enrollment cycle. Enrollment for any part of a month is considered enrollment for the entire month.
   A. TRUE
   B. FALSE

9. Except as provided in other sections of Circular 230, a practitioner will be presumed to have exercised due diligence if the practitioner relies on the work product of another person and the practitioner used reasonable care in engaging, supervising, training, and evaluating the person, taking proper account of the nature of the relationship between the practitioner and the person.
   A. TRUE
   B. FALSE

10. An unenrolled return preparer may represent any taxpayer before a revenue officer of the IRS, provided that the unenrolled return preparer has prepared at least one return for any taxpayer in the last three years.
    A. TRUE
    B. FALSE

11. A practitioner must exercise due diligence in determining the correctness of oral or written representations made by the practitioner to clients with reference to any matter administered by the IRS.
    A. TRUE
    B. FALSE

12. Written advice is a *reliance opinion* if the advice has more than 50 % likelihood that one or more significant Federal tax issues would be resolved in the taxpayer's favor.
    A. TRUE
    B. FALSE

13. Joseph Smith, an enrolled agent, has represented Stephen Francis before the IRS and also prepared returns for Stephen in each of the last three years. Stephen was divorced last year, and his ex-wife, Lindsay, stops by Joseph's office and asks Joseph to represent her before the IRS with respect to the examination of her return that she filed separately from her husband in a year in which they were separated but not yet divorced. Because the representation involves a tax return for which Lindsay filed separately, and Lindsay was separated at the time, Joseph may undertake the representation of Lindsay without considering whether a conflict of interest exists between Lindsay and her former spouse.
    A. TRUE
    B. FALSE

14. In order to be absolutely certain that she will not be sanctioned for failing to exercise due diligence, an enrolled agent must complete all tasks involved with the representation of a taxpayer herself.
    A. TRUE
    B. FALSE

15. An enrolled agent cannot be sanctioned for a materially false or misleading statement that the client decides to make on a document submitted to the IRS, provided that it is the client who makes the final decision to submit the document containing the false or misleading statement.
    A. TRUE
    B. FALSE

16. Practice before the IRS comprehends all matters connected with a presentation to the IRS or any of its officers or employees relating to a taxpayer's rights, privileges, or liabilities under laws or regulations administered by the IRS. Such presentations include, but are not limited to, preparing and filing documents, corresponding and communicating with the IRS, and representing a client at conferences, hearings, and meetings.
    A. TRUE
    B. FALSE

17. A conflict of interest exists if the representation of one client will be directly adverse to another client, or there is a significant risk that the representation of one or more clients will be materially limited by the practitioner's responsibilities to another client, a former client, or a third person or by a personal interest of the practitioner.
    A. TRUE

B. FALSE

18. Whenever the Office of Professional Responsibility determines that a practitioner violated any provision of the laws or regulations in Circular 230, the Office of Professional Responsibility may reprimand the practitioner or institute a proceeding for censure, suspension, or disbarment of the practitioner. A proceeding for censure, suspension, or disbarment of a practitioner is instituted by the filing of a complaint. Except in unusual circumstances, a proceeding will not be instituted unless the proposed respondent previously has been advised in writing of the law, facts, and conduct warranting such action and has been accorded an opportunity to dispute facts, assert additional facts, and make arguments.
    A. TRUE
    B. FALSE

19. The Office of Professional Responsibility will make available for public inspection at the Office of Professional Responsibility, the roster of all persons enrolled to practice. The roster of all persons censured, suspended, or disbarred from practice before the IRS, and the roster of all disqualified appraisers will be kept confidential.
    A. TRUE
    B. FALSE

20. A representative qualified to practice before the IRS can prepare and sign a formal written protest on behalf of a client to request an appeals conference.
    A. TRUE
    B. FALSE

21. For purposes of Circular 230 (regulations governing practice), the definition of 'tax return' includes an amended return and a claim for refund.
    A. TRUE
    B. FALSE

22. The same practitioner may not represent former spouses John and Jane, each claiming their son Jason as a dependent child on their individual tax returns, for audits of those returns.
    A. TRUE
    B. FALSE

23. Circular 230 (regulations governing practice), contains special rules for professional conduct with respect to tax shelter opinions. (Add to notes)
    A. TRUE
    B. FALSE

24. An individual who prepares income tax returns for compensation will not be treated as an income tax return preparer under the Internal Revenue Code unless the individual is an enrolled agent, a lawyer, a CPA, or an enrolled actuary.
    A. TRUE
    B. FALSE

25. An unenrolled preparer can represent the taxpayer before any function of the IRS.
    A. TRUE
    B. FALSE

26. John prepares tax returns. John is not an enrolled agent, enrolled actuary, CPA, or attorney. In 2000, new clients, Mr. and Mrs. Black, engage John to prepare their 1999 joint income tax return. John prepares the Black's 1999 joint income tax return and signs it as the preparer. This is the only return John has prepared for the Blacks. In March of 2001, Mr. and Mrs. Black received a notice from the IRS with regard to their 1998 joint income tax return. Mr. and Mrs. Black ask John to contact the IRS to resolve the matter with regard to their 1998 joint income tax return, but do not provide John with a power of attorney. John is not permitted to represent or advocate a position before the IRS on behalf of Mr. and Mrs. Black concerning their 1998 return.
    A. TRUE
    B. FALSE

27. Under Circular 230, an applicant who wishes to challenge the Director of Practice's denial of his or her application for enrollment is required to file a written appeal with the Secretary of the Treasury.
    A. TRUE
    B. FALSE

28. Ms. Smith hired Tom, an enrolled agent, to prepare her Federal income tax return for 2001. While gathering information to prepare the return, Tom discovered that although Ms. Smith was required to file Federal income tax returns for the 1999 tax year and the 2000 tax year under the Federal tax laws, she did not file these returns. Circular 230 requires that Tom promptly advise Ms. Smith that she did not comply with the Internal Revenue laws by failing to file her Federal income tax returns for the 1999 tax year and the 2000 tax year.
    A. TRUE
    B. FALSE

29. The Circular 230 requirement that a practitioner exercise due diligence in preparing, approving, and filing returns does not apply if the practitioner is merely assisting in preparing, approving, or filing returns.
    A. TRUE
    B. FALSE

30. A practitioner is subject to sanction under Circular 230 if he or she does not receive proper consent to represent conflicting interests before the IRS.
    A. TRUE
    B. FALSE

31. Circular 230 permits an enrolled agent to cash a taxpayer's refund check if the amount of the check is less than the amount of the total fee outstanding on the date the check is cashed.
    A. TRUE
    B. FALSE

32. Circular 230 does not contain separate rules for the preparation of tax shelter opinions.
    A. TRUE
    B. FALSE

33. Circular 230 never permits a practitioner to sign a return as a preparer if the return contains a frivolous position.
    A. TRUE
    B. FALSE

34. A criminal conviction under State law for embezzlement is not disreputable conduct under Circular 230 because the crime of embezzlement, although a crime involving dishonesty, is not a crime under the Federal revenue laws.
    A. TRUE
    B. FALSE

35. Circular 230 permits an individual charged with violating the regulations under Circular 230 to appear in person or to be represented by counsel or other representative.
    A. TRUE
    B. FALSE

36. To be timely, the respondent has 30 days from the date of the decision to appeal an initial decision ordering disbarment.
    A. TRUE
    B. FALSE

37. The Director of Practice is permitted to notify appropriate officers and employees of the IRS, interested departments and agencies of the Federal government and the State where a practitioner is licensed, that a practitioner has been disbarred or suspended from practice before the IRS.
    A. TRUE
    B. FALSE

38. Able was requested by his client to represent him in connection with an IRS audit. Able is therefore practicing before the IRS.
    A. TRUE
    B. FALSE

39. If the Director of Practice denies an application for enrollment, the applicant has the right to appeal the decision by filing a written protest within 60 days of receipt of the notice.
    A. TRUE
    B. FALSE

40. Charlie, a certified public accountant, is required in all circumstances to submit records or information upon the lawful request by an IRS representative.
    A. TRUE
    B. FALSE

41. Donald, an enrolled agent, has knowledge that a client has not complied with the revenue law of the United Sates. Donald must advise the client of such noncompliance.
    A. TRUE
    B. FALSE

42. Edward, an enrolled agent, may not, knowingly employ a person or accept employment from a person who has been disbarred or suspended by the Director of Practice.
    A. TRUE
    B. FALSE

43. Harold, an enrolled agent, must at all times exercise due diligence when preparing any document involving IRS matters.
    A. TRUE
    B. FALSE

44. Leonore, an enrolled agent, who prepares an income tax return, has no right to endorse an IRS refund check payable to the client, notwithstanding the fact that the check was sent directly to her.
    A. TRUE
    B. FALSE

45. Diane, an enrolled agent, who is required to render an opinion on material issues involving a tax shelter investment, must determine whether it is certain that the investor will prevail on the merits of material tax issues, which may be challenged by the IRS.

A. TRUE
B. FALSE

46. If a position on a tax return has approximately a one in three, or greater, likelihood of being sustained on its merits, then there is a realistic possibility of its being sustained on the merits.
    A. TRUE
    B. FALSE

47. Harold, an enrolled agent, advises prospective clients that he is able to obtain approval of qualified retirement plans with unique vesting provisions because of his close relationship with the IRS territory manager of the Tax Exempt Government Entities operating unit in his locality. This type of employment solicitation does not constitute disreputable conduct subjecting Harold to potential disbarment or suspension from IRS practice.
    A. TRUE
    B. FALSE

48. Jake, an attorney, is charged by the Director of Practice with acts of misconduct and a complaint is served upon him. Jake has 10 days from the date of service to file an answer.
    A. TRUE
    B. FALSE

49. Annie Holt, an enrolled agent, was issued findings of fact, conclusions of law, and a decision ruling that she committed acts of misconduct, which were volatile under Circular 230, and, therefore, a decision as entered ruling that she should be disbarred. Annie Holt has a right to appeal the decision to the Secretary of the Treasury.
    A. TRUE
    B. FALSE

50. The regulations in Circular 230 governing the practice of attorneys, certified public accountants, enrolled agents, enrolled actuaries and appraisers before the IRS can be found in the Code of Federal Regulations.
    A. TRUE
    B. FALSE

51. The Office of Director of Practice is prohibited from maintaining a roster of all persons enrolled to practice, disbarred or suspended from practice, and disqualified appraisers, for public inspection.
    A. TRUE
    B. FALSE

52. Enrolled actuaries are authorized to practice before the IRS for all matters connected with a presentation to the IRS or any of its offices or employees relating to a client's rights, privileges, or liabilities under the Internal Revenue laws.
    A. TRUE
    B. FALSE

53. A person is eligible to be an enrolled agent only by demonstrating a special competence in tax matters by a written IRS examination and by refraining from engaging in any conduct that would justify suspension or disbarment.
    A. TRUE
    B. FALSE

54. Attorneys and accountants licensed to practice in a particular state who are in good standing in that state may practice before the IRS only in that state.
    A. TRUE
    B. FALSE

55. There is no right to appeal a decision of suspension or disbarment of practice before the IRS.
    A. TRUE
    B. FALSE

56. A non-signing preparer of an individual's tax return is eligible to represent the taxpayer involving an IRS examination for the taxable year covered by that return without being eligible to practice before the IRS.
    A. TRUE
    B. FALSE

57. A Circular 230 practitioner must, when requested by the Director of Practice, provide the Director with any information he may have concerning violation of Circular 230 regulations by any person. An exception to this duty is made if the practitioner believes in good faith and on reasonable grounds that such information is privileged or that the request therefore is of doubtful legality.
    A. TRUE
    B. FALSE

58. An enrolled agent can accept the client's statement in preparing a tax return without making any inquiries.
    A. TRUE
    B. FALSE

59. If an enrolled agent has knowledge that a client has filed an erroneous tax return, the client must be advised to correct the error.
    A. TRUE
    B. FALSE

60. An enrolled agent may not, in practice before the IRS, knowingly and directly or indirectly accept employment as associate, correspondent, or subagent from, or share fees with, any person who is under disbarment or suspension from practice before the IRS.
    A. TRUE
    B. FALSE

61. A Circular 230 practitioner may not, under any circumstances, charge a contingent fee for preparing a tax return or claim for refund.
    A. TRUE
    B. FALSE

62. An enrolled agent is permitted to charge any amount of fee to represent a client before the IRS.
    A. TRUE
    B. FALSE

63. An advertisement by an enrolled agent depicting the official IRS insignia is proper as long as the enrolled agent is currently enrolled with the Director of Practice.
    A. TRUE
    B. FALSE

64. An enrolled agent is permitted to publish the availability of a written schedule of fees for representation of the taxpayer before the IRS.
    A. TRUE
    B. FALSE

65. A certified public accountant who is suspended from practice in Puerto Rico can continue to practice before the IRS in Alaska.
    A. TRUE
    B. FALSE

66. A person disbarred from practice before the IRS can apply for reinstatement within 10 years following such disbarment.
    A. TRUE
    B. FALSE

67. An enrolled agent, in order to avoid disbarment or suspension proceedings, may offer his consent to suspension or his resignation. The Director of Practice must accept this offer.
    A. TRUE
    B. FALSE

68. The hearing for suspension or disbarment of a person authorized to practice before the IRS is before the U.S. Tax Court.
    A. TRUE
    B. FALSE

69. A disbarment or suspension proceeding against an individual is begun with a complaint signed by the Director of Practice and delivered or mailed to the individual.
    A. TRUE
    B. FALSE

70. An enrolled agent is unqualifiedly permitted to represent the partnership and all of its individual partners involving an IRS examination of the partnership return.
    A. TRUE
    B. FALSE

71. Advice on non-criminal tax matters from a federally authorized practitioner has the same confidentiality protection as communication with an attorney.
    A. TRUE
    B. FALSE

72. "Practice before the IRS," means preparation of a tax return, furnishing information at the request of the IRS and appearing as a witness for the taxpayer.
    A. TRUE
    B. FALSE

73. An applicant whose application for enrollment has been denied may file an appeal within 30 days of receipt of the notice to the Secretary of the Treasury.
    A. TRUE
    B. FALSE

74. A parent has authority to represent his/her child only if the child is present.
    A. TRUE
    B. FALSE

75. A disciplinary proceeding will not be instituted until the facts or conduct which may warrant such action have been called to the attention of the respondent and he has

been accorded opportunity to demonstrate or achieve compliance with all lawful requirements.
- A. TRUE
- B. FALSE

76. With regards to complaints filed against enrolled agents, all papers must be filed in duplicate.
    - A. TRUE
    - B. FALSE

77. A preparer is considered to have recklessly or intentionally disregarded a rule or regulation if a position contrary to a rule or regulation is taken on a return or claim for refund and if the preparer knows of, or is reckless in not knowing of, the rule or regulation in question.
    - A. TRUE
    - B. FALSE

78. In any case in which a recognized representative is unable or unwilling to declare his/her own knowledge that the facts are true and correct, the IRS may require the taxpayer to make such a declaration under penalty of perjury.
    - A. TRUE
    - B. FALSE

MULTIPLE CHOICE QUESTIONS:
Please select the most appropriate answer.

79. With respect to unenrolled return preparers, which of the following statements is **correct**?
    - A. An unenrolled return preparer is an individual other than an attorney, CPA, enrolled agent, or enrolled actuary who prepares and signs a taxpayer's return as the preparer, or who prepares a return but is not required (by the instructions to the return or regulations) to sign the return.
    - B. An unenrolled return preparer is only permitted to appear as a taxpayers' representative before a Customer Service Representative of the IRS.
    - C. An unenrolled preparer may receive refund checks on behalf of the taxpayer if Form 8821 has been executed.
    - D. An unenrolled preparer is permitted to represent a taxpayer over the telephone with the Automated Collection System unit.

80. Margaret Smith is a CPA who is representing John & Mary Jones before the Wage and Investment Division of the IRS. The Service is questioning John & Mary on

contributions that were listed on page 2 of their 2004 Form 1040. While reviewing the documentation provided by John & Mary, Margaret discovers contributions that were made to a non-qualified organization. What is the appropriate action for Margaret to take?
   A. Margaret must advise John & Mary on how to keep the omission from being discovered by the IRS.
   B. Margaret must notify the IRS that she is no longer representing John & Mary by withdrawing her Form 2848.
   C. Margaret must advise John & Mary promptly of the omission and the consequences provided by the Internal Revenue Code and Regulations for such omission.
   D. Margaret must immediately advise the IRS examiner of the non-qualified contributions.

81. The Office of Professional Responsibility can censure, suspend or disbar a practitioner from practice before the IRS for incompetence?
    A. Conviction of any criminal offense under the revenue laws of the United States.
    B. Conviction of any criminal offense involving dishonesty or breach of trust.
    C. Giving false or misleading information or participating in any way in the giving of false or misleading information to the Department of the Treasury or any officer or employee thereof.
    D. All of the above.

82. Josephine Jones, an Enrolled Agent, received a complaint from the Office of Professional Responsibility. Select the statement below that is **correct** with respect to the contents of the answer that Josephine will file in rebuttal to the complaint.
    A. Josephine may only state a general denial of the allegations.
    B. Josephine must specifically admit or deny each allegation set forth in the complaint, and may not state that she is without sufficient information to admit or deny a specific allegation.
    C. Josephine may deny a material allegation in the complaint even though she knows it to be true.
    D. Josephine must specifically admit or deny each allegation set forth in the complaint, except that she may state that she is without sufficient information to admit or deny a specific allegation.

83. How long must each practitioner maintain records of their completed CPE credits?
    A. CPE credit information does not have to be retained by the Enrolled Agent since the qualifying organization provides the Office of Professional Responsibility a list of each participant that completed CPE credits.

B. CPE credit information must be maintained for a period of three (3) years from the date they are completed.
C. CPE credit information must be retained for a period of three (3) years following the date of renewal of enrollment
D. CPE credit information must be retained for a period of one (1) year following the year they are completed.

84. To maintain active enrollment to practice before the IRS, each individual enrolled is required to have his or her enrollment renewed. The Office of Professional Responsibility will notify the individual of his or her renewal of enrollment and will issue the individual a card to evidence enrollment. Which of the following statements about renewal of enrollment is **correct?**
    A. A reasonable refundable fee may be charged for each application for renewal of enrollment filed with the Office of Professional Responsibility.
    B. Failure by an individual to receive notification from the Office of Professional Responsibility of the renewal requirement will not be justification for the failure to timely renew enrollment.
    C. Forms required for renewal may only be obtained from the National Association of Enrolled Agents.
    D. The enrollment cycle is a 3 year period and all Enrolled Agents must renew at the same time, no matter when they first became Enrolled Agents.

85. Of the following statements below, which one **is not** considered practice before the IRS?
    A. Communicating with the IRS for a taxpayer regarding the taxpayer's rights, privileges, or liabilities under laws and regulation administered by the IRS.
    B. Representing a taxpayer at conferences, hearings, or meetings with the IRS.
    C. Preparing a tax return or furnishing information at the request of the IRS.
    D. Preparing and filing necessary documents at the request of the IRS for a taxpayer and discussing issues.

86. Which of the following statements is **correct** with respect to the limited practice of an unenrolled return preparer:
    A. An unenrolled return preparer may represent the taxpayer, before certain types of IRS personnel, with respect to an examination regarding the return that he or she prepared.
    B. An unenrolled return preparer is permitted to appear as a taxpayers' representative before any function of the IRS as long as he or she prepared the return.
    C. If authorized by the taxpayer, an unenrolled return preparer can sign consents to extend the statutory period for assessment or collection of tax.

D. An unenrolled preparer may receive a refund check on behalf of the taxpayer if permission has been granted to the unenrolled preparer with a Form 8821.

87. Frank Maple, a Certified Public Accountant, represents his brother Joe Maple and Joe's business partner Bill Smith. Joe Maple and Bill Smith are equal shareholders in the Joe & Bill Corporation. The IRS examined the corporation and determined that one of the shareholders committed fraud, but could not determine which shareholder it was. Frank has made an appointment with the IRS to determine which partner was guilty. Which of the following statements reflects what Frank should do in accordance with Circular 230?
    A. Frank should meet with the IRS and try to convince the examiner that each shareholder is equally guilty.
    B. Advise Joe & Bill that they should dissolve the corporation thereby making it difficult for the IRS to pursue the issue.
    C. Advise Joe & Bill that he cannot represent them because there is a conflict of interest.
    D. Advise Joe & Bill on creating documents that will convince the IRS that neither shareholder is guilty of fraud.

88. Stuart Light, an Enrolled Agent, received a complaint from the Office of Professional Responsibility for disreputable conduct. Which one of the following items was **not** required to be listed in the complaint:
    A. A demand for an answer to the charges
    B. The unit and employee of the IRS that recommended the action against Stuart.
    C. The specific sanctions that are recommended against Stuart
    D. The charges against Stuart

89. Sara Birch became an Enrolled Agent on March 12, 2005. Sara is ordering business cards and advertising for her accounting and tax practice. Of the following presentations listed below, which one will violate the Circular 230 rules for advertising?
    A. Sara Birch, Enrolled Agent, Certified to practice before the IRS.
    B. Sara Birch, Enrolled Agent, representing taxpayers before the IRS.
    C. Sara Birch, enrolled to represent taxpayers before the IRS.
    D. Sara Birch, EA, admitted to practice before the IRS.

90. Rich, an enrolled agent, is currently representing Dana before the IRS. Mike, Dana's former business partner, asks Rich to represent him before the IRS. Notwithstanding the existence of a conflict of interest between Dana and Mike, Rich may still represent Mike before the IRS if certain requirements are met. Which of the

following statements is **not** a requirement that Rich has to satisfy before he can represent Mike?
- A. Dana and Mike must each give informed consent, confirmed in writing, to Rich.
- B. Rich must reasonably believe that he will be able to provide competent and diligent representation to both Dana and Mike.
- C. Rich must immediately notify the Office of Professional Responsibility in writing that he is representing both Dana and Mike.
- D. The representation of Dana must not be prohibited by law.

91. Which of the following statements is **correct** with respect to a client's request for records of the client that are necessary for the client to comply with his or her Federal tax obligations?
    - A. The practitioner may never return records of the client to the client even if the client requests prompt return of the records.
    - B. The existence of a dispute over fees always relieves the practitioner of his or her responsibility to return records of the client to the client.
    - C. The practitioner must, at the request of the client, promptly return the records of the client to the client unless applicable state law provides otherwise.
    - D. The practitioner must, at the request of the client, return the records of the client to the client within three months of receiving the request.

92. Larry Smith passed all parts of the Special Enrollment Examination in October of 2003. Larry submitted the required forms to become an Enrolled Agent. Larry failed the suitability test performed by the IRS and the Office of Professional Responsibility informed Larry that he was denied participation and provided him with the reasons for the denial. Larry received the notice on January 20, 2004. What action should Larry take to appeal the denial received from the Office of Professional Responsibility?
    - A. Larry must file a written appeal no later than the 19th of February with the Commissioner of IRS or his delegate.
    - B. Larry must file a petition no later than the 30th of January with the District Court.
    - C. Larry must file a written appeal no later than the 30th of January with the Secretary of the Treasury or his delegate.
    - D. Larry must file a written appeal no later than the 19th of February with the Secretary of the Treasury or his delegate.

93. Which of the following statements is **correct** with respect to the limited practice of an unenrolled return preparer?

A. An unenrolled return preparer may represent the taxpayer for any year the taxpayer provides authorization, whether or not the unenrolled preparer prepared the return in question.
B. An unenrolled return preparer is only permitted to represent taxpayers before the examination and collection functions of the IRS.
C. If authorized by the taxpayer, an unenrolled return preparer can sign consents to extend the statutory period for assessment or collection of tax.
D. An unenrolled preparer cannot receive refund checks.

94. Sam, an Enrolled Agent, is representing Fred before the Examination Division of the IRS. The IRS is questioning Fred on his Schedule C gross income that is listed on the 2002 tax return. While reviewing the documentation Fred provided, Sam discovers income that was omitted from the tax return. What is the appropriate action for Sam to take?
    A. Sam must immediately advise the IRS examiner of the omitted income.
    B. Sam must notify the IRS that he is no longer representing Fred by withdrawing his Form 2848.
    C. Sam must advise Fred promptly of the omission and the consequences provided by the Internal Revenue Code and regulations for such omission.
    D. Sam must advise Fred on how to keep the omission

95. John Bright recently passed the Special Enrollment Examination and is advertising for his business. Which of the following presentations will violate the Circular 230 rules for advertising?
    A. John Bright, enrolled to practice before the IRS
    B. John Bright, Certified Enrolled Agent
    C. John Bright, enrolled to represent taxpayers before the IRS
    D. John Bright, admitted to practice before the IRS

96. Circular 230, discusses standards for advising clients with respect to tax return positions and for preparing or signing returns. Which of the statements below is **true**?
    A. A practitioner may not sign a tax return as a preparer if the practitioner determines that the tax return contains a position that does not have a realistic possibility of being sustained on its merits (the realistic possibility standard) unless the position is not frivolous and is adequately disclosed to the IRS.
    B. A practitioner advising a client to take a position on a tax return, or preparing or signing a tax return as a preparer, must inform the client of the penalties reasonably likely to apply to the client with respect to the position advised, prepared, or reported.

C. A practitioner advising a client to take a position on a tax return, or preparing or signing a tax return as a preparer, generally may rely in good faith without verification upon information furnished by the client. The practitioner may not, however, ignore the implications of information furnished to, or actually known by, the practitioner, and must make reasonable inquiries if the information as furnished appears to be incorrect, inconsistent with an important fact or another factual assumption, or incomplete.
D. All of the above.

97. The Office of Professional Responsibility can censure, suspend, or disbar a practitioner from practice before the IRS for incompetence and/or disreputable conduct.
Which one of the following is considered disreputable conduct?
A. Being indicted for any criminal offense under the revenue laws of the United States
B. Having your motor vehicle license suspended as a result of numerous traffic violations
C. Being indicted of any felony under federal or state law for which the conduct involved renders the practitioner unfit to practice before the IRS
D. Giving false or misleading information, or participating in any way in the giving of false or misleading information to the Department of the Treasury or any officer or employee thereof

98. Select the statement below that is **correct** with respect to the contents of an answer that is filed in rebuttal to a complaint filed by the Office of Professional Responsibility.
A. The answer must be written and general denials are permitted.
B. The respondent does not have to admit or deny all of the allegations set forth in the complaint and can state they are without sufficient information to admit or deny a specific allegation.
C. The respondent may not deny a material allegation in the complaint that the respondent knows to be true, or state that the respondent is without sufficient information to form a belief, when the respondent possesses the required information.
D. The respondent does not have to state affirmatively any special matters of defense on which he or she relies.

99. John Jones prepared a return for a client that contained a frivolous position that could not be defended under any circumstances. The examiner who conducted the examination referred Mr. Jones to the Office of Professional Responsibility. After all procedural requirements had been met; the Office of Professional Responsibility

filed a complaint against John Jones. Which statement below is **correct** with respect to the hearing that will take place for the complaint filed against Mr. Jones?
- A. An Administrative Law Judge will preside at the hearing on a complaint filed for the censure, suspension, or disbarment of a practitioner or disqualification of an appraiser.
- B. A request by a practitioner or appraiser that a hearing in a disciplinary proceeding concerning him or her be public, and that the record of such disciplinary proceeding be made available for inspection by interested persons may be granted by a United States District Court judge.
- C. The United States District Court judge assigned to the case will determine the location of the hearing.
- D. If either party to the proceeding fails to appear at the hearing, after notice of the proceeding has been sent to him or her, the party will be deemed to have waived the right to a hearing and the United States District Court judge may make his or her decision against the absent party by default.

100. After a decision has been made on a complaint filed by the Office of Professional Responsibility, the practitioner or Office of Professional Responsibility may appeal the decision. Which statement is **correct** with respect to filing an appeal of the decision?
- A. Within 30 days from the date of the District Court Judge's decision, either party may appeal to the Secretary of the Treasury, or his or her delegate.
- B. Within 30 days from the date of the District Court Judge's decision, either party may appeal to the Supreme Court.
- C. Within 30 days from the date of the Administrative Law Judge's decision, either party may appeal to the Secretary of the Treasury, or his or her delegate.
- D. Within 45 days from the date of the Administrative Law Judge's decision, either party may appeal to the Secretary of the Treasury, or his or her delegate.

101. Each individual applying for renewal as an Enrolled Agent must complete CPE credits during each year of enrollment. How long must each practitioner maintain records of their completed CPE credits?
- A. CPE credits do not have to be retained by the Enrolled Agent since the qualifying organization provides the Office of Professional Responsibility a list of each participant that completed CPE credits.
- B. The Enrolled Agent does not have to retain any proof of CPE credits because they must be submitted to the Office of Professional Responsibility as they are completed.
- C. The Enrolled Agent must retain for a period of 1 year, from the date they completed the CPE credit, information required (as listed in Circular 230) that documents successful completion of qualified CPE credits.

D. The Enrolled Agent applying for renewal must retain the information required (as listed in Circular 230) which documents successful completion of qualified CPE credits, for a period of 3 years following the date of renewal of enrollment.

102. Sam is an enrolled agent and a partner in the firm of Taxes-R-Us, LLP. One of Sam's former partners is under investigation by the Office of Professional Responsibility for disreputable conduct. Sam has been asked by the Office of Professional Responsibility to provide information regarding his former partner. Sam must provide all the information requested **unless**:
    A. He has credible evidence that Sam is not guilty of the disreputable conduct.
    B. He believes in good faith and on reasonable grounds that the information requested is privileged or that the request is of doubtful legality.
    C. The partnership agreement prohibits him from providing the information. The conduct in question relates to one of Sam's clients.
    D. The conduct in question relates to one of Sam's clients.

103. Mike is an enrolled agent. Widget, Inc. is an accrual basis taxpayer. In 2002, while preparing Widget's 2001 return, Mike discovered that Widget failed to include income on its 2000 return that Widget received in 2001, but that should have been included in income in 2000 under the accrual method of accounting. What must Mike do?
    A. Advise Widget of the error and the consequences of the error.
    B. Include the income on the 2001 return.
    C. Refuse to prepare Widget's 2001 return until Widget agrees to amend its 2000 return to include the amount in income.
    D. Change Widget to the cash method of accounting.

104. John, a CPA, is a sole proprietor of a practice that represents taxpayers in IRS examinations and appeals proceedings. Sally, an enrolled agent, is an associate in John's firm and paid by John as an employee. On February 1, 2003, John is disbarred from practice before the IRS by the Office of Professional Responsibility. What, if anything, must Sally do after John is disbarred?
    A. Nothing.
    B. Quit.
    C. Become John's partner.
    D. Report all of John's activities to the Office of Professional Responsibility on a quarterly basis.

105. Sandy is an enrolled agent. He is preparing a brochure to hand to prospective clients and would like to explain the designation "enrolled agent." Which of the following language is Sandy **not** permitted to use?
    A. "I am permitted to practice before the IRS."
    B. "I am enrolled to represent taxpayers before the IRS."
    C. "I am certified by the IRS."
    D. "I am admitted to practice before the IRS."

106. Mike is an enrolled agent. For the past five years, the information that Anne provided Mike to prepare her return included a Schedule K-1 from a partnership showing significant income. However, Mike did not see a Schedule K-1 from the partnership among the information Anne provided to him this year. What does due diligence require Mike to do?
    A. Without talking to Anne, Mike should estimate the amount that would be reported as income on the Schedule K-1 based on last year's Schedule K-1 and include that amount on Anne's return.
    B. Call Anne's financial advisor and ask him about Anne's investments.
    C. Nothing, because Mike is required to rely only on the information provided by his client, even if he has a reason to know the information is not accurate.
    D. Ask Anne about the fact that she did not provide him with a Schedule K-1.

107. Phil, an enrolled agent, prepares William's income tax return. William gives Phil power of attorney, including the authorization to receive his federal income tax refund check. Accordingly, the IRS sends William's $100 refund check to Phil's office. William is very slow in paying his bills and owes Phil $500 for tax services. Phil should:
    A. Use William's check as collateral for a $100 loan to tide him over until William pays him.
    B. Refuse to give William the check until William pays him the $500.
    C. Get William's written authorization to endorse the check, cash the check, and reduce the amount William owes him to $400.
    D. Turn the check directly over to William.

108. Sandra, an enrolled agent, prepares Linda's income tax return. Linda sold some stock in a corporation and believes the proceeds of the stock are all a return to capital, and therefore, not included in her gross income. After research, Sandra determines that there is reasonable basis for Linda's position, but she does not believe there is a realistic possibility of success on the merits. Under what circumstances can Sandra sign Linda's return if the proceeds are **not** included in income reported on the return?
    A. If the position is not frivolous and is adequately disclosed on the return.

B. If Sandra documents her disagreement with Linda's position and keeps it in her file.
C. If Linda agrees in writing not to dispute any IRS challenge to the position.
D. Under no circumstances.

109. A practitioner who is disbarred by the Office of Professional Responsibility may seek reinstatement after:
    A. 1 year.
    B. 2 years.
    C. 4 years.
    D. 5 years.

110. Ray was suspended from practice for four months by the Office of Professional Responsibility. Which of the following is Ray permitted to do during the period of suspension?
    A. Prepare tax returns.
    B. Sign closing agreements regarding tax liabilities.
    C. Represent taxpayers before IRS with respect to returns Ray did **not** prepare.
    D. Sign a consent to extend the statute of limitations for the assessment and collection of tax.

111. Matt, an enrolled agent, provided tax advice to XYZ corporation on a federal tax matter. The Securities and Exchange Commission ("SEC") is reviewing a required filing of the XYZ Corporation and asks to see a copy of Matt's tax advice. The tax advice is not protected by the federally authorized tax practitioner privilege under IRC section 7525 from disclosure to the SEC because:
    A. Matt is not a lawyer.
    B. Matt is not a CPA.
    C. The federally authorized tax practitioner privilege protects advice only against disclosure to the IRS, not other government agencies.
    D. The federally authorized tax practitioner privilege protects only advice to individuals.

112. Who is authorized to practice before the IRS if they hold power of attorney?
    A. Any person considered an enrolled agent under Circular 230, who is not currently under suspension or disbarment from practice before the IRS who files a written declaration that he or she is currently qualified as an enrolled agent and is authorized to represent the particular party on whose behalf he or she acts.

B. Any attorney who is **not** currently under suspension or disbarment from practice before the IRS who files a written declaration that he or she is currently qualified as an attorney and is authorized to represent the particular party on whose behalf he or she acts.
C. Both A and B.
D. Neither A or B.

113. Janet is not an enrolled agent, CPA, attorney, or enrolled actuary. In 1999, the president of Widgets-R-Us engaged Janet to prepare the company's 1998 Form 1120-S. Janet prepared the 1998 income tax return for Widgets-R-Us and signed it as the preparer. This is the only return Janet prepared for Widgets-RUs. In December 2000, the IRS began an examination of Widgets-R-Us' 1997 and 1998 Federal income tax returns. Janet has a power of attorney to represent Widgets-R-Us for 1997 and 1998. Under Circular 230, Janet is permitted to represent Widgets-R-Us during the examination with regard to its:
    A. 1997 Form 1120-S only.
    B. 1998 Form 1120-S only.
    C. 1997 and 1998 Forms 1120-S.
    D. None of the above.

114. The IRS began an examination of Mr. Jones' 2000 income tax return. Mr. Jones hired Tyler, an enrolled agent and former IRS employee, to represent him before the IRS. Tyler wrote a memorandum to Mr. Jones outlining the issues that might be raised by the IRS and how to address these issues. Tyler correctly marked this memorandum as confidential and privileged under Section 7525 of the Internal Revenue Code. During the examination, the Revenue Officer assigned to the case asked Tyler for a copy of the memorandum. Mr. Jones, invoking the Section 7525 privilege, told Tyler not to disclose it to the Revenue Officer. Tyler is **not** required to provide the Revenue Officer with a copy of the memorandum because:
    A. The Revenue Officer did not issue a summons requesting it.
    B. Section 7525 extends the attorney client privilege to federally authorized tax practitioners.
    C. Circular 230 does not authorize officers or employees of the IRS to request any documents other than a tax return.
    D. The IRS cannot request documents during an examination.

115. Ms. Smith hired Tom, an enrolled agent, to prepare her Federal income tax return for 2001. While gathering information to prepare the return, Tom discovered that Ms. Smith failed to file Federal income tax returns for the 1999 and 2000 tax years. Circular 230 requires that Tom do the following:

A. Promptly advise Ms. Smith that she did not comply with the Internal Revenue laws by failing to file Federal income tax returns for the 1999 and the 2000 tax years.
  B. Refuse to prepare Ms. Smith's 2000 Federal income tax return unless she files her 1999 and 2000 Federal income tax returns.
  C. Inform the IRS that Ms. Smith did not file Federal income tax returns for the 1999 and 2000 tax years.
  D. Both B and C.

116. Failure to file an answer to a complaint instituting a proceeding for disbarment by the original or extended deadline constitutes:
  A. An admission of the allegations in the complaint and a waiver of a hearing.
  B. An error that can be corrected by filing the answer with the Administrative Law Judge within one year of the original (or extended) deadline.
  C. Grounds for criminal sanctions.
  D. Equitable estoppel against the practitioner.

117. How is a proceeding for violation of the regulations in Circular 230 instituted against an attorney, certified public accountant, enrolled agent, or enrolled actuary?
  A. An aggrieved taxpayer files a petition with the United States Tax Court stating a claim against the attorney, certified public accountant, enrolled agent, or enrolled actuary.
  B. The Commissioner of the IRS files a complaint against the attorney, certified public accountant, enrolled agent, or enrolled actuary with the United States Tax Court.
  C. The Director of Practice signs a complaint naming the attorney, certified public accountant, enrolled agent, or enrolled actuary and files the complaint in the Director's office.
  D. The Secretary of the Treasury files a complaint against the attorney, certified public accountant, enrolled agent, or enrolled actuary in the United States District Court for the District of Columbia.

118. Who presides over a hearing on a complaint for disbarment based on a violation of the laws or regulations governing practice before the IRS?
  A. The Commissioner of IRS.
  B. An Administrative Law Judge.
  C. A United States Tax Court Judge.
  D. The Secretary of the Treasury.

119. An appeal from the initial decision ordering disbarment is made to which of the following:
    A. The Secretary of the Treasury.
    B. The Administrative Law Judge.
    C. The United States District Court for the District of Columbia.
    D. The United States Tax Court.

120. Treasury Circular 230:
    A. Contains rules of conduct applicable to enrolled agents and enrolled actuaries, but not attorneys or certified public accountants.
    B. Contains rules regarding disciplinary actions for tax return preparers who are not enrolled agents, CPA's or attorneys
    C. Contains the rules regarding eligibility to become an enrolled agent and renewal of enrollment.
    D. All of the above.

121. Arnie is a Certified Public Accountant who prepares income tax returns for his clients. One of his clients submitted a list of expenses to be claimed on Schedule C of the tax return. Arnie qualifies as a return preparer and, as such, is required to comply with which one of the following conditions?
    A. Arnie is required to independently verify the client's information.
    B. Arnie can ignore implications of information known by him.
    C. Inquiry is not required if the information appears to be incorrect or incomplete.
    D. Appropriate inquiries are required to determine whether the client has substantiation for travel and entertainment expenses.

122. Which of the following individuals qualify as a practitioner under Circular 230?
    A. Certified public accountant
    B. Enrolled actuary
    C. Attorney
    D. All of the above

123. Frank, a certified public accountant, has the right to make the following solicitations of employment involving IRS matters:
    A. Seeking new business from a former client
    B. Communicating with a family member
    C. Targeting mailings
    D. All of the above

124. Maude, an attorney, has been charged by the Director of Practice with acts of misconduct. Which of the following forms of evidence is Maude not permitted to introduce at the hearing:
    A. Depositions
    B. Exhibits
    C. Letters
    D. All of the above.

125. A notice of disbarment or suspension of a certified public accountant from practice before the IRS is issued to which of the following:
    A. IRS employees
    B. Interested departments and agencies of the Federal government
    C. State authorities
    D. All of the above

126. Enrolled agents generally must complete continuing education credits for renewed enrollment. Which of the following describes the credit requirements?
    A. A minimum of 72 hours must be completed in each year of an enrollment cycle
    B. A minimum of 24 hours must be completed in each year of an enrollment cycle
    C. A minimum of 80 hours must be completed, overall, for the entire enrollment cycle
    D. A minimum of 16 hours must be completed in each year of the enrollment cycle

127. Generally, each individual who applies for renewal to practice before the IRS must retain the information required with regard to qualifying Continuing Professional Education hours: How long must verification of CPE taken be retained?
    A. For a period of one year following the date of renewal of enrollment
    B. For a period of three years following the date of renewal of enrollment
    C. For a period of five years if it is an initial enrollment
    D. The individual is not required to retain the information if the Continuing Professional Education sponsor has agreed to retain it

128. The Director of Practice notified Sally in February 1999 that she passed the Special Enrollment Examination. She submitted her application for enrollment, and received the initial enrollment on June 15, 1999. Her Continuing Professional Education requirements until the first full renewal cycle are:
    A. She does not have to complete any Continuing Professional Education requirements until the first full renewal cycle
    B. She must complete two hours of credit for each full month and each part of a month left in the current renewal cycle

C. She must complete a minimum of 72 hours of Continuing Professional Education unless she is within less than a year before the end of the current cycle
D. She must complete two hours of credit for only each full month left in the current renewal cycle.

129. Identify the item below that is **not** considered practice before the IRS:
    A. Corresponding with the IRS on behalf of a client.
    B. Preparing a tax return for an individual.
    C. Representing a client at an audit.
    D. Calling the IRS to discuss a letter received by a client.

130. Identify the individual below who is **not** eligible to practice before the IRS. None of the individuals are under suspension or disbarment.
    A. Enrolled actuary, with respect to specified statutory issues.
    B. Attorney.
    C. Certified public accountant.
    D. Certified financial planner.

131. Identify the individual below who would **not** be eligible to practice before the IRS under the limited practice rules.
    A. An unenrolled tax preparer who works for a firm. The taxpayer's return was prepared by another individual who also works for the firm.
    B. An unenrolled tax preparer who prepared and signed the tax return.
    C. An unenrolled preparer who appears as a witness for the taxpayer.
    D. An unenrolled tax preparer who represents taxpayers before IRS personnel who are outside of the U.S.

132. The following persons are authorized to represent a taxpayer before the IRS:
    A. An individual representing a member of his/her immediate family.
    B. A regular full-time employee of an individual employer representing the employer.
    C. An officer or full-time employee of a corporation representing the corporation.
    D. All of the above.

133. Identify the appropriate action that a practitioner should take when he or she becomes aware of an error or omission on a client's return.
    A. Amend the return and provide it to the client.
    B. Inform the IRS of the noncompliance, error, or omission.

C. Do nothing.
D. Promptly advise the client of such noncompliance, error, or omission.

134. Identify the individual below from whom an enrolled agent, in practice before the IRS, may knowingly accept assistance:
    A. An individual who is under disbarment from practice before the IRS.
    B. An individual who is under suspension from practice before the IRS.
    C. An individual who has temporary recognition to practice before the IRS.
    D. A former government employee where any Federal law would be violated.

135. Which of the following mailings, offering your tax preparation or representation services, would not be classified as a targeted direct mail solicitation?
    A. A mailing with an attached gift certificate to all new home owners in a specific zip code area.
    B. A mailing to all taxpayers who have filed for bankruptcy in the past year.
    C. A mailing to all taxpayers for whom you prepared a Schedule C last year, offering to explain the advantages of establishing a Keogh account before the end of the year.
    D. A mailing to all dentists listed in the yellow pages for your office.

136. An enrolled agent may be disbarred or suspended from IRS practice for which of the following conduct:
    A. Criminal conviction of an offense under the Internal Revenue Code.
    B. Misappropriation of funds received from a client for the purpose of tax payments.
    C. Disbarment or suspension from the practice as an attorney, C.P.A, accountant, or actuary.
    D. All of the above.

137. The Director of Practice has documentation that an enrolled agent has violated the law or regulations governing practice before the IRS. He or She may:
    A. Reprimand such person.
    B. Institute proceedings for disbarment.
    C. Institute proceedings for suspension.
    D. All of the above.

138. An enrolled agent can recommend a position on the client's tax return as long as the position is:
    A. Reasonable.

B. Not frivolous.
C. Adequately disclosed.
D. All of the above.

139. All of the following individuals are eligible to practice (on a limited basis) before the IRS except:
    A. A regular full-time employee of an individual may represent the employer.
    B. A bona fide officer of a corporation may represent the corporation.
    C. A limited partner in a partnership may represent the partnership.
    D. A trustee of a trust may represent the trust.

140. All of the following are considered examples of disreputable conduct for which an enrolled agent can be disbarred or suspended except:
    A. Directly or indirectly attempting to influence the official action of any employee of the IRS by use of threats, false accusations, or by bestowing any gift, favor or thing of value.
    B. Misappropriation or failure to remit funds received from a client for the purpose of payment of taxes or other obligations due the United States.
    C. Knowingly aiding and abetting another person to practice before the IRS during a period of suspension or disbarment.
    D. Failure to timely pay personal income taxes.

141. Which of the following is an income tax return preparer?
    A. Neighbor who assists with preparation of depreciation schedule.
    B. Son who enters income tax return information into computer program and prints return.
    C. Woman who prepares income tax returns in her home during filing season and accepts payment for her services.
    D. Volunteer at a local church who prepares income tax returns but accepts no payment

142. Which of the following Forms is used by applicants to apply to take the special enrollment examination?
    A. Form 2848
    B. Form 23
    C. Form 2587
    D. Form 8554

143. Which of the following Forms is used to apply for enrollment by applicants who have passed the special enrollment examination?

A. Form 2848
B. Form 23
C. Form 2587
D. Form 8554

144. Which of the following Forms is used to apply for Renewal of Enrollment to Practice before the IRS?
    A. Form 8554
    B. Form 23
    C. Form 2587
    D. Form 2848

145. To qualify for CPE credit for an enrolled agent, a course of learning must be a qualifying program designed to enhance professional knowledge. Which one of the following courses would **not** be acceptable as qualifying course?
    A. Accounting
    B. Tax preparation software
    C. Ethics
    D. Economics

146. Which of the following situations is protected by section 7525 confidentiality privilege?
    A. Information disclosed to a tax practitioner for the purpose of preparing a return.
    B. Criminal tax matters before the IRS or in federal court.
    C. Noncriminal tax matters before the IRS or in federal court.
    D. Written communications made in connection with the promotion of direct or indirect participation in a tax shelter.

1.08 UNIT 1: ANSWERS

1. **(B) Correct**
    Just preparing a tax return, furnishing information at the request of the IRS, or appearing as a witness for the taxpayer is not practice before the IRS. These acts can be performed by anyone.

2. **(B) Correct**
    According to circular 230, a practitioner may not, knowingly and directly or indirectly accept assistance from or assist any person who is under disbarment or suspension from practice before the IRS.

3. **(B) Correct**
    The Secretary of the Treasury (rather than Office of Professional Responsibility) may censure (public reprimand), suspend, or disbar any practitioner from practice before the IRS.

4. **(B) Correct**
    Practicing before the IRS include all off the following:
    (a) Communicating with the IRS for a taxpayer regarding the taxpayer's rights, privileges, or liabilities under laws and regulations administered by the IRS.
    (b) Representing a taxpayer at conferences, hearings, or meetings with the IRS.
    (c) Preparing and filing documents with the IRS for a taxpayer.
    (d) Corresponding and communicating with the IRS.
    Preparing or signing a formal written protest on behalf of a client to request an appeals conference is part of all the four items above.

5. **(A) Correct**
    Under Code Sec. 6695, a preparer is required to furnish a completed copy of the return or claim for refund to the taxpayer before (or at the same time) the return or claim for refund is presented to the taxpayer for signature. A penalty applies if the preparer fails to furnish a copy to Taxpayer.

6. **(A) Correct**
    The Director of the Office of Professional Responsibility will maintain *rosters* of all enrolled agents, as well as individuals who have been censured, suspended or disbarred from practice before the IRS or upon whom a monetary penalty was imposed.

7. **(B) Correct**

    Section 7525 provides a privilege of confidentiality for communications between a taxpayer and a *federally authorized tax practitioner* that has essentially the same scope as the federal attorney-client privilege. Section 7525 confidentiality privilege does **not** protect against criminal tax matters before the I.R.S. or in federal court.

8. **(A) Correct**

    An individual who receives initial enrollment during an enrollment cycle must complete 2 hours of qualifying continuing education credit for each month enrolled during the enrollment cycle. Enrollment for any part of a month is considered enrollment for the entire month.

9. **(A) Correct**

    A practitioner will be presumed to have exercised due if the practitioner relies on the work product of another person and the practitioner used reasonable care in engaging, supervising, training, and evaluating the person, taking proper account of the nature of the relationship between the practitioner and the person.

10. **(B) Correct**

    An unenrolled return preparer is permitted to appear as a representative only before *customer service representatives*, *revenue agents*, and *examination officers*, with respect to an examination regarding the return he or she prepared. Thus, the unenrolled return preparer cannot represent clients concerning a return they have not prepared. It must be for a *specific* tax return he or she prepared.

11. **(A) Correct**

    A practitioner must exercise due diligence when performing the following duties:
    (a) Preparing or assisting in the preparing, approving, and filing of returns, documents, affidavits, and other papers relating to IRS matters.
    (b) Determining the correctness of oral or written representations made by him or her to the Department of the Treasury.
    (c) Determining the correctness of oral or written representations made by him or her to clients with reference to any matter administered by the IRS.

12. **(A) Correct**

    Written advice is a *reliance opinion* if the advice has more than 50 % likelihood that one or more significant Federal tax issues would be resolved in the taxpayer's favor. Written advice is not treated as a *reliance opinion* if the practitioner discloses in the written advice that it was not intended or written by the practitioner to be used, and that it cannot be used by the taxpayer, for the purpose of avoiding penalties that may be imposed on the taxpayer.

13. **(B) Correct**
A practitioner is not allowed to represent a client before the IRS if the representation involves a conflict of interest. A conflict of interest exists if:
   (a) The representation of one client will be directly adverse to another client, or
   (b) There is a significant risk that the representation of one or more clients will be materially limited by the practitioner's responsibilities to another client, a former client or a third person, or by a personal interest of the practitioner.

14. **(B) Correct**
So long as due diligence is used in determining the correctness of oral or written representations made by the practitioner to clients with reference to any matter administered by the IRS, the practitioner does not have to complete all tasks related to the representation.

15. **(B) Correct**
Any practitioner or unenrolled return preparer may be disbarred or suspended from practice before the IRS, or censured, for disreputable conduct. Knowingly giving false or misleading information in connection with federal tax matters, or participating in such activity is one of the examples of disreputable conduct.

16. **(A) Correct**
Practice before the IRS covers all matters relating to any of the following:
   (a) Communicating with the IRS for a taxpayer regarding the taxpayer's rights, privileges, or liabilities under laws and regulations administered by the IRS.
   (b) Representing a taxpayer at conferences, hearings, or meetings with the IRS.
   (c) Preparing and filing documents with the IRS for a taxpayer.
   (d) Corresponding and communicating with the IRS.

17. **(A) Correct**
See answer # 13)

18. **(A) Correct**
Whenever the Director of the Office of Professional Responsibility determines that a practitioner violated any laws governing practice before IRS, the Director may do one of the following:
   1) Reprimand the practitioner, or
   2) Institute a proceeding for a sanction (a proceeding is instituted by the filing of a complaint).

Usually, a proceeding will not be instituted unless the practitioner has been notified in writing about the law, facts, and conduct warranting such action and has been accorded an opportunity to dispute the facts, assert additional facts, and make arguments.

19. **(B) Correct**
    The Director of the Office of Professional Responsibility will maintain *rosters* of the following people, and may make available for public inspection:
    1. Enrolled agents, including individuals:
        (a) People who have been granted active enrollment to practice.
        (b) People have their enrollment placed in inactive status for failure to meet the requirements for renewal for enrollment.
        (c) People who have their enrollment placed in inactive retirement status.
        (d) Whose offer of consent to resign from enrollment has been accepted by the Director of the Office of Professional Responsibility
    2. Individuals who have been censured, suspended or disbarred from practice before the IRS or upon whom a monetary penalty was imposed.

20. **(A) Correct**
    Practicing before the IRS include all off the following:
    a) Communicating with the IRS for a taxpayer regarding the taxpayer's rights, privileges, or liabilities under laws and regulations administered by the IRS.
    b) Representing a taxpayer at conferences, hearings, or meetings with the IRS.
    c) Preparing and filing documents with the IRS for a taxpayer.
    d) Corresponding and communicating with the IRS

    Preparing or signing a formal written protest on behalf of a client to request an appeals conference is part of all the four items above.

21. **(A) Correct**
    A tax return includes income tax, estate tax, gift tax, excise tax, employment tax and certain information returns. A tax return also includes an amended or adjusted return. A tax return also includes any information return.

22. **(A) Correct**
    A practitioner is not allowed to represent a client before the IRS if the representation involves a conflict of interest. A conflict of interest exists if:
    a) The representation of one client will be directly adverse to another client, or
    b) There is a significant risk that the representation of one or more clients will be materially limited by the practitioner's responsibilities to another client, a former client or a third person, or by a personal interest of the practitioner.

23. **(A) Correct**
    Circular 230 (regulations governing practice), contains special rules for professional conduct with respect to tax avoidance or tax evasion opinions. Even

though the circular does not explicitly mention the word 'tax-shelter', it has been mostly associated with tax avoidance/evasion schemes. Abusive tax shelters are now also referred to as abusive tax avoidance transactions.

24. **(B) Correct**
An Income tax return preparer is defined as person (including a partnership or corporation) who prepares for compensation all or a substantial portion of a tax return or claim for refund under the income tax provisions of the Code.

25. **(B) Correct**
An unenrolled return preparer is permitted to appear as a representative only before *customer service representatives*, *revenue agents*, and *examination officers*, with respect to an examination regarding the return he or she prepared. Thus, the unenrolled return preparer cannot represent clients concerning a return they have not prepared. It must be for a *specific* tax return he or she prepared.

26. **(A) Correct**
See answer # 10

27. **(A) Correct**
The Director of the Office of Professional Responsibility must inform the applicant as to the reason(s) for any denial of an application for enrollment. The applicant may, within 30 days after receipt of the notice of denial of enrollment, file a written appeal of the denial of enrollment with the Secretary of the Treasury or his or her delegate.

28. **(A) Correct**
A practitioner who knows that his or her client has not complied with the revenue laws or has made an error or omission in any return, document, affidavit, or other required paper, has the responsibility to advise the client promptly of the noncompliance, error, or omission, and the consequences of the noncompliance, error, or omission.

29. **(B) Correct**
A practitioner must exercise due diligence when performing the following duties:
   a) Preparing or assisting in the preparing, approving, and filing of returns, documents, affidavits, and other papers relating to IRS matters.
   b) Determining the correctness of oral or written representations made by him or her to the Department of the Treasury.
   c) Determining the correctness of oral or written representations made by him or her to clients with reference to any matter administered by the IRS.

30. **(A) Correct**
    A practitioner may be subject to the sanction of either suspension or censure for failure to advise his or her clients about a potential conflict of interest or for failure to obtain the clients' written consents.

31. **(B) Correct**
    Practitioners who are income tax return preparers may not endorse or otherwise negotiate (cash) any refund check issued to the taxpayer.

32. **(B) Correct**
    Circular 230 (regulations governing practice), contains special rules for professional conduct with respect to tax avoidance or tax evasion opinions. Even though the circular does not explicitly mention the word 'tax-shelter', it has been mostly associated with tax avoidance/evasion schemes. Abusive tax shelters are now also referred to as abusive tax avoidance transactions.

33. **(A) Correct**
    A practitioner may not sign a tax return as a preparer, or advise a client to take a position on a tax return if the practitioner determines that the tax return or the position on a tax return contains a position that does not have a realistic possibility of being sustained on its merits unless the position is **not** frivolous and is adequately disclosed to the IRS.

34. **(B) Correct**
    Disreputable conduct listed on circular 230 includes misappropriation, or failing to properly and promptly remit, funds received from clients for payment of taxes or other obligations due the United States. This carries the same definition as embezzlement, which is a criminal offense.

35. **(A) Correct**
    During the proceedings before the Administrative Law Judge, a respondent (practitioner) may appear in person, be represented by a practitioner, or be represented by an attorney who has not filed a declaration with the IRS.

36. **(A) Correct**
    An appeal and brief must be filed (in duplicate) with the Director of the Office of Professional Responsibility within 30 days of the date that the decision of the Administrative Law Judge is made. Then the Director will immediately furnish a copy of the appeal to the Secretary of the Treasury or delegate who decides appeals.

37. **(A) Correct**

Upon the issuance of a final order censuring, suspending, or disbarring a practitioner or a final order disqualifying an appraiser, the Director of the Office of Professional Responsibility may give notice of the censure, suspension, disbarment, or disqualification to appropriate officers and employees of the IRS and to interested departments and agencies of the Federal government, including state authorities.

38. **(A) Correct**
    Practice before the IRS covers all matters relating to any of the following:
    (1) Communicating with the IRS for a taxpayer regarding the taxpayer's rights, privileges, or liabilities under laws and regulations administered by the IRS.
    (2) Representing a taxpayer at conferences, hearings, or meetings with the IRS.
    (3) Preparing and filing documents with the IRS for a taxpayer.
    (4) Corresponding and communicating with the IRS.

39. **(B) Correct**
    The Director of the Office of Professional Responsibility must inform the applicant as to the reason(s) for any denial of an application for enrollment. The applicant may, within 30 days after receipt of the notice of denial of enrollment, file a written appeal of the denial of enrollment with the Secretary of the Treasury or his or her delegate.

40. **(B) Correct**
    A practitioner must promptly submit records or information in any matter before the IRS, *unless* the practitioner believes in good faith and on reasonable grounds that the records or information are privileged.

41. **(A) Correct**
    A practitioner who knows that his or her client has not complied with the revenue laws or has made an error or omission in any return, document, affidavit, or other required paper, has the responsibility to advise the client promptly of the noncompliance, error, or omission, and the consequences of the noncompliance, error, or omission.

42. **(A) Correct**
    According to circular 230, a practitioner may not, knowingly and directly or indirectly accept assistance from or assist any person who is under disbarment or suspension from practice before the IRS.

43. **(A) Correct**
    A practitioner must exercise due diligence when performing the following duties:
    (1) Preparing or assisting in the preparing, approving, and filing of returns, documents, affidavits, and other papers relating to IRS matters.

(2) Determining the correctness of oral or written representations made by him or her to the Department of the Treasury.
(3) Determining the correctness of oral or written representations made by him or her to clients with reference to any matter administered by the IRS.

44. **(A) Correct**
Practitioners who are income tax return preparers may not endorse or otherwise negotiate (cash) any refund check issued to the taxpayer.

45. **(B) Correct**
A list of requirements for covered opinions is listed on page 21.

46. **(A) Correct**
A position has a realistic possibility of being sustained if a reasonable and well-informed analysis by a person knowledgeable in tax law would lead such a person to conclude that the position has approximately a one-in-three, or greater, likelihood of being sustained on its merits.

47. **(B) Correct**
Any practitioner or unenrolled return preparer may be disbarred or suspended from practice before the IRS, or censured, for disreputable conduct. Soliciting employment by prohibited means as discussed in section 10.30 of Treasury Department Circular No. 230 is one of the disreputable conducts listed. Section 10.30 states that a practitioner may not make, directly or indirectly, an uninvited written or oral solicitation of employment in matters related to the IRS if the solicitation violates Federal or State law or other applicable rule.

48. **(B) Correct**
The Director of the Office of Professional Responsibility must do the following within the complaint:
   (i) Notify the respondent (practitioner) of the time for answering the complaint, which may not be less than 30 days from the date of *service of the complaint*.
   (ii) Include the name and address of the Administrative Law Judge with whom the answer must be filed.
   (iii) Include the name and address of the person representing the Director to whom a copy of the answer must be served.
   (iv) Note that a decision by default may be rendered against the respondent (practitioner) in the event an answer is not filed as required.

49. **(A) Correct**
Appeal of the Administrative Law Judge decision is made with the Secretary of the Treasury or his/her delegate.

50. **(A) Correct**
Circular No. 230 is a Treasury Department Circular that sets forth the regulations governing practice before the IRS. These regulations in Circular 230 governing the practice of attorneys, certified public accountants, enrolled agents, enrolled actuaries and appraisers before the IRS are found under *Title 31 Code of Federal Regulations, Subtitle A, Part 10.*

51. **(B) Correct**
The Director of the Office of Professional Responsibility will maintain *rosters* of the following people, and may make available for public inspection:
   1. Enrolled agents, including individuals:
      (i) People who have been granted active enrollment to practice.
      (ii) People have their enrollment placed in inactive status for failure to meet the requirements for renewal for enrollment.
      (iii) People who have their enrollment placed in inactive retirement status.
      (iv) Whose offer of consent to resign from enrollment has been accepted by the Director of the Office of Professional Responsibility
   2. Individuals who have been censured, suspended or disbarred from practice before the IRS or upon whom a monetary penalty was imposed.

52. **(B) Correct**
Enrolled actuaries must be enrolled as an actuary by the Joint Board for the Enrollment of Actuaries and must not currently be under suspension or disbarment from practice before the IRS. Practice as an enrolled actuary is limited to issues involving categories outlined on page 14.

53. **(B) Correct**
There are two way of becoming an enrolled agent:
   1) Written examination
   2) IRS experience

54. **(B) Correct**
The IRS is a Federal unit and therefore representation is not limited by states. Attorneys and accountants that are in good standing are recognized practitioners authorized to practice before the IRS. Thus, they can practice anywhere in the United States including its territories.

55. **(B) Correct**
Appeal of the Administrative Law Judge decision is made with the Secretary of the Treasury or his/her delegate.

56. **(A) Correct**

An unenrolled return preparer is permitted to appear as a representative only before customer service representatives, revenue agents, and examination officers, with respect to an examination regarding the return he or she prepared. A non-signing preparer is an unenrolled return preparer.

57. **(A) Correct**
A practitioner must promptly submit records or information in any matter before the IRS, <u>unless</u> the practitioner believes in good faith and on reasonable grounds that the records or information are privileged.

58. **(B) Correct**
A practitioner advising a client to take a position on a tax return, or preparing or signing a tax return as a preparer, generally may rely in good faith without verification upon information furnished by the client. The practitioner may not, however, ignore the implications of information furnished to, or actually known by the practitioner, and must make reasonable inquiries if the information as furnished appears to be incorrect, inconsistent with an important fact or another factual assumption, or incomplete.

59. **(B) Correct**
A practitioner who knows that his or her client has not complied with the revenue laws or has made an error or omission in any return, document, affidavit, or other required paper, has the responsibility to advise the client promptly of the noncompliance, error, or omission, and the consequences of the noncompliance, error, or omission. Advising the client to *correct* the error is not mandatory.

60. **(A) Correct**
According to circular 230, a practitioner may not, knowingly and directly or indirectly accept assistance from or assist any person who is under disbarment or suspension from practice before the IRS.

61. **(B) Correct**
Circular 230 permits charge of contingent fee in the following situations:
(1) A practitioner may charge a contingent fee for services rendered in connection with the Service's examination of, or challenge to:
   a) An original tax return, or
   b) An amended return or claim for refund or credit where the amended return or claim for refund or credit was filed within 120 days of the taxpayer receiving a written notice of the examination of, or a written challenge to the original tax return.
(2) A practitioner may charge a contingent fee for services rendered in connection with a claim for credit or refund filed solely in connection with the determination of statutory interest or penalties assessed by the IRS.

(3) A practitioner may charge a contingent fee for services rendered in connection with any judicial proceeding arising under the IRS.

62. **(B) Correct**
In general, a practitioner may not charge an unconscionable (excessive) fee in connection with any matter before the IRS. A practitioner may not charge a contingent fee for preparing an original tax return or for any advice rendered in connection with a position taken or to be taken on an original tax return.

63. **(B) Correct**
Enrolled agents are not allowed to use the term of art *'certified'* or imply an employer/employee relationship with the IRS when describing their professional designation. However, the following descriptions are acceptable for enrolled agents:
   (a) Enrolled to represent taxpayers before the IRS
   (b) enrolled to practice before the IRS
   (c) admitted to practice before IRS

Though not explicitly stated on circular 230, practitioners are not allowed to carry out an advertisement depicting the official IRS insignia (logo).

64. **(A) Correct**
Practitioners are allowed to publish the availability of a written schedule of fees and disseminate the following fee information:
   (a) Fixed fees for specific routine services.
   (b) Hourly rates.
   (c) Range of fees for particular services.
   (d) Fee charged for an initial consultation.

65. **(B) Correct**
A certified public accountant means any person who is duly qualified to practice as a certified public accountant in any state, territory, or possession of the United States, including a Commonwealth, or the District of Columbia. Therefore, any suspension will bar the CPA from practicing in all the jurisdictions mentioned here.

66. **(B) Correct**
The Director of the Office of Professional Responsibility may allow a petition for reinstatement from any person disbarred from practice before the IRS after 5 years have expired from the date of the disbarment or disqualification.

67. **(B) Correct**
Director of the Office of Professional Responsibility may confer with a practitioner on issues concerning allegations of misconduct irrespective of whether a proceeding has been instituted. A practitioner may voluntarily *consent* to be sanctioned instead of going through the proceedings. The Director may

either accept or decline the *offer of consent*, or may request that some revisions to be made to the offer of consent.

68. **(B) Correct**
Proceedings on complaints for the sanction of a practitioner will be conducted by an Administrative Law Judge.

69. **(A) Correct**
A proceeding for disbarment or suspension will not be instituted unless the practitioner has been *notified in writing* about the law, facts, and conduct warranting such action and has been accorded an opportunity to dispute the facts, assert additional facts, and make arguments. In general, the complaint must be served on the respondent or his agent by one of the following ways:
   1) Certified or first class mail to the last known address
   2) In person - Proof of service in person must:
   3) Be a written statement, sworn or affirmed by the person who served the complaint and:
      (i) Identify the manner of service
      (ii) Include the name of recipient,
      (iii) Identify the relationship of the recipient to the respondent (practitioner).
      (iv) Include the Place, date and time of service.
      (v) Other means agreed to by the respondent (practitioner).
   4) Within 10 days of serving the complaint, copies of the *evidence* in support of the complaint must be served on the respondent.

70. **(A) Correct**
An Enrolled agent is any individual, other that an attorney or CPA, that is enrolled to practice before the IRS without any limitations. Thus, enrolled agents can represent the partnership and all of its individual partners during an IRS examination of the partnership return.

71. **(B) Correct**
The confidentiality privilege under section 7525 applies only to communications related to *tax advice*. Confidentiality privilege does **not** protect the following situations:
   (a) Information disclosed to a tax practitioner for the purpose of preparing a return.
   (b) Criminal tax matters before the I.R.S. or in federal court.
   (c) Written communications made in connection with the promotion of direct or indirect participation in a tax shelter.
   (d) Information that is also available from non-privileged sources.
   (e) Communication between the taxpayer's tax practitioner and a third-party who provides information about the taxpayer to the practitioner

72. **(B) Correct**
Just preparing a tax return, furnishing information at the request of the IRS, or appearing as a witness for the taxpayer is not practice before the IRS. These acts can be performed by anyone.

73. **(A) Correct**
The Director of the Office of Professional Responsibility must inform the applicant as to the reason(s) for any denial of an application for enrollment. The applicant may, within 30 days after receipt of the notice of denial of enrollment, file a written appeal of the denial of enrollment with the Secretary of the Treasury or his or her delegate.

74. **(B) Correct**
An individual can represent members of his or her immediate family. Immediate family means a spouse, child, parent, brother, or sister of the individual. During representation, the party being represented does not have to be present.

75. **(B) Correct**
Usually, a proceeding for disbarment or suspension will not be instituted unless the practitioner has been *notified in writing* about the law, facts, and conduct warranting such action and has been accorded an opportunity to dispute the facts, assert additional facts, and make arguments.

76. **(B) Correct**
The only time a duplicate filing of documents is required is when filing an appeal of the decision of the Administrative Law Judge with the Secretary of the Treasury. Circular 230 does not require that all papers be filed in duplicate with regards to complaints filed against enrolled agents.

77. **(A) Correct**
A practitioner may not advise a client to submit a document, affidavit or other paper to the IRS that:
   a) The purpose of which is to delay or impede the administration of the Federal tax laws.
   b) That is frivolous.
   c) That contains or omits information in a manner that demonstrates an intentional disregard of a rule or regulation unless the practitioner also advises the client to submit a document that evidences a good faith challenge to the rule or regulation.

78. **(A) Correct**

When a recognized representative is unable or unwilling to declare his/her own knowledge that the facts are true and correct, the Internal Revenue Service may require the taxpayer to make such a declaration under penalty of perjury.

79. **(A) Correct**
An unenrolled return preparer is an individual other than an attorney, CPA, enrolled agent, or enrolled actuary who prepares and signs a taxpayer's return as the preparer, or who prepares a return but is not required (by the instructions to the return or regulations) to sign the return.
Answer B is wrong because an unenrolled return preparer is permitted to appear as a representative before customer service representatives, revenue agents, and examination officers, with respect to an examination regarding the return he or she prepared.
Answer C is wrong because receiving of refund checks on behalf of the taxpayers is limited only to those authorized to practice before the IRS (Attorneys, CPAs, and EAs).
Answer D is wrong because representing a taxpayer over the telephone with the Automated Collection System unit is not regarded as practicing before the IRS.

80. **(C) Correct**
A practitioner who knows that his or her client has not complied with the revenue laws or has made an error or omission in any return, document, affidavit, or other required paper, has the responsibility to advise the client promptly of the noncompliance, error, or omission, and the consequences of the noncompliance, error, or omission.

81. **(D) Correct**
Any practitioner or unenrolled return preparer may be disbarred or suspended from practice before the IRS, or censured, for disreputable conduct. Page 25 contains a detailed list of examples of conduct that is considered disreputable.

82. **(D) Correct**
An answer must be written and contain a statement of facts that constitute the respondent's grounds of defense. General denials are not permitted. The respondent must *specifically admit or deny* each allegation set forth in the complaint. Otherwise, the respondent may state that he or she is without sufficient information to admit or deny a specific allegation.

83. **(C) Correct**
Each individual applying for renewal for enrollment must retain the required information with regard to qualifying CPE credit hours for a period of 3 years, following the date of renewal of enrollment.

84. **(B) Correct**

To maintain active enrollment to practice before the IRS, each individual is required to have his or her enrollment renewed. Failure to receive notification from the Director of the Office of Professional Responsibility of the renewal requirement will not be justification for the individual's failure to satisfy this requirement.

Answer A is wrong because the renewal fee is *nonrefundable*.

Answer C is wrong because these renewal forms are available through the IRS website.

Answer D is wrong because renewal cycles are determined by the last digit of the Social Security Number.

85. **(C) Correct**
Practice before the IRS covers all matters relating to any of the following:
      (1) Communicating with the IRS for a taxpayer regarding the taxpayer's rights, privileges, or liabilities under laws and regulations administered by the IRS.
      (2) Representing a taxpayer at conferences, hearings, or meetings with the IRS.
      (3) Preparing and filing documents with the IRS for a taxpayer.
      (4) Corresponding and communicating with the IRS

    Just preparing a tax return, furnishing information at the request of the IRS, or appearing as a witness for the taxpayer is not practice before the IRS. These acts can be performed by anyone.

86. **(A) Correct**
An unenrolled return preparer is permitted to appear as a representative only before customer service representatives, revenue agents, and examination officers, with respect to an examination regarding the return he or she prepared.
Answer B is wrong because an unenrolled return preparer is limited to only customer service representatives, revenue agents, and examination officers.
Answer C is wrong because an unenrolled return preparer are non-signing return preparer and therefore not authorized to sign consents to extend the statutory period for assessment or collection of tax.
Answer D is wrong because an unenrolled return preparer is not authorized to receive a refund check on behalf of the taxpayer. This privilege is only for practitioners authorized to practice before the IRS (Attorneys, CPAs, EAs).

87. **(C) Correct**
A practitioner is not allowed to represent a client before the IRS if the representation involves a conflict of interest. A conflict of interest exists if:
      a) The representation of one client will be directly adverse to another client, or

b) There is a significant risk that the representation of one or more clients will be materially limited by the practitioner's responsibilities to another client, a former client or a third person, or by a personal interest of the practitioner.

Conflict of interest exists because Frank is related to Joe.

88. **(B) Correct**

The following must be contained in a complaint made against a practitioner:
1) Charges
2) Specification of sanction
3) Demand for answer

89. **(A) Correct**

Advertising and solicitation by practitioners is permitted by circular 230, however, several restrictions exist:
1) A practitioner may not use solicitation containing a false, fraudulent, or coercive statement or claim.
2) Enrolled agents are not allowed to use the term '*certified*' or imply an employer/employee relationship with the IRS when describing their professional designation. However, the following descriptions are acceptable for enrolled agents:
   a) Enrolled to represent taxpayers before the IRS
   b) Enrolled to practice before the IRS
   c) Admitted to practice before IRS

90. **(C) Correct**

A practitioner may represent a client in a conflict of interest situation if the following conditions are met:
(1) The practitioner reasonably believes that the practitioner will be able to provide competent and diligent representation to each affected client.
(2) The representation is not prohibited by law.
(3) Each affected client waives the conflict of interest and gives informed consent, confirmed in writing by each affected client, at the time the existence of the conflict of interest is known by the practitioner. The confirmation may be made within a reasonable period of time after the informed consent, but not later than 30 days.

91. **(C) Correct**

A practitioner must (at the request of a client) promptly return any and all records of the client that are necessary for the client to comply with his or her Federal tax obligations, even if there is a dispute over fees between the practitioner and the client. However, the practitioner may retain copies of the records returned to a client.

92. **(D) Correct**
    The Director of the Office of Professional Responsibility must inform the applicant as to the reason(s) for any denial of an application for enrollment. The applicant may, within 30 days after receipt of the notice of denial of enrollment, file a written appeal of the denial of enrollment with the Secretary of the Treasury or his or her delegate.

93. **(D) Correct**
    An unenrolled return preparer is permitted to appear as a representative only before customer service representatives, revenue agents, and examination officers, with respect to an examination regarding the return he or she prepared. An unenrolled return preparer <u>cannot</u>:
        (a) Represent a taxpayer before other offices of the IRS, such as Collection or Appeals. This includes the Automated Collection System (ACS) unit.
        (b) Execute closing agreements.
        (c) Extend the statutory period for tax assessments or collection of tax.
        (d) Execute waivers.
        (e) Execute claims for refund.
        (f) Receive refund checks.
        (g) Take any acknowledgements, oaths, or certification as a Notary Public relating to any tax return, protest, or other document that the preparer has prepared or that the preparer has assisted in preparing.

94. **(C) Correct**
    A practitioner who knows that his or her client has not complied with the revenue laws or has made an error or omission in any return, document, affidavit, or other required paper, has the responsibility to advise the client promptly of the noncompliance, error, or omission, and the consequences of the noncompliance, error, or omission.

95. **(B) Correct**
    1) A practitioner may not use solicitation containing a false, fraudulent, or coercive statement or claim.
    2) Enrolled agents are not allowed to use the term of art '*certified*' or imply an employer/employee relationship with the IRS when describing their professional designation. However, the following descriptions are acceptable for enrolled agents:
        (a) Enrolled to represent taxpayers before the IRS
        (b) Enrolled to practice before the IRS
        (c) Admitted to practice before IRS

96. **(D) Correct**
    - A practitioner may not sign a tax return as a preparer or advise a client to take a position on a tax return if the practitioner determines that the tax

return or the position on a tax return contains a position that does not have a realistic possibility of being sustained on its merits (the realistic possibility standard) <u>unless</u> the position is not frivolous and is adequately disclosed to the IRS.
- A practitioner advising a client to take a position on a tax return, or preparing or signing a tax return as a preparer, generally may rely in good faith without verification upon information furnished by the client. The practitioner may not, however, ignore the implications of information furnished to, or actually known by the practitioner, and must make reasonable inquiries if the information as furnished appears to be incorrect, inconsistent with an important fact or another factual assumption, or incomplete.
- A practitioner advising a client to take a position on a tax return, or preparing or signing a tax return as a preparer, generally may rely in good faith without verification upon information furnished by the client. The practitioner may not, however, ignore the implications of information furnished to, or actually known by, the practitioner, and must make reasonable inquiries if the information as furnished appears to be incorrect, inconsistent with an important fact or another factual assumption, or incomplete.

97. **(D) Correct**
Any practitioner or unenrolled return preparer may be disbarred or suspended from practice before the IRS, or censured, for disreputable conduct. The list on page 25 contains examples of conduct that is considered disreputable:

98. **(C) Correct**
    - The answer must be written and contain a statement of facts that constitute the respondent's grounds of defense. General denials are not permitted. The respondent must *specifically admit or deny* each allegation set forth in the complaint. Otherwise, the respondent may state that he or she is without sufficient information to admit or deny a specific allegation.
    - The respondent may not deny a material allegation in the complaint that he or she knows to be true, or state that the respondent is without sufficient information to form a belief, when he or she possesses the required information. The respondent also must state affirmatively any special matters of defense on which he or she relies.

99. **(A) Correct**
Proceedings on complaints for the sanction of a practitioner are conducted by an Administrative Law Judge. The Administrative Law Judge has the authority to:
    (1) Administer oaths and affirmations.
    (2) Make rulings on motions and requests.

(3) Determine the time and place of hearing and regulate its course and conduct.
(4) Adopt rules of procedure and modify them from time to time for the orderly disposition of the proceedings.
(5) Rule on offers of proof, receive relevant evidence, and examine witnesses.
(6) Take or authorize the taking of depositions or answers to requests for admission.
(7) Receive and consider oral or written argument on facts or law.
(8) Hold or provide for the holding of conferences for the settlement or simplification of the issues with the consent of the parties.
(9) Act and take measures that are necessary or appropriate to the efficient conduct of any proceeding.
(10) Make decisions.

100. **(C) Correct**
 1) Appeal of the Administrative Law Judge's decision is made with the Secretary of the Treasury or his/her delegate.
 2) The appeal must include a brief that states exceptions to the decision of the Administrative Law Judge and supporting reasons for such exceptions.
 3) The appeal and brief must be filed (in duplicate) with the Director of the Office of Professional Responsibility within 30 days of the date that the decision of the Administrative Law Judge is made. Then the Director will immediately furnish a copy of the appeal to the Secretary of the Treasury or delegate who decides appeals.
 4) A copy of the appeal for review must be sent to any non-appealing party.

101. **(D) Correct**
Each individual applying for renewal for enrollment must retain the required information with regard to qualifying CPE credit hours for a period of 3 years, following the date of renewal of enrollment.

102. **(B) Correct**
Practitioners must promptly submit records or information requested by officers or employees of the IRS. When the Office of Professional Responsibility requests information concerning possible violations of the regulations by other parties, the practitioner must provide the information and be prepared to testify in disbarment or suspension proceedings. A practitioner can be exempted from these rules if he or she believes in good faith and on reasonable grounds that the information requested is privileged or that the request is of doubtful legality.

103. **(A) Correct**

A practitioner who knows that his or her client has not complied with the revenue laws or has made an error or omission in any return, document, affidavit, or other required paper, has the responsibility to advise the client promptly of the noncompliance, error, or omission, and the consequences of the noncompliance, error, or omission.

104. **(A) Correct**

    Since Sally is an enrolled agent, she is authorized to represent clients before the IRS regardless of who her employer is. There is no explicit requirement within circular 230 for Sally to report john's activities quarterly. However, john's name is included in a roster furnished by the Office of Professional Responsibility.

105. **(C) Correct**

    Enrolled agents are not allowed to use the term of *'certified'* or imply an employer/employee relationship with the IRS when describing their professional designation. However, the following descriptions are acceptable for enrolled agents:

    (a) Enrolled to represent taxpayers before the IRS.
    (b) Enrolled to practice before the IRS.
    (c) Admitted to practice before IRS.

106. **(D) Correct**

    A practitioner must exercise due diligence when performing the following duties:

    (a) Preparing or assisting in the preparing, approving, and filing of returns, documents, affidavits, and other papers relating to IRS matters.
    (b) Determining the correctness of oral or written representations made by him or her to the Department of the Treasury.
    (c) Determining the correctness of oral or written representations made by him or her to clients with reference to any matter administered by the IRS.

107. **(D) Correct**

    Practitioners who are income tax return preparers may not endorse or negotiate (cash) any refund check issued to the taxpayer.

108. **(A) Correct**

    A practitioner may not sign a tax return as a preparer or advise a client to take a position on a tax return if the practitioner determines that the tax return or the position on a tax return contains a position that does not have a realistic possibility of being sustained on its merits (the realistic possibility standard) unless the position is not frivolous and is adequately disclosed to the IRS.

109. **(D) Correct**

The Director of the Office of Professional Responsibility may allow a petition for reinstatement from any person disbarred from practice before the IRS after 5 years have expired from the date of the disbarment or disqualification.

110. **(A) Correct**
Ray is not allowed to practice before the IRS. Just preparing a tax return, furnishing information at the request of the IRS, or appearing as a witness for the taxpayer is not practice before the IRS. These acts can be performed by anyone. *Answers (B), (C), and (D) are wrong because these acts are considered as* practicing before the IRS.

111. **(C) Correct**
Section 7525 provides a privilege of confidentiality for communications between a taxpayer and a *federally authorized tax practitioner* that has essentially the same scope as the federal attorney-client privilege. The privilege applies only to communications related to *tax advice*. Tax Advice is defined as advice given by a federally authorized tax practitioner with respect to a matter that is within the scope of the practitioner's authority to practice before the IRS.

112. **(C) Correct**
A recognized representative is an individual that meets the following three criteria:
1) Is appointed as an *attorney-in-fact* under a power of attorney.
2) Files a declaration of representative
3) Is one of the following:
    (a) Attorney, Certified public accountant (CPA), Enrolled agent, Enrolled actuary, Any individual who is granted temporary recognition by the Director of Practice
    (b) Any individual authorized to represent a taxpayer with whom a special relationship exists
    (c) Unenrolled return preparer actuary who prepares and signs a taxpayer's return as the preparer, or who prepares a return but is not required (by the instructions to the return or regulations) to sign the return.

113. **(B) Correct**
Unenrolled return preparers are limited to representation of a taxpayer before revenue agents and examining officers of the Examination Division in the offices of District Director with respect to the tax liability of the taxpayer for the taxable year or period covered by a return prepared by the unenrolled return preparer.

114. **(B) Correct**

Section 7525 provides a privilege of confidentiality for communications between a taxpayer and a *federally authorized tax practitioner* that has essentially the same scope as the federal attorney-client privilege. The privilege applies only to communications related to *tax advice*. Tax Advice is defined as advice given by a federally authorized tax practitioner with respect to a matter that is within the scope of the practitioner's authority to practice before the IRS.

115. **(A) Correct**

A practitioner who knows that his or her client has not complied with the revenue laws or has made an error or omission in any return, document, affidavit, or other required paper, has the responsibility to advise the client promptly of the noncompliance, error, or omission, and the consequences of the noncompliance, error, or omission.

116. **(A) Correct**

Failure to file an answer within the time prescribed constitutes an admission of the allegations of the complaint and a waiver of hearing, therefore the Administrative Law Judge may make the decision by default without a hearing or further procedure.

117. **(C) Correct**

Whenever the Director of the Office of Professional Responsibility determines that a practitioner violated any laws governing practice before IRS, the Director may do one of the following:

    (a) Reprimand the practitioner, or

    (b) Institute a proceeding for a sanction (a proceeding is instituted by the filing of a complaint).

Usually, a proceeding for disbarment or suspension will not be instituted unless the practitioner has been *notified in writing* about the law, facts, and conduct warranting such action and has been accorded an opportunity to dispute the facts, assert additional facts, and make arguments.

118. **(B) Correct**

Proceedings on complaints for the sanction of a practitioner are conducted by an Administrative Law Judge.

119. **(A) Correct**

    (i) Appeal of the Administrative Law Judge decision is made with the Secretary of the Treasury or his/her delegate.

    (ii) The appeal must include a brief that states exceptions to the decision of the Administrative Law Judge and supporting reasons for such exceptions.

    (iii) The appeal and brief must be filed (in duplicate) with the Director of the Office of Professional Responsibility within 30 days of the date that the decision of the Administrative Law Judge is made. Then the Director will immediately furnish a copy of the appeal to the Secretary of the Treasury or delegate who decides appeals.

(iv) A copy of the appeal for review must be sent to any non-appealing party.

120. **(C) Correct**
Circular No. 230 is a Treasury Department Circular that sets forth the regulations governing practice before the IRS. These regulations in Circular 230 governing the practice of attorneys, certified public accountants, enrolled agents, enrolled actuaries and appraisers before the IRS are found under *Title 31 Code of Federal Regulations, Subtitle A, Part 10.* The circular also contains rules regarding eligibility to become an enrolled agent and renewal of enrollment.

121. **(D) Correct**
A practitioner advising a client to take a position on a tax return, or preparing or signing a tax return as a preparer, generally may rely in good faith without verification upon information furnished by the client. The practitioner may not, however, ignore the implications of information furnished to, or actually known by the practitioner, and must make reasonable inquiries if the information as furnished appears to be incorrect, inconsistent with an important fact or another factual assumption, or incomplete.

122. **(D) Correct**
An attorney, Certified public accountant (CPA), Enrolled agent, and Enrolled actuary all qualify as practitioners under Circular 230.

123. **(D) Correct**
A practitioner has the right to make the following solicitations of employment involving IRS matters:
    (a) Seeking new business from a former client.
    (b) Communicating with a family member.
    (c) Targeting mailings.

124. **(C) Correct**
Letters are not a permissible form of evidence at the hearing.

125. **(D) Correct**
Upon the issuance of a final order censuring, suspending, or disbarring a practitioner or a final order disqualifying an appraiser, the Director of the Office of Professional Responsibility may give notice of the censure, suspension, disbarment, or disqualification to appropriate officers and employees of the IRS and to interested departments and agencies of the Federal government, including state authorities.

126. **(D) Correct**
    - In order to qualify for renewal of enrollment, an individual enrolled to practice before the IRS must complete 72 hours of Continuing Professional Education (CPE) over the 3-year enrollment cycle to remain active. This must include at least 2 hours of Ethics CPE each year.
    - A minimum of 16 hours of continuing education credit, including 2 hours of ethics or professional conduct, must be completed during each enrollment year of an enrollment cycle.
    - An individual who receives initial enrollment during an enrollment cycle must complete 2 hours of qualifying continuing education credit for each month enrolled during the enrollment cycle. Enrollment for any part of a month is considered enrollment for the entire month.

127. **(B) Correct**
    - An Enrollment year is a calendar year (January 1 to December 31).
    - An Enrollment cycle means 3 successive enrollment years preceding the effective date of renewal.
    - The effective date of renewal is the 1st day of the 4th month following the close of the period for renewal

128. **(B) Correct**
An individual who receives initial enrollment during an enrollment cycle must complete 2 hours of qualifying continuing education credit for each month enrolled during the enrollment cycle. Enrollment for any part of a month is considered enrollment for the entire month.

129. **(B) Correct**
Just preparing a tax return, furnishing information at the request of the IRS, or appearing as a witness for the taxpayer is not practice before the IRS. These acts can be performed by anyone.

130. **(D) Correct**
An attorney, Certified public accountant (CPA), Enrolled agent, and Enrolled actuary all qualify as practitioners under Circular 230 authorized to practice before the IRS. A Certified financial planner is not authorized to practice before the IRS.

131. **(A) Correct**
An unenrolled return preparer is permitted to appear as a representative only before customer service representatives, revenue agents, and examination officers, with respect to an examination regarding the return he or she prepared.

132. **(D) Correct**
    Unenrolled Agents – The IRS may authorize an individual to represent a taxpayer with whom a special relationship exists. The following unenrolled people may be authorized to represent an individual or entity before the IRS:
    A. **Employee** - An employee. A regular full-time employee can represent his or her employer. An employer can be, but is not limited to, an individual, partnership, corporation (including a parent, subsidiary, or other affiliated corporation), association, trust, receivership, guardianship, estate, organized group, governmental unit, agency, or authority.
    B. **Family** - An individual can represent members of his or her immediate family. Immediate family means a spouse, child, parent, brother, or sister of the individual.
    C. **Corporation** – A bona fide officer of a corporation (including a parent, subsidiary, or other affiliated corporation), association, or organized group can represent the corporation, association, or organized group. An officer of a governmental unit, agency, or authority, in the course of his or her official duties, can represent the organization before the IRS.
    D. **Unenrolled return preparers** - Unenrolled return preparers are limited to representation of a taxpayer before revenue agents and examining officers of the Examination Division in the offices of District Director with respect to the tax liability of the taxpayer for the taxable year or period covered by a return prepared by the unenrolled return preparer.
    E. **Partnership** – A general partner may represent a partnership.
    F. **Fiduciary** – A trustee, receiver, guardian, administrator, executor stands in the position of a taxpayer and acts as the taxpayer, NOT as a representative.
    G. **Others** – In general an individual who is granted temporary recognition by the Director of Practice may represent a taxpayer on specific matters even if the taxpayer is not present, provided the individual presents satisfactory identification and proof of his or her authority to represent the taxpayer.
    H. **Representing one-self** - Individuals may appear on their own behalf before the IRS provided they present satisfactory identification. The individual does not have to file a written declaration of qualification and authority.

133. **(D) Correct**
    A practitioner who knows that his or her client has not complied with the revenue laws or has made an error or omission in any return, document, affidavit, or other required paper, has the responsibility to advise the client promptly of the noncompliance, error, or omission, and the consequences of the noncompliance, error, or omission.

134. **(C) Correct**

According to circular 230, a practitioner may not, knowingly and directly or indirectly accept assistance from or assist any person who is under disbarment or suspension from practice before the IRS or from any former government employee where the provisions in circular 230 or any federal law would be violated.

135. **(C) Correct**

A targeted direct mail solicitation is a direct mail campaign targeted to *non-clients* whose unique situation would be the main reason for the solicitation. *Answers (A), (B), and (D)* are all good examples of a targeted direct mail solicitation because they are all directed to non-client with unique situations. The solicitation in *Answer (C)* is directed to current clients and their need for assistance with Schedule C issues is not related directly related to the solicitation for Keogh plans.

136. **(D) Correct**

Any practitioner or unenrolled return preparer may be disbarred or suspended from practice before the IRS, or censured, for disreputable conduct. The following list contains examples of conduct that is considered disreputable:
   a) Being convicted of any criminal offense under the revenue laws or of any offense involving dishonesty or breach of trust.
   b) Knowingly giving false or misleading information in connection with federal tax matters, or participating in such activity.
   c) Soliciting employment by prohibited means as discussed in Circular No. 230.
   d) Willfully failing to file a tax return, evading or attempting to evade any federal tax or payment, or participating in such actions.
   e) Misappropriating, or failing to properly and promptly remit, funds received from clients for payment of taxes or other obligations due the United States.
   f) Directly or indirectly attempting to influence the official action of IRS employees by the use of threats, false accusations, duress, or coercion, or by offering gifts, favors, or any special inducements.
   g) Being disbarred or suspended from practice as an attorney, CPA, public accountant, or actuary, by the District of Columbia or any state, possession, territory, commonwealth, or any federal court, or any body or board of any federal agency.
   h) Knowingly aiding and abetting another person to practice before the IRS during a period of suspension, disbarment, or ineligibility.
   i) Using abusive language, making false accusations and statements knowing them to be false, circulating or publishing malicious or libelous matter, or engaging in any contemptuous conduct in connection with practice before the IRS.
   j) Giving a false opinion knowingly, recklessly, or through gross incompetence; or following a pattern of providing incompetent opinions in questions arising under the federal tax laws.

137. **(D) Correct**
Whenever the Director of the Office of Professional Responsibility determines that a practitioner violated any laws governing practice before IRS, the Director may do one of the following:
1) Reprimand the practitioner, or
2) Institute a proceeding for a sanction of disbarment or suspension (a proceeding is instituted by the filing of a complaint).

138. **(D) Correct**
A practitioner may not sign a tax return as a preparer or advise a client to take a position on a tax return if the practitioner determines that the tax return or the position on a tax return contains a position that does not have a realistic possibility of being sustained on its merits (the realistic possibility standard) *unless* the position is not frivolous and is adequately disclosed to the IRS.

139. **(C) Correct**
A general partner may represent a partnership. A limited partner in a partnership may not represent the partnership.

140. **(D) Correct**
Failure to timely pay personal income taxes' is not one of the listed examples of disreputable conducts outlined on page 25 of the study notes.
Answers A, B, and C are all among the examples of disreputable conducts outlined on page 25 of the study notes.

141. **(C) Correct**
An income tax return preparer is defined as person (including a partnership or corporation) who prepares for *compensation* all or a substantial portion of a tax return or claim for refund under the income tax provisions of the Code.
Answer A is wrong because a depreciation schedule is not a substantial portion of the tax return. Also, there was not compensation.
Answers B and D are wrong because there was no compensation.

142. **(C) Correct**
Applicants can apply to take the special enrollment examination (SEE) by filing Form 2587.

143. **(B) Correct**
Individuals who have passed the examination or are applying on the basis of past service and technical experience with the IRS can apply for enrollment by filing Form 23 (*Application for Enrollment to Practice before the IRS*).

144. **(A) Correct**

Applicants for renewal of enrollment must file Form 8554 (*Application for Renewal of Enrollment to Practice before the IRS*). To qualify for renewal, applicants must complete the necessary hours of continuing professional education during each 3-year enrollment cycle.

145. **(D) Correct**

    To qualify for CPE credit for an enrolled agent, a course of learning must:
    (1) Be a *qualifying program* designed to enhance professional knowledge in any of the following:
    - (a) Federal taxation or Federal tax related matters
    - (b) Accounting
    - (c) Tax preparation software
    - (d) Taxation
    - (e) Ethics
    (2) Be a qualifying program consistent with the Internal Revenue Code and effective tax administration.
    (3) Be sponsored by a qualifying sponsor.

146. **(C) Correct**

    Section 7525 confidentiality privilege does **not** protect the following situations:
    (1) Information disclosed to a tax practitioner for the purpose of preparing a return.
    (2) Criminal tax matters before the I.R.S. or in federal court.
    (3) Written communications made in connection with the promotion of direct or indirect participation in a tax shelter.
    (4) Information that is also available from non-privileged sources.
    (5) Communication between the taxpayer's tax practitioner and a third-party who provides information about the taxpayer to the practitioner.

UNIT 2: PREPARER PENALTIES, TAXPAYER PENALTIES, AND EITC

Unit 2 Contents:
2.01   TAX RETURN PREPARER
2.02   PREPARER PENALTIES
2.03   TAXPAYER PENALTIES
2.04   EARNED INCOME TAX CREDIT (EITC)
2.05   UNIT 2: QUESTIONS
2.06   UNIT 2: ANSWERS

2.01   TAX RETURN PREPARER

An Income tax return preparer is defined as person (including a partnership or corporation), who prepares for *compensation,* or employs one or more persons to prepare for compensation, all or a *substantial portion* of a tax return or claim for refund under the income tax provisions of the Code. This includes a person who prepares a United States tax return for a fee outside the United States.

Preparers include people who:
1. Furnish sufficient advice or information so that the completion of the return by another individual is a mechanical process.
2. Supply computerized tax return preparation services to tax practitioners or offer services or programs that make substantive tax determinations.
3. Software companies or other persons that prepare computer programs and sell those programs to taxpayers for use in preparing their returns may also be an income tax return preparer for purposes of the return preparer penalties.
4. For the purposes of IRC section 6694 penalties, no more than one individual associated with a firm (i.e., an employee or partner) is treated as a preparer of the same return or claim (one-preparer-per-firm rule). NOTE: The one-preparer-per-firm rule does not mean that an IRC section 6694 penalty cannot also be asserted against the firm, as an employer. It also does not mean that there can never be more than one preparer per return. For example, if a CPA receives advice from an attorney (who is not associated with the same firm) and the advice constitutes a substantial portion of the return; both the CPA and the attorney are income tax return preparers with respect to that return.
5. A non-signing preparer who prepares a schedule or entry that constitutes a substantial portion of the return may be considered a tax return preparer. In making the decision as to what constitutes a substantial portion, examiners should consider the relation of the entry or schedule to the tax liability, the complexity of the return as a whole, and the relative time involved in preparing it.

6. An electronic return originator may be a return preparer under IRC section 7701(a)(36) and who could be liable for these penalties. However, an electronic filer who is primarily a transmitter with services limited to typing, reproduction or other mechanical assistance in the preparation of a return or claim for refund is not an income tax preparer for purposes for these penalties.
7. A general partner who prepares a partnership return can be an income tax return preparer of a limited partner's return in certain situations.
8. A preparer (1st preparer) can be a preparer of a return prepared by another preparer (2nd preparer) if the 2nd preparer relied on information contained on the return prepared by the 1st preparer. This occurs, for example, when the 1st preparer negligently overstates the expenses on a prior year's return, thus creating an NOL, and the 2nd preparer, in good faith, applies the NOL carryover in preparing the subsequent year's return.
9. The definition of income tax preparer is slightly altered for purposes of IRC section 6695(g). Preparers who merely give advice or prepare another return that affects the EITC return or refund claim are not considered preparers. The due diligence standards are imposed only on paid preparers who prepare the EITC return or claim.

Persons Who Are Not Income Tax Return Preparers

The following persons are **not** income tax return preparers:
1. A person who prepares a return or claim for refund with no explicit or implicit agreement for compensation even though the person receives a gift or return service or favor.
2. A person who only provides mechanical assistance in the preparation of an income tax return or claim for refund (e.g., provides typing or copying services).
3. A person who prepares an income tax return or claim for refund of a person, or an officer, general partner, or employee of a person, by whom the individual is regularly and continuously employed or in which the individual is a general partner.
4. A person who prepares an income tax return or claim for refund for an estate or a trust, but only if such person is a fiduciary or is an officer, general partner, or employee of the fiduciary.
5. A person who prepares a claim for refund for a taxpayer in response to a deficiency notice or a waiver of restriction after initiation of an examination of the taxpayer or another taxpayer.
6. Any person who provides tax assistance under the Volunteer Income Tax Assistance (VITA) program established by the IRS.
7. Any person who provides tax assistance as part of a qualified Low-Income Taxpayer Clinic (LITC). The assistance must be directly related to a controversy with the IRS or as part of an LITC's English as a Second Language (ESL) outreach program. The LITC cannot charge a separate fee or vary a fee based on whether

the LITC provides assistance with a return or claim, and the LITC cannot charge more than a nominal fee for its service.

Substantial Portion

Only a person who prepares *all* or a *substantial* portion of a return or claim for refund will be considered to be a tax return preparer of the return or claim for refund. A person who renders tax advice on a position that is directly relevant to the determination of the existence, characterization, or amount of an entry on a return or claim for refund will be regarded as having prepared that entry. Whether a schedule, entry, or other portion of a return or claim for refund is a substantial portion is determined based upon whether the person knows or reasonably should know that the tax attributable to the schedule, entry, or other portion of a return or claim for refund is a substantial portion of the tax required to be shown on the return or claim for refund. A single tax entry may constitute a substantial portion of the tax required to be shown on a return. Factors to consider in determining whether a schedule, entry, or other portion of a return or claim for refund is a substantial portion include:
1) The size and complexity of the item relative to the taxpayer's gross income.
2) The size of the understatement attributable to the item compared to the taxpayer's reported tax liability.

A schedule or other portion is not considered to be a *substantial portion* if the schedule, entry, or other portion of the return or claim for refund involves amounts of gross income, amounts of deductions, or amounts on the basis of which credits are determined that are:
(1) Less than $10,000, or
(2) Less than $400,000 and also less than 20% of the gross income as shown on the return or claim for refund (or, for an individual, the individual's adjusted gross income).

If more than one schedule, entry or other portion is involved, all schedules, entries or other portions shall be aggregated.

A tax return preparer is <u>not</u> considered to be a tax return preparer of another return merely because an entry or entries reported on the first return may affect an entry reported on the other return, unless the entry or entries reported on the first return are directly reflected on the other return and constitute a substantial portion of the other return. For example, the sole preparer of a partnership's or small business corporation's income tax return is considered a tax return preparer of a partner's or a shareholder's return if the entry or entries on the partnership or small business corporation return reportable on the partner's or shareholder's return constitute a substantial portion of the partner's or shareholder's return.

<u>EXAMPLE 1:</u>
Accountant C prepares a Form 8886, "Reportable Transaction Disclosure Statement" that is used to disclose reportable transactions. C does not prepare the tax return or

advise the taxpayer regarding the tax return reporting position of the transaction to which the Form 8886 relates. The preparation of the Form 8886 is not directly relevant to the determination of the existence, characterization, or amount of an entry on a tax return or claim for refund. Rather, the Form 8886 is prepared by C to disclose a reportable transaction. C has not prepared a substantial portion of the tax return and is <u>not</u> considered a tax return preparer under section 6694.

EXAMPLE 2:
Accountant D prepares a schedule for an individual taxpayer's Form 1040, "U.S. Individual Income Tax Return", reporting $4,000 in dividend income and gives oral or written advice about Schedule A, which results in a claim of a medical expense deduction totaling $5,000, but does not sign the tax return. D is <u>not</u> a non-signing tax return preparer because the total aggregate amount of the deductions is less than $10,000 (Reg. Sec. 301.7701-15).

What Is a Return of Tax or Claim for Refund?

A tax return includes income tax, estate tax, gift tax, excise tax, employment tax and certain information returns. A tax return also includes an amended or adjusted return. A tax return also includes any information return:
   (1) That reports items that are or may be reported on another taxpayer's return, and
   (2) Any item reported on the information return or other document is a substantial portion of the taxpayer's return.

A claim for a tax refund includes a claim for credit against any tax.

Information Returns of Tax Preparers

Any person who employs one or more signing tax return preparers to prepare any return or claim for refund at any time during a return period must:
   1) Retaining a record of:
      (i) Name,
      (ii) Taxpayer identification number, and
      (iii) Place of work of each tax return preparer employed by him
   2) Make the record available for inspection upon request by the Commissioner

The return required must be filed on or before the first July 31 following the end of such return period. The term 'return period' means the 12-month period beginning on July 1 of each year. The records must be retained and kept available for inspection for the 3-year period following the close of the return period to which that record relates.
- A sole proprietor must retain and make available a record with respect to him or herself.

- A partnership is treated as the employer of the partners and must retain and make available a record with respect to the partners and other tax return preparers employed or engaged by the partnership (Reg. Sec. 1.6060-1).

2.02   PREPARER PENALTIES

Penalty Steering Committee (PSC)

The PSC is a multifunctional group that is established by the Area Planning and Special Programs (PSP) Territory Manager. The PSC members can include among others:
1) Electronic Filer Coordinator
2) Examination Return Preparer Coordinator
3) Representative designated by the Area Director
4) Criminal Investigations representative

The PSC identifies patterns of preparer abuse, recommends the initiation of a project on potentially abusive return preparers, and reviews the appropriateness and accuracy of return preparer penalty assertion.

Internal Revenue Manual (IRM)

The IRM is the official source for IRS policies, directives, guidelines, procedures and delegations of authority in the IRS.
The IRM consists of the following:
- *Policy statements* - major decisions of the Commissioner and other specified executives that govern and guide personnel in the administration of the tax laws.
- *Procedures and guidelines* - tell IRS employees how to serve taxpayers in administering the nations' tax laws.
- *Delegations of authority* - official notification by the Commissioner of certain rights and responsibilities delegated to subordinate officials. Delegations of authority effecting taxpayers are also published in the Federal Register.

IRS has penalty and injunctive authority to address improper income tax return preparation. The Internal Revenue Code (IRC) provides the following penalties to stop fraudulent, unscrupulous and/or incompetent tax return preparers and abusive transaction promoters. Penalty assertion is the key enforcement vehicle for noncompliant preparers and promoters.

Income tax return preparers are subject to penalties for failure to comply with internal revenue codes and regulation. The IRS Criminal Investigation Return Preparer Program (RPP) was implemented and established procedures to foster compliance by identifying, investigating and prosecuting abusive return preparers. The program was developed to enhance compliance in the return-preparer community by engaging in enforcement actions and/or asserting appropriate civil penalties against unscrupulous or incompetent return preparers.

The IRS Return Preparer Program focuses on enhancing compliance in the return-preparer community by investigating and referring criminal activity by return preparers to the Department of Justice for prosecution and/or asserting appropriate civil penalties against unscrupulous return preparers.

Return preparer fraud generally involves the preparation and filing of false income tax returns by preparers who:
- Claim inflated personal or business expenses.
- Claim false deductions.
- Claim unallowable credits or excessive exemptions.
- Manipulate income figures to fraudulently obtain tax credits, such as the Earned Income Tax Credit.

Some return preparers have been convicted of, or have pleaded guilty to, felony charges. Return-related preparer penalties can also result in:
a) Disciplinary action by the IRS Office of Professional Responsibility
b) Suspension or expulsion of the preparer's firm from participation in IRS e-file

Burden of Proof for IRC Penalties
The preparer bears the burden of proof on issues such as:
1) Whether the preparer knew or reasonably should have known that the questioned position was taken on the return or claim for refund.
2) Whether there is reasonable cause and good faith with respect to the position.
3) Whether the position was adequately disclosed
4) Whether the preparer recklessly or intentionally disregarded a rule or regulation.

Understatement
A preparer is considered to have recklessly or intentionally disregarded a rule or regulation if the preparer takes a position on the return or claim that is contrary to a rule or regulation and the preparer knows of, or is reckless in not knowing of, the rule or regulation. A penalty predicated on reckless or intentional disregard would not be imposed if there is adequate disclosure of a non-frivolous position and, in the case of a regulation; the position represents a good faith challenge to the regulation's validity.

A final administrative or judicial determination concerning the taxpayer's return is not required in order to assert return preparer penalties. However, the penalties will be abated if a subsequent judicial or administrative determination concludes that no understatement exists (IRC section 6694(d)). For purposes of the return preparer penalties, the net amount payable is not reduced by any carry-back.

There are two types of understatements as outlined in IRC Section 6694.
1) Understatement due to unreasonable positions

2) Understatement due to willful or reckless conduct

If there is a final administrative determination or a final judicial decision that there was no understatement of liability in the case of any return or claim for refund and a penalty has been assessed, the assessment will be abated, and if any portion of such penalty has been paid the amount so paid will be refunded to the person who made such payment as an overpayment of tax (Code Sec. 6694(d)).

Code Sec. 6694(b)(3) states that the amount of any penalty payable by any person by reason of *understatement due to willful or reckless conduct* for any return or claim for refund will be reduced by the amount of the penalty paid by such person by reason of *understatement due to unreasonable positions*.

1. Penalty for Understatement due to unreasonable positions

Under (Code Sec. 6694(a)), If a tax return preparer prepares any return or claim of refund in which any part of an understatement of liability is due to *unreasonable position*, and the preparer knew, or should have reasonably known about the position, the preparer will pay a penalty for each return or claim in the amount of:

The greater of:
   a) $1,000
      or
   b) 50% of the income derived (or to be derived) by the tax return preparer with respect to the return or claim.

A position is considered to have a realistic possibility of being sustained on its merits if a reasonable and well-informed analysis by a person knowledgeable in tax law would lead such a person to conclude that the position has approximately a one-in-three or greater, likelihood of being sustained on its merits

A penalty will not be imposed if, considering all the facts and circumstances, it is determined that the understatement was due to reasonable cause and that the preparer acted in good faith. There must substantial authority to sustain the position taken on the return.

EXAMPLE 1:
A new statute is unclear as to whether a certain transaction that a taxpayer has engaged in will result in favorable tax treatment. Prior law, however, supported the taxpayer's position. There are no regulations under the new statute and no authority other than the statutory language and committee reports. The committee reports state that the intent was not to adversely affect transactions similar to the taxpayer's transaction. The taxpayer's position satisfies the realistic possibility standard.

EXAMPLE 2:
A taxpayer has engaged in a transaction that is adversely affected by a new statutory provision. Prior law supported a position favorable to the taxpayer. The preparer believes that the new statute is inequitable as applied to the taxpayer's situation. The statutory language is unambiguous as it applies to the transaction (e.g., it applies to all manufacturers and the taxpayer is a manufacturer of widgets). The committee reports do not specifically address the taxpayer's situation. A position contrary to the statute does not satisfy the realistic possibility standard.

EXAMPLE 3:
The facts are the same as in Example 2, except the committee reports indicate that Congress did not intend to apply the new statutory provision to the taxpayer's transaction (e.g., to a manufacturer of widgets). Thus, there is a conflict between the general language of the statute, which adversely affects the taxpayer's transaction, and a specific statement in the committee reports that transactions such as the taxpayer's are not adversely affected. A position consistent with either the statute or the committee reports satisfies the realistic possibility standard. However, a position consistent with the committee reports constitutes a disregard of a rule or regulation and, therefore, must be adequately disclosed in order to avoid an IRC penalty.

EXAMPLE 4:
The instructions to an item on a tax form published by the IRS are incorrect and are clearly contrary to the regulations. Before the return is prepared, the IRS publishes an announcement acknowledging the error and providing the correct instruction. Under these facts, a position taken on a return which is consistent with the regulations satisfies the realistic possibility standard. On the other hand, a position taken on a return which is consistent with the incorrect instructions does not satisfy the realistic possibility standard. However, if the preparer relied on the incorrect instructions and was not aware of the announcement or the regulations, the reasonable cause and good faith exception may apply depending on all facts and circumstances.

EXAMPLE 5:
A statute is silent as to whether a taxpayer may take a certain position on the taxpayer's 2003 Federal income tax return. Three private letter rulings issued to other taxpayers in 2000 and 2001 support the taxpayer's position. However, proposed regulations issued in 2002 are clearly contrary to the taxpayer's position. After the issuance of the proposed regulations, the earlier private letter rulings cease to be authorities and are not taken into account in determining whether the taxpayer's position satisfies the realistic possibility standard. The taxpayer's position may or may not satisfy the realistic possibility standard, depending on an analysis of all the relevant authorities (Reg. Sec. 1.66942(b)(3).

2. Penalty for Understatement due to willful or reckless conduct

Any understatement of the net amount payable for any tax due or any overstatement of the net amount creditable or refundable for any tax may subject a preparer to a penalty. A preparer is subject the penalty if any part of any understatement of liability with respect to any return or claim for refund is due to a willful attempt by the preparer to understate the liability for tax, or to the preparer's reckless or intentional disregard of rules or regulations.

Under Code Sec. 6694(b), a tax return preparer who prepares any return or claim for refund in which any part of an understatement of liability is due to *willful or reckless conduct*, the preparer will pay a penalty for each return or claim in the amount of:

The greater of:
1) $5,000
   or
2) 50% of the income derived (or to be derived) by the tax return preparer with respect to the return or claim.

There is no statute of limitation period for assessing the penalty against an income tax return preparer for willful or reckless conduct that results in an understatement of liability (Code Sec. 6696(d))

EXAMPLE 1:
A taxpayer provided a preparer with detailed check registers reflecting personal and business expenses. One of the expenses was for domestic help, and this expense was identified as personal on the check register. The preparer knowingly deducted the expenses of the taxpayer's domestic help as wages paid in the taxpayer's business. The preparer is subject to the penalty.

EXAMPLE 2:
A taxpayer provided a preparer with detailed check registers to compute the taxpayer's expenses. However, the preparer knowingly overstated the expenses on the return. After adjustments by the examiner, the tax liability increased significantly. Because the preparer disregarded information provided in the check registers, the preparer is subject to the penalty.

EXAMPLE 3:
A revenue ruling holds that certain expenses incurred in the purchase of a business must be capitalized. The Code is silent as to whether these expenses must be capitalized or may be deducted currently, but several cases from different courts hold that these particular expenses may be deducted currently. There is no other authority. Under these facts, a position taken contrary to the revenue ruling on a return or claim for refund is not a reckless or intentional disregard of a rule, since the position contrary to the revenue ruling has a realistic possibility of being sustained on its merits. Therefore, the preparer will not be subject to a penalty.

EXAMPLE 4:
Final regulations provide that certain expenses incurred in the purchase of a business must be capitalized. One Tax Court case has expressly invalidated that portion of the regulations. Under these facts, a position contrary to the regulation will subject the preparer to an IRC section 6694(b) penalty even though the position may have a realistic possibility of being sustained on its merits. However, because the contrary position on these facts represents a good faith challenge to the validity of the regulations, the preparer will not be subject to an IRC section 6694(b) penalty if the position is adequately disclosed in the manner provided in Treas. Reg. 1.66943(e).

Penalties of $50 (Each Occurrence)

The following are subject to $50 for each failure per return. (The maximum penalty imposed with respect to any return period may not exceed $25,000) (Code Sec. 6695):
1) Failure to furnish copy to taxpayer
2) Failure to sign return/claim for refund
3) Failure to furnish identifying number
4) Failure to retain copy or list
5) Failure to file correct information returns

The only exception is if the preparer can show reasonable cause for the failure.

1. Failure to furnish copy to taxpayer

A preparer is required to furnish a completed copy of the return or claim for refund to the taxpayer before (or at the same time) the return or claim for refund is presented to the taxpayer for signature. A penalty of $50 applies if the preparer fails to furnish a copy to Taxpayer.

If there is an employment arrangement between two or more preparers, the requirement to furnish a copy only applies to the person who employs (or engages) one or more other preparers. Similarly, if there is a partnership arrangement, the requirement to furnish a copy only applies to the partnership.

The penalty will also not be imposed where a preparer deletes certain information from the copy furnished to the taxpayer if the taxpayer holds an elected or politically appointed position with the government of the United States or a State or political subdivision thereof and who in order to carry out their official duties, has arranged their affairs so that they have less than full knowledge of the property they hold or of the debts for which they are responsible.

The penalty does not apply if the failure was due to reasonable cause and not due to willful neglect.

2. Failure to sign return/claim for refund

A $50 penalty applies if the preparer, who is required by regulations to sign the taxpayer's return or claim for refund, fails to sign the return or claim for refund. Preparers must sign the return/claim for refund using the appropriate method prescribed by the Secretary after it is completed and before it is presented to the taxpayer for signature.

A manual signature is no longer required. The signature requirement may be satisfied if the preparer used a computer program to sign the return or claim for refund or if the preparer signs the completed return, makes a photocopy of the return, and the taxpayer signs and files the photocopy.

If a preparer is physically unable to sign a return because of a temporary or permanent disability, the penalty will not be imposed if the words "Unable to Sign" are printed, typed, or stamped on the preparer signature line. Also, the preparer's name must be printed, typed, or stamped under the signature line after the return is completed, and before it is presented to the taxpayer for signature.

In general, a facsimile signature stamp or signed gummed label is not acceptable.
Except:
   a) A preparer of a return or claim for refund for a nonresident alien may use a facsimile signature to sign as preparer if the preparer is authorized to sign for the taxpayer using a facsimile signature.
   b) A preparer of Forms 1041 may use a facsimile signature to sign the Forms 1041 if certain conditions are met.

If the preparer required to sign the return or claim for refund is unavailable to sign, another preparer must review the return or claim for refund and then manually sign the return/claim for refund.

If more than one preparer is involved in the preparation of the return/claim for refund, the preparer with primary responsibility for the overall substantive accuracy of the return/claim for refund is the preparer who must sign the return/claim for refund.

If the mechanical preparation of the return/claim for refund is done by a computer not under the control of the individual preparer, the signature requirement may be satisfied by a signed attestation by the individual preparer that all the information in the return was obtained from the taxpayer and is true and correct to the best of the preparer's knowledge. The attestation must be attached to the return/claim for refund and the information contained in the return or claim for refund must not be altered by another person. A preparer is not required to sign and affix an identification number to the taxpayer's copy of the return.

The penalty does not apply if the failure was due to reasonable cause and not due to willful neglect.

3. Failure to furnish identifying number

A $50 penalty applies if the preparer fails to furnish an identifying number of the return preparer. The return/claim for refund must contain:
   a) The identifying number of the preparer required to sign the return/claim for refund.
   b) The identifying number of the partnership or employer.

The penalty does not apply if the failure was due to reasonable cause and not due to willful neglect.

4. Failure to retain copy or list

A $50 penalty applies if the preparer fails to retain copy or list. A preparer must:
   1) Retain a completed copy of the return/claim for refund, or alternatively retain a record (by list, card file, electronically, or otherwise) of all the taxpayers, their taxpayer identification numbers, the taxable years, and the type of returns/claims for refund prepared.
   2) Retain a record (by copy of the return/claim for refund or by a list, card file, electronically, or otherwise) of the name of the preparer required to sign the return/claim for refund for each return/claim for refund presented to the taxpayer.
   3) Make such copy or list available for inspection upon request by the IRS for a 3-year period following the close of the return period

The penalty does not apply if the failure was due to reasonable cause and not due to willful neglect.

5. Failure to file correct information returns

A $50 penalty applies if the preparer fails to file Information Returns of Income Tax Return Preparers. Each person who employs (or engages) one or more income tax return preparers must retain a record of the name, taxpayer identification number and place of work of each income tax return preparer employed (or engaged) by him. A partnership is treated as the employer of the partners.
- The record may be in any form of documentation so long as it discloses which individuals were employed (or engaged) as income tax return preparers during that period.
- The record must be retained and made available for inspection for a 3-year period following the close of the return period to which it relates. The term "return period" means the 12-month period beginning on July 1st of each year.

If an income tax return preparer is not employed by another preparer, such preparer is treated as his own employer for purposes of this penalty. Therefore, if a preparer is a sole proprietor, he/she must retain and make available a record with respect to him or herself.

The penalty does not apply if the failure was due to reasonable cause and not due to willful neglect.

Penalty for Negotiation of check

A penalty applies if the preparer endorses or otherwise negotiates (directly or through an agent) a refund check issued to a taxpayer (other than the preparer).

Any preparer who endorses or otherwise negotiates any check made to a taxpayer shall pay a penalty of $500 with respect to each such check. The penalty does not apply with respect to deposit by a bank of the full amount of the check in the taxpayer's account for the benefit of the taxpayer.

A preparer that is also a financial institution, but has not made a loan to the taxpayer on the basis of the taxpayer's anticipated refund, may:
   a) Cash a refund check and remit all of the cash to the taxpayer
   b) Accept a refund check for deposit in full to the taxpayer's account, provided the bank does not initially endorse or negotiate the check (unless the bank has made a loan to a taxpayer on the basis of the anticipated refund).
   c) Endorse a refund check for deposit in full to the taxpayer's account pursuant to a written authorization of the taxpayer (unless the bank has made a loan to the taxpayer on the basis of the anticipated refund).
   d) Endorse or negotiate a refund check as part of the check clearing process after initial endorsement or negotiation

There is **no reasonable cause exception for negotiation of check penalty.

Penalty for Aiding and Abetting Understatement of Tax Liability

This penalty applies to any person who knowingly aids and abets in the understatement of the tax liability of another person.

Under (Code Sec. 6701), a person who aids or assists in, procures, or advises with respect to, the preparation or presentation of any portion of a return, affidavit, claim, or other document, and knows that such portion would result in an understatement of the liability for tax of another person shall pay a penalty of $1,000 for each return, affidavit, claim, or other document. The penalty is $10,000 if the prohibited conduct relates to a corporation's tax return.

The penalty is imposed on a person who:

1) Aids or assists in, procures or advises with respect to, the preparation or presentation of any portion of a return, affidavit, claim or other document.
2) Knows (or has reason to know) that such portion will be used in connection with any material matter arising under the internal revenue laws.
3) Knows that such portion (if used) would result in an understatement of another person's tax liability.

This penalty has been broadened to cover people who only *have reason to believe* that the document will be used in connection with a material matter arising under the tax laws. Initially, the penalty required that a person have actual knowledge that the document would be used in connection with a material matter arising under the tax laws. The burden of proof for this penalty is on the Government. Most court decisions hold that the Government need only establish its proof by a *preponderance of evidence* rather than the clear and convincing evidence standard.

The key words in the penalty are '**document**,' '**knows**,' and '**understatement**.' For the penalty to be imposed, the person penalized must be implicated in the preparation or presentation of a document, some portion of which he or she knows or has reason to know, will be used in connection with a material matter arising under the tax laws and knows that such position would result in an understatement of tax liability if so used.

There is no statute of limitation on assessment of aiding and abetting penalty because the penalty does not depend on the filing of a return.

A husband and wife who make a joint return of income tax are considered to be the same taxpayer for the taxable year. Example: Someone who assists two taxpayers in preparing false documents would be liable for a $2,000 penalty whereas the penalty would be only $1,000 if he had advised in the preparation of two false documents for the same taxpayer. Similarly, an advisor who prepares a false partnership return and then false Schedules K1 for 10 individual partners would be subject to a $10,000 penalty.

The following are examples of aiding and abetting penalty:

EXAMPLE 1:
A tax advisor would not be subject to the penalty for suggesting an aggressive but supportable filing position to a client even though that position was later rejected by the courts and even though the client was subjected to the substantial understatement penalty.

EXAMPLE 2:
If the tax advisor, in example 1 above, suggested a position which he or she knew could not be reasonably supported by statute or regulation, and the advisor prepared (or assisted in the preparation of) a document for the underlying tax return reflecting that

insupportable position, the penalty could apply. Thus, if a person prepares a return (or a schedule or other portion of a return) for a client reflecting a deduction of an amount the preparer knows is not deductible, the preparer could be subject to the penalty. However, if a person prepares a schedule or other portion of a return that reflects positions reasonably supported by rules or regulations, the person will not be subject to penalty even if other portions of the return are erroneous or fraudulent.

EXAMPLE 3:
Taxpayer B was given a winning horse race ticket at a race course by taxpayer A, the ticket owner. The race course, using information supplied by Taxpayer B, prepared a Form 1099 in Taxpayer B's name. Taxpayer B received the proceeds from the winning ticket and returned the proceeds to Taxpayer A for a 6% fee. Taxpayer B is a person who has aided, assisted in the preparation of, or procured a document (the Form 1099) that Taxpayer B knows, or has reason to know, will be used in connection with material matters under the Internal Revenue laws.
   a) Taxpayer B knows that, if used, the document would result in an understatement of Taxpayer A's income tax liability. Thus, Taxpayer B is liable for the IRC section 6701 penalty.

EXAMPLE 4:
Mr. C, an accountant, prepared a 2000 return for Taxpayer D, a client. Mr. C knowingly overstated D's expenses on the return, thereby creating a NOL for the year. Mr. C prepared amended returns for Taxpayer D for 1998 and 1999, claiming refunds for those years based on the 2000 NOL carryback. The carryback was not exhausted in 1999. Mr. E, another accountant, prepared Taxpayer D's 2001 return using the information presented to Mr. E by Taxpayer D, including copies of the document prepared by Mr. C. Mr. E is unaware of the overstatement of expenses by Mr. C and deducted the remaining unused NOL on Taxpayer D's 2001 return.
   1) Mr. C is liable for three separate IRC section 6701 penalties for his role in preparing Taxpayer D's 1998, 1999, and 2000 returns, which Mr. C knew, or had reason to know would result in understatements of Taxpayer's D's 1998, 1999, and 2000 federal income tax liabilities.
   2) Mr. E, however, was unaware of the overstatement of expenses on the 2000 return and is unaware of the understatement of tax liability on the 2001 return. Thus, Mr. E is not liable for an IRC section 6701 penalty.

EXAMPLE 5:
On January 15, 2000, A, an individual, offers to donate a painting to museum X. B, the curator of the museum, agrees to accept the painting. B offers to backdate a receipt for the donation to December 30, 1999. B knows that the receipt will be used to substantiate A's charitable deduction. A uses the backdated receipt to claim a charitable deduction for 1999.

a) B has aided in the preparation of a federal tax document knowing that it will be used in connection with a material tax matter and that it will result in an understatement of tax.
b) Mr. G. has aided in the preparation of a document knowing that it will be used in connection with a material tax matter and that it will result in the understatement of tax liability. Thus, Mr. G. is liable for the IRC section 6701 penalty.

EXAMPLE 6:
Taxpayer F retains Mr. G., an appraiser, to appraise rare books that she wishes to donate to a university. Mrs. F tells Mr. G. that she needs the appraisal to substantiate a charitable contribution deduction for federal income tax purposes. Mr. G. knows that the fair market value of the books may be any amount between $50,000 and $75,000. Mr. G. offers to provide Mrs. F an appraisal, for a fee, indicating the books are worth $100,000. Mr. G. indicates to Mrs. F that if the IRS challenges the valuation, the appraisal of $100,000 can be used to negotiate a fair market value of $75,000.
1) Mrs. F agrees to pay the fee for the appraisal indicating the books are worth $100,000, and Mr. G. prepares the appraisal.
2) Mr. G. has aided in the preparation of a document knowing that it will be used in connection with a material tax matter and that it will result in the understatement of tax liability. Thus, Mr. G. is liable for the IRC section 6701 penalty.

EXAMPLE 7:
Mrs. H, an accountant, overstates the value of depreciable property on an estate tax return. Mrs. H knows there is no reasonable basis for the valuation. Mrs. H also knows that the valuation claimed on the estate tax return will not understate the tax liability of the estate because of the application of the unified credit. Mrs. H, however, intends that the value claimed on the return will be used by the beneficiary of the estate in computing depreciation deductions. Mrs. H has aided in the preparation of a tax document and knows that the estate tax return will result in an understatement of the tax liability of the beneficiary. The IRC section 6701 penalty therefore applies.

EXAMPLE 8:
Mr. A, an attorney, knowingly understates an item of partnership income in preparing a partnership return for calendar-year 2000. Mr. A prepares and transmits to the partners Schedules K1 for the 10 individual partners for the same calendar-year reflecting the understated income. Mr. A is subject to ten separate $1,000 IRC section 6701 penalties for his preparation of ten Schedules K1 which Mr. A knew would, if used, result in understatements of the federal tax liabilities of the ten partners on their federal income tax returns. Mr. A will not be subject to an eleventh penalty in connection with the partnership return itself, since the partnership itself is not liable for income tax and the only understatements of tax liability are the understatements of tax liability on the ten partners' individual returns.

EXAMPLE 9:
Mrs. B, an officer of an S corporation under section 1361(a)(1), prepares the corporation's tax return for calendar-year 2000. Mrs. B intentionally understates the corporation's net capital gain for the taxable year, resulting in an understatement of the corporation's tax liability under section 1374. Mrs. B also prepares Schedules K1 for the individual shareholders for the same calendar-year reflecting the understated capital gain. Mrs. B is subject to a $10,000 penalty for her aid in the preparation of the small business corporation return and a $1,000 penalty for each Schedule K1 prepared.

EXAMPLE 10:
Mrs. C, an accountant, prepares false income and gift tax returns for client Mr. D. Each of the returns is prepared for calendar-year 2000. The calendar-year 2000, however, relates to a period for which different taxes are imposed. Thus, there are two taxable periods for purposes of application of the penalty under IRC section 6701: the calendar-year 2000 which is the period for which the income tax is imposed, and the calendar-year 2000 which is the period for which the gift tax is imposed. Mrs. C is subject to a penalty of $2,000.

Penalty for Unauthorized Preparer Disclosure

Under IRC section 6713, any preparer that discloses any information furnished to him for, or in connection with, the preparation of a tax return, or uses any such information for any purpose other than to prepare, or assist in preparing such return shall pay a penalty of $250 for each such disclosure or use. The total amount imposed for any calendar-year may not exceed $10,000 per person per calendar-year. There is no statute of limitations for this penalty.

Tax Return Information:
Tax return information is all the information tax return preparers obtain from taxpayers or other sources in any form or manner that is used to prepare tax returns or is obtained in connection with the preparation of returns. It also includes all:
   (a) Computations, worksheets, and printouts preparers create.
   (b) Correspondence from IRS during the preparation, filing and correction of returns. Statistical compilations of tax return information.
   (c) Tax return preparation software registration information.
All tax return information is protected by Code. Sec. 7216 and the regulations.

Disclosing SSNs outside the United States:
Generally, tax return preparers may not obtain *consents* to disclose social security numbers to tax return preparers located outside the United States or any territory or possession of the United States. If SSNs are included in documents for which the tax return preparer has obtained the consent of the taxpayer to disclose, the tax return preparer must *redact* or *mask* any SSN before disclosing the tax return information to a return preparer outside the United States.

Exception: SSNs may be disclosed to tax return preparers located outside the United States if taxpayer consent is obtained and both the sending and receiving tax return preparers maintain adequate data protection safeguards defined in Revenue Procedure 2008-35, Sec. 4.07.

The following will not subject a preparer to the penalties for *disclosure of information*:
- (i) Disclosure for use in revenue investigations or court proceedings.
- (ii) Disclosure to a taxpayer's fiduciary.
- (iii) Disclosure by a tax return preparer to a tax return processor.
- (iv) Disclosure by one officer, employee, or member to another.
- (v) Disclosure of identical information obtained from other sources.
- (vi) Disclosure or use of information in preparation or audit of state returns.
- (vii) Disclosure or use in preparation of other returns for the taxpayer.
- (viii) Disclosure or use to prepare lists to solicit tax return business (Reg. Sec. 301.7216-2).

Penalty for Promoting Abusive Tax Shelters

Under IRC section 6700, a penalty applies to any person who organizes, assists in the organization of, or participates in the sale of any interest in any plan or arrangement, and who, in connection with such sale or organization, either:
1) Makes or furnishes a false or fraudulent statement with respect to the allowability of any deduction or credit, exclusion of any income, or the securing any tax benefit by reason of participating in the entity, plan or arrangement, or
2) Makes or furnishes a gross valuation overstatement as to any material matter.

The penalty amount is:
> *The lesser of:*
> a) $1,000 per activity
> or
> b) 100% of the gross income derived from the activity.

Anyone who participates in the sale of an interest in the shelter *indirectly* and anyone who cause another person to make false statements or gross overvaluation may be subject to the penalty.

Abusive tax shelters are now also referred to as abusive tax avoidance transactions.

2.03   TAXPAYER PENALTIES

Criminal and Civil Penalties

Criminal penalties impose imprisonment and may also require monetary penalties as well. Civil penalties require monetary penalties. A taxpayer may be liable for both criminal and civil penalties for the same acts

Civil penalties are divided into two categories:
1) Penalties subject to the deficiency procedures (which means the penalty may be challenged administratively and in the United States Tax Court before payment of the penalty), and
2) Assessable penalties (to which the deficiency procedures do not apply and that generally are due within 10 days of demand for payment).

Tax penalties are not deductible as a trade or business expense because they are a fine or similar penalty paid to a government for violation of any law. A fine or similar penalty includes additions to tax and assessable penalties imposed. (Code Sec. 162(f)

Claim for Penalties

If a penalty is proposed against a preparer that the preparer does not agree with, the following actions are available for the preparer:
a) Request a conference with the agent and present additional information and explanations showing that the penalty is not warranted.
b) Wait for the penalty to be assessed and for a notice and demand statement to be issued, then pay the penalty within 30 days and file a claim for refund.
c) Wait for the penalty to be assessed and for a notice and demand statement to be issued, then pay at least 15% of the penalty within 30 days and file a claim for refund.
d) If the refund claim is denied, the preparer must begin a proceeding in the appropriate U.S. district court for the determination of his liability for such penalty within 30 days after date of denial.

Abatement of Penalties by the IRS (Reduction in Amount Owed)

The IRS may abate the unpaid portion an assessment of any tax or any liability concerning tax that:
1) Is in excess of the correct tax liability;
2) Is assessed after the expiration of the applicable period of limitation; or
3) Has been erroneously or illegally assessed (Code Sec. 6404(a)).

The IRS may also abate any penalty or addition to tax that is attributable to *erroneous* advice furnished to the taxpayer by an officer or employee of the IRS. A written response issued to a taxpayer by an officer or employee of the IRS is advice *only* if the response *applies the tax laws* to the specific written facts submitted by the taxpayer and *provides a conclusion* as to the tax treatment of the taxpayer, based upon application of the tax laws to those facts (Code Sec. 6404(f)). Abatement in this situation is applicable if:
a) The advice was furnished in response to a specific written request from the taxpayer;
b) The taxpayer reasonably relied upon the written advice from the IRS; and

c) The taxpayer furnished adequate and accurate information in making the request (Code Sec. 6404(f)(2)).

Abatement requests must be filed within the period allowed for collection of the penalty or, if the penalty has been paid, the period allowed for claiming a credit or refund of the penalty (Reg. 301.6404-3(e)).

A taxpayer may rely on advice issued by the IRS until put on notice that the advice may no longer be relied upon. This is done by any of the following ways:
1) Correspondence from the IRS stating the advice no longer represents IRS position.
2) Enactment of legislation or ratification of a tax treaty.
3) A decision of the United States Supreme Court.
4) The issuance of temporary or final regulations.
5) The publication of a revenue ruling or revenue procedure.
6) Statement in the Internal Revenue Bulletin (Reg. Sec. 1.6404-3(b)(2)).

An abatement request is competed on Form 843 and filed with either:
a) The IRS Service Center where the return was filed, when the request relates to an item reported on a tax return.
b) The IRS Service Center where the taxpayer's return was filed for the tax-year during which the taxpayer relied on the erroneous advice, when the request does not relate to an item reported on a tax return (Reg. 301.6404-3(d)).

Form 843 must be accompanied by the following copies:
(i) The taxpayer's written request for advice.
(ii) The erroneous written advice furnished by the IRS.
(iii) Any tax adjustments report that identifies the penalty or addition to tax and the item relating to the erroneous written advice (Reg. 301.6404-3(d)).

Criminal Penalties
In addition to civil tax penalties, the Internal Revenue Code imposes several criminal tax penalties. In a criminal tax case the government must prove each element of the offense beyond a *reasonable doubt*. In civil penalty cases, the IRS's burden of proof is based on *preponderance of evidence.*

Penalties for Criminal Tax Evasion
The IRC imposes criminal penalties for the willful attempt by any person to evade or defeat any tax or the payment of any tax. The elements of such offense are:
1) The existence of a tax deficiency
2) A willful attempt on the part of the defendant to evade taxes or the payment of any tax.

3) An affirmative act constituting an evasion or attempted evasion of the tax (Code Sec. 7201).

The following acts are regarded as *tax evasion* when the taxpayer also failed to file a return:
- (i) Keeping a double set of books.
- (ii) Making false entries or alterations, or false invoices or documents.
- (iii) Destruction of books or records.
- (iv) Concealment of assets or covering up sources of income.
- (v) Conducting business so as to avoid making records.
- (vi) Overstated deductions.
- (vii) Untruthful or misleading conduct during an IRS investigation.

Conviction for Criminal Tax Evasion is punishable by a fine of up to $100,000 ($500,000 for corporations) or imprisonment for not more than five years, or both (Code Sec. 7201).

False Return Penalties

Any person who *willfully* makes and subscribes a false return, statement, or other document that is verified under *penalty of perjury*, or who willfully aids or assists in, or procures, counsels, or advises in the preparation or presentation of a false tax related document, is guilty of a *felony*. The maximum penalty for conviction is a fine of up to $100,000 ($500,000 for corporations) or imprisonment for up to three years, or both (Code Sec. 7206).

Penalties for Failure to File or Pay Taxes

The IRC provides penalties of up to one year imprisonment or a fine of up to $25,000 ($100,000 for a corporation) or both, for:
1) *Willful* failure to pay tax,
2) Failure to file a return,
3) Failure to keep required records, or
4) Failure to supply required information (Code Sec. 7203).

This provision does not apply to the failure to pay estimated tax unless the defendant is liable for civil penalties for underpayment of estimated tax. A *willful* act has the same meaning in this particular misdemeanor statute just as in the felony statutes; thus, the element of voluntary, intentional violation of a known legal duty is must exist.

The following addition taxpayer penalties and will be discussed accordingly:
- A. Penalty for late filing
- B. Penalty for failure to pay tax shown on the return
- C. Penalty for failure to pay a tax required to be but not shown on a return
- D. Accuracy-related penalty
- E. Fraud penalty

F. Penalty for failure to collect and pay over tax (responsible person penalty)
G. Deposit-related penalties
H. Failure to file required information returns
I. Penalty for bounced checks

A. Penalty for Late Filing

The failure-to-file penalty is imposed if the return is not filed on or before the prescribed due date, considering all permitted extensions of the time for filing the return (Code Sec. 6651(a)(1)).

A taxpayer who files a tax return late is liable for a penalty between 5% and 25% of the amount required to be shown on the return. The penalty is 5% for a delinquency of not more than one month, with an additional 5% for each month (or part of a month) thereafter until the maximum of 25% is reached (Code Sec. 6651(a)).

The penalty rate is applied to the amount of tax required to be shown on the return, which is the net amount due. The net amount due is the total tax due reduced by:
1) Payments made before the due date of payment, and
2) Credits against tax that may be claimed on the return (Reg. Sec. 301.6651-1(d)).

If the taxpayer fails to file the required return and also fails to pay the tax due, the amount of the failure-to-pay penalty is offset against the failure-to-file penalty with respect to the tax. This prevents an overlap of these two penalties.

If the return is more than 60 days late, the *minimum* penalty imposed is:
The lesser of:
1. $135,

   or
2. 100% of the tax required to be shown on the return

If a failure to file a return is fraudulent, the amount of the failure-to-file penalty is increased to 15% of the net amount of tax due for each month the return is not filed (up to a maximum of 5 months) for a maximum penalty rate of 75% (Code Sec. 6651(f)).

EXAMPLE:
Income tax returns of individuals on a calendar-year basis must be filed on or before the 15th day of April following the close of the calendar-year. Assume an individual filed his income tax return for the calendar-year 2009 on July 20, 2010, and the failure to file on or before the prescribed date is <u>not</u> due to reasonable cause. The tax shown on the return is $800 and a deficiency of $200 is subsequently assessed, making the tax required to be shown on the return, $1,000. Of this amount, $300 has been paid by withholding from wages and $400 has been paid as estimated tax. The balance due as shown on the return of $100 ($800 shown as tax on the return less $700 previously paid) is paid on August 21, 2010. The failure to pay on or before the prescribed date is

not due to reasonable cause. There will be imposed, in addition to interest, an additional amount under section 6651(a)(2) of $2.50, which is 2.5% (2% for the 4 months from April 16 through August 15, and 0.5% for the fractional part of the month from August 16 through August 21) of the net amount due as shown on the return of $100 ($800 shown on the return less $700 paid on or before April 15). There will also be imposed an additional amount under section 6651(a)(1) of $58, determined as follows:

20% (5% per month for the 3 months from April 16 through July 15 and 5% for the fractional part of the month from July 16 through July 20) of the net amount due of $300 ($1,000 required to be shown on the return less $700 paid on or before April 15) $60.00

Reduced by the amount of the addition imposed under section 6651(a)(2) for those months................2.00

Addition to tax under section 6651(a)(1)..**$58.00**

Failure Due to Reasonable Cause

When a taxpayer's late filing was due to *reasonable cause* and not due to *willful neglect*, the penalty is not imposed.

Reasonable cause may exist when:
   a) The delinquency was due to the death, serious illness, or unavoidable absence of the taxpayer or member of his or her immediate family.
   b) The taxpayer is unable to obtain records.
   c) Reliance is on erroneous advice from the IRS.
   d) Reliance is on a tax adviser.
   e) Failure to file resulted from a fire, casualty, natural disaster, or other disturbance. (IRM 20.1.1.3)

B. Penalty For Failure to Pay Tax <u>Shown</u> on The Return

This penalty does not apply if the delinquency payment is due to *reasonable cause* and not due to willful neglect. The penalty applies only to the amount due stated on the return and not paid. It does not apply to an underpayment not stated on the return (Code Sec. 6651(b)).

The penalty period begins on the payment due date (due date of the related return, including extensions) and ends with payment of the tax.

The penalty is .05% for each month (or part of a month) up to a maximum of 25%. The .05% rate is increased to 1% if the taxpayer fails to pay after the IRS notifies the taxpayer (Code Sec. 6651(d)). The penalty rate is reduced to .25% per month during the period of an installment payment agreement with the IRS (Code Sec. 6651(h)).

The appropriate penalty rate is applied to the net tax shown on the return. The net tax is the total tax, reduced by:
   1) Any part of the tax paid on or before the beginning of the month, and
   2) Any tax credit that may be claimed on the return.

If the tax on the return is overstated, the failure-to-pay penalty is calculated using the actual tax due, not the tax erroneously shown on the return (Code Sec. 6651(c)).

An offset is allowed against the failure-to-file penalty for the amount of the failure-to-pay penalty for any month (or part thereof) to which both penalties apply. Accordingly, if the taxpayer fails to timely file the return and also fails to pay the tax shown as due on the late filed return, then both the failure-to-file and the failure-to-pay penalties may apply with respect to the same month, but the failure-to-file penalty is reduced by the failure-to-pay penalty (Code Sec. 6651(c)(1)).

EXAMPLE:
An individual files his income tax return for the calendar-year 2009 on December 2, 2010, and such delinquency is <u>not</u> due to reasonable cause. The balance due, as shown on the return, of $500 is paid when the return is filed on December 2, 2010. In addition to interest and the addition for failure to pay under section 6651(a)(2) of $20, (8 months at 0.5% per month, 4%) there will also be imposed an additional amount under section 6651(a)(1) of $112.50, determined as follows:

Penalty at 5% for maximum of 5 months, 25% of $500 ....$125.00

Less reduction for the amount of the addition under section 6651(a)(2):
Amount imposed under section 6651(a)(2) for failure to pay for the months in which there is also an addition for failure to file—2½% for the 5 months April 16 through September 15 of the net amount due ($500) 12.50

Addition to tax under section 6651(a)(1)..**$112.50**

C. Penalty for Failure to Pay Tax <u>Not Shown</u> on Return

The IRC penalizes a taxpayer for failure to pay the tax required to be, but not shown on a return after notice and demand for payment. Generally a taxpayer has 21 calendar days after such notice to pay the tax. However, taxpayers that owe $100,000 or more must pay the tax within 10 business days. The penalty does not apply if the taxpayer can show that the failure to pay was due to reasonable cause and not due to willful neglect (Code Sec. 6651(a)(3)).

The penalty begins to accrue after the prescribed number of days has expired. The penalty is ½% of the assessed amount not shown on the return for each month (or fraction of a month), up to a maximum of 25% (Code Sec. 6651(a)). The ½% rate is increased to 1% when the taxpayer does not pay after the IRS notifies the taxpayer. The penalty rate is reduced to .25% per month during the period of an installment payment agreement with the IRS (Code Sec. 6651(h)).

The penalty rate is applied to the tax required to be but not shown on a return and that has been assessed. The amount required to be shown on the return is the net amount due, which is the total amount of tax required to be shown reduced by the amount of such tax paid before the beginning of the month.

D. Accuracy-Related Penalty

The accuracy-related penalty applies only if a return is filed. If no return is filed, the delinquency penalty applies instead. The accuracy-related penalty is a flat <u>20% of the underpayment.</u> This penalty applies only to:
   a) Underpayments attributable to negligence or disregard of rules or regulations.
   b) A substantial understatement of income tax.
   c) Certain valuation misstatements (Code Sec. 6662).

Negligence
A 20% penalty is imposed only on the portion of any underpayment of tax that is due to negligence or disregard of rules or regulations (Code Sec. 6662(b)(1)).

EXAMPLE:
Maria owes 5,000 of additional taxes for tax-year 2010. It has been ascertained that 2,000 of the amount is due to negligence. The negligence penalty is $400 (0.20 x $2,000)

Negligence is defined as failure to:
   1. Make a reasonable attempt to comply with the internal revenue laws.
   2. Exercise ordinary and reasonable care in preparation of a tax return.
   3. Keep adequate books and records or to substantiate items properly.

A taxpayer is negligent if he is careless, reckless, or intentionally disregards the rules or regulations. Negligence connotes a lack of due care or a failure to do what a reasonable and prudent person would do under the circumstances. Negligence includes both a taxpayer's affirmative acts and well as the failures to act.
Rules or regulations include:
   (i) Provisions of the Code.
   (ii) Temporary or final regulations.
   (iii) Revenue rulings or notices published in the Internal Revenue Bulletin.

The IRS has the burden of proving that the negligence penalty is appropriate only if the taxpayer challenges the penalty.

Action to Enjoin Tax Return Prepares
If the court finds that a tax return preparer has:
   1) Recklessly or intentionally disregarded rules or regulations, or willfully understated tax liability
   2) Misrepresented his or her eligibility to practice before the IRS
   3) Guaranteed a tax refund or the allowance of a tax credit, or
   4) Engaged in other fraudulent or deceptive conduct that substantially interferes with the administration of the Internal Revenue laws,

The court may enjoin the preparer from further engaging in the above-mentioned conduct.

If the court finds that a tax return preparer has continually or repeatedly engaged in any conduct mentioned above, the court may enjoin such person from acting as a tax return preparer.

Definition of Underpayment
An underpayment is the amount by which the tax imposed exceeds:
1) The sum of:
   (i) The amount of tax shown on the return,
       plus
   (ii) Amounts not shown on the return but previously assessed,
        minus
2) The amount of rebates made (Code Sec. 6664).

The definition of underpayment also may be expressed as:
Underpayment = W − (X + Y − Z)
   Where:
   W = the amount of income tax imposed
   X = the amount shown as the tax by the taxpayer on his return
   Y = amounts not so shown previously assessed (or collected without assessment)
   Z = the amount of rebates made.

W = Income Tax Imposed
The tax imposed is the income tax imposed on the taxpayer for the tax-year, determined without regard to:
1. The credits for tax withheld.
2. The taxpayer's tax or estimated tax payments.
3. Any amounts collected as the result of a termination or jeopardy assessment.
4. Any tax that the taxpayer is not required to show on the return, such as the accumulated earnings tax (Reg. Sec. 1.6664-2(b)).

X = Amount Shown as Tax on Return
The amount shown on a return is:
1. The total tax liability shown by the taxpayer on his return *reduced by*:
   (i) Credits,
   (ii) Estimated tax, and
   (iii) Other payments claimed by taxpayer on the return, *minus*
2. Amounts actually withheld, paid or applied from a prior year.

Y = Amounts Not So Shown Previously Assessed *(or collected without assessment)*

"*Amounts not so shown previously assessed*" means only amounts assessed before the return is filed that were not shown on the return, such as termination assessments and jeopardy assessments made prior to the filing of the return for the taxable year.

The amount "*collected without assessment*" is the amount by which:
The sum of:
  a) Credits relating to tax withheld on wages,
  b) Credits relating to tax withheld at source on nonresident aliens and foreign corporations,
  c) estimated tax payments, and
  d) other payments in satisfaction of tax liability made before the return is filed,

….*exceed* the tax shown on the return (provided such excess has not been refunded or allowed as a credit to the taxpayer).

Z = Amount of Rebates Made

The term "*rebate*" means an abatement credit, refund or other repayment, so much as was made on the ground that the tax imposed was less than the excess of:
1. *The sum of:*
   a) The amount shown as the tax by the taxpayer on his return,
      <u>plus</u>
   b) Amounts not so shown previously assessed (or collected without assessment),
      <u>divided by</u>
2. Rebates previously made.

EXAMPLE 1:

A Taxpayer's 2010 return showed a tax liability of $18,000. The taxpayer had no amounts previously assessed (or collected without assessment) and received no rebates of tax. Taxpayer claimed a credit in the amount of $23,000 for income tax withheld, which resulted in a refund received of $5,000. It is later determined that the taxpayer should have reported additional income and that the correct tax for the taxable year is $25,500. There is an underpayment of $7,500, determined as follows:

Tax imposed under subtitle A.	$25,500
Tax shown on return	$18,000
Tax previously assessed (or collected without assessment)	0
Amount of rebates made	0
Balance	$18,000
Underpayment	**$7,500**

EXAMPLE 2:

The facts are the same as in *Example 1* except that the taxpayer failed to claim on the return a credit of $1,500 for income tax withheld. This $1,500 constitutes an amount collected without assessment. The underpayment is $6,000, determined as follows:

Tax imposed under subtitle A		$25,500
Tax shown on return	$18,000	
Tax previously assessed (or collected without assessment)	1,500	
Amount of rebates made	0	
Balance		$19,500
Underpayment		**$6,000**

EXAMPLE 3:

On Form 1040 filed for tax-year 2010, a taxpayer reported a tax liability of $10,000, estimated tax payments of $15,000, and received a refund of $5,000. Estimated tax payments actually made with respect to tax-year 2010 were only $7,000. For purposes of determining the amount of underpayment subject to a penalty, the tax shown on the return is $2,000 (reported tax liability of $10,000 reduced by the overstated estimated tax of $8,000 ($15,000 – $7,000)). The underpayment is $8,000, determined as follows:

Tax imposed under subtitle A		$10,000
Tax shown on return	$2,000	
Tax previously assessed (or collected without assessment)	0	
Amount of rebates made	0	
Balance		$2,000
Underpayment		**$8,000**

(Reg. Sec. 1.6664-2.)

E. Fraud Penalty

In general, fraud is a taxpayer's specific and actual intent to evade payment of a tax due and owing. Code Sec. 6663 imposes a penalty equal to 75% of the portion of any underpayment due to fraud. If the IRS establishes by clear and convincing evidence that any portion of an underpayment is attributable to fraud, the entire underpayment is attributable to fraud. The taxpayer must then produce evidence to show that any or all of the underpayment was not due to fraud and must establish the portion not attributable to fraud by a preponderance of the evidence.

Elements of Fraud

Fraud is established when the following exist:
1. Knowing falsehood by the taxpayer
2. An intent to evade tax
3. An underpayment of tax

A taxpayer's failure to file tax returns by itself is not enough to establish fraud. However, an extended period of non-filing along with some affirmative indication of fraudulent intent will support imposition of the fraud penalty.

Criminal Penalty vs. Civil Penalty on Fraud

Generally, the IRS will pursue a taxpayer on criminal charges first and then pursue civil penalties. The reason behind this is because the taxpayer could assert his Fifth Amendment rights against self-incrimination during the civil investigation.

When criminal tax proceedings are followed by civil proceedings, the doctrine of collateral estoppel may apply.

Collateral estoppel prevents a person from re-litigating an issue that a court has already decided on. Collateral estoppel doctrine applies only to issues that were actually presented and determined in the first proceeding. The imposition of civil fraud penalty, in addition to either imprisonment or criminal monetary penalties, <u>does not</u> constitute double-jeopardy, and therefore does not violate the U.S. Constitution. Criminal fines or penalties paid for income tax evasion and/or conspiracy to defraud the United States do not reduce any civil fraud penalty.

In a criminal tax fraud proceeding, the IRS must establish fraud *beyond a reasonable doubt.* However, in a civil tax fraud proceeding, the IRS must only prove fraud by *clear and convincing evidence.* The following is the order of hierarchy on burden of proof, 1st being the highest:
- ➢ 1st Beyond a reasonable doubt
- ➢ 2nd Clear and convincing evidence
- ➢ 3rd Preponderance of the evidence

F.   Frivolous Return Penalty

Any person (including most entities) that files a *frivolous federal tax return* is subject to a penalty of $5,000. In addition, a penalty of $5,000 is imposed on any person that submits a *specified frivolous submission.*

The penalty for frivolous federal tax returns is imposed when:
1) An individual files what purports to be a tax return but that:
    a) Does not contain information on which the substantial correctness of the self-assessment may be judged, or
    b) Contains information indicating on its face that the self-assessment is substantially incorrect, and
2) The lack of or incorrect information on the filed return:
    a) Is based on a position that the IRS has identified as frivolous, or
    b) Reflects a desire to delay or impede the administration of the federal tax laws.

The frivolous return penalty is in *addition* to any other penalty provided by law.
A specified submission is:
1) A request for a hearing after the IRS files a notice of lien or the taxpayer receives a pre-levy Collection Due Process Hearing Notice, and

2) An application relating to agreements for payment of tax liability in installments, compromises, or taxpayer assistance orders (Code Sec. 6702).

G. Penalty for Failure to Collect and Pay Over Tax

A *responsible person* who fails to withhold taxes or pay them to the government may be personally liable for 100% of the taxes required to be withheld and paid. This penalty is commonly known as the Responsible Person or Trust Fund Recovery Penalty (TFRP). A responsible person is anyone who has a duty to withhold and/or pay the taxes. A responsible person is liable for the penalty when the person *willfully* fails to:
   a) Collect
   b) Account for
   c) Pay employees' withheld taxes to the government

The trust fund recovery penalty is designed to collect all of the unpaid taxes withheld from employees' wages. Other penalties may also apply (Code Sec. 6672).

Responsible Person Liable for TFRP

A responsible person who knows that withholding taxes are owed but pays other creditors instead is considered to have acted *willful* a matter of law and is subject to the penalty.

A responsible person may be a corporate officer, a partner, an LLC member, or an employee. Generally, a responsible person can pay or direct payment to the business's creditors. When determining whether a person is responsible for the trust fund recovery penalty, a court will look at whether the person's business position included the:
   1. Duty to collect, account for, and pay over withheld taxes; and
   2. Actual ability to control payments to creditors.

A responsible person is usually someone who has:
   (1) Financial authority under a corporation's bylaws, an LLC's operating agreement, or a partnership agreement.
   (2) Authority to sign or co-sign the business's checks.
   (3) Authority to direct expenditure of the business's funds.
   (4) Signed the business's employment or other tax returns.
   (5) Provided operating capital to or guaranteed loans for the business.
   (6) Hired and fired business employees.
   (7) Responsibility for preparing and paying payroll.
   (8) Responsibility for day-to-day operations of the business.
   (9) Controlled the business's financial affairs.

Withheld Taxes

An employer is required to withhold income and FICA taxes from an employee's wages. The employer is liable to the IRS for the amount withheld.

When the employer fails to remit amounts required to be withheld to the IRS, any individuals responsible for collecting and paying the taxes for the employer may be personally liable for the taxes. A responsible person who *willfully* attempts to evade or defeat payment of withheld taxes is also liable for the trust fund recovery penalty.

Exempt Organization Trustees and Board Members
An honorary, unpaid trustee or board member of an exempt organization generally is not liable for the responsible person penalty. The trustee or board member must:
    (1) Be serving in an honorary capacity.
    (2) Not participate in the day-to-day or financial activities of the organization.
    (3) Not have any knowledge of the failure to collect or remit withholding taxes.

Trust Fund Recovery Penalty Enforcement
The IRS will review the following information when seeking to enforce the trust fund recovery penalty:
1. *Corporate records* - Articles of Incorporation, bylaws and minutes, to determine directors' and officers' identities and duties;
2. *Financial records* - Financial statements, bank statements and cancelled checks, to determine who had the authority to sign checks, make deposits and borrow money;
3. *Tax records* - Form 941, to determine who was responsible for filing tax returns and paying taxes; and,
4. *Payroll records* - Time cards and employee ledgers, to determine whether taxes were withheld and amounts (IRM 5.7.4).

H. Penalty for Failure to Deposit Withheld Taxes

A taxpayer who makes total federal tax deposits of more than $200,000 is required to make those deposits electronically beginning with the 2nd succeeding calendar-year. Taxes that are subject to electronic deposit requirements include:
    (a) FICA taxes
    (b) Withheld income taxes
    (c) FUTA tax, excise taxes
    (d) Corporate income taxes

Beginning 2010, a taxpayer must make tax deposits *electronically*, using the Electronic Federal Tax Payment System (EFTPS), if either:
    (1) The taxpayer exceeded the $200,000 threshold in 2008 or
    (2) The taxpayer was required to use EFTPS in 2009 (Pub. 15)

Required Deposits
The following is a list of some of the required deposits:
- FICA taxes and income tax withheld;
- FUTA tax;
- Federal excise taxes;
- 30% withholding on a nonresident alien's income;

- 30% withholding on a foreign partnership, or a foreign corporation's income;
- Corporate income and estimated income taxes;
- Railroad retirement act taxes;
- Withholding on designated distributions from certain pension plans, and
- Backup withholding (Code Sec. 6656).

The penalty amount depends on how much time it takes a taxpayer to correct a failure-to-deposit. A taxpayer is subject to a penalty equal to:
1) 2% of the underpayment if the failure is corrected within 5 days of the due date. The underpayment is the amount the taxpayer was required to deposit minus any amount actually deposited on or before the due date.
2) 5% of the underpayment if the failure is corrected after five days but not more than 15 days after the due date;
3) 10% of the underpayment if the failure is not corrected by the 15th day after the due date; and
4) 15% of the underpayment if the tax is not deposited on or before the earlier of:
   a) 10 days after the date of the first delinquency notice to the taxpayer, or
   b) The day on which notice and demand for immediate payment is given under the Code's jeopardy assessment provisions or levy provisions (Code Sec. 6656(b)).

Safe Harbor Rule

A safe harbor provision is available under which employers may avoid a failure-to-deposit penalty. Under the safe harbor provision, an employer is deemed to have satisfied deposit obligation if:
   a) The amount of any shortfall does not exceed the greater of $100 or 2% of the amount of employment taxes required to be deposited, *and*
   b) The employer deposits the shortfall on or before the shortfall make-up date.

A shortfall is the employment taxes that must be deposited minus the amount actually deposited for the period.

A depositor required to make monthly deposits must deposit or remit a shortfall no later than the due date for the quarterly return, in accordance with the applicable form and instructions. A shortfall in a semiweekly deposit or a deposit required to be made under the one-day rule must be deposited by
The earlier of:
1) The first Wednesday or Friday falling on or after the 15th day of the month following the deposit month, or
2) The return due date for the return period (Rev. Proc. 2001-58).

When the total amount of accumulated employment taxes for the return period is less than $2,500 and the amount is fully deposited or remitted with a timely filed return for the return period, the amount deposited or remitted is deemed to have been timely deposited (Pub. 15)

First-Time Depositors
The IRS may waive the failure-to-deposit penalty on a person's inadvertent failure to deposit any employment tax if:
1) The person meets certain net worth requirements;
2) The failure either:
    a) Occurs during the first quarter that the person was required to deposit any employment tax, or
    b) If the person is required to change the frequency of deposits of any employment tax, relates to the first deposit to which the change applies.
3) The return of tax was filed on or before the due date (Code Sec. 6656(c)).

I. Failure to File Required Information Returns:
The following penalties may be imposed for failure to file required information returns:
(1) Failure to file correct returns penalty.
(2) Failure to comply with specific information reporting requirements penalty.
(3) Failure to provide correct payee statements penalty.

For purposes of these penalties, an *information return* is any statement of the amount of payments to another person. These forms include:
   a) Form W-2, for wages.
   b) 1098 and 1099 series forms.
   c) Form 8027, for tip reporting.
   d) Form 5498, for IRA and qualified plans reporting. (Code Sec. 6724(d)).

The IRS must issue a deficiency notice and the penalty may be contested in the Tax Court before payment of the penalty. The IRS may not collect penalties while a Tax Court proceeding is pending. The IRS will assess a deficiency within 3 years from the date a return is filed. A taxpayer seeking a refund due to an abated or waived penalty must file his claim within two years from the date the penalty is paid (Code Sec. 6511(a))

1. Failure to File Correct Returns Penalty.
This penalty punishes both *late filing* and *incorrect information returns* that are <u>not</u> payee statements. It applies to any:
1. Failure to file an information return by the required filing date.
2. Failure to include all of the information required to be shown on the return.
3. Incorrect information included on the return.
4. Failure to file returns electronically or on magnetic media when this is required.

NOTE: As of December 31, 2008, the IRS no longer accepts any form of magnetic media. Forms 1098, 1099, 5498 and W-2G must be filed electronically through the IRS FIRE System (Rev. Proc. 2009-30).

- The penalty generally is $50 for each return, with a maximum penalty of $250,000 ($100,000 for small taxpayer) for each calendar-year.

- The penalty is reduced to $15 per information return when the taxpayer corrects the failure within 30 days after the required filing date, with a maximum penalty of $75,000 ($25,000 for small taxpayer) for the calendar-year.

- When the taxpayer corrects the failure more than 30 days after the required filing date, but before August 1 of the same calendar-year, the penalty is $30 per return, with a maximum penalty of $150,000 (50,000 for small taxpayer) per calendar-year. (Code Sec. 6721).

*A small taxpayer is one that has less than $5,000,000 annual gross receipts for the 3 most recent tax-years.

EXAMPLE 1:
Corporation R fails to timely file 11,000 Forms 1099-MISC (relating to miscellaneous income) for the 2010 calendar-year. 5,000 of these returns are filed with correct information within 30 days, and 6,000 after 30 days but on or before August 1, 2011. For the same year R fails to timely file 400 Forms 1099-INT (relating to payments of interest) which R eventually files on September 28, 2011, after the period for reduction of the penalty has elapsed.
R is subject to a penalty of $245,000 computed as follows:

400 forms which were not filed by August 1 ($50 × 400)	$20,000
6,000 forms filed after 30 days ($30 × 6,000) = $180,000 but limited to $150,000	$150,000
5,000 forms filed within 30 days ($15 × 5,000)	$75,000
Total penalty	**$245,000**

EXAMPLE 2:
Corporation T fails to file timely 6,000 Forms 1099-MISC for the 2010 calendar-year. T files the 6000 Forms 1099-MISC on September 1, 2011. Because T does not correct the failure by August 1, 2011, T is subject to a penalty of $250,000, the maximum penalty. Without any limitation, T would be subject to a $300,000 penalty ($50 × 6,000 = $300,000).

EXAMPLE 3:
Corporation U files timely 300 Forms 1099-MISC on paper for the 2010 calendar-year with correct information. Under section 6011(e)(2) a person required to file at least 250 returns during a calendar-year must file those returns on magnetic media. U does not

correct its failures to file these returns on magnetic media by August 1, 2011. It is therefore subject to a penalty for a failure to file timely. However, the penalty for a failure to file timely on magnetic media applies only to the extent the number of returns *exceeds* 250. As U was required to file 300 returns on magnetic media, U is subject to a penalty of $2,500 for 50 returns ($50 × 50 = $2,500).

EXAMPLE 4:
Corporation V files 300 Forms 1099-MISC on paper for the 2010 calendar-year. The forms were filed on March 15, 2011, rather than on the required filing date of February 28, 2011. A person required to file at least 250 returns during a calendar-year must file those returns on magnetic media. V does not correctly file these returns on magnetic media by August 1, 2011. V is subject to a penalty of $3,750 for filing 250 of the returns late ($15 × 250) and $2,500 for failing to file 50 returns on magnetic media ($50 × 50) for a total penalty of $6,250. (Reg. Sec. 301.6721-1(a)(1)).

2. Failure to Include All Information Required To Be Shown on the Return.

The penalty for failure to file a correct information return because of intentional disregard of the requirements is $100 per return or more depending on the return involved (Code Sec. 6721).

Generally, the penalty is:
1) 10% of the total amount required to be reported correctly on a return or
2) 5% of the total amount required to be reported correctly on a return required if the return is related to:
    (i) Brokers.
    (ii) Exchanges of certain partnership interests.
    (iii) Certain dispositions of donated property.
3) $25,000 per transaction or the amount received up to $100,000 for a return required if the return is related to cash receipts of more than $10,000.

There is <u>no</u> limit on the maximum penalty per calendar-year for intentional disregard of the filing requirements

The facts and circumstances to be considered when determining whether a reporting failure is due to intentional disregard include:
   a) Whether the filer has a history of failure to timely file or failure to include correct information on returns.
   b) Whether the failure was promptly corrected upon discovery.
   c) Whether the filer corrects a failure to file or a failure to include correct information within 30 days after the date of any written request from the IRS to do so.
   d) Whether the information reporting penalties are less than the cost to file timely or to include correct information on a return.

3. Penalty for Failure to Provide Correct Payee Statements.

The penalty for *non-intentional* failure to provide a correct payee statement applies to the following acts:
1) Failing to furnish a payee statement by the due date.
2) Failing to include all the required information on a payee statement
3) Incorrect information on a payee statement (Code Sec. 6722(b)(2)).

The *non-intentional* penalty generally is $50 per return with a maximum for any calendar-year of $100,000

The penalty for *intentionally* disregarding the requirement to furnish a correct payee statement is for each failure to provide a statement, which is:

The greater of:
1) $100, or
2) either
   a) 10% of the amount required to be correctly reported, or
   b) 5% of the amount required to be correctly reported for a payee statement related to:
      (i) Brokers.
      (ii) Exchanges of certain partnership interests.
      (iii) Certain dispositions of donated property.

In addition, the $100,000 annual limitation on information filing penalties <u>does not</u> apply. The intentional disregard penalty is on top of the $100,000 limit for non-intentional failures (Code Sec. 6722(c)(2)).

Inconsequential Errors on Payee Statements

An inconsequential error or omission is <u>not</u> a failure to include correct information. An inconsequential error or omission is any failure that <u>cannot</u> reasonably be expected to prevent or hinder the payee from timely receiving correct information and reporting it on his or her return or from otherwise putting the statement to its intended use.

The following errors or omissions are never inconsequential:
a) Reporting the wrong dollar amounts.
b) Reporting the wrong address for the payee.
c) Using the wrong form for the information reported (i.e., whether or not the form is an acceptable substitute for an official form of the IRS).
d) Furnishing an incorrect dividend or interest statement, a statement from a cooperative, or a royalty statement.

EXAMPLE 1:
A payor furnishes a statement with respect to a Form 1099-MISC (relating to miscellaneous income). The payee statement is complete and correct, except the word "boulevard" is misspelled in the payee's address. The error cannot reasonably be expected to prevent or hinder the payee from timely receiving correct information and

reporting it on his or her tax return or from otherwise putting the statement to its intended use. Therefore, no penalty is imposed.

EXAMPLE 2:
Assume the same facts as in Example 1, except that the only error on the payee statement is that the payee's street address, '4821 Grant Boulevard' is reported incorrectly as '8421 Grant Boulevard'. A penalty is imposed with respect to the payee statement because the error can reasonably be expected to prevent or hinder the payee from timely receiving correct information and reporting it on his or her tax return or from otherwise putting the statement to its intended use.

A filer may correct a failure to provide or an incorrect payee statement by filing or correcting the payee statement. For penalty purposes, a correction is prompt if it is made:
1) Within 30 days of the date the failure is discovered or any impediment to filing a correct statement is removed, or
2) When a regular correction submission is made. Regular submissions are made at intervals of 30 days or less.

J.   Penalty for bounced checks
When a taxpayer writes a check to pay taxes and the check bounces, the IRS may impose a penalty. The penalty is either 2% of the amount of the check (unless the check is under $1,250, in which case the penalty is the amount of the check) or $25, whichever is less.

2.04   EARNED INCOME TAX CREDIT (EITC)

Penalty for Failure to Be Diligent in Determining Eligibility for EITC
EITC return preparers that fail to meet the knowledge standard and other due diligence requirements are subject to an array of civil penalties. Their clients whose returns made false EITC claims also could face penalties, in addition to repayment and interest on any erroneous refunds received (Code Sec. 6695(g)).

Penalties include:
1) $100 penalty for each due diligence failure to comply assessed against return preparers or their employers.
2) A minimum $1,000 penalty against return preparers who prepare EITC claims for which any part of an understatement of tax liability is due to an unreasonable position.
3) A minimum $5,000 penalty against return preparers who prepare EITC claims for which any part of an understatement of tax liability is due to reckless or intentional disregard of rules or regulations by the tax preparer.

4) Clients, whose returns are examined and found to be incorrect, could be subject to:
   (i) Accuracy or fraud penalties
   (ii) 2 to 10 years ban from claiming EITC

EITC Due Diligence Requirements

Paid preparers must meet four due diligence requirements on returns with EITC claims or face possible penalties. New expanded regulations clarify these requirements and set a performance standard for the "knowledge" requirement, i.e. what a reasonable and well-informed tax return preparer, knowledgeable in the law, would do.

When preparing EITC returns and claims for refund, paid preparers must:
1. Evaluate information received from clients
2. Apply a consistency and reasonableness standard to the information
3. Ask additional questions if the information appears incorrect, inconsistent or incomplete
4. Document and retain the record of inquiries made and client responses

The <u>four</u> due diligence requirements are that tax preparers must do:
(a) Completion of Eligibility checklist
(b) Computation of the Credit
(c) Knowledge
(d) Record Retention

A. Completion of Eligibility checklist
   a) Either complete Form 8867 or its equivalent
   b) Complete checklist based on information provided by the taxpayer for the preparer

B. Computation of the Credit
   a) Keep the EIC worksheet or an equivalent that demonstrates how the EIC was computed

C. Knowledge
   a) Know or have reason to know that any information used in determining the taxpayer's eligibility for, or the amount of, the EIC is incorrect, incomplete or inconsistent
   b) Do not ignore the implications of information furnished or known
   c) Make reasonable inquiries if a reasonable and well-informed tax return preparer, knowledgeable in the law, would conclude the information furnished appears to be incorrect, inconsistent or incomplete
   d) Document in your records any additional inquiries made and your client's responses.

D. Record Retention
   a) Retain Form 8867 and EIC worksheet or the equivalent

b) Maintain record of how and when the information used to complete these forms was obtained
c) Verify the identity of the person furnishing the information
d) Retain records for 3 years after the June 30th following the date the return or claim was presented for signature

Examples of situations when preparer should ask additional questions to meet due diligence knowledge requirement:

A. A client wants to use his niece and nephew to claim EITC.
   ✓ Preparer should ask questions to determine whether the children meet EITC qualifying child requirements for the client. Preparer should ask questions to ensure the children's parents or other relatives will not, or cannot claim the children.

B. An 18 year-old client with an infant has $3,000 in earned income and states she lives with her parents. She wants to claim the infant as a qualifying child for the EITC.
   ✓ This information seems incomplete and inconsistent because the 18 year old lives with her parents and earns very little income. Preparer must ask additional questions to determine if the 18 year old is the qualifying child of her parents. If she is the qualifying child of her parents, she is not eligible to claim the EITC.

C. A 22 year-old client wants to claim two sons, ages 10 and 11, as qualifying children for FITC.
   ✓ Preparer must make additional reasonable inquiries regarding the relationship between the client and the children since the age of the client seems inconsistent with the ages of the children claimed as sons.

D. A client has two qualifying children and wants to claim the EITC. She tells you she had a Schedule C business and earned $10,000 in income and had no expenses.
   ✓ This information appears incomplete because it is unusual that someone who is self-employed has no business expenses. Preparer must ask additional reasonable questions to determine if the business exists and if the information about her income and expenses is correct.

Knowledge Requirement for EITC
IRS assesses most due diligence penalties for failure to comply with the knowledge requirement. To meet the knowledge requirement, a preparer should:
   (a) Apply a common sense standard to the information provided by the client.
   (b) Evaluate whether the information is complete and gather any missing facts.
   (c) Determine if the information is consistent. Recognize contradictory statements and statements you know not to be true.
   (d) Conduct a thorough in-depth interview with every client every year.
   (e) Ask enough questions to reasonably know the return is correct and complete.
   (f) Document in the file any questions asked and client's responses as they happen.

Most Common EITC Errors

The following are four most common errors account for more than 80% of erroneous claims. Due diligence must be exercised by preparers in order to avoid them:
1. Qualifying Children
2. Filing Status
3. Income Reporting Errors
4. Incorrect Social Security Numbers

1. Qualifying Child EITC Error

The most common EITC error is the "*Qualifying Child*" issue. This is where taxpayers claim a child that does not meet the *age*, *relationship* or *residency* requirements.

A "*Qualifying Child*" must meet all relationship, age, <u>and</u> residency requirements. If two people filing separate tax returns claim the same child, tie-breaker rules determine which person has the valid claim

Tax preparers should be aware of the following potential qualifying child problem areas. If a preparer believes the given information furnished is incorrect, inconsistent or incomplete, he or she should <u>ask additional questions</u>:
1) Claiming qualifying children other than son or daughter
2) Age of primary taxpayer compared to the age of qualifying children is inconsistent
3) Very young taxpayers with qualifying children who could potentially be qualifying children themselves
4) Single taxpayer with young qualifying child and no childcare expenses
5) Claiming a disabled adult as a qualifying child

Qualifying Child Requirements
An individual is a qualifying child if:
a) He or she meets the relationship, age, and residency tests, *and*
b) Has not filed a joint return other than to claim a refund (New for 2009), *and*
c) If a child is a qualifying child of a parent and another person who is not a parent of the child, the person who is not a parent can claim the child for EITC only if their AGI is higher than the AGI of any parent (New for 2009 tax-year).

Relationship Test – The child must be your client's:
a) Son, daughter, adopted child, stepchild, or a descendant of any of them, or
b) Brother, sister, stepbrother, stepsister, or
c) A descendant of any of them, or
d) Eligible foster child

Age Test – The child must be younger than your client (New for 2009 tax-year), and:
a) Under the age of 19 at the end of 2009, or

b) A full-time student under the age of 24 at the end of 2009, or
  c) Any age and permanently and totally disabled at any time during 2009.

Residency Test - The child must have:
  a) Lived with your client for more than half the year and the home must be in the United States.
  b) Periods of temporary absence due to special circumstances may count as periods of residency. See special rules.
  c) A child who was born or died is treated as having lived with you for all of 2009 if your home was the child's home the entire time he or she was alive in 2009.

Additional Rules for Qualifying Child
A qualifying child can be any age if the qualifying child is permanently and totally disabled. A child is considered permanently and totally disabled for tax purposes if both of the following apply:
  1) He or she cannot engage in any substantial gainful activity because of a physical or mental condition
  2) A doctor determines the condition has lasted or can be expected to last continuously for at least a year or can lead to death

If a parent qualifies to claim a child, any person other than the parent claiming the child must have an AGI higher than the parent.
- This rule applies before the tie-breaker rules
- This rule is new for 2009 tax-year

If the child is a qualifying child of more than one person for EITC and the parent AGI rule is met, they can choose. If more than one person claims the same child, IRS applies the tie-breaker rules.

Tie-Breaker Rules
More than one person may be eligible to claim a child as a qualifying child. If more than one person claims the child, IRS applies the following rules:
  1. If only one person is the child's parent then only that parent can treat the child as a qualifying child.
  2. If two of the persons are parents of the child and they do not file a joint return together then only the parent with whom the child lived the longest during the year can treat the child as a qualifying child.
  3. If two of the persons are parents of the child, the child lived with each parent the same amount of time during the year, and the parents do not file a joint return then only the parent with the highest AGI can treat the child as a qualifying child.
  4. If none of the persons are the child's parent, then only the person with the highest AGI can treat the child as a qualifying child.

2. Filing Status Errors

Some married taxpayers intentionally claim single or Head of Household (HOH) filing status in order to claim more EITC. The tax law defining HOH filing status is complex and the exception that allows some married taxpayers to claim HOH status, is confusing and therefore preparers must ask additional questions.

The following are some potential filing status problem areas that need additional questioning by a preparer:
1) Taxpayers who state they are separated and qualify for HOH filing status.
2) Taxpayers who state they are HOH or single when they are married.
3) Taxpayers claiming HOH when they should be claiming single.
4) More than one Head of Household (HOH) taxpayer at the same address.

EITC Filing Statuses
EITC has four filing statuses:
1. Married Filing Joint (MFJ)
2. Qualified Widower
3. Single
4. Head of Household (HOH)

A married taxpayer <u>may not</u> file as Married Filing Separate (MFS) and receive the EITC. A taxpayer who has lived apart from his or her spouse for the last 6 months of the year, had a child living in the same house, and paid for more than half the cost of keeping up the home <u>may</u> file as HOH.

3. Income Reporting Errors

When qualifying for EITC, over-reporting or under-reporting earned income or under-reporting investment income can cause misreported income issues. Taxpayers may over-report or under-report income to qualify for or maximize the amount of EITC.

Over or Under-Reporting Income
Income reporting errors include:
a) Schedule C's with large losses, thereby lowering income to qualify for EITC;
b) Schedule C's with bogus or inflated income to maximize the amount of EITC; and
c) Schedule C's without expenses
d) Self-employed taxpayers filing a Schedule C, Profit or Loss from Business, must report the correct gross income and all allowable deductions on their return

Preparers must be aware of the following potential misreported income problem areas and make sure there is enough information to prepare a correct and complete return:
1) Questionable Schedule C income to qualify for EITC, specifically income that is not reported on a Form 1099
2) Questionable Schedule C losses that qualify the taxpayer for EITC
3) Insufficient income to support taxpayer and qualifying children

4) Schedule C's where the taxpayer has no record for income or expenses
5) Schedule C businesses with no expenses when it is reasonable for the taxpayer to have incurred expenses

4. Incorrect Social Security Numbers

Potential problem areas related to social security card include:
- (a) Returns claiming EITC with social security cards not valid for work within the U.S.
- (b) Returns claiming EITC with social security numbers that do not match SSA data
- (c) Returns claiming EITC with social security names that do not match SSA data

If the IRS rejects a return due to an invalid SSN or name, the preparer should notify his or her client of the following actions:
- (1) If the name or SSN number submitted on the original return was incorrect, the taxpayer information will need to be corrected. The client needs to submit a new return or respond to the math error notice with the correct information.
- (2) If the name or SSN is correct, the client needs to contact the Social Security Administration to correct any SSN and name mismatch and then respond to IRS with either a new return or respond to the math error notice.

2.05   UNIT 2: QUESTIONS

TRUE/FALSE
Please select either (A) for TRUE or (B) for FALSE

1. An income tax return preparer that is required to sign a tax return but fails to do so is subject to a penalty.
    A. TRUE
    B. FALSE

2. A paid preparer must give the taxpayer a copy of his or her tax return in addition to the copy filed with the IRS.
    A. TRUE
    B. FALSE

3. If a person is paid to prepare, assist in preparing, or review a tax return then he/she must sign that return. He/she may, however, choose whether or not to provide the other information in the paid preparer's area of the tax return.
    A. TRUE
    B. FALSE

4. A tax return preparer may use the tax return information of a client to solicit from the client any additional current business, in matters not related to the IRS, that the preparer provides and offers to the public; provided the preparer has the client's written consent.
    A. TRUE
    B. FALSE

5. Nancy had e-mail correspondence in 2009 with her longtime tax return preparer, an enrolled agent. The correspondence related to tax advice on the depreciation of rental property Nancy had acquired in 2009. Nancy never filed the 2009 or subsequent returns. Nancy was notified by the IRS that she is the subject of a criminal investigation for the failure to file her returns. The IRS has issued a subpoena to obtain the e-mails as part of its investigation. The e-mails with her preparer are confidential communications between Nancy and her federally authorized practitioner and are therefore protected under Internal Revenue Code Section 7525.
    A. TRUE
    B. FALSE

6. An income tax return preparer who is required to sign a tax return but fails to do so is subject to a penalty.
    A. TRUE

B. FALSE

7. A penalty assessed on a preparer under Sec. 6694 must be abated or refunded, if in the final judicial decision, there is no understatement of liability.
    A. TRUE
    B. FALSE

8. There is no limitation period for assessing the penalty against an income tax return preparer for willful or reckless conduct that results in an understatement of tax liability.
    A. TRUE
    B. FALSE

9. Jurgen, a tax return preparer, intentionally disregarded regulations in preparing a return for a client. As a consequence, the tax liability shown on the return was understated. The client's return was subsequently audited by the IRS, and the penalty for willful or reckless conduct was assessed against Jurgen. Jurgen's client appealed the IRS's audit determination. An appeals officer determined that the client did not take several allowable deductions. These deductions eliminated the understatement produced by Jurgen's intentional disregard of regulations. The IRS will abate the penalty, and any amount Jurgen may have paid will be refunded.
    A. TRUE
    B. FALSE

10. If the IRS decides to assess a preparer penalty, a report of the examination must be furnished to the preparer, and the preparer must be given 90 days to respond and receive further consideration before the penalty is assessed and billed.
    A. TRUE
    B. FALSE

11. If a return preparer penalty is proposed because of an understatement of tax liability and that understatement includes a change to earned income credit, two separate penalties may be imposed -- one for understatement of tax liability and a second for failure to be diligent in claiming earned income credit.
    A. TRUE
    B. FALSE

12. Joan is preparing Kimball's 2009 tax return. Kimball complains about the very small amount of compensation he received for serving on jury duty for all of May in 2009. Joan does not report any income from jury duty on Kimball's tax return. Joan is subject to a penalty for willful understatement.
    A. TRUE

B. FALSE

13. If an income tax return preparer knows or reasonably should have known that the tax on a return he/she prepared is understated due to a position for which there was not a realistic possibility of being sustained on its merits, a penalty of $250 may be asserted by the IRS.
    A. TRUE
    B. FALSE

14. An income tax return preparer who operates a check cashing agency that cashes, endorses, or negotiates income tax refund checks of taxpayers for whom the preparer had prepared returns is exempted from the penalty asserted on income tax return preparers for negotiating checks as provided by IRC Sec. 6695(f).
    A. TRUE
    B. FALSE

15. The term "negligence" includes a failure to make a reasonable attempt to comply with the tax law or to exercise ordinary and reasonable care in preparing a return.
    A. TRUE
    B. FALSE

16. A penalty applies to an income tax return preparer if (s)he does not (1) keep for 3 years a copy of the tax return, or a list regarding certain taxpayer information, and a record of the individual preparer who was required to sign the return and (2) make available such information to the IRS upon its request, unless the preparer can show reasonable cause for the failure.
    A. TRUE
    B. FALSE

17. Mary is a tax return preparer who also acts as a business manager for her clients. In this capacity, she requires her clients to maintain checking accounts under which she is authorized to sign checks on their behalf. Mary's clients' refund checks are mailed to her. She then obtains their endorsements and deposits the refunds in the checking accounts. Based on these facts, Mary is not subject to a penalty for negotiation of a check under Sec. 6695.
    A. TRUE
    B. FALSE

18. Sec. 6694(a) provides for a penalty against a return preparer for understatement of tax liability due to an unrealistic position. Sec. 6694(b) provides for a penalty if any part of the understatement is due to willful or reckless conduct. Both of

these penalties may be assessed simultaneously on a given return, but the total amount of the penalties cannot exceed the Sec. 6694(b) penalty.
   A. TRUE
   B. FALSE

19. An income tax return preparer takes a position on a return that is contrary to a revenue ruling that is published by the IRS in the Internal Revenue Bulletin. The position has a realistic possibility of being sustained on its merits; however, the preparer did not adequately disclose this position on the return. The preparer is considered to have recklessly or intentionally disregarded the revenue ruling and is subject to the $1,000 penalty under Sec. 6694(b).
   A. TRUE
   B. FALSE

20. In the absence of reasonable cause, a tax return preparer is subject to a penalty for failure to retain and keep available, for a 5-year period, a copy of any return prepared or a record of the name, taxpayer identification number, and taxable year of the taxpayer for whom the return was prepared and the type of return prepared.
   A. TRUE
   B. FALSE

21. An income tax return preparer, who is not a preparer bank, who collects return preparation fees by endorsing and cashing income tax refund checks for clients and withholding the amount of the fee will be subject to a $500 penalty for each check negotiated in this manner.
   A. TRUE
   B. FALSE

22. If a district court finds that an income tax return preparer has continually or repeatedly engaged in guaranteeing the payment of tax refunds to his/her client-taxpayers, the court may enjoin such person from acting as an income tax return preparer.
   A. TRUE
   B. FALSE

23. The penalty for a preparer who fails to retain a copy or record of income tax returns and claims for refunds under Internal Revenue Code Sec. 6695(d) is $25 for each failure up to a maximum of $25,000 for a single return period.
   A. TRUE
   B. FALSE

24. Preparers who fail to properly sign the returns they prepared, or who do not furnish the required tax preparer identification numbers, may be fined $50 for

each improper signature and an additional $50 for each identification number omitted.
   A. TRUE
   B. FALSE

25. A taxpayer, during an interview conducted by the preparer, stated that he had paid $6,500 in doctor bills and $5,000 in deductible travel and entertainment expenses during the tax year, when in fact he had paid smaller amounts. On the basis of this information, the preparer properly calculated the deductions for medical expenses and for travel and entertainment expenses, which resulted in an understatement of tax liability. The preparer had no reason to believe that the medical expenses and the travel and entertainment expenses were incorrect or incomplete. The preparer did not ask for underlying documentation of the medical expenses but inquired about the existence of travel and entertainment expense records. The preparer was reasonably satisfied by the taxpayer's representations that the taxpayer had adequate records (or other corroborative evidence) for the deduction of $5,000 for travel and entertainment expenses. The preparer is not subject to a penalty under Sec. 6694.
   A. TRUE
   B. FALSE

26. An income tax return preparer who fails to furnish a copy of the return or claim for refund to the taxpayer shall be subject to a $50 penalty for the failure unless it is shown that the failure is due to reasonable cause and not due to willful neglect.
   A. TRUE
   B. FALSE

27. The willful or reckless conduct penalty under Sec. 6694(b) is reduced by the amount of the penalty paid for any understatement due to an unrealistic position under Sec. 6694(a).
   A. TRUE
   B. FALSE

28. If you work for a firm as a tax preparer, you may be assessed a penalty of $50 per return for failure to furnish a copy of the tax return to the taxpayer.
   A. TRUE
   B. FALSE

29. Barbara is an enrolled agent who only prepares tax returns. One of her clients was audited by the IRS and a substantial income tax deficiency resulted. Barbara was determined by the IRS to be an income tax return preparer and a preparer

penalty was assessed. Barbara can contest the validity of the penalty in Tax Court without making any payment of the penalty.
- A. TRUE
- B. FALSE

30. An income tax return preparer can satisfy the regulation requiring the preparer to retain a copy or record of each return prepared by retaining a photocopy of only the completed first page of each return.
- A. TRUE
- B. FALSE

31. Any person who employs one or more income tax return preparers must retain a record of the name, taxpayer identification number, and place of work of each return preparer who is employed during the year.
- A. TRUE
- B. FALSE

32. A signature stamp is sufficient to meet the return preparer signature requirement.
- A. TRUE
- B. FALSE

33. If a person is paid to prepare, assist in preparing, or review a tax return then he/she must sign that return. He/she may, however, choose whether or not to provide the other information in the paid preparer's area of the tax return.
- A. TRUE
- B. FALSE

34. A paid preparer must give the taxpayer a copy of his or her tax return in addition to the copy filed with the IRS.
- A. TRUE
- B. FALSE

35. Diane, an enrolled agent who is required to render an opinion on material issues involving a tax shelter investment, must determine whether it is certain that the investor will prevail on the merits of material tax issues, which may be challenged by the IRS.
- A. TRUE
- B. FALSE

36. Paul is a barber who prepares federal tax returns during the tax-filing season. Paul charges $25.00 for each return. Paul qualifies as a return preparer.
- A. TRUE
- B. FALSE

37. An income tax preparer is required to retain a record, by retention of a copy of the return, maintenance of a list, or card file of each tax return completed.
    A. TRUE
    B. FALSE

38. Each person who employs (or engages) one or more income tax return preparers to prepare returns other than for the employer must retain a record of the name, taxpayer identification number, and principal place of work during the return period (the 12-month period beginning on July 1 of each year) of each income tax return preparer employed at any time during that period. The record must be kept available for inspection for a 3-year period, which includes the return period to which, that record relates.
    A. TRUE
    B. FALSE

39. Each person who employs (or engages) one or more income tax return preparers to prepare returns other than for the employer must retain a record, to be kept available for inspection for the 2-year period following the close of the return period to which that record relates, of the name, taxpayer identification number, and principal place of work during the return period (the 12-month period beginning July 1 of each year) of each income tax return preparer employed at any time during that period.
    A. TRUE
    B. FALSE

40. Lillie is a partner in LAB Partnership. She is responsible for the overall substantive accuracy of all income tax returns prepared by the employees. Lillie does not collect the necessary information nor does she prepare tax returns. Lillie should sign the returns as the preparer.
    A. TRUE
    B. FALSE

41. Each person who employs (or engages) one or more income tax return preparers to prepare returns other than for that person must retain a record of the name, taxpayer identification number, and principal place of work during the return period (the 12-month period beginning on July 1 of each year) of each income tax return preparer employed at any time during that period. The record must be kept available for inspection for the 3-year period following the close of the return period to which that record relates.
    A. TRUE
    B. FALSE

42. An income tax return preparer must furnish a completed copy of the original return to the taxpayer not later than the time the original return is presented for the signature of the taxpayer.
    A. TRUE
    B. FALSE

43. A person shall not be an income tax return preparer merely because a person furnishes typing, reproducing, or other mechanical assistance.
    A. TRUE
    B. FALSE

44. A person who prepares a return or claim for refund for a taxpayer with no explicit or implicit agreement for compensation is not a preparer, even though the person receives a gift, return service, or favor.
    A. TRUE
    B. FALSE

45. B is a college student working his way through school. During the tax season, he is paid to prepare his friends' tax returns. B was paid $250. B is not an income tax preparer.
    A. TRUE
    B. FALSE

46. Anyone who prepares a return or claim for a refund as a fiduciary is not covered by the preparer rules.
    A. TRUE
    B. FALSE

47. A person who prepares only a portion of a return will not be considered a preparer if that portion involves gross income, deductions, or the basis for determining tax credits of Under $2,000 or Under $100,000 and less than 20% of gross income (or 20% of adjusted gross income on an individual return) of the return as a whole.
    A. TRUE
    B. FALSE

48. Completion of a single schedule of a tax return will be considered a "substantial portion" if that schedule is the dominant portion of the entire tax return.
    A. TRUE
    B. FALSE

49. Preparers of information returns such as Form 1099-DIV are not covered by the preparer rules.
    A. TRUE

B. FALSE

50. An income tax return preparer can satisfy the regulation requiring the preparer to retain a copy or record of each return prepared by retaining a photocopy of only the completed first page of each return prepared.
    A. TRUE
    B. FALSE

51. An income tax return preparer includes any person who prepares, for compensation, an estate tax return or a gift tax return.
    A. TRUE
    B. FALSE

52. A preparer who willfully, recklessly, and/or intentionally understates the tax liability on a return he or she prepares is subject to a penalty of $500.
    A. TRUE
    B. FALSE

53. Joan is preparing Kimball's 2009 tax return. Kimball complains about the very small amount of compensation he received for serving on jury duty for all of May in 2009. Joan does not report any income from jury duty on Kimball's tax return. Joan is subject to a penalty for willful understatement.
    A. TRUE
    B. FALSE

54. Joni is a tax return preparer. She's not a preparer bank. Joni prepared Judy's income tax return and then cashed Judy's refund check. Joni is subject to a penalty of $500.
    A. TRUE
    B. FALSE

55. Trent's Tax Service prepared the 1998 return of George Dell and was paid $100 by Mr. Dell. The return was audited and changes were made to both income and expenses on the return but no additional tax was due. These changes were the direct result of negligent actions on the part of Trent's Tax Service. Trent's Tax Service may be liable for a $250 penalty for understatement of taxpayer's liability due to an unrealistic position under IRC Section 6694.
    A. TRUE
    B. FALSE

56. If a return preparer penalty is proposed because of an understatement of tax liability and that understatement includes a change to earned income credit, two separate penalties may be imposed - one for understatement of tax liability and a second penalty for failure to be diligent in claiming earned income credit.

A. TRUE
B. FALSE

57. A penalty assessed on a preparer under Section 6694 must be abated or refunded, if in the final judicial decision, there is no understatement of liability.
    A. TRUE
    B. FALSE

58. If you work for a firm as a tax preparer, you may be assessed a penalty of $50 per return for failure to furnish a copy of the tax return to the taxpayer.
    A. TRUE
    B. FALSE

59. Barbara is an enrolled agent who only prepares tax returns. One of her clients was audited by the IRS and a substantial income tax deficiency resulted. Barbara was determined by the IRS to be an income tax return preparer and a preparer penalty was assessed. Barbara can contest the validity of the penalty in Tax Court without making any payment of the penalty.
    A. TRUE
    B. FALSE

60. Donna is a secretary who prepares income tax returns during the tax filing season. Donna does not keep a copy of the returns she prepares but she does keep a record of her clients' names, identification numbers, tax year and type of return prepared. Donna is subject to a civil penalty in the amount of $50 for each copy of a tax return she does **not** retain up to a maximum of $25,000 for each year.
    A. TRUE
    B. FALSE

61. The penalty, if you understate your income tax because you show negligence or disregard of the rules or regulations, is 20% of the underpayment. Negligence includes the failure to keep adequate books and records.
    A. TRUE
    B. FALSE

MULTIPLE CHOICE QUESTIONS:
Please select the most appropriate answer.

62. Which of the following statements is FALSE regarding tax return preparers?
    A. Only a person who signs a return as the preparer may be considered the preparer of the return.

B. Unpaid preparers, such as volunteers who assist low-income individuals, are not considered to be preparers for purposes of preparer penalties.
C. An employee who prepares the return of his/her employer does not meet the definition of an income tax preparer.
D. The preparation of a substantial portion of a return for compensation is treated as the preparation of that return.

63. Which of the following is considered an income tax return preparer?
    A. A neighbor who assists with preparation of depreciation schedule.
    B. A son who enters income tax return information into a computer program and prints a return.
    C. A woman who prepares income tax returns in her home during filing season and accepts payment for her services.
    D. A volunteer at a local church who prepares income tax returns but accepts no payment.

64. Sandra, an enrolled agent, prepares Linda's income tax return. Linda sold some stock in a corporation and believes the proceeds of the stock are all a return to capital, and therefore, not included in her gross income. After research, Sandra determines that there is reasonable basis for Linda's position, but she does not believe there is a realistic possibility of success on the merits. Under what circumstances can Sandra sign Linda's return if the proceeds are not included in income reported on the return?
    A. If the position is not frivolous and is adequately disclosed on the return.
    B. If Sandra documents her disagreement with Linda's position and keeps it in her file.
    C. If Linda agrees in writing not to dispute any IRS challenge to the position.
    D. Under no circumstances.

65. Identify the FALSE statement below.
    A. Joachim provides tax assistance under a Volunteer Income Tax Assistance (VITA) program established by the IRS. Joachim is not a tax preparer.
    B. "Prep Free" is an organization sponsoring a Volunteer Income Tax Assistance (VITA) program and provides free tax preparation through VITA. Prep Free is not a tax preparer for returns that it prepares through the VITA program it sponsors.
    C. Jonathan is the paid preparer of Form 1120S for Cow Bells, Inc., a small business corporation. He does not prepare the individual return for Jaime, a Cow Bells shareholder who does not work for Cow Bells but who has pass-through income of $600. Jaime's return also includes $54,000 of income from other sources. Jonathan is not a tax preparer with respect to Jaime's return.
    D. Terry is the paid preparer of Form 1065 for Winter Wiggles, a partnership. She does not prepare the individual return for Thelma, who owns a partnership interest in Winter Wiggles. Thelma's individual return includes

pass-through earnings of $26,000 from Winter Wiggles. Thelma's return also includes income from other sources consisting of $38,000 wages and $3,000 alimony. Terry is not a tax preparer with respect to Thelma's return.

66. Ernie is a principal of an international CPA firm. One of the firm's clients owns seven businesses and is a member of over 100 flow-through entities. Several members of Ernie's firm assist in the preparation of the client's individual income tax return. Which one of the following is TRUE with regard to the member of the firm who qualifies as the return preparer?
   A. The signatory is the individual preparer who has the primary responsibility for the overall substantive accuracy of the reporting positions on the return.
   B. A photocopy of a manually signed copy of the return satisfies the manual signature requirement.
   C. If the individual preparer is physically unable to sign the return due to a disability, (s)he can indicate "unable to sign" as the signature.
   D. All of the answers are correct.

67. With regard to the requirements for preparers signing returns under Sec. 6695, which of the following statements is FALSE?
   A. A $50 penalty is imposed on any preparer who does not inscribe his/her employer's identification number on the return.
   B. If more than one preparer is involved in the preparation of the return, the individual with primary responsibility for the overall accuracy of the preparation of the return must sign it.
   C. If a substitute preparer has reviewed both the information obtained by the original preparer and the original preparer's preparation of the return, the substitute preparer may sign the return (assume the original preparer is available to sign).
   D. A facsimile signature stamp or gummed label will not satisfy the signature requirement for individual income tax returns.

68. Which of the following is considered an income tax preparer under the income tax preparer regulations?
   A. An individual who prepares a return for a friend, free of charge, and then receives a gift of gratitude from the friend.
   B. An individual who prepares a return for his/her employer if (s)he is regularly and continuously employed by the employer.
   C. An individual who prepares, as a fiduciary, a return or claim for refund for any person.
   D. Someone who employs another person to prepare, for compensation, a substantial portion of any return of tax under the income tax provisions of the Code.

69. Arnie is a Certified Public Accountant who prepares income tax returns for his clients. One of his clients submitted a list of expenses to be claimed on Schedule C of the tax return. Arnie qualifies as a return preparer and, as such, is required to comply with which one of the following conditions?
   A. Arnie is required to independently verify the client's information.
   B. Arnie can ignore implications of information known by him.
   C. Inquiry is not required if the information appears to be incorrect or incomplete.
   D. Appropriate inquiries are required to determine whether the client has substantiation for travel and entertainment expenses.

70. Mike is an enrolled agent. For the past five years, the information that Anne provided Mike to prepare her return included a Schedule K-1 from a partnership showing significant income. However, Mike did not see a Schedule K-1 from the partnership among the information Anne provided to him this year. What does due diligence require Mike to do?
   A. Without talking to Anne, Mike should estimate the amount that would be reported as income on the Schedule K-1 based on last year's Schedule K-1 and include that amount on Anne's return.
   B. Call Anne's financial advisor and ask him about Anne's investments.
   C. Nothing, because Mike is required to rely only on the information provided by his client, even if he has a reason to know the information is not accurate.
   D. Ask Anne about the fact that she did not provide him with a Schedule K-1.

71. Sam, an Enrolled Agent, is representing Fred before the Examination Division of the IRS. The IRS is questioning Fred on his Schedule C gross income that is listed on the 2009 tax return. While reviewing the documentation Fred provided, Sam discovers income that was omitted from the tax return. What is the appropriate action for Sam to take?
   A. Sam must immediately advise the IRS examiner of the omitted income.
   B. Sam must notify the IRS that he is no longer representing Fred by withdrawing his Form 2848.
   C. Sam must advise Fred promptly of the omission and the consequences provided by the Internal Revenue Code and regulations for such omission.
   D. Sam must advise Fred on how to keep the omission from being discovered by the IRS.

72. When must an income tax return preparer provide a copy of an income tax return to a taxpayer?
   A. Within 45 days after the return is filed, including extensions.
   B. Within 48 hours after the taxpayer requests a copy of the income tax return.
   C. Not later than the time the original return is presented to the taxpayer for signature.
   D. None of the answers are correct.

73. Circular 230, Sec. 10.34, discusses standards for advising clients with respect to tax return positions and for preparing or signing returns. Which of the statements below is TRUE?
    A. A practitioner may not sign a tax return as a preparer if the practitioner determines that the tax return contains a position that does not have a realistic possibility of being sustained on its merits (the realistic possibility standard) unless the position is not frivolous and is adequately disclosed to the IRS.
    B. A practitioner advising a client to take a position on a tax return, or preparing or signing a tax return as a preparer, must inform the client of the penalties reasonably likely to apply to the client with respect to the position advised, prepared, or reported.
    C. A practitioner advising a client to take a position on a tax return, or preparing or signing a tax return as a preparer, generally may rely in good faith without verification upon information furnished by the client. The practitioner may not, however, ignore the implications of information furnished to, or actually known by, the practitioner and must make reasonable inquiries if the information as furnished appears to be incorrect, inconsistent with an important fact or another factual assumption, or incomplete.
    D. All of the answers are correct.

74. Which of the following is not an income tax return preparer?
    A. Someone who employs one or more persons to prepare for compensation, other than for the employer, all or a substantial portion of any tax return under Subtitle A of the Code.
    B. Someone who prepares a substantial portion of a return or claim for refund under Subtitle A of the Code.
    C. Someone who prepares an information return for a person or entity under Subtitle A of the Code.
    D. Someone who prepares, as a fiduciary, a return or claim for refund for any person.

75. Identify the item below that does not describe information a preparer must maintain about every return prepared.
    A. The taxpayer's name and taxpayer identification number.
    B. The date the return or claim for refund was prepared.
    C. The taxable year of the taxpayer (or nontaxable entity) for which the return was prepared.
    D. The type of return or claim for refund prepared.

76. Which of the following is FALSE regarding the filing of information returns concerning employees who prepare tax returns?
    A. Annual listings of preparers, identification numbers, and place of work are required for preparers who employ others to prepare returns.

B. The period for which the information return is required is a 12-month period beginning July 1 of each year.
C. No information return is actually required to be submitted; a list is made and kept by the employing preparer.
D. Information returns of income tax return preparers must be maintained by the preparer for 2 years.

77. Jack, a return preparer, did not retain copies of all returns that he prepared but did keep a list that reflected the taxpayer's name, identification number, tax year, and type of return for each of his clients. Which of the following statements best describes this situation?
    A. Jack is in compliance with the provisions of Sec. 6107 if he retains the list for a period of 1 year after the close of the return period in which the return was signed.
    B. Jack is in compliance with the provisions of Sec. 6107 provided he retains the list for a 3-year period after the close of the return period in which the return was signed.
    C. Jack is not in compliance with Sec. 6107 since he must retain copies of all returns filed.
    D. Jack is not in compliance with Sec. 6107 since he has not kept all the information required by the Code.

78. Joe, a calendar-year taxpayer, filed his federal income tax return, with a refund due, for tax year 2004 on April 1, 2005. The last day to timely file a claim for refund with respect to that return is
    A. April 1, 2007
    B. April 15, 2007
    C. April 1, 2008
    D. April 15, 2008

79. With regard to the reporting requirements for income tax return preparers under Sec. 6060, which of the following statements is FALSE?
    A. The provisions in this section apply to preparers who employ five or more income tax preparers. A.
    B. For purposes of this section, the term "return period" means the 12-month period beginning on July 1 of each year.
    C. For purposes of this section, a sole proprietor shall retain and make available a record with respect to him or herself.
    D. For purposes of this section, a partnership is treated as the employer of the partners and shall retain and make available a record with respect to the partners and other tax return preparers employed or engaged by the partnership.

80. A tax return preparer must complete the paid preparer's area of the return if
    A. The taxpayer prepares his own return.
    B. The individual volunteers to complete the return for no cost.
    C. The individual was paid to prepare, assist in preparing, or review the tax return.
    D. An employee prepares a tax return for his employer by whom he is regularly and continuously employed.

81. Which of the following statements is TRUE regarding records required to be maintained by return preparers?
    A. Tax return preparers are required to maintain a complete copy of each return or claim for refund they have filed for 3 years after the return period.
    B. Tax return preparers are required to maintain a list of the names, identification numbers, and tax years for which returns are prepared and to keep this list for 3 years after the return period.
    C. Tax return preparers are required to maintain a complete copy of each return or claim for refund they have filed for 3 years after the return period, or are required to maintain a list of the names, identification numbers, and tax years for which returns are prepared and to keep this list for 3 years after the return period.
    D. Tax return preparers are required to maintain a complete copy of each return or claim for refund they have filed for 3 years after the return period and are required to maintain a list of the names, identification numbers, and tax years for which returns are prepared and to keep this list for 3 years after the return period.

82. Identify the item below that is accurate regarding preparer retention of records.
    A. The preparer must retain a completed copy of each return or claim for refund prepared or retain a record by list, card file, or otherwise, of information, as required by regulation, about each return prepared.
    B. The preparer must retain information about the preparer of each return presented to a taxpayer for signature. This information may be retained via retention of a copy of the return or claim for refund, maintenance of a list or card file, or otherwise.
    C. The preparer must make the copy or record of returns and claims for refund and record of the individuals required to sign available for inspection upon request by the district director.
    D. All of the answers are correct.

83. Jane is a Certified Public Accountant who specializes in preparing federal tax returns. Which of the following returns would qualify Jane as an income tax return preparer?
    A. Estate or gift tax returns.
    B. Excise tax returns.

C. Withholding tax returns.
D. None of the answers are correct.

84. Preparers of which of the following returns are not covered by the preparer rules?
   A. Individual income tax.
   B. Corporate income tax.
   C. Fiduciary income tax.
   D. Estate tax.

85. Which of the following is an income tax return preparer according to the tax return preparer rules?
   A. Mr. A engages a number of persons to prepare income tax returns on a commission basis but he himself does not prepare returns.
   B. Mr. B, controller of Corporation X, prepares and files X's corporate tax return.
   C. Mr. C owns and operates a payroll service. Services provided to clients include the preparation of all employment tax returns.
   D. Mr. D, an attorney, regularly advises clients in arranging future business transactions to minimize income tax.

86. All of the following are income tax return preparers except
   A. A person who prepares a substantial portion of the return for a fee.
   B. A person who prepares a claim for a refund for a fee.
   C. A person who gives an opinion about theoretical events that have not occurred.
   D. A person who prepares a United States return for a fee outside the United States.

87. The duties in the preparation of XYZ Corporation's income tax return were assigned and completed as follows:

   Joe-----The employee who obtained the information, applied the tax law to the information, and performed the necessary calculations.
   Sue-----Joe's supervisor, who reviews Joe's work. In her review, Sue reviews the information provided and the application of the tax laws.
   Co. A---A computer tax service, which takes the information provided by Sue, verifies the mathematical accuracy, and prints the return form.
   Pat-----A partner in the public accounting firm where Joe and Sue work. Pat reviews the return and the information provided and applies this information to XYZ's affairs. Pat also verifies that the partnership's policies have been followed and makes the final determination.

   Who is the preparer of XYZ's return and therefore is required to sign it?
   A. Joe.

B. Sue.
C. Company A.
D. Pat.

88. Mr. K employs X, Y, and Z to prepare income tax returns for taxpayers. X and Y collect the information from taxpayers and apply the tax laws. The return forms are completed by a computer service. One day, when certain returns prepared by X and Y were ready for their signatures, X was out of town for 2 weeks and Y was out of the office for the day. Which one of the following statements is TRUE?
    A. Z may sign the returns prepared by X and Y if Z reviews the information obtained by X and Y from the taxpayers and reviews the preparation of the returns.
    B. Z may sign the returns prepared by X if Z reviews the information obtained by X from the taxpayers and reviews the preparation of the returns.
    C. Z may sign the returns prepared by Y if he reviews the information obtained by Y from the taxpayers and reviews the preparation of the returns.
    D. X and Y must sign the returns that each one prepared.

89. Which one of the following individuals would qualify as a tax return preparer under the return preparer regulations?
    A. Someone who prepares as a fiduciary a return or claim for refund for any person.
    B. Someone who prepares a return or claim for refund without compensation.
    C. Someone who employs one or more persons to prepare for compensation all or a substantial portion of a tax return under Subtitle A of the Internal Revenue Code.
    D. Someone who does not prepare the entire return of a person but, rather, prepares a schedule for interest income that totals $700 and gives advice, making him a preparer of a schedule of interest expenses, which results in a deduction for interest expenses of $800.

90. Which of the following is not an income tax return preparer?
    A. Someone who does not physically prepare an income tax return but offers enough advice that completion of the return is largely a mechanical matter.
    B. Someone who prepares a substantial portion of a return or claim for refund under Subtitle A of the Code.
    C. A firm who offers computer tax preparation services if the program makes substantive tax determinations.
    D. Someone who prepares a return or claim for refund for his/her employer.

91. By what date must a tax return preparer furnish a copy of the original return to a taxpayer?
    A. By the date the taxpayer pays for the preparation of the return.

B. By the date the tax return is presented for the signature of the taxpayer.
C. By the date the tax return is due to be filed with the IRS.
D. By the seventh work day after the preparer signs the completed return.

92. A penalty may be assessed on any preparer or
    A. Any person who prepares and signs a tax return or claim for refund.
    B. Any member of a firm who gives advice (written or oral) to a taxpayer or to a preparer not associated with the same firm.
    C. Any person who prepares and signs a tax return or claim for refund and the individual with overall supervisory responsibility for the advice given by the firm with respect to the return or claim.
    D. The individual with overall supervisory responsibility for the advice given by the firm with respect to the return or claim.

93. Which one of the following would result in a penalty against the preparer for failure to sign a tax return?
    A. L, a law firm, employs A, an attorney, to prepare tax returns. A obtained information from X, L's client, and determined X's tax liability. A signed the tax returns instead of his employer.
    B. N, an individual, has an arrangement with C, a corporation, to prepare tax returns for compensation. C does not provide office space, supplies, etc. N used forms provided by C, which N sent back to C to be reviewed by E, C's employee, for math and proper application of tax law. N signed the return instead of C or E.
    C. D, who is not an enrolled agent, an attorney, or a CPA, prepares and signs income tax returns for compensation.
    D. P prepares income tax returns for compensation and signs the extension request with a facsimile signature stamp.

94. If you are employed as a tax preparer employee by a tax preparation firm, which of the following penalties may be assessed to you as a tax preparer?
    A. $50 per return for failure to furnish a copy of the return to the taxpayer.
    B. $50 per return for failure to furnish preparer's identifying number to the taxpayer.
    C. $50 per return for failure to maintain copies of returns prepared or maintain a listing of clients.
    D. None of the answers are correct.

95. Which of the following persons would be subject to the penalty for improperly negotiating a taxpayer's refund check?
    A. An income tax return preparer who operates a check cashing agency that cashes, endorses, or negotiates income tax refund checks for returns he prepared.

- B. An income tax return preparer who operates a check cashing business and cashes checks for her clients as part of a second business.
- C. The firm that prepared the tax return and is authorized by the taxpayer to receive an income tax refund but not to endorse or negotiate the check.
- D. A business manager who prepares income tax returns for clients who maintain special checking accounts against which the business manager is authorized to sign certain checks on their behalf. The clients' federal income tax refunds are mailed to the business manager, who has the clients endorse the checks and then deposits them in the special accounts.

96. Which one of the following would result in a penalty against the tax return preparer for failure to furnish a copy of the 2009 tax return to the taxpayer?
    - A. The paid preparer's copy machine broke in December 2009, and he or she was not able to get it fixed until after filing season.
    - B. The paid preparer prepared one return that affected amounts reported on another return.
    - C. Failure was due to reasonable cause and not due to willful neglect.
    - D. The preparer gave advice on a specific issue of law.

97. Bernard is an income tax return preparer. While preparing a 2009 tax return for a client, Bernard determines the client owes a substantial amount of tax. In order to generate a refund for the client, Bernard substantially overstates itemized deductions and expenses claimed on the Schedule C. Bernard is subject to a penalty of
    - A. $5,000
    - B. $500
    - C. $200
    - D. $1,000

98. Which of the following statements is FALSE with respect to tax return preparer penalties?
    - A. For tax returns that are due (without extension) after December 31, 1989, the penalty for an understatement due to the preparer's negligent or intentional disregard of one or more rules or regulations is $250; for willful understatement of liability, the penalty is $1,000.
    - B. If a preparer in good faith and with reasonable basis takes the position that a rule or regulation does not accurately reflect the Code, he/she is not subject to either penalty.
    - C. The IRS has the burden of proof that a preparer has negligently or intentionally disregarded a rule or regulation.
    - D. Many Code sections require the existence of specific facts and circumstances. In order to avoid a penalty, a preparer shall make appropriate inquiries of the taxpayer to determine that the requirements have been met incident to claiming a deduction.

99. During an interview conducted by the tax return preparer, the client stated that he had paid $1,500 for deductible travel expenses and $3,000 for charitable contributions. The preparer asked if documentation existed in support of the deductions and was assured by the client that adequate documentation did exist. When the client's return was later examined by the IRS, a tax deficiency resulted due to the client's lack of supporting documentation for the travel expenses. Which of the following statements best describes this situation?
    A. The preparer is subject to a penalty under Sec. 6694 because she did not verify that her client had supporting documentation.
    B. The preparer is subject to a penalty under Sec. 6694 because she did not verify the existence of the documentation and a tax deficiency resulted from the examination.
    C. The preparer is not subject to a penalty under Sec. 6694 because she is not required to examine or review the client's books and records in order to verify the client's information.
    D. The preparer is not subject to a penalty under Sec. 6694 due to the dollar amounts of the adjustments in the examination.

100. Delores is an income tax return preparer. While preparing a return for a client, she knowingly took an unrealistic position that she did not disclose. She also intentionally disregarded rules and regulations. The position Delores took caused an understatement of her client's liability. With regard to the penalties that may be assessed against Delores, which of the following statements is TRUE?
    A. Only the penalty for understatement of liability due to unrealistic positions may be assessed against Delores.
    B. Only the penalty for willful or reckless conduct may be assessed against Delores.
    C. Delores must pay both the penalty for understatement of liability due to an unrealistic position and the penalty for willful or reckless conduct. C.
    D. Delores is liable for both penalties, but the penalty for willful or reckless conduct will be reduced by the amount of the penalty for understatement due to unrealistic positions.

101. When a prepared return claims the earned income credit, which of the following is FALSE?
    A. Due diligence requirements apply.
    B. No special requirements apply to returns claiming earned income credit.
    C. The preparer may be penalized $100 if no attempt is made to determine eligibility for the credit.
    D. The preparer must take additional steps to ensure that a client is eligible for earned income credit.

102. With respect to a penalty proposed pursuant to Sec. 6694 of the Internal Revenue Code, which of the following statements is TRUE?
    A. The IRS must send a letter to the tax return preparer at least 30 days before the statute of limitations expires.
    B. After the IRS sends the tax return preparer a letter, that preparer has 10 days to request further consideration.
    C. If the IRS assesses either the Sec. 6694(a) or Sec. 6694(b) penalty, the preparer can, within 30 days, either pay the entire amount and then file for refund or pay at least 15% of the entire amount and then file a claim for the amount paid.
    D. The preparer cannot bring suit in district court to determine liability for the penalty if the claim for refund is denied.

103. To satisfy the earned income credit due diligence requirements, a preparer must retain all of the following except
    A. A copy of the completed Eligibility Checklist or Alternative Eligibility Record.
    B. A copy of the Computation Worksheet or Alternative Computation Record.
    C. A copy of the social security cards for the taxpayer and each qualifying child.
    D. A record of how and when the information used to complete the Eligibility Checklist or Alternative Eligibility Record and the Computation Worksheet or Alternative Computation Record was obtained by the preparer, including the identity of any person furnishing the information. D.

104. Frankie is a truck driver who is also a licensed return preparer and specializes in preparing income tax returns claiming the Earned Income Credit (EIC). Frankie will not be subject to a preparer penalty for an erroneously claimed EIC if he complies with which one of the following?
    A. Completion of an eligibility checklist based upon information provided by the client.
    B. Completion of the computation worksheet for the EIC based upon information provided by the client.
    C. Knowledge or reason to know that the information used to determine eligibility for an amount of the EIC is correct.
    D. All of the answers are correct.

105. Willie is the owner of an accounting firm. One of Willie's employees prepares an income tax return for a client and believes that a deduction can be claimed for a bad debt. If the return is examined and the deduction is disallowed, Willie will not be subject to a preparer penalty under which of the following circumstances?

    A. The position on the return had a realistic possibility of being sustained on the merits.

B. The position on the return had at least a one-in-three chance of being sustained on its merits.
C. There is substantial authority to sustain the position taken on the return. C.
D. All of the answers are correct.

106. John is an income tax return preparer. He prepares a tax return for a client and takes a position that he knows does not have a realistic possibility of being sustained on its merits. He does not disclose this position on the tax return. The position John takes causes the client's tax liability to be substantially understated. John is subject to a penalty of
A. $50
B. $100
C. $1000
D. $5,000

107. A penalty may be assessed against an income tax return preparer who takes an unrealistic position that causes an understatement of liability on a return. For purposes of assessing the penalty, "understatement of liability" means
A. Any understatement of tax liability greater than $100.
B. Any understatement of the tax liability or overstatement of the amount to be refunded or credited.
C. Any understatement that exceeds 10% of the tax liability shown on the return.
D. Any overstatement of the amount refundable that exceeds 10% of the amount refundable shown on the claim for refund.

108. If a penalty is proposed against a preparer that the preparer does not agree with, what actions are available to the preparer?
e) Request a conference with the agent and present additional information and explanations showing that the penalty is not warranted.
f) Wait for the penalty to be assessed and for a notice and demand statement to be issued, then pay the penalty within 30 days and file a claim for refund.
g) Wait for the penalty to be assessed and for a notice and demand statement to be issued, then pay at least 15% of the penalty within 30 days and file a claim for refund.
h) All of the answers are correct.

109. In which of the following situations may the tax return preparer disclose the tax return information requested without first obtaining the consent of the taxpayer/client?
A. The preparer receives a state grand jury subpoena requesting copies of federal and state income tax returns.

B. An IRS agent, in his/her official capacity, visits the preparer and requests copies of state and federal income tax returns, related returns, schedules, and records of the taxpayer used in the preparation of the tax returns.
C. A partner in a partnership, who was not involved with the return preparation or partnership records, requests a copy of the partnership return, including the Schedule K-1s for all partners.
D. All of the answers are correct.

110. Matt, an enrolled agent, provided tax advice to XYZ corporation on a federal tax matter. The Securities and Exchange Commission ("SEC") is reviewing a required filing of the XYZ corporation and asks to see a copy of Matt's tax advice. The tax advice is not protected by the federally authorized tax practitioner privilege under IRC Section 7525 from disclosure to the SEC because
A. Matt is not a lawyer.
B. Matt is not a CPA.
C. The federally authorized tax practitioner privilege protects advice only against disclosure to the IRS, not other government agencies.
D. The federally authorized tax practitioner privilege protects only advice to individuals.

111. Which of the following situations describes a disclosure of tax return information by a tax return preparer that would subject the preparer to a penalty?
A. A grandfather's tax information is made available to his granddaughter to inform her that she will be claimed as a dependent on the grandfather's return.
B. An employee of the tax return preparer makes corporate return information available to shareholders.
C. After a client files for bankruptcy, the tax return preparer provides a copy of the last return filed to the court-appointed fiduciary without written permission.
D. None of the answers are correct.

112. Which of the following situations describes a disclosure of tax information by an income tax preparer that would subject the preparer to a penalty?
A. Ron died after furnishing tax return information to his tax return preparer. Ron's tax return preparer disclosed the information to Jerry, Ron's nephew, who is not the fiduciary of Ron's estate.
B. In the course of preparing a return for Duck Company, Jan obtained information indicating the existence of illegal kickbacks. Jan gave the information to Bill, an auditor in her firm, who was performing a financial audit of the company. Bill confirmed illegal kickbacks were occurring and brought the information to the attention of Duck Company officers.
C. Glade informed the proper federal officials of actions he mistakenly believed to be illegal.

D. Les, a return preparer, obtained information from Tom while selling Tom life insurance. The information was identical to tax return information that had been furnished to him previously. Les discussed this information with Mary, his wife, who was not an employee of any of his businesses.

113. If there is an underpayment of tax on your return due to fraud, how much is the penalty added to your tax?
   A. 20 % of the underpayment due to fraud
   B. 20% of the underpayment, reduced for those items for which there was adequate disclosure
   C. $500 added to any other penalty provided by law
   D. 75% of the underpayment due to fraud

114. A frivolous income tax return is one that does not include enough information to figure the correct tax or that certain information clearly showing that the tax that was reported is substantially incorrect. If a taxpayer files a frivolous return, which penalty applies specifically to the taxpayer for the frivolous return?
   A. $50 for failure to supply your social security number..
   B. 20% of the underpayment, reduced for those items for which there was adequate disclosure made.
   C. $5,000 frivolous return penalty, applied in addition to any other applicable penalty or penalties.
   D. $100 for the failure to furnish the tax shelter registration number.

115. Isaac's income tax return for 2009 was examined. This resulted in an income tax deficiency in the amount of $50,000 from two $25,000 adjustments. The Revenue Agent determined that Isaac was negligent involving the first adjustment and proposed an accuracy-related penalty. The second adjustment was discovered by the Revenue Agent based upon a disclosure statement in the tax return and did not relate to a tax shelter. What is the amount of penalty that the Revenue Agent can propose?
   A. $2,500
   B. $5,000
   C. $10,000
   D. None of the above.

116. Ron's tax returns were examined for 2007, 2008, and 2009, all of which resulted in adjustments increasing income reported on Schedule C of the returns. The Revenue Agent determined that the failure to report the income was intentional. The Revenue Agent proposed a fraud penalty. The adjustment for each year was in the amount of $100,000. The fraud penalty for **each year** should be in which of the following amounts?
   A. $50,000
   B. $75,000

C. $18,800
D. $28,200

117. Willie is the owner of an accounting firm. One of Willie's employees prepares an income tax return for a client and opines that a deduction can be claimed for a bad debt. If the return is examined and the deduction is disallowed, Willie will **not** be subject to a preparer penalty under which of the following circumstances?
   A. The position on the return had a realistic possibility of being sustained on the merits.
   B. The position on the return had at least a one in- three chance of being sustained on its merits.
   C. There is substantial authority to sustain the position taken on the return.
   D. All of the above.

118. Frankie is a truck driver who is also a licensed return preparer and specializes in preparing income tax returns claiming the Earned Income Credit (EIC). Frankie will not be subject to a preparer penalty for an erroneously claimed EIC if he complies with which one of the following?
   A. Completion of an eligibility checklist based upon information provided by the client.
   B. Completion of the computation worksheet for the EIC based upon information provided by the client.
   C. Knowledge or reason to know that the information used to determine eligibility for an amount of the EIC is correct.
   D. All of the above.

119. A penalty may be assessed on any preparer or:
   A. Any person who prepares and signs a tax return or claim for refund
   B. Any member of a firm who gives advice (written or oral) to a taxpayer or to a preparer not associated with the same firm
   C. Both A and D
   D. The individual with overall supervisory responsibility

120. If a penalty is proposed against a preparer that the preparer does not agree with, what actions are available to the preparer?
   A. Request a conference with the agent and present additional information and explanations showing that the penalty is not warranted.
   B. Wait for the penalty to be assessed and a notice and demand statement to be issued then pay the penalty within 30 days and file a claim for refund.
   C. Wait for the penalty to be assessed and a notice and demand statement to be issued, then pay at least 15% of the penalty within 30 days and file a claim for refund.
   D. Any of the above.

121. If a reasonable and well-informed tax return preparer, knowledgeable in the law, concludes that the information provided by a taxpayer appears to be incorrect, inconsistent or incomplete, the preparer must make reasonable inquiries to satisfy due diligence.
   A. TRUE
   B. FALSE

122. Which of the following is not a due diligence requirement that you as a preparer must meet?
   A. Computation of the Credit
   B. Record Retention
   C. Completion of Eligibility Checklist
   D. Review of Social Security cards
   E. "Knowledge" Requirement

123. Barbara wishes to have her taxes prepared. Her information is as follows:
   - Her 22 year old daughter, Julie, graduated from college in August
   - Julie lived with her until Julie got married in November
   - She wants to claim EITC
   - Her W-2 indicates earnings of $27,000

   Should the preparer ask additional questions to satisfy due diligence in this situation?
   A. Yes
   B. No

124. Steven wishes to have his taxes prepared. His information is as follows:
   - He is 22 years old
   - He has step-sons, ages 10 and 11
   - The boys lived with him all year
   - Their mother moved in with them in August
   - He divorced the boy's mother two years ago
   - His W-2 earnings are $20,000

   Should the preparer ask additional questions to satisfy due diligence in this situation?
   A. Yes
   B. No

2.06 UNIT 2: ANSWERS

1. **(A) Correct**
   A $50 penalty applies if the preparer, who is required by regulations to sign the taxpayer's return or claim for refund, fails to sign the return or claim for refund. Preparers must sign the return/claim for refund using the appropriate method prescribed by the Secretary after it is completed and before it is presented to the taxpayer for signature.

2. **(A) Correct**
   A preparer is required to furnish a completed copy of the return or claim for refund to the taxpayer before (or at the same time) the return or claim for refund is presented to the taxpayer for signature. A $50 penalty applies if the preparer fails to furnish a copy to Taxpayer.

3. **(B) Correct**
   Preparers must sign the return/claim for refund using the appropriate method prescribed by the Secretary after it is completed and before it is presented to the taxpayer for signature.

4. **(A) Correct**
   A tax preparer may use tax return information of a client to solicit from the client any additional current business in matters not related to the IRS that the preparer provides and offers to the public; provided the preparer has the client's written consent. However, the practitioner may not persist in attempting to contact a prospective client if the prospective client has made it known to the practitioner that he or she does not desire to be solicited.

5. **(B) Correct**
   Section 7525 provides a privilege of confidentiality for communications between a taxpayer and a *federally authorized tax practitioner* that has essentially the same scope as the federal attorney-client privilege. Section 7525 confidentiality privilege does **not** protect against criminal tax matters before the I.R.S. or in federal court. (Unit 1. Pg. 13)

6. **(A) Correct**
   A $50 penalty applies if the preparer, who is required by regulations to sign the taxpayer's return or claim for refund, fails to sign the return or claim for refund. Preparers must sign the return/claim for refund using the appropriate method prescribed by the Secretary after it is completed and before it is presented to the taxpayer for signature.

7. **(A) Correct**
A penalty predicated on reckless or intentional disregard would not be imposed if there is adequate disclosure of a non-frivolous position and, in the case of a regulation; the position represents a good faith challenge to the regulation's validity. A final administrative or judicial determination concerning the taxpayer's return is not required in order to assert return preparer penalties. However, the penalties will be abated if a subsequent judicial or administrative determination concludes that no understatement exists (IRC section 6694(d)).

8. **(A) Correct**
There is no statute of limitation period for assessing the penalty against an income tax return preparer for willful or reckless conduct that results in an understatement of liability (Code Sec. 6696(d))

9. **(A) Correct**
If there is a final administrative determination or a final judicial decision that there was no understatement of liability in any return or claim for refund, and a penalty had been assessed, the assessment will be abated, and if any portion of such penalty has been paid, the amount paid will be refunded to the person who made such payment as an overpayment of tax (Code Sec. 6694(d)).

10. **(A) Correct**
Tax return preparers may file a claim for Penalties assessed under section 6700, 6701, or 6694 upon paying 15% of the penalty within 30 days from the date of notice and demand. The refund claim is filed on Form 6118 with the IRS service center or IRS office that sent the statement(s).

11. **(A) Correct**
Earned Income Tax Credit (EITC) penalties include:
1) $100 penalty for each due diligence failure to comply assessed against return preparers or their employers.
2) A minimum $1,000 penalty against return preparers who prepare EITC claims for which any part of an understatement of tax liability is due to an unreasonable position.
3) A minimum $5,000 penalty against return preparers who prepare EITC claims for which any part of an understatement of tax liability is due to reckless or intentional disregard of rules or regulations by the tax preparer.
4) Clients, whose returns are examined and found to be incorrect, could be subject to:
    (i) Accuracy or fraud penalties
    (ii) 2 to 10 years ban from claiming EITC

12. **(A) Correct**
    A preparer is subject to penalty if any part of any understatement of liability with respect to any return or claim for refund is due to a willful attempt by the preparer to understate the liability for tax, or to the preparer's reckless or intentional disregard of rules or regulations.

13. **(B) Correct**
    Under Code Sec. 6694(a), if a tax return preparer prepares any return or claim of refund in which any part of an understatement of liability is due to *unreasonable position* and the preparer knew, or should have reasonably known about the position, the preparer will pay a penalty for each return or claim in the amount of:

    The greater of:
    a) $1,000
        or
    b) 50% of the income derived (or to be derived) by the tax return preparer with respect to the return or claim.

    A position is considered to have a realistic possibility of being sustained on its merits if a reasonable and well-informed analysis by a person knowledgeable in tax law would lead such a person to conclude that the position has approximately a one-in-three, or greater, likelihood of being sustained on its merits.

14. **(B) Correct**
    Any preparer who endorses or otherwise negotiates any check made to a taxpayer shall pay a penalty of $500 with respect to each such check. The penalty does not apply with respect to deposit by a bank of the full amount of the check in the taxpayer's account in such bank for the benefit of the taxpayer.

15. **(A) Correct**
    A taxpayer is negligent if he is careless, reckless, or intentionally disregards the rules or regulations. Negligence connotes a lack of due care or a failure to do what a reasonable and prudent person would do under the circumstances. Negligence includes both a taxpayer's affirmative acts and well as the failures to act.
    Rules or regulations include:
    (i) Provisions of the Code.
    (ii) Temporary or final regulations.
    (iii) Revenue rulings or notices published in the Internal Revenue Bulletin.

16. **(A) Correct**

    The following are subject to $50 penalty for each failure per return. (The maximum penalty imposed with respect to any return period may not exceed $25,000) (Code Sec. 6695):
    1) Failure to furnish copy to taxpayer
    2) Failure to sign return/claim for refund
    3) Failure to furnish identifying number
    4) Failure to retain copy or list
    5) Failure to file correct information returns

17. **(A) Correct**

    A preparer that is also a financial institution, but has not made a loan to the taxpayer on the basis of the taxpayer's anticipated refund, may:
    a) Cash a refund check and remit all of the cash to the taxpayer
    b) Accept a refund check for deposit in full to the taxpayer's account, provided the bank does not initially endorse or negotiate the check (unless the bank has made a loan to a taxpayer on the basis of the anticipated refund).
    c) Endorse a refund check for deposit in full to the taxpayer's account pursuant to a written authorization of the taxpayer (unless the bank has made a loan to the taxpayer on the basis of the anticipated refund).
    d) Endorse or negotiate a refund check as part of the check clearing process after initial endorsement or negotiation

18. **(A) Correct**

    Code Sec. 6694(b)(3) states that the amount of any penalty payable by any person by reason of *understatement due to willful or reckless conduct* for any return or claim for refund will be reduced by the amount of the penalty paid by such person by reason of *understatement due to unreasonable positions*.

19. **(B) Correct**

    A taxpayer is negligent if he is careless, reckless, or intentionally disregards the rules or regulations. Negligence connotes a lack of due care or a failure to do what a reasonable and prudent person would do under the circumstances. Negligence includes both a taxpayer's affirmative acts and well as the failures to act.
    Rules or regulations include:
    (i) Provisions of the Code.
    (ii) Temporary or final regulations.
    (iii) Revenue rulings or notices published in the Internal Revenue Bulletin.

    Under Code Sec. 6694(a), if a tax return preparer prepares any return or claim of refund in which any part of an understatement of liability is due to *unreasonable position* and the preparer knew, or should have reasonably known about the position, the preparer will pay a penalty for each return or claim in the amount of:

The greater of:
    a) $1,000
        or
    b) 50% of the income derived (or to be derived) by the tax return preparer with respect to the return or claim.

A position is considered to have a realistic possibility of being sustained on its merits if a reasonable and well-informed analysis by a person knowledgeable in tax law would lead such a person to conclude that the position has approximately a one-in-three, or greater, likelihood of being sustained on its merits.

20. **(B) Correct**
A $50 penalty applies if the preparer fails to retain copy or list. A preparer must:
1) Retain a completed copy of the return/claim for refund, or alternatively retain a record (by list, card file, electronically, or otherwise) of all the taxpayers, their taxpayer identification numbers, the taxable years, and the type of returns/claims for refund prepared.
2) Retain a record (by copy of the return/claim for refund or by a list, card file, electronically, or otherwise) of the name of the preparer required to sign the return/claim for refund for each return/claim for refund presented to the taxpayer.
3) Make such copy or list available for inspection upon request by the IRS for a 3-year period following the close of the return period

The penalty does not apply if the failure was due to reasonable cause and not due to willful neglect.

21. **(A) Correct**
This penalty generally applies if the preparer endorses or otherwise negotiates (directly or through an agent) a refund check issued to a taxpayer (other than the preparer).

Any preparer who endorses or otherwise negotiates any check made to a taxpayer shall pay a penalty of $500 with respect to each such check. The penalty does not apply with respect to deposit by a bank of the full amount of the check in the taxpayer's account in such bank for the benefit of the taxpayer.

A preparer that is also a financial institution, but has not made a loan to the taxpayer on the basis of the taxpayer's anticipated refund, may:
    a) Cash a refund check and remit all of the cash to the taxpayer

b) Accept a refund check for deposit in full to the taxpayer's account, provided the bank does not initially endorse or negotiate the check (unless the bank has made a loan to a taxpayer on the basis of the anticipated refund).
c) Endorse a refund check for deposit in full to the taxpayer's account pursuant to a written authorization of the taxpayer (unless the bank has made a loan to the taxpayer on the basis of the anticipated refund).
d) Endorse or negotiate a refund check as part of the check clearing process after initial endorsement or negotiation

22. **(A) Correct**
If the court finds that a tax return preparer has:
1) Recklessly or intentionally disregarded rules or regulations, or willfully understated tax liability
2) Misrepresented his or her eligibility to practice before the IRS
3) Guaranteed a tax refund or the allowance of a tax credit, or
4) Engaged in other fraudulent or deceptive conduct that substantially interferes with the administration of the Internal Revenue laws,

The court may enjoin the preparer from further engaging in the above-mentioned conduct.

If the court finds that a tax return preparer has *continually* or *repeatedly* engaged in any conduct mentioned above, the court may enjoin such person from acting as a tax return preparer.

23. **(B) Correct**
The following are subject to $50 penalty for each failure per return. (The maximum penalty imposed with respect to any return period may not exceed $25,000) (Code Sec. 6695):
1) Failure to furnish copy to taxpayer
2) Failure to sign return/claim for refund
3) Failure to furnish identifying number
4) Failure to retain copy or list
5) Failure to file correct information returns

The only exception is if the preparer can show reasonable cause for the failure.

24. **(A) Correct**
The following are subject to $50 penalty for each failure per return. (The maximum penalty imposed with respect to any return period may not exceed $25,000) (Code Sec. 6695):
1) Failure to furnish copy to taxpayer
2) Failure to sign return/claim for refund
3) Failure to furnish identifying number
4) Failure to retain copy or list
5) Failure to file correct information returns

The only exception is if the preparer can show reasonable cause for the failure.

25. **(A) Correct**
A preparer is considered to have recklessly or intentionally disregarded a rule or regulation if the preparer takes a position on the return or claim that is contrary to a rule or regulation and the preparer knows of, or is reckless in not knowing of, the rule or regulation. Since the preparer inquired about the existence of travel and entertainment expense records and was reasonably satisfied by the taxpayer's representations that the taxpayer had adequate records (or other corroborative evidence) for the deduction of $5,000 for travel and entertainment expenses, his position is considered to have a realistic possibility. The understatement was due to reasonable cause and the preparer acted in good faith. Travel and entertainment expense is one of the high audit areas, thus, requires more and accurate substantiation that medical expense.

26. **(A) Correct**
The following are subject to $50 penalty for each failure per return. (The maximum penalty imposed with respect to any return period may not exceed $25,000) (Code Sec. 6695):
    1) Failure to furnish copy to taxpayer
    2) Failure to sign return/claim for refund
    3) Failure to furnish identifying number
    4) Failure to retain copy or list
    5) Failure to file correct information returns
The only exception is if the preparer can show reasonable cause for the failure.

27. **(A) Correct**
Code Sec. 6694(b)(3) states that the amount of any penalty payable by any person by reason of *understatement due to willful or reckless conduct* for any return or claim for refund will be reduced by the amount of the penalty paid by such person by reason of *understatement due to unreasonable positions*.

28. **(B) Correct**
If there is an employment arrangement between two or more preparers, the requirement to furnish a copy only applies to the person who employs (or engages) one or more other preparers. Similarly, if there is a partnership arrangement, the requirement to furnish a copy only applies to the partnership. In this case, the firm is responsible for the penalty because it employed/engaged the preparer.

29. **(B) Correct**
Tax return preparers may file a claim for Penalties assessed under section 6700, 6701, or 6694 <u>upon</u> paying 15% of the penalty within 30 days from the date of

notice and demand. The refund claim is filed on Form 6118 with the IRS service center or IRS office that sent the statement(s) (Code Sec. 6694(c)(1)).

30. **(A) Correct**
A preparer must retain a record (by copy of the return/claim for refund or by a list, card file, electronically, or otherwise) of the name of the preparer required to sign the return/claim for refund for each return/claim for refund presented to the taxpayer. The first page of form 1040 contains all the required information to satisfy the document retention requirement.

31. **(A) Correct**
Each person who employs (or engages) one or more income tax return preparers must retain a record of the name, taxpayer identification number and place of work of each income tax return preparer employed (or engaged) by him.

32. **(B) Correct**
In general, a facsimile signature stamp or signed gummed label is not acceptable. Except:
    a) A preparer of a return or claim for refund for a nonresident alien may use a facsimile signature to sign as preparer if the preparer is authorized to sign for the taxpayer using a facsimile signature.
    b) A preparer of Forms 1041 may use a facsimile signature to sign the Forms 1041 if certain conditions are met

33. **(B) Correct**
Information in the paid preparer's area of the tax return is mandatory. A $50 penalty applies if the preparer fails to furnish an identifying number of the return preparer. The return/claim for refund must contain:
    a) The identifying number of the preparer required to sign the return/claim for refund.
    b) The identifying number of the partnership or employer.

34. **(A) Correct**
A preparer is required to furnish a completed copy of the return or claim for refund to the taxpayer before (or at the same time) the return or claim for refund is presented to the taxpayer for signature. A penalty of $50 applies if the preparer fails to furnish a copy to Taxpayer.

35. **(B) Correct**
Circular 230 states that practitioner must provide an opinion whether it is more likely than not that an investor will prevail on the merits of each material tax issue presented by the offering which involves a reasonable possibility of a challenge by the IRS. Where such an opinion cannot be given with respect to any

material tax issue, the opinion should fully describe the reasons for the practitioner's inability to make an opinion as to the likely outcome.

36. **(A) Correct**
An Income tax return preparer is defined as person (including a partnership or corporation) who prepares for compensation all or a substantial portion of a tax return or claim for refund under the income tax provisions of the Code. Since Paul is receiving compensation for his tax preparation services, he is considered to be tax return preparer.

37. **(A) Correct**
A $50 penalty applies if the preparer fails to retain copy or list. A preparer must:
1) Retain a completed copy of the return/claim for refund, or alternatively retain a record (by list, card file, electronically, or otherwise) of all the taxpayers, their taxpayer identification numbers, the taxable years, and the type of returns/claims for refund prepared.
2) Retain a record (by copy of the return/claim for refund or by a list, card file, electronically, or otherwise) of the name of the preparer required to sign the return/claim for refund for each return/claim for refund presented to the taxpayer.
3) Make such copy or list available for inspection upon request by the IRS for a 3-year period following the close of the return period

The penalty does not apply if the failure was due to reasonable cause and not due to willful neglect.

38. **(A) Correct**
Any person who employs a tax return preparer to prepare any return or claim for refund at any time during a return period must make a return indicating the:
1) Name
2) Taxpayer identification number
3) Place of work of each tax return preparer employed by him

The return required must be filed on or before the first July 31 following the end of such return period. The term '*return period*' means the 12-month period beginning on July 1 of each year. The records must be retained and kept available for inspection for the 3-year period following the close of the return period to which that record relates.

39. **(B) Correct**
Any person who employs a tax return preparer to prepare any return or claim for refund at any time during a return period must make a return indicating the:
1) Name
2) Taxpayer identification number
3) Place of work of each tax return preparer employed by him

The return required must be filed on or before the first July 31 following the end of such return period. The term 'return period' means the 12-month period beginning on July 1 of each year. The records must be retained and kept available for inspection for the 3-year period following the close of the return period to which that record relates.

40. **(A) Correct**
    If more than one preparer is involved in the preparation of the return/claim for refund, the preparer with primary responsibility for the overall substantive accuracy of the return/claim for refund is the preparer who must sign the return/claim for refund.

41. **(A) Correct**
    Any person who employs a tax return preparer to prepare any return or claim for refund at any time during a return period must make a return indicating the:
    1) Name
    2) Taxpayer identification number
    3) Place of work of each tax return preparer employed by him

    The return required must be filed on or before the first July 31 following the end of such return period. The term 'return period' means the 12-month period beginning on July 1 of each year. The records must be retained and kept available for inspection for the 3-year period following the close of the return period to which that record relates. (Reg. Sec. 1.6060-1).

42. **(A) Correct**
    A preparer is required to furnish a completed copy of the return or claim for refund to the taxpayer before (or at the same time) the return or claim for refund is presented to the taxpayer for signature. A penalty of $50 applies if the preparer fails to furnish a copy to Taxpayer.

43. **(A) Correct**
    A person who only provides mechanical assistance in the preparation of an income tax return or claim for refund (e.g., provides typing or copying services) is not an income tax return preparer.

44. **(A) Correct**
    An Income tax return preparer is defined as person (including a partnership or corporation) who prepares for *compensation* all or a *substantial portion* of a tax return or claim for refund under the income tax provisions of the Code.

45. **(B) Correct**
    An Income tax return preparer is defined as person (including a partnership or corporation), who prepares for *compensation,* all or a *substantial portion* of a tax return or claim for refund under the income tax provisions of the Code.

46. **(A) Correct**
    A person who prepares an income tax return or claim for refund for an estate or a trust, but only if such person is a fiduciary or is an officer, general partner, or employee of the fiduciary is <u>not</u> an income tax return preparer.

47. **(B) Correct**
    An Income tax return preparer is defined as person (including a partnership or corporation), who prepares for *compensation,* all or a *substantial portion* of a tax return or claim for refund under the income tax provisions of the Code. *A schedule or other portion* is not considered to be a *substantial portion* if the schedule, entry, or other portion of the return or claim for refund involves amounts of gross income, amounts of deductions, or amounts on the basis of which credits are determined that are:
    (1) Less than $10,000, or
    (2) Less than $400,000 and also less than 20 percent of the gross income as shown on the return or claim for refund (or, for an individual, the individual's adjusted gross income).
    If more than one schedule, entry or other portion is involved, all schedules, entries or other portions shall be aggregated (Reg. Sec. 301.7701-15).

48. **(A) Correct**
    Only a person who prepares *all* or a *substantial* portion of a return or claim for refund will be considered to be a tax return preparer of the return or claim for refund. A person who renders tax advice on a position that is directly relevant to the determination of the existence, characterization, or amount of an entry on a return or claim for refund will be regarded as having prepared that entry. Whether a schedule, entry, or other portion of a return or claim for refund is a substantial portion is determined based upon whether the person knows or reasonably should know that the tax attributable to the schedule, entry, or other portion of a return or claim for refund is a substantial portion of the tax required to be shown on the return or claim for refund. A single tax entry may constitute a substantial portion of the tax required to be shown on a return. Factors to consider in determining whether a schedule, entry, or other portion of a return or claim for refund is a substantial portion include:
    3) The size and complexity of the item relative to the taxpayer's gross income; and
    4) The size of the understatement attributable to the item compared to the taxpayer's reported tax liability

49. **(A) Correct**
    A person who prepares *all* or a *substantial* portion of a return or claim for refund will be considered to be a tax return preparer of the return or claim for refund. Factors to consider in determining whether a schedule, entry, or other portion of a return or claim for refund is a substantial portion include:

> 1) The size and complexity of the item relative to the taxpayer's gross income
> 2) The size of the understatement attributable to the item compared to the taxpayer's reported tax liability

Form 1099-DIV (Dividends and Distributions) is a subsidiary of schedule B (Interest and Ordinary Dividends), which is a schedule related to Form 1040. In order of hierarchy, the size and complexity of the item relative to the taxpayer's gross income makes it <u>not</u> substantial, thus not covered by the preparer rules.

50. (A) Correct

A preparer must retain a record (by copy of the return/claim for refund or by a list, card file, electronically, or otherwise) of the name of the preparer required to sign the return/claim for refund for each return/claim for refund presented to the taxpayer. The first page of form 1040 contains all the required information to satisfy the document retention requirement.

51. (B) Correct

A person who prepares an income tax return or claim for refund for an estate or a trust, but only if such person is a fiduciary or is an officer, general partner, or employee of the fiduciary is <u>not</u> an income tax return preparer.

52. (B) Correct

Under (Code Sec. 6694(b)), any tax return preparer who prepares any return or claim for refund in which which any part of an understatement of liability is due to *willful or reckless conduct,* the preparer will pay a penalty for each return or claim in the amount of:

The greater of:
1) $5,000
   or
2) 50% of the income derived (or to be derived) by the tax return preparer with respect to the return or claim.

53. (A) Correct

A preparer is subject to penalty if any part of any understatement of liability with respect to any return or claim for refund is due to a willful attempt by the preparer to understate the liability for tax, or to the preparer's reckless or intentional disregard of rules or regulations. Under the IRC, income is taxed at its original source. Jury duty compensation is taxable income.

54. (A) Correct

This penalty generally applies if the preparer endorses or otherwise negotiates (directly or through an agent) a refund check issued to a taxpayer (other than the preparer). Any preparer who endorses or otherwise negotiates any check made to a taxpayer shall pay a penalty of <u>$500</u> with respect to each such check. The

penalty does not apply with respect to deposit by a bank of the full amount of the check in the taxpayer's account in such bank for the benefit of the taxpayer. A preparer that is also a financial institution, but has not made a loan to the taxpayer on the basis of the taxpayer's anticipated refund, may:
   a) Cash a refund check and remit all of the cash to the taxpayer
   b) Accept a refund check for deposit in full to the taxpayer's account, provided the bank does not initially endorse or negotiate the check (unless the bank has made a loan to a taxpayer on the basis of the anticipated refund).
   c) Endorse a refund check for deposit in full to the taxpayer's account pursuant to a written authorization of the taxpayer (unless the bank has made a loan to the taxpayer on the basis of the anticipated refund).
   d) Endorse or negotiate a refund check as part of the check clearing process after initial endorsement or negotiation

55. **(B) Correct**
A preparer is subject to penalty if any part of any understatement of liability with respect to any return or claim for refund is due to a willful attempt by the preparer to understate the liability for tax, or to the preparer's reckless or intentional disregard of rules or regulations. Under Code Sec. 6694(b), any tax return preparer who prepares any return or claim for refund in which any part of an understatement of liability is due to *willful or reckless conduct,* the preparer will pay a penalty for each return or claim in the amount of:
   The greater of:
   1) $5,000
      or
   2) 50% of the income derived (or to be derived) by the tax return preparer with respect to the return or claim.

56. **(A) Correct**
EITC return preparers that fail to meet the knowledge standard and other due diligence requirements are subject to an array of civil penalties. Their clients whose returns made false EITC claims also could face penalties, in addition to repayment and interest on any erroneous refunds received (Code Sec. 6695(g)). Penalties include:
   1) $100 penalty for each due diligence failure to comply assessed against return preparers or their employers.
   2) A minimum $1,000 penalty against return preparers who prepare EITC claims for which any part of an understatement of tax liability is due to an unreasonable position.
   3) A minimum $5,000 penalty against return preparers who prepare EITC claims for which any part of an understatement of tax liability is due to reckless or intentional disregard of rules or regulations by the tax preparer.

        4) Clients, whose returns are examined and found to be incorrect, could be subject to:
- (i) Accuracy or fraud penalties
- (ii) 2 to 10 years ban from claiming EITC

57. (A) Correct

If there is a final administrative determination or a final judicial decision that there was no understatement of liability in any return or claim for refund, and a penalty had been assessed, the assessment will be abated, and if any portion of such penalty has been paid, the amount paid will be refunded to the person who made such payment as an overpayment of tax (Code Sec. 6694(d)).

58. (B) Correct

If there is an employment arrangement between two or more preparers, the requirement to furnish a copy only applies to the person who employs (or engages) one or more other preparers. Similarly, if there is a partnership arrangement, the requirement to furnish a copy only applies to the partnership.

59. (B) Correct

Tax return preparers may file a claim for Penalties assessed under section 6700, 6701, or 6694 upon paying 15% of the penalty within 30 days from the date of notice and demand. The refund claim is filed on Form 6118 with the IRS service center or IRS office that sent the statement(s).

60. (B) Correct

A $50 penalty applies if the preparer fails to retain copy or list. A preparer must retain a completed copy of the return/claim for refund, or alternatively retain a record (by list, card file, electronically, or otherwise) of all the taxpayers, their taxpayer identification numbers, the taxable years, and the type of returns/claims for refund prepared.

61. (A) Correct

The accuracy-related penalty applies only if a return is filed. If no return is filed, the delinquency penalty applies instead. The accuracy-related penalty is a flat 20% of the underpayment. This penalty applies only to:
- a) Underpayments attributable to negligence or disregard of rules or regulations.
- b) A substantial understatement of income tax.
- c) Certain valuation misstatements (Code Sec. 6662).

62. (A) Correct

An Income tax return preparer is defined as person (including a partnership or corporation), who prepares for *compensation*, all or a substantial portion of a tax return or claim for refund under the income tax provisions of the Code.

The following persons are **not** income tax return preparers:
a) A person who prepares a return or claim for refund with no explicit or implicit agreement for compensation even though the person receives a gift or return service or favor.
b) A person who only provides mechanical assistance in the preparation of an income tax return or claim for refund (e.g., provides typing or copying services).
c) A person who prepares an income tax return or claim for refund of a person, or an officer, general partner, or employee of a person, by whom the individual is regularly and continuously employed or in which the individual is a general partner.
d) A person who prepares an income tax return or claim for refund for an estate or a trust, but only if such person is a fiduciary or is an officer, general partner, or employee of the fiduciary.
e) A person who prepares a claim for refund for a taxpayer in response to a deficiency notice or a waiver of restriction after initiation of an examination of the taxpayer or another taxpayer
f) Any person who provides tax assistance under the VITA program.
g) Any person who provides tax assistance as part of a qualified Low-Income Taxpayer Clinic (LITC). The assistance must be directly related to a controversy with the IRS or as part of an LITC's English as a Second Language (ESL) outreach program. The LITC cannot charge a separate fee or vary a fee based on whether the LITC provides assistance with a return or claim, and the LITC cannot charge more than a nominal fee for its service.

63. **(C) Correct**
Accepting payment is part of compensation. An Income tax return preparer is defined as person (including a partnership or corporation), who prepares for *compensation,* all or a substantial portion of a tax return or claim for refund under the income tax provisions of the Code.

Answer A is wrong because preparation of depreciation schedule is not a substantial portion of a tax return or claim for refund under the income tax provisions of the Code.
Answer B is wrong because a person who only provides mechanical assistance in the preparation of an income tax return or claim for refund is not a preparer. Also compensation was not received
Answer D is wrong because there was no compensation.

64. **(A) Correct**
A position is considered to have a realistic possibility of being sustained on its merits if a reasonable and well-informed analysis by a person knowledgeable in tax law would lead such a person to conclude that the position has

approximately a one-in-three, or greater, likelihood of being sustained on its merits. A penalty will not be imposed if, considering all the facts and circumstances, it is determined that the understatement was due to reasonable cause and that the preparer acted in good faith.

65. **(D) Correct**

    Answers A and B are True because a person who provides tax assistance under the Volunteer Income Tax Assistance (VITA) program established by the IRS is not a tax preparer. Thus, answers A and B are true.

    Answer C is also True because Reg. Sec. 301.7701-15 states that the sole preparer of a partnership's or small business corporation's income tax return is considered a tax return preparer of a partner's or a shareholder's return if the entry or entries on the partnership or small business corporation return reportable on the partner's or shareholder's return constitute a substantial portion of the partner's or shareholder's return. In this situation, the $600 pass-through income is <u>not</u> substantial, relative to the $54,000 of income from other sources.

    D is False because any person who prepares only a portion of a return is <u>not</u> be considered a preparer if that portion contains gross income, deductions, or the basis for determining tax credits of:
    (i) Less than $10,000, or
    (ii) Less than $400,000 and also less than 20% of the gross income as shown on the return or claim for refund (or, for an individual, the individual's adjusted gross income).

    If more than one schedule, entry or other portion is involved, all schedules, entries or other portions shall be aggregated (Reg. Sec. 301.7701-15).

66. **(D) Correct**
    (a) A manual signature is no longer required. The signature requirement may be satisfied if the preparer used a computer program to sign the return or claim for refund or if the preparer signs the completed return, makes a photocopy of the return, and the taxpayer signs and files the photocopy.
    (b) If a preparer is physically unable to sign a return because of a temporary or permanent disability, the penalty will not be imposed if the words "Unable to Sign" are printed, typed, or stamped on the preparer signature line. Also, the preparer's name must be printed, typed, or stamped under the signature line after the return is completed, and before it is presented to the taxpayer for signature.
    (c) If more than one preparer is involved in the preparation of the return/claim for refund, the preparer with primary responsibility for the overall substantive accuracy of the return/claim for refund is the preparer who must sign the return/claim for refund.

- (d) If the preparer required to sign the return/claim for refund is unavailable to sign, another preparer must review the return/claim for refund and then manually sign the return/claim for refund.
- (e) In general, a facsimile signature stamp or signed gummed label is not acceptable.

67. (C) Correct
See answer #66.

68. (D) Correct
See answer #62.

69. (D) Correct
A preparer is considered to have recklessly or intentionally disregarded a rule or regulation if the preparer takes a position on the return or claim that is contrary to a rule or regulation and the preparer knows of, or is reckless in not knowing of, the rule or regulation. The preparer should inquire about the existence of travel and entertainment expense. Travel and entertainment expense is one of the high audit areas, thus, requires more and accurate substantiation as part of due diligence.

70. (D) Correct
A practitioner must exercise due diligence when performing the following duties:
- (a) Preparing or assisting in the preparing, approving, and filing of returns, documents, affidavits, and other papers relating to IRS matters.
- (b) Determining the correctness of oral or written representations made by him or her to the Department of the Treasury.
- (c) Determining the correctness of oral or written representations made by him or her to clients with reference to any matter administered by the IRS.

71. (C) Correct
A practitioner who knows that his or her client has not complied with the revenue laws or has made an error or omission in any return, document, affidavit, or other required paper, has the responsibility to advise the client promptly of the noncompliance, error, or omission, and the consequences of the noncompliance, error, or omission.

72. (C) Correct
A preparer is required to furnish a completed copy of the return or claim for refund to the taxpayer before (or at the same time) the return or claim for refund is presented to the taxpayer for signature. A penalty of $50 applies if the preparer fails to furnish a copy to Taxpayer.

73. **(D) Correct**
    (i) A practitioner may not sign a tax return as a preparer if the practitioner determines that the tax return contains a position that does not have a realistic possibility of being sustained on its merits (the realistic possibility standard) unless the position is not frivolous and is adequately disclosed to the IRS.
    (ii) A practitioner advising a client to take a position on a tax return, or preparing or signing a tax return as a preparer, must inform the client of the penalties reasonably likely to apply to the client with respect to the position advised, prepared, or reported.
    (iii) A practitioner advising a client to take a position on a tax return, or preparing or signing a tax return as a preparer, generally may rely in good faith without verification upon information furnished by the client. The practitioner may not, however, ignore the implications of information furnished to, or actually known by, the practitioner and must make reasonable inquiries if the information as furnished appears to be incorrect, inconsistent with an important fact or another factual assumption, or incomplete.

74. **(D) Correct**
    See answer #62.

75. **(B) Correct**
    A preparer must retain a completed copy of the return/claim for refund, or alternatively retain a record (by list, card file, electronically, or otherwise) of all the taxpayers, their taxpayer identification numbers, the taxable years, and the type of returns/claims for refund prepared.

76. **(D) Correct**
    Any person who employs a tax return preparer to prepare any return or claim for refund at any time during a return period must make a return indicating the:
    (a) Name
    (b) Taxpayer identification number
    (c) Place of work of each tax return preparer employed by him
    The return required must be filed on or before the first July 31 following the end of such return period. The term 'return period' means the 12-month period beginning on July 1 of each year. The records must be retained and kept available for inspection for the 3-year period following the close of the return period to which that record relates (Reg. Sec. 1.6060-1).

77. **(B) Correct**
    A preparer must:
    1) Retain a completed copy of the return/claim for refund, or alternatively retain a record (by list, card file, electronically, or otherwise) of all the

taxpayers, their taxpayer identification numbers, the taxable years, and the type of returns/claims for refund prepared.
2) Retain a record (by copy of the return/claim for refund or by a list, card file, electronically, or otherwise) of the name of the preparer required to sign the return/claim for refund for each return/claim for refund presented to the taxpayer.
3) Make such copy or list available for inspection upon request by the IRS for a 3-year period following the close of the return period

78. **(D) Correct**

A claim for tax refund must be filed 3 years from the date of filing the return or 2 years after the tax was paid, whichever is later. An early return is treated as filed on the due date. Since the due date for the 2004 tax-year was April 15, 2005, the claim for tax refund must be filed 3 years from April 15, 2005, thus April 15, 2008 is the correct answer.

79. **(A) Correct**

Any person who employs one or more signing tax return preparers to prepare any return or claim for refund at any time during a return period must:
1) Retaining a record of:
    (i) Name,
    (ii) Taxpayer identification number, and
    (iii) Place of work of each tax return preparer employed by him
2) Make the record available for inspection upon request by the Commissioner

The return required must be filed on or before the first July 31 following the end of such return period. The term 'return period' means the 12-month period beginning on July 1 of each year. The records must be retained and kept available for inspection for the 3-year period following the close of the return period to which that record relates.
- A sole proprietor must retain and make available a record with respect to him or herself.
- A partnership is treated as the employer of the partners and must retain and make available a record with respect to the partners and other tax return preparers employed or engaged by the partnership (Reg. Sec. 1.6060-1).

80. **(C) Correct**

A tax return preparer must complete the paid preparer's area of the return if the individual was paid to prepare, assist in preparing, or review the tax return.

81. **(C) Correct**

See answer #77.

82. **(D) Correct**
    See answer #77.

83. **(D) Correct**
    A person who prepares an income tax return or claim for refund for an estate or a trust, but only if such person is a fiduciary or is an officer, general partner, or employee of the fiduciary is <u>not</u> a tax preparer.

84. **(D) Correct**
    See answer #83.

85. **(A) Correct**
    An Income tax return preparer is defined as person (including a partnership or corporation), who prepares for *compensation,* or employs one or more persons to prepare for compensation, all or a *substantial portion* of a tax return or claim for refund under the income tax provisions of the Code.

86. **(C) Correct**
    An Income tax return preparer is defined as person (including a partnership or corporation), who prepares for *compensation,* or employs one or more persons to prepare for compensation, all or a *substantial portion* of a tax return or claim for refund under the income tax provisions of the Code. This includes a person who prepares a United States tax return for a fee outside the United States. Giving an opinion about theoretical events that have not occurred is not part of the definition of a tax preparer.

87. **(D) Correct**
    An Income tax return preparer is defined as person (including a partnership or corporation), who prepares for *compensation,* or employs one or more persons to prepare for compensation, all or a *substantial portion* of a tax return or claim for refund under the income tax provisions of the Code. If more than one preparer is involved in the preparation of the return/claim for refund, the preparer with primary responsibility for the overall substantive accuracy of the return/claim for refund is the preparer who must sign the return/claim for refund. Because Pat meets all the criteria within the definition of a preparer, *answer D is* the most suitable answer.

88. **(B) Correct**
    If the preparer required to sign the return/claim for refund is unavailable to sign, another preparer must review the return/claim for refund and then manually sign the return/claim for refund. Therefore Z may sign the returns prepared by X if Z reviews the information obtained by X from the taxpayers and reviews the preparation of the returns.

89. **(C) Correct**

An Income tax return preparer is defined as person (including a partnership or corporation), who prepares for *compensation,* or employs one or more persons to prepare for compensation, all or a *substantial portion* of a tax return or claim for refund under the income tax provisions of the Code. This includes a person who prepares a United States tax return for a fee outside the United States. *Answer C* is the only answer that fits this definition.

90. **(D) Correct**

Preparers include people who:
   a) Furnish sufficient advice or information so that the completion of the return by another individual is a mechanical process.
   b) Supply computerized tax return preparation services to tax practitioners, or offers services or programs that make substantive tax determinations.
   c) Software companies or other persons that prepare computer programs and sell those programs to taxpayers for use in preparing their returns may also be an income tax return preparer for purposes of the return preparer penalties.
   d) For the purposes of IRC section 6694 penalties, no more than one individual associated with a firm (i.e., an employee or partner) is treated as a preparer of the same return or claim (one-preparer-per-firm rule). NOTE: The one-preparer-per-firm rule does not mean that an IRC section 6694 penalty cannot also be asserted against the firm, as an employer. It also does not mean that there can never be more than one preparer per return. For example, if a CPA receives advice from an attorney (who is not associated with the same firm) and the advice constitutes a substantial portion of the return; both the CPA and the attorney are income tax return preparers with respect to that return.
   e) A non-signing preparer who prepares a schedule or entry that constitutes a substantial portion of the return may be considered a tax return preparer. In making the decision as to what constitutes a substantial portion, examiners should consider the relation of the entry or schedule to the tax liability, the complexity of the return as a whole, and the relative time involved in preparing it.
   f) An electronic return originator may be a return preparer under IRC section 7701(a)(36) and who could be liable for these penalties. However, an electronic filer who is primarily a transmitter with services limited to typing, reproduction or other mechanical assistance in the preparation of a return or claim for refund is not an income tax preparer for purposes for these penalties.
   g) A general partner who prepares a partnership return can be an income tax return preparer of a limited partner's return in certain situations.
   h) A preparer (1st preparer) can be a preparer of a return prepared by another preparer (2nd preparer) if the 2nd preparer relied on

information contained on the return prepared by the 1st preparer. This occurs, for example, when the 1st preparer negligently overstates the expenses on a prior year's return, thus creating an NOL, and the 2nd preparer, in good faith, applies the NOL carryover in preparing the subsequent year's return.

i) The definition of income tax preparer is slightly altered for purposes of IRC section 6695(g). Preparers who merely give advice or prepare another return that affects the EITC return or refund claim are not considered preparers. The due diligence standards are imposed only on paid preparers who prepare the EITC return or claim.

91. **(B) Correct**

    A preparer is required to furnish a completed copy of the return or claim for refund to the taxpayer before (or at the same time) the return or claim for refund is presented to the taxpayer for signature.

92. **(C) Correct**

    A penalty may be assessed on any preparer or any person who prepares and signs a tax return or claim for refund and the individual with overall supervisory responsibility for the advice given by the firm with respect to the return or claim.

93. **(D) Correct**

    In general, a facsimile signature stamp or signed gummed label is not acceptable. Except:
    a) A preparer of a return or claim for refund for a nonresident alien may use a facsimile signature to sign as preparer if the preparer is authorized to sign for the taxpayer using a facsimile signature.
    b) A preparer of Forms 1041 may use a facsimile signature to sign the Forms 1041 if certain conditions are met.

    Therefore P would be subject to a preparer penalty of $50 for failure to adequately sign the extension.

94. **(D) Correct**

    If there is an employment arrangement between two or more preparers, the requirement to furnish a copy only applies to the person who employs (or engages) one or more other preparers. Similarly, if there is a partnership arrangement, the requirement to furnish a copy only applies to the partnership. In this case, the firm is responsible for the penalty because it employed/engaged the preparer.

95. **(A) Correct**

    A penalty applies if the preparer endorses or otherwise negotiates (directly or through an agent) a refund check issued to a taxpayer (other than the preparer). Any preparer who endorses or otherwise negotiates any check made to a taxpayer shall pay a penalty of $500 with respect to each such check. The penalty does not apply with respect to deposit by a bank of the full amount of the check in the taxpayer's account for the benefit of the taxpayer.

96. **(A) Correct**
A preparer is required to furnish a completed copy of the return or claim for refund to the taxpayer before (or at the same time) the return or claim for refund is presented to the taxpayer for signature. A penalty of $50 applies if the preparer fails to furnish a copy to Taxpayer. The penalty does not apply if the failure was due to reasonable cause and not due to willful neglect. Waiting until after the filing season to fix the copier would be construed as willful neglect.

97. **(A) Correct**
Any understatement of the net amount payable for any tax due or any overstatement of the net amount creditable or refundable for any tax may subject a preparer to a penalty.
A preparer is subject the penalty if any part of any understatement of liability with respect to any return or claim for refund is due to a willful attempt by the preparer to understate the liability for tax, or to the preparer's reckless or intentional disregard of rules or regulations.

Under Code Sec. 6694(b), a tax return preparer who prepares any return or claim for refund in which any part of an understatement of liability is due to *willful or reckless conduct*, the preparer will pay a penalty for each return or claim in the amount of:
The greater of:
a) $5,000
   or
b) 50% of the income derived (or to be derived) by the tax return preparer with respect to the return or claim.

98. **(A & C) Correct**
The *Taxpayer* has the burden of proof that a preparer has negligently or intentionally disregarded a rule or regulation. Also, the penalty for an understatement due to the preparer's negligent or intentional disregard of one or more rules or regulations has changed since 1989 and was modifies in 2007 from $1,000 to $5,000 (Code Sec. 6694).

99. **(B) Correct**
A preparer is considered to have recklessly or intentionally disregarded a rule or regulation if the preparer takes a position on the return or claim that is contrary to a rule or regulation and the preparer knows of, or is reckless in not knowing of, the rule or regulation. The preparer should verify the existence of travel and entertainment expense through substantiation of taxpayer documents. Travel

and entertainment expense is one of the high audit areas, thus, requires more and accurate substantiation as part of due diligence.

100. **(D) Correct**
Code Sec. 6694(a) provides a penalty of $1,000 to be assessed against a return preparer who takes an unrealistic position that causes an understatement of liability. The penalty is applicable if the preparer knew, or reasonably should have known, that the position was unrealistic and the preparer did not disclose the position, or if the position was frivolous. Sec. 6694(b) assesses a $5,000 penalty against a return preparer whose willful or reckless conduct causes an understatement of liability. The penalty is applicable if the understatement of liability is due to the preparer's willful attempt to understate the tax liability or his/her reckless or intentional disregard of rules or regulations. Code Sec. 6694(b) also states that the $5,000 penalty is to be reduced by the $1,000 penalty assessed under Sec. 6694(a) if the preparer is subject to both. Therefore, a preparer who is subject to both the penalty for understatement due to unrealistic positions and the penalty for willful or reckless conduct will pay a total penalty of $5,000 [($5,000 + $1,000) - $1,000].

101. **(B) Correct**
EITC return preparers that fail to meet the knowledge standard and other due diligence requirements are subject to an array of civil penalties. Their clients whose returns made false EITC claims also could face penalties, in addition to repayment and interest on any erroneous refunds received (Code Sec. 6695(g)).
Penalties include:
   (a) $100 penalty for each due diligence failure to comply assessed against return preparers or their employers.
   (b) A minimum $1,000 penalty against return preparers who prepare EITC claims for which any part of an understatement of tax liability is due to an unreasonable position.
   (c) A minimum $5,000 penalty against return preparers who prepare EITC claims for which any part of an understatement of tax liability is due to reckless or intentional disregard of rules or regulations by the tax preparer.
   (d) Clients, whose returns are examined and found to be incorrect, could be subject to:
      (i) Accuracy or fraud penalties
      (ii) 2 to 10 years ban from claiming EITC

When preparing EITC returns and claims for refund, paid preparers must:
   1. Evaluate information received from clients
   2. Apply a consistency and reasonableness standard to the information

3. Ask additional questions if the information appears incorrect, inconsistent or incomplete
4. Document and retain the record of inquiries made and client responses

102. **(C) Correct**
Tax return preparers may file a claim for Penalties assessed under section 6700, 6701, or 6694 <u>upon</u> paying 15% of the penalty within 30 days from the date of notice and demand. The refund claim is filed on Form 6118 with the IRS service center or IRS office that sent the statement(s) (Code Sec. 6694(c)(1)). If the refund claim is denied, the preparer must begin a proceeding in the appropriate U.S. district court for the determination of his liability for such penalty within 30 days after date of denial.

103. **(C) Correct**
To satisfy the earned income credit due diligence requirements, a preparer must retain all of the following:
a) Keep the EIC worksheet or an equivalent that demonstrates how the EIC was computed.
b) Retain Form 8867 and EIC worksheet or the equivalent.
c) Maintain record of how and when the information used to complete these forms was obtained.
d) Retain records for 3 years after the June 30th following the date the return or claim was presented for signature.

The retention of a copy of the Social Security cards for the taxpayer and each qualifying child is not required because the IRS has an internal system of matching the social security names with Social Security Administration data.

104. **(D) Correct**
When preparing EITC returns and claims for refund, paid preparers must:
a) Evaluate information received from clients
b) Apply a consistency and reasonableness standard to the information
c) Ask additional questions if the information appears incorrect, inconsistent or incomplete
d) Document and retain the record of inquiries made and client responses

The <u>four</u> due diligence requirements are that tax preparers must do:
(a) Completion of Eligibility checklist
(b) Computation of the Credit
(c) Knowledge
(d) Record Retention

105. **(D) Correct**
Under (Code Sec. 6694(a)), If a tax return preparer prepares any return or claim of refund in which any part of an understatement of liability is due to *unreasonable position*, and the preparer knew, or should have reasonably known about the position, the preparer will pay a penalty for each return or claim in the amount of:
   The greater of:
   a) $1,000
      or
   b) 50% of the income derived (or to be derived) by the tax return preparer with respect to the return or claim.

   A position is considered to have a realistic possibility of being sustained on its merits if a reasonable and well-informed analysis by a person knowledgeable in tax law would lead such a person to conclude that the position has approximately a one-in-three, or greater likelihood of being sustained on its merits. A penalty will not be imposed if, considering all the facts and circumstances, it is determined that the understatement was due to reasonable cause and that the preparer acted in good faith.

106. **(C) Correct**
See answer #105.

107. **(B) Correct**
Code Sec. 6694(e) defines "understatement of liability" as any understatement of the tax liability or overstatement of the amount to be refunded or credited.

108. **(D) Correct**
If a penalty is proposed against a preparer that the preparer does not agree with, the following actions are available for the preparer:
   a) Request a conference with the agent and present additional information and explanations showing that the penalty is not warranted.
   b) Wait for the penalty to be assessed and for a notice and demand statement to be issued, then pay the penalty within 30 days and file a claim for refund.
   c) Wait for the penalty to be assessed and for a notice and demand statement to be issued, then pay at least 15% of the penalty within 30 days and file a claim for refund.
   d) If the refund claim is denied, the preparer must begin a proceeding in the appropriate U.S. district court for the determination of his liability for such penalty within 30 days after date of denial.

109. **(D) Correct**
The following will not subject a preparer to the penalties for disclosure of information if:
- a) The preparer receives a state grand jury subpoena requesting copies of federal and state income tax returns (Court order).
- b) An IRS agent, in his or her official capacity, visits the preparer and requests copies of state and federal income tax returns, related returns, schedules, and records of the taxpayer used in the preparation of the tax returns.
- c) A partner in a partnership, who was not involved with the return preparation or partnership records, requests a copy of the partnership return, including the Schedule K-1s for all partners.

110. **(C) Correct**
Section 7525 provides a privilege of confidentiality for communications between a taxpayer and a *federally authorized tax practitioner* that has essentially the same scope as the federal attorney-client privilege. The privilege applies only to communications related to *tax advice*. Tax Advice is defined as advice given by a federally authorized tax practitioner with respect to a matter that is within the scope of the practitioner's authority to practice before the IRS. The taxpayer must assert the confidentiality privilege because it is not automatic.

Section 7525 confidentiality privilege does **not** protect the following situations:
1) Information disclosed to a tax practitioner for the purpose of preparing a return.
2) Criminal tax matters before the IRS or in federal court.
3) Written communications made in connection with the promotion of direct or indirect participation in a tax shelter.
4) Information that is also available from non-privileged sources.
5) Communication between the taxpayer's tax practitioner and a third-party who provides information about the taxpayer to the practitioner.

111. **(D) Correct**
The following will not subject a preparer to the penalties for *disclosure of information*:
- (i) Disclosure for use in revenue investigations or court proceedings.
- (ii) Disclosure to a taxpayer's fiduciary.
- (iii) Disclosure by a tax return preparer to a tax return processor.
- (iv) Disclosure by one officer, employee, or member to another.
- (v) Disclosure of identical information obtained from other sources.

  (vi) Disclosure or use of information in preparation or audit of state returns.
  (vii) Disclosure or use in preparation of other returns for the taxpayer.
  (viii) Disclosure or use to prepare lists to solicit tax return business (Reg. Sec. 301.7216-2).

112. **(A) Correct**
See answer #111

113. **(D) Correct**
In general, fraud is a taxpayer's specific and actual intent to evade payment of a tax due and owing. Code Sec. 6663 imposes a penalty equal to 75% of the portion of any underpayment due to fraud.

114. **(C) Correct**
Any person (including most entities) that files a *frivolous federal tax return* is subject to a penalty of $5,000. In addition, a penalty of $5,000 is imposed on any person that submits a *specified frivolous submission*.

The penalty for frivolous federal tax returns is imposed when:
1) An individual files what purports to be a tax return but that:
   a) Does not contain information on which the substantial correctness of the self-assessment may be judged, or
   b) Contains information indicating on its face that the self-assessment is substantially incorrect, and
2) The lack of or incorrect information on the filed return:
   a) Is based on a position that the IRS has identified as frivolous, or
   b) Reflects a desire to delay or impede the administration of the federal tax laws.

The frivolous return penalty is in *addition* to any other penalty provided by law.

115. **(B) Correct**
The accuracy-related penalty is a flat 20% of the underpayment. This penalty applies only to:
 a) Underpayments attributable to negligence or disregard of rules or regulations.
 b) A substantial understatement of income tax.
 c) Certain valuation misstatements (Code Sec. 6662).

The agent proposed an accuracy-related penalty first adjustment, thus $5,000 (25,000 x 0.20). Under IRC section 6713, any preparer that discloses any information furnished to him for, or in connection with, the preparation of a tax return, or uses any such information for any purpose other than to prepare, or assist in preparing such return shall pay a penalty of $250 for each such disclosure or use. Because the second adjustment was based upon a disclosure statement in the tax return and did not relate to a tax shelter, code. Sec. 6662 allows a reduction by the amount of disclosure penalty, thus: $5,000 [($5,000 + $250) – 250]

116. **(B) Correct**
Code Sec. 6663 imposes a penalty equal to 75% of the portion of any underpayment due to fraud. Thus: $75,000 ($100,000 x 0.75) for each year.

117. **(D) Correct**
A position is considered to have a realistic possibility of being sustained on its merits if a reasonable and well-informed analysis by a person knowledgeable in tax law would lead such a person to conclude that the position has approximately a one-in-three, or greater, likelihood of being sustained on its merits. A penalty will not be imposed if, considering all the facts and circumstances, it is determined that the understatement was due to reasonable cause and that the preparer acted in good faith. There must substantial authority to sustain the position taken on the return.

118. **(D) Correct**
When preparing EITC returns and claims for refund, paid preparers must:
   a) Evaluate information received from clients
   b) Apply a consistency and reasonableness standard to the information
   c) Ask additional questions if the information appears incorrect, inconsistent or incomplete
   d) Document and retain the record of inquiries made and client responses

The <u>four</u> due diligence requirements are that tax preparers must do:
   (a) Completion of Eligibility checklist
   (b) Computation of the Credit
   (c) Knowledge
   (d) Record Retention

119. **(C) Correct**
A penalty may be assessed on any preparer or any person who prepares and signs a tax return or claim for refund and the individual with overall supervisory responsibility for the advice given by the firm with respect to the return or claim. A person giving advice in not considered as tax preparer.

120. **(D) Correct**

If a penalty is proposed against a preparer that the preparer does not agree with, the following actions are available for the preparer:
   a) Request a conference with the agent and present additional information and explanations showing that the penalty is not warranted.
   b) Wait for the penalty to be assessed and for a notice and demand statement to be issued, then pay the penalty within 30 days and file a claim for refund.
   c) Wait for the penalty to be assessed and for a notice and demand statement to be issued, then pay at least 15% of the penalty within 30 days and file a claim for refund.
   d) If the refund claim is denied, the preparer must begin a proceeding in the appropriate U.S. district court for the determination of his liability for such penalty within 30 days after date of denial.

121. **(A) Correct**

Due diligence Knowledge requirements:
   a) Know or have reason to know that any information used in determining the taxpayer's eligibility for, or the amount of, the EIC is incorrect, incomplete or inconsistent
   b) Do not ignore the implications of information furnished or known
   c) Make reasonable inquiries if a reasonable and well-informed tax return preparer, knowledgeable in the law, would conclude the information furnished appears to be incorrect, inconsistent or incomplete
   d) Document in the records any additional inquiries made and the client's responses.

122. **(D) Correct**

The following are *four due diligence requirements* that all tax preparers are required to perform:
   a) Completion of Eligibility checklist
   b) Computation of the Credit
   c) Knowledge
   d) Record Retention

123. **(A) Correct**

The preparer ask additional questions to satisfy due diligence in this situation. The facts as presented are incomplete. To determine whether Barbara may claim EITC, the preparer must make sufficient inquiries to determine whether Barbara's newly married daughter is her qualifying child. The preparer should ask appropriate questions to determine if the newly married qualifying child has filed a joint return other than to claim a refund; based on the 2009 tax law changed, the child is a qualifying

child, only if the child has not filed a joint return other than to claim a refund. The preparer must ask Barbara the following questions:
   a) Did your daughter file a joint return with her husband?
   b) Did your daughter have a filing requirement?

124. **(B) Correct**
Based on the initial interview, Steven can claim the boys as qualifying children for EITC. He is their step-father so they meet the relationship requirement. Since the boys are below 19 years of age and lived with Steven all year, they met the age and residency tests.

UNIT 3: THIRD-PARTY AUTHORIZATION

Unit 3 Contents:
3.01 UNIT DEFINITIONS
3.02 THIRD-PARTY AUTHORIZATION
3.03 POWER-OF-ATTORNEY (POA)
3.04 THE CENTRALIZED AUTHORIZATION FILE (CAF)
3.05 UNIT 3: QUESTIONS
3.06 UNIT 3: ANSWERS

3.01 UNIT DEFINITIONS

Power-of-Attorney - A document signed by the taxpayer, as principal, by which an individual is appointed as attorney-in-fact to perform certain specified act(s) or kinds of act(s) on behalf of the principal.

General Power-of-Attorney – An attorney-in-fact is authorized to perform any or all acts the taxpayer can perform.

Durable Power-of-Attorney - A Power-of-Attorney which specifies that the appointment of the attorney-in-fact will not end due to either the *passage of time* (the authority conveyed will continue until the death of the taxpayer) or *incompetency* of the principal (e.g., the principal becomes unable or is adjudged incompetent to perform his or her business affairs).

Limited Power-of-Attorney – This type of Power-of-Attorney is limited in any facet (a type of Power-of-Attorney authorizing the attorney-in-fact to perform only *certain specified* acts as contrasted to a general Power-of-Attorney authorizing the representative to perform any and all acts the taxpayer can perform).

Practice before the IRS - Practice before the IRS encompasses all matters connected with presentation to the IRS or any of its personnel relating to a taxpayer's rights, privileges, or liabilities under laws or regulations administered by the IRS. Such presentations include the preparation and filing of necessary documents, correspondence with and communications to the IRS, and the representation of a taxpayer at conferences, hearings, and meetings.

Principal - A person (taxpayer) who appoints an attorney-in-fact under a Power-of-Attorney.

Recognized Representative - An individual who is recognized to practice before the IRS under the provisions of the Internal Revenue Code

Representation - Acts performed on behalf of a taxpayer by a representative in practice before the IRS. Note: Any person may prepare a tax return, appear as a witness for the taxpayer before the IRS, or furnish information at the request of the IRS or any of its officers or employees.

Substitution of Representative - An act performed by an attorney-in-fact whereby authority given under a Power-of-Attorney is transferred to another recognized representative. After a substitution is made, only the newly recognized representative will be considered the taxpayer's representative.

Tax Information Authorization (TIA) - A document signed by the taxpayer authorizing any individual or entity designated by the taxpayer to receive or inspect confidential tax return information in a specified matter (IRM 21.3.7.1).

3.02   THIRD-PARTY AUTHORIZATION

A third-party authorization is a *signed document* and/or an *oral statement* made by a taxpayer granting a third-party the authority to perform specified acts on behalf of the taxpayer. Third-party authorizations include:
   (1)   Form 2848 (Power-of-Attorney and Declaration of Representative).
   (2)   Form 8821 (Tax Information Authorization).
   (3)   Non-written tax information authorization.
   (4)   Oral Disclosure Consent.
   (5)   Third-party Designee (Checkbox).
   (6)   Estate Tax Return Power-of-Attorney.
   (7)   E-services Disclosure Authorization.

The <u>Checkbox election</u> is made directly on the tax form. Checkbox authority:
   a) Does not allow a designee to represent the taxpayer.
   b) Is not recorded on the CAF.
   c) Is recorded directly to the taxpayers account,.
   d) Mirrors Form 8821 authority.
   e) Allows the designee to provide or receive information on any issue in connection with the tax period covered by the return on which the designation was made for a period not to exceed one year.
   f) Allows the designee to receive written account information/transcripts upon request for a period not to exceed one year.
   g) Is available on Forms 720, 941, 941PR, 941SS, 1040, 1041, 1120, 2290 and CT-1
   h) Can co-exist with a Power-of-Attorney for the same tax period.

If the taxpayer uses the checkbox authority on an original return to designate a person to receive return information, the designee's authority also extends to any amended return filed with respect to that return, provided the request for the return or return information is made by the designee within one year from the date the original return was due without regard to any extension of time. This includes Business Master File (BMF) returns which only carry the checkbox authority. More than one person can be designated on a Tax Information Authorization.

3.03 POWER-OF-ATTORNEY (POA)

Form 2848, Power-of-Attorney and Declaration of Representative, is a legal document used to authorize an individual to represent a taxpayer before the IRS and authorize the IRS to release confidential tax information to an individual for the account matters(s) specified. Form 2848 (Power-of-Attorney and Declaration of Representative) can only be granted to an individual eligible to practice before the IRS (e.g. Attorney, CPA or Enrolled Agent).

Taxpayers have the right to represent themselves or have someone else represent them before the IRS in connection with a Federal tax matter. If a taxpayer wants someone to represent him/her before the IRS, the taxpayer must file Form 2848 (Power-of-Attorney and Declaration of Representative) with the IRS office where he/she wants the representative to act. The representative must be a person authorized to practice before the IRS. The taxpayer's signature on Form 2848 allows the individual named to *represent* the taxpayer before the IRS and to *receive* tax information. The IRS will accept a copy of a Power-of-Attorney that is submitted by facsimile transmission (fax). Guidelines on Power-of-Attorney are set forth on publication 947.

A properly executed Power-of-Attorney can be used in connection with more than one particular type of tax matter or more than one taxable year. The Power-of-Attorney must clearly express the taxpayer's intention as to the scope of the authority of the representative and must also clearly specify the tax matter(s) to which the authority relates.

Scope of Power-of-Attorney

Any representative, other than an unenrolled preparer, can perform the following acts requiring Power-of-Attorney, on behalf of the taxpayer:

(1) Represent taxpayer before any office of the IRS.
(2) Record the interview.
(3) Sign an offer or a waiver of restriction on assessment or collection of a tax deficiency, or a waiver of notice of disallowance of claim for credit or refund.
(4) Sign a consent to extend the statutory time period for assessment or collection of a tax.
(5) Execute a closing agreement under Sec. 7121.
(6) Receive, but not endorse or cash, a refund check drawn on the U.S. Treasury. The taxpayer must specifically *initial* Form 2848 showing the name of the individual designated to receive the refund check.
(7) Authorize the extension of the statute of limitations.

- Form 2848, Power-of-Attorney and Declaration of Representative, can be used to appoint an unenrolled return preparer as a taxpayer's representative before revenue agents and examining officers of the Examination Division of the IRS.
- A document other than Form 2848 can be used to appoint a Power-of-Attorney if it contains the information required by the IRS.
- A taxpayer can execute a durable Power-of-Attorney, which specifies that the appointment of the attorney-in-fact will not end due to the incapacity or incompetency of the taxpayer.

- The issuance of a CAF number <u>does not</u> indicate that a person is either recognized or authorized to practice before the IRS.
- The purpose of the CAF number is to facilitate the processing of a Power-of-Attorney or a tax information authorization submitted by a recognized representative or designee.
- A recognized representative or a designee should include the same CAF number on every Power-of-Attorney or tax information authorization filed.

- For taxpayers that want someone to represent them in their absence at an examination or at an appeal within the IRS, the taxpayer must furnish that representative with written authorization on Form 2848, Power-of-Attorney and Declaration of Representative, or any other properly written authorization. The representative can be an attorney, certified public accountant, or an enrolled agent. Even if the taxpayer appointed a representative, the taxpayer may attend the examination or appeals conference and may act on his or her own behalf.

Declaration of the representative on a power or attorney

Within the power of attorney, the representative must declare the following:

(1) I am not currently under suspension or disbarment from practice before the Internal Revenue Service;

(2) I am aware of regulations contained in Circular 230 (31 CFR, Part 10), as amended, concerning the practice of attorneys, certified public accountants, enrolled agents, enrolled actuaries, and others;

(3) I am authorized to represent the taxpayer(s) identified in Part I for the tax matter(s) specified there; and

(4) I am one of the following:

    (a) **Attorney**—a member in good standing of the bar of the highest court of the jurisdiction (state) shown below.

    (b) **Certified Public Accountant**—duly qualified to practice as a certified public accountant in the jurisdiction (state) shown below.

    (c) **Enrolled Agent**—enrolled as an agent under the requirements of Circular 230.

    (d) **Officer**—a bona fide officer of the taxpayer's organization.

    (e) **Full-Time Employee**—a full-time employee of the taxpayer.

    (f) **Family Member**—a member of the taxpayer's immediate family (for example, spouse, parent, child, brother, or sister).

    (g) **Enrolled Actuary**—enrolled as an actuary by the Joint Board for the Enrollment of Actuaries under 29 U.S.C. 1242

    (h) **Unenrolled Return Preparer**—the authority to practice before the Internal Revenue Service is limited by Circular 230, section. One must have prepared the return in question and the return must be under examination by the IRS.

    (i) **Student Attorney**—student who receives permission to practice before the IRS by virtue of their status as a law student under section 10.7(d) of Circular 230.

    (j) **Student CPA**—student who receives permission to practice before the IRS by virtue of their status as a CPA student under section 10.7(d) of Circular 230.

(k) **Enrolled Retirement Plan Agent**—enrolled as a retirement plan agent under the requirements of Circular 230.

Tax Years

The taxpayer may list any tax years or periods that have already ended as of the date of signing the Power-of-Attorney. However, the taxpayer may include on a Power-of-Attorney only future tax periods that end no later than 3 years after the date the Power-of-Attorney is received by the IRS. The 3 future periods are determined starting after December 31 of the year the Power-of-Attorney is received by the IRS. However, one should avoid general references such as all years or all periods.

Content

A Power-of-Attorney or tax information authorization should contain the following information:
(a) Type of tax involved.
(b) Specific year(s)/period(s) involved.
(c) Name and mailing address of the recognized representative(s).
(d) The taxpayer's intent as to the scope of authority of the representative.

Identification number of the representative, like SSNs or EIN is not required on the Power-of-Attorney.

Signing taxpayer's Return

The representative named under a Power-of-Attorney is not permitted to sign the taxpayer's personal income tax return unless both of the following exist:
(a) The signature is permitted under the Internal Revenue Code and the related regulations.
(b) The taxpayer *specifically* authorizes the representative's signature through the Power-of-Attorney.

Example, the regulation permits a representative to sign a return if the taxpayer is unable to sign the return for any of the following reasons:
(i) Disease or injury.
(ii) Continuous absence from the U. S. (including Puerto Rico) for a period of at least 60 days prior to the date required by law for filing the return.
(iii) Other good cause if specific permission is requested of and granted by the IRS.

When a return is signed by a representative, it must be accompanied by a Power-of-Attorney (or copy) authorizing the representative to sign the return. A taxpayer's signature on a Power-of-Attorney does not have to be notarized or witnessed.

When a taxpayer signs and dates the Form 2848 before the representative, the signature dates of the taxpayer(s) and representative(s) must be within 45 days for domestic authorizations and within 60 days for authorizations of taxpayers/representatives residing abroad. Otherwise, the Form 2848 will be returned. If the taxpayer's dated signature is more current than the representative's signature, the 45 and 60 day rule does not apply. The IRS must receive Form

8821 within 120 days of the taxpayer's signature date unless the Form 8821 covers tax matters only.

Substitution or Delegation

A recognized representative can substitute or delegate authority under the Power-of-Attorney to another recognized representative *only if* the act is specifically authorized under the Power-of-Attorney. After a substitution has been made, *only* the newly recognized representative will be recognized as the taxpayer's representative. If a delegation of power has been made, <u>both</u> the original and the delegated representative will be recognized by the IRS to represent the taxpayer.

To make a substitution or delegation, the representative must file the following items with the IRS office(s) where the Power-of-Attorney was filed:
1. A written notice of substitution or delegation signed by the recognized representative.
2. A written declaration of representative made by the new representative.
3. A copy of the Power-of-Attorney that specifically authorizes the substitution or delegation.

A representative cannot execute consents that will allow the IRS to disclose tax return or return information to a third-party unless this authority is specifically delegated to the representative on line 5 of Form 2848.

Termination

A Power-of-Attorney is generally terminated if the taxpayer becomes incapacitated or incompetent. The Power-of-Attorney can continue, however, in the case of taxpayer's incapacity or incompetency if the taxpayer authorizes this on Form 2848, or if the taxpayer's *non-IRS durable Power-of-Attorney* meets all the requirements for acceptance by the IRS.

Non-IRS Powers of Attorney

The IRS will accept a *non-IRS Power-of-Attorney*, but a completed transmittal Form 2848 must be attached in order for the Power-of-Attorney to be entered on the *Centralized Authorization File* (CAF) system.

If a taxpayer wants to use a Power-of-Attorney document other than Form 2848, the document must contain the following information of the taxpayer:
 (1) Name and mailing address.
 (2) Social security number and/or employer identification number.
 (3) Employee plan number, if applicable.
 (4) The name and mailing address of the representative.
 (5) The types of tax involved.
 (6) The federal tax form number.
 (7) The specific year(s) or period(s) involved.
 (8) For estate tax matters, the decedent's date of death.

(9) A clear expression of taxpayer's intention concerning the scope of authority granted to the representative.
(10) Signature and date.

The taxpayer must also attach (to the non-IRS Power-of-Attorney) a signed and dated statement made by the representative. This statement is referred to as the _Declaration of Representative_ and is contained in *Part II* of Form 2848. The statement should read:
1) I am not currently under suspension or disbarment from practice before the IRS or other practice of my profession by any other authority,
2) I am aware of the regulations contained in Treasury Department Circular No. 230 (31 CFR, Part 10) concerning the practice of attorneys, certified public accountants, enrolled agents, enrolled actuaries, and others,
3) I am authorized to represent the taxpayer(s) identified in the Power-of-Attorney; and
4) I am authorized to practice before the IRS as an individual described in 26 CFR 601.502(b).

The IRS will not accept a non-IRS Power-of-Attorney if it does not contain all the information listed above.

Procedure for Non-IRS Power-of-Attorney

The attorney-in-fact named in the taxpayer's non-IRS Power-of-Attorney can sign a Form 2848 on the taxpayer's behalf if:
1. The original non-IRS Power-of-Attorney grants authority to handle federal tax matters (for example, general authority to perform any acts).
2. The attorney-in-fact attaches a statement (signed under penalty of perjury) to the Form 2848 stating that the original non-IRS Power-of-Attorney is valid under the laws of the governing jurisdiction.

The Form 2848 prepared by the attorney-in-fact should be signed in the following manner: "John Doe (Taxpayer's name), by Jane Attorney (Taxpayer's attorney-in-fact's name) under authority of the attached Power-of-Attorney."

The individual named as representative on Form 2848 must sign and date Part II of the form. This can be the attorney-in-fact named in the original Power-of-Attorney or any other individual recognized to practice before the IRS.

Revocation of Prior Power-of-Attorney

A newly filed Power-of-Attorney concerning the same matter will revoke a previously filed Power-of-Attorney. However, the new Power-of-Attorney will not revoke the prior Power-of-Attorney if it specifically states it does not revoke such prior Power-of-Attorney and either of the following is attached to the new Power-of-Attorney:
(a) A copy of the unrevoked prior Power-of-Attorney, or

(b) A statement signed by the taxpayer listing the name and address of each representative authorized under the prior unrevoked Power-of-Attorney.

Revocation or Withdrawal of Representative

If a taxpayer wishes to revoke an existing Power-of-Attorney and he/she does not want to name a new representative, or if a representative wants to withdraw from a representation, the taxpayer must send a copy of the previously executed Power-of-Attorney to the IRS. The copy of the Power-of-Attorney must have a current signature (under the original signature on line 9) of the taxpayer if the taxpayer is *revoking* or of the representative if the representative is *withdrawing*. Taxpayer must write "**REVOKE**" across the top of Form 2848.

One can revoke a Power-of-Attorney for which a Form 2848 was not filed by writing a letter to that effect and sending it, along with a copy of the original Power-of-Attorney, to each office of the IRS where you originally filed it. A new Power-of-Attorney revokes a prior Power-of-Attorney if it is granted by the taxpayer to another recognized representative with respect to the same matter, unless the new Power-of-Attorney states otherwise and another condition is met. The filing of Form 2848 will not revoke any Form 8821 that is in effect, and vice versa.

If the taxpayer does not have a copy of the Power-of-Attorney needing to be revoked or withdrawn, he or she must send a statement to the office of the IRS where the taxpayer originally filed the Power-of-Attorney.

The statement of revocation or withdrawal must:
    (1) Indicate that the authority of the Power-of-Attorney is revoke.
    (2) List the tax matters and periods.
    (3) Be signed and dated by the taxpayer or representative.

    (i) The taxpayer must list the name and address of each recognized representative whose authority is revoked.
    (ii) When the taxpayer is *completely* revoking authority, the form should state "remove all years/periods", instead of listing the specific tax matters, years, or periods.
    (iii) If the representative is withdrawing, he or she must list the name, TIN, and address (if known) of the taxpayer.
    (iv) A Power-of-Attorney held by a student of a Low Income Taxpayer Clinic (LITC) is valid for only 130 days from the received date and will automatically be revoked. If the taxpayer is authorizing a student to represent him/her after the valid time, a second Form 2848 should be filed for valid representation.

When Power-of-Attorney is **not** required

The following situations <u>do not</u> require a Power-of-Attorney:
    (1) Providing information to the IRS.
    (2) Authorizing the disclosure of tax return information through Form 8821.
    (3) Allowing the IRS to discuss return information with a third-party designee.
    (4) Allowing a tax matters partner or person (TMP) to perform acts for the partnership.

(5) Allowing the IRS to discuss return information with a fiduciary.
(6) Representing a taxpayer through a non-written consent.

Form 8821

Form 8821 authorizes any individual, corporation, firm, organization, or partnership a taxpayer designates, to inspect and/or receive your confidential information in any office of the IRS for the type of tax and the years or periods taxpayers list on Form 8821.

Differences between Form 2848 and Form 8821

Form 2848 (POA)	Form 8821 (TIA)
• Referred to as "Representative"	• Referred to as "Appointee"
• Must be an individual	• May be an individual or a business entity
• Based on eligibility to practice	• Does not have representational authority
• Recorded on Centralized Authorization File (CAF)	• Recorded on the Centralized Authorization File (CAF)
• May allow substitution or re-delegation of representation	
• Taxpayer retains accountability	• Taxpayer retains accountability
• More than three individuals can be designated as representatives.	• More than one individual or business entity can be designated as an appointee.
• If more than three individuals need to be designated as representatives, indicate on Line 2, attach additional Forms 2848 and check line 8.	• If more than one individual/business entity is designated, a list may be attached to the Form 8821, naming the additional appointee(s).

Joint Returns

In the case of any matter concerning a joint return in which both husband and wife are not to be represented by the same recognized representative(s), the Power-of-Attorney must be executed by the spouse who is to be represented.

A Form 2848 and Form 8821 for a jointly filed authorization will be processed by the IRS if after researching each tax year(s), it is determined the tax-year(s) are filed jointly. The year(s) that are not filed jointly will be processed separately, as though each spouse filed a separate Form 2848 or 8821, and will be recorded to their individual taxpayer account. This includes future years covered by the forms.

EXAMPLE:
John and Mary Doe submitted Form 2848 or Form 8821 as joint for tax-years 2002 to 2010. During research, IRS records indicate John and Mary filed single for tax-year 2002. The authorization will be processed as joint for tax-years 2003 through 2009, as John and Mary filed jointly for these years. The authorization will be processed as separate for tax year 2002 and 2010 as John and Mary did not file a joint return together.

Partnerships and Corporations

In the case of a partnership, a Power-of-Attorney must be executed by all partners, or if executed in the name of the partnership, by the partner or partners duly authorized to act for the partnership. The partner or partners must certify that they have such authority. If a dissolved partnership is involved, each of the former living partners must execute a Power-of-Attorney. If a corporation is involved, the Power-of-Attorney must be executed by an officer of the corporation having authority to legally bind the corporation. The officer must certify that (s)he has such authority.

3.04 THE CENTRALIZED AUTHORIZATION FILE (CAF)

The Centralized Authorization File (CAF) is an electronic database containing tax practitioner records. A CAF number is assigned to a tax practitioner when a Form 2848 or Form 8821 is filed. This number represents a file that contains information regarding the type of authorization that taxpayers have given representatives for the various modules within their accounts.

The CAF contains:
(1) Minimal taxpayer information (name and taxpayer information number). Taxpayer's address and phone information are <u>not</u> recorded on the CAF.
(2) Third-party name, address, telephone number, fax number, types of authorization levels, and CAF status information such as revocations, deletions, suspension, disbarment, and undeliverable.
(3) A summary of the types of tax form and tax period(s).

The CAF maintains an electronic record of an authorization. An authorization which has already been recorded on the CAF may be updated at any time. The authorization must contain current dated signatures from both the taxpayer(s) and their representative(s) to evidence current intent.

Information recorded onto the CAF system enables IRS personnel who do not have a copy of the actual Power-of-Attorney or tax information authorization to verify the authority of the taxpayer's representative. If a representative wants his/her non-IRS Power-of-Attorney entered into the CAF, the representative should attach it to a completed "transmittal" Form 2848 and submit it to the IRS. A Power-of-Attorney will not be rejected based on the absence of a CAF number.

The maximum number of third-party representatives that may be recorded on the CAF per tax module is 50. A maximum of 2 third-parties can be designated to receive notices; however, only one representative may receive refunds per tax module. The CAF database accepts up to 3 future years.

Entry onto the Centralized Authorization File (CAF) system enables IRS employees who do not have access to the actual Power-of-Attorney or tax information authorization to:

a) Determine whether a recognized representative or appointee is authorized to discuss specific confidential tax information;
b) Determine the extent to which a recognized representative or appointee has been authorized to represent a taxpayer; and
c) Send copies of notices and other IRS communications to the person (individual or other entity) designated on the form.

CAF Number

- A CAF number is a unique number that will be assigned to any person who files with the IRS a Power-of-Attorney and a written declaration that (s)he is currently qualified to practice before the IRS and is authorized to represent the particular party on whose behalf (s)he acts. A CAF number will be assigned to any person who files with the IRS a tax information authorization.
- A third-party can request multiple CAF numbers in order to differentiate between multiple office addresses.
- Requests for multiple locations or CAF numbers must be received as separate correspondence. The request must be in writing and contain:
    (1) third-party name, name variations, and aliases
    (2) Existing CAF numbers and corresponding address(es)
    (3) A request for additional CAF number(s) and corresponding address(es)
    (4) A third-party dated signature
- A third-party can also request multiple CAF numbers in order to differentiate between related entities, e.g., "John Smith" versus "The Firm of John Smith" and/or "the Firm of John Smith".

Authorizations Recorded on the CAF

1. Authorizations recorded on the CAF are generally submitted on Form 2848 (Power-of-Attorney and Declaration of Representative), Form 706 (U.S. Estate Tax Return), and Form 8821 (Tax Information Authorization). Form 2848 and Form 8821 can be processed directly to the CAF by qualifying representatives via the Internet using the Disclosure Authorization (DA) program.
2. CAF examiners do not verify the credentials or practice status of the party listed as a representative on Form 2848. The Office of Professional Responsibility determines credentials and practice status. A Power-of-Attorney that <u>does not</u> include a CAF number will <u>not be</u> rejected.
3. Authorizations <u>not</u> processed to the CAF include but are not limited to:
    (a) Checkbox Authority
    (b) Form 8655
    (c) CP 2000
    (d) Requests for a private letter ruling or technical advice.
    (e) Applications for an employer identification number (EIN).
    (f) Claims filed on Form 843, Claim for Refund and Request for Abatement.
    (g) Corporate dissolutions.

(h) Requests for change of accounting method.
(i) Requests for change of accounting period.

E-Services Disclosure Authorization

Form 2848 and Form 8821, can be processed directly to the CAF by qualifying representatives via the Internet using the *Disclosure Authorization* (DA) program.

Only the following 3 types of practitioners qualify for Disclosure Authorization through e-Services:
   (1) Attorney - Any person who is a member in good standing of the bar of the highest court of any State, territory, or possession of the United States, including a Commonwealth or the District of Columbia.
   (2) Certified Public Accountant (CPA) - Any person who is duly qualified to practice as a certified public accountant in any State, territory, or possession of the United States, including a Commonwealth, or the District of Columbia.
   (3) Enrolled Agent - Any person who has earned the privilege of practicing or representing taxpayers before the IRS. Enrolled agents, like attorneys and certified public accountants (CPAs), are unrestricted as to which taxpayers they can represent, what types of tax matters they can handle, and before which IRS offices they can practice.

Eligible tax professionals may electronically submit Form 2848 and Form 8821 as well as view and modify existing forms online. Disclosure Authorization allows tax professionals to expedite processing and issues a real-time acknowledgement of accepted submissions. Form 8655 (Reporting Agent Authorization for Magnetic Tape/Electronic Filers) cannot be submitted using Disclosure Authorization (IRM 21.3.7.1).

3.05 UNIT 3: QUESTIONS

TRUE/FALSE
Please select either (A) for True or (B) for False

1. Dave operates a retail business as a sole proprietorship with stores in several locations in the Toledo, Ohio area. The books and records for all of the stores are maintained at the main store near his residence. Dave's tax returns have always been prepared by his long time accountant in Toledo. Dave has been notified that his 2009 Income tax return has been selected for an examination. Dave's brother-in-law in Detroit, Michigan, a district away, has just passed the Enrolled Agent's examination and Dave's wife would like him to handle the examination. The IRS will likely approve a transfer to the Detroit office, provided a properly executed form 2848 is submitted with the request.
    A. TRUE
    B. FALSE

2. A representative named under a Power-of-Attorney is not permitted to sign your personal tax return unless
   (i) The signature is permitted under the Internal Revenue Code, and
   (ii) You authorize the signature in your Power-of-Attorney.
    A. TRUE
    B. FALSE

3. A representative having a Power-of-Attorney is permitted to endorse a refund check if the taxpayer authorizes the representative to receive it.
    A. TRUE
    B. FALSE

4. Any notice or other written communication required or permitted to be given to a taxpayer in any matter before the IRS may be given to the representative instead of the taxpayer.
    A. TRUE
    B. FALSE

5. Only an attorney, certified public accountant, or enrolled agent may use Form 2848, Power-of-Attorney and Declaration of Representatives.
    A. TRUE
    B. FALSE

6. Form 8821, Tax Information Authorization, can be used when you want to authorize an individual to represent you before the IRS.
    A. TRUE
    B. FALSE

7. A taxpayer's representative who is enrolled to practice before the IRS and has the taxpayer's properly executed general Power-of-Attorney, Form 2848, can sign a waiver agreeing to a tax adjustment on behalf of the taxpayer.
    A. TRUE
    B. FALSE

8. A Power-of-Attorney is required to be submitted by an individual other than the attorney of record in any matter before the IRS concerning a case docketed in the United States Tax Court.
    A. TRUE
    B. FALSE

9. An enrolled agent who is an income tax return preparer may endorse or otherwise negotiate a check that is payable to a taxpayer/client as long as the Power-of-Attorney signed by the taxpayer/client expressly authorizes such acts.
    A. TRUE
    B. FALSE

10. A Form 2848, "Power-of-Attorney and Declaration of Representative," has a provision that will allow the taxpayer to authorize an Attorney, CPA, and Enrolled Agent to receive and endorse a refund check on behalf of the taxpayer.
    A. TRUE
    B. FALSE

11. The filing of Form 8821 will revoke any Form 2848 that is in effect.
    A. TRUE
    B. FALSE

12. Entry onto the Centralized Authorization File (CAF) system enables IRS employees who do not have access to the actual Power-of-Attorney or tax information authorization to do **all** of the following:
    (i) Determine whether a recognized representative or appointee is authorized to discuss specific confidential tax information;
    (ii) Determine the extent to which a recognized representative or appointee has been authorized to represent a taxpayer; and
    (iii) Send copies of notices and other IRS communications to the person (individual or other entity) designated on the form.
    A. TRUE
    B. FALSE

13. Form 8821, "Tax Information Authorization," is used to allow disclosure of tax return information to third parties and limited representation by an unenrolled preparer.
    A. TRUE

B. FALSE

14. John Bitter wants his associate, Bill Sweet, to be informed about his business tax account. John wants to disclose only this information, and grant no other authority. Form 8821 Tax Information Authorization should not be used in this situation because it would allow Bill to represent John.
    A. TRUE
    B. FALSE

15. A Power-of-Attorney is required when you want to authorize another to represent you at a conference with the IRS, or prepare and file a written response to the IRS.
    A. TRUE
    B. FALSE

16. Generally a newly filed Power-of-Attorney concerning the same matter does **not** revoke the previous Power-of-Attorney. The new representative is automatically added to the list of authorized representatives.
    A. TRUE
    B. FALSE

17. A representative may be added to an existing Power-of-Attorney by telephoning the IRS service center where the related return or the original Power-of-Attorney was filed.
    A. TRUE
    B. FALSE

18. A practitioner, who holds a Power-of-Attorney, may cash a taxpayer's federal income tax refund check.
    A. TRUE
    B. FALSE

19. John prepares tax returns. John is **not** an enrolled agent, enrolled actuary, CPA, or attorney. In 2000, new clients, Mr. and Mrs. Black, engage John to prepare their 1999 joint income tax return. John prepares the Black's 1999 joint income tax return and signs it as the preparer. This is the only return John has prepared for the Blacks. In March of 2001, Mr. and Mrs. Black received a notice from the IRS with regard to their 1998 joint income tax return. Mr. and Mrs. Black ask John to contact the IRS to resolve the matter with regard to their 1998 joint income tax return, but do not provide John with a Power-of-Attorney. John is not permitted to represent or advocate a position before the IRS on behalf of Mr. and Mrs. Black concerning their 1998 return.
    A. TRUE
    B. FALSE

20. A Power-of-Attorney may be filed with the IRS by a facsimile transmission (FAX).
    A. TRUE
    B. FALSE

21. A Power-of-Attorney may **not** be used to authorize a recognized representative to receive the original of notices sent to the taxpayer by the IRS.
    A. TRUE
    B. FALSE

22. Each new Power-of-Attorney (Form 2848) revokes all prior Power-of-Attorneys regardless of the matter it pertains to.
    A. TRUE
    B. FALSE

23. A tax representative may be authorized to receive a refund check for a client if that authorization is on Form 2848.
    A. TRUE
    B. FALSE

24. A Centralized Authorization File (CAF) is an automated file containing information regarding the authority of an individual appointed under a Power-of-Attorney or person designated under a tax information authorization.
    A. TRUE
    B. FALSE

25. The issuance of a CAF number does not indicate that a person is either recognized or authorized to practice before the IRS.
    A. TRUE
    B. FALSE

26. The filing of a Form 2848 terminates all previously filed tax information authorizations.
    A. TRUE
    B. FALSE

27. Jim, a tax return preparer, has several clients who travel extensively. They have requested that all returns and correspondence with the IRS bear their preparer's address so that he can handle their tax matters timely. Several have given Jim power-of-attorney. From time-to-time, a refund check will be received for one of these clients and Jim will deposit it to that client's account. Jim has not violated the prohibition against endorsing or otherwise negotiating a refund check of a return he prepared.
    A. TRUE
    B. FALSE

28. The purpose of a CAF number is to give IRS personnel quicker access to authorization information.
    A. TRUE
    B. FALSE

29. Only under very limited circumstances, as described in the instructions to Form 2848, may a taxpayer authorize an Attorney, CPA or Enrolled Agent to receive and endorse a refund check on behalf of the taxpayer.
    A. TRUE
    B. FALSE

30. Form 2848 is used to appoint a representative to act on a taxpayer's behalf before the IRS. Form 2848 is filed only if the taxpayer wants to name a person(s) to represent them, and that person is a person recognized to practice before the IRS.
    A. TRUE
    B. FALSE

31. Form 2848, Power-of-Attorney and Declaration of Representative, properly executed by the taxpayer, permits the taxpayer's representative to make substitution of representatives without the taxpayer's specific grant of authority to do so.
    A. TRUE
    B. FALSE

32. A properly executed Power-of-Attorney can be used in connection with more than one particular type of tax.
    A. TRUE
    B. FALSE

33. A tax information authorization is not required of a taxpayer's representative at a conference with IRS officials that is also attended by the taxpayer.
    A. TRUE
    B. FALSE

34. An attorney, a certified public accountant, or a person enrolled to practice before the IRS is not required to file a Power-of-Attorney in any form to receive or inspect confidential information about his/her client's tax matters.
    A. TRUE
    B. FALSE

35. A Power-of-Attorney is not required for a practitioner to sign a waiver of notice of disallowance of a claim for credit or a refund.
    A. TRUE
    B. FALSE

36. A single Form 2848, Power-of-Attorney and Declaration of Representative, may not cover more than one tax matter or more than one taxable year.
    A. TRUE
    B. FALSE

37. If a Power-of-Attorney has been filed, a new Power-of-Attorney must be filed if the taxpayer changes the authority granted to a representative.
    A. TRUE
    B. FALSE

38. A taxpayer may revoke a Power-of-Attorney without authorizing a new representative by filing a statement of revocation with those offices of the IRS where the taxpayer originally filed the Power-of-Attorney.
    A. TRUE
    B. FALSE

MULTIPLE CHOICE QUESTIONS:
Please select the most appropriate answer.

39. A properly executed Form 2848, Power-of-Attorney and Declaration of Representative, is required to allow a representative to perform all of the following except
    A. Sign a waiver agreeing to an income tax adjustment.
    B. Sign a consent to extend the statutory time period for assessment of tax.
    C. Execute closing agreements.
    D. Request the disclosure of confidential tax return information.

40. A Power-of-Attorney is required in all of the following situations except to:
    A. Represent an individual at a conference with the IRS.
    B. File a written response to the IRS on behalf of another individual.
    C. Sign a consent to extend the statute of limitations on behalf of another individual.
    D. Furnish copies of preexisting documents at the request of the IRS.

41. With respect to powers of attorney, which of the following statements is false?
    A. The IRS will accept a facsimile (fax) copy of a Power-of-Attorney if the appropriate IRS office is equipped to receive it.
    B. IRS Form 2848, Power-of-Attorney and Declaration of Representative, cannot be used by a taxpayer to appoint an unenrolled return preparer to act as the taxpayer's representative before agents and examining officers of the Examination Division of the IRS.
    C. A taxpayer's signature on a Power-of-Attorney does not have to be notarized or witnessed.

D. A taxpayer can execute a durable Power-of-Attorney, which specifies that the appointment of the attorney-in-fact will not end due to the incapacity or incompetency of the taxpayer.

42. If a representative chooses to use a non-IRS Power-of-Attorney form, which of the following "Declaration of Representative" statements is not required in order for the Power-of-Attorney to be valid?

    A. A declaration that the representative is not currently under suspension or disbarment from practice before the IRS or other practice of his/her profession by any other authority.
    B. A declaration that the representative is aware of the regulations contained in Treasury Department Circular 230 concerning the practice of enrolled agents, attorneys, CPAs, etc.
    C. A declaration that the representative is not currently under investigation by the IRS.
    D. A declaration that the representative is authorized to practice before the IRS in his/her capacity as an attorney, a certified public accountant, an enrolled agent, etc.

43. Which of the following is true regarding a refund check?
    A. Form 2848, Power-of-Attorney, may be used to authorize cashing of a refund check.
    B. Form 2848, Power-of-Attorney, may be used to authorize receipt of a refund check.
    C. Form 8821, Tax Information Authorization, must be signed before a refund check may be applied to a fee for electronic filing.
    D. Both Form 2848 and Form 8821 must be used to authorize cashing a refund check.

44. A declaration of representative, which accompanies a Power-of-Attorney, includes all of the following statements except
    A. I am authorized to represent the taxpayer(s) identified in the Power-of-Attorney.
    B. I am aware of the regulations in Circular 230.
    C. I am an individual described in 26 CFR 601.502(a) (such as an attorney, a CPA, an enrolled agent, etc.).
    D. I have never been sanctioned (e.g., reprimand, suspension, or disbarment) by the Director of Practice.

45. A representative who signs a Form 2848, Power-of-Attorney, declares under penalty of perjury that he or she is aware of which of the following?
    A. The federal income tax regulations.
    B. The regulations in Treasury Department Circular No. 230.

- C. Recent tax law developments that relate to the tax matter(s) listed on line 3 of the Form 2848.
- D. All of the answers are correct.

46. A taxpayer must use a Power-of-Attorney to do which of the following?
    A. Authorize an individual to prepare the taxpayer's return.
    B. Authorize an individual to represent a taxpayer at a conference with the IRS.
    C. Authorize the IRS to disclose tax information to an individual.
    D. Authorize an individual to provide information to the IRS.

47. Who is authorized to practice before the IRS if (s)he holds Power-of-Attorney?
    A. Any person considered an enrolled agent under Circular 230, who is not currently under suspension or disbarment from practice before the IRS who files a written declaration that he or she is currently qualified as an enrolled agent and is authorized to represent the particular party on whose behalf he or she acts.
    B. Any attorney who is not currently under suspension or disbarment from practice before the IRS who files a written declaration that he or she is currently qualified as an attorney and is authorized to represent the particular party on whose behalf he or she acts.
    C. Any person considered an enrolled agent under Circular 230 or an attorney who is not currently under suspension or disbarment from practice before the IRS who files a written declaration that he or she is currently qualified as an enrolled agent or an attorney and is authorized to represent the particular party on whose behalf (s)he acts.
    D. None of the answers are correct.

48. A Power-of-Attorney is required when a taxpayer wishes to authorize a recognized representative to perform one or more of the following services on behalf of the taxpayer, except to
    A. Execute a closing agreement.
    B. Request confidential tax return information.
    C. Represent the taxpayer before an appeals officer.
    D. Execute a consent to extend the statutory period of assessment.

49. With regard to revoking a Power-of-Attorney, which of the following statements is false?
    A. You can revoke a Form 2848 Power-of-Attorney by sending a copy of the original Form 2848 to each office of the IRS where you originally filed the form. You must write the word "REVOKE" at the top center of page 1 and sign and date the form at the bottom of page 2.
    B. A new Power-of-Attorney revokes a prior Power-of-Attorney if it is granted by the taxpayer to another recognized representative with respect to the same

matter, unless the new Power-of-Attorney states otherwise and another condition is met.
C. You can revoke a Power-of-Attorney for which a Form 2848 was not filed by writing a letter to that effect and sending it, along with a copy of the original Power-of-Attorney, to each office of the IRS where you originally filed it.
D. A recognized representative may revoke a Power-of-Attorney by filing a statement to that effect and sending it to each office of the IRS where the Power-of-Attorney was originally filed. The statement must be signed by the representative and the taxpayer.

50. A Power-of-Attorney is required when you want to authorize any individual to do the following.
A. To represent you at a conference with the IRS.
B. To prepare and file a written response to the IRS.
C. To sign the offer or a waiver of restriction on assessment or collection of tax deficiency.
D. All of the answers are correct.

51. According to the Conference and Practice Requirements, all of the following tax matters may be reflected on a Power-of-Attorney except
A. Forms 1040 for all years.
B. 2002, 2003, 2004 Forms 1040.
C. Forms 941 for all 4 tax quarters of 2004.
D. 2003 Form 940.

52. Phil, an enrolled agent, prepares William's income tax return. William gives Phil Power-of-Attorney, including the authorization to receive his federal income tax refund check. Accordingly, the IRS sends William's $100 refund check to Phil's office. William is very slow in paying his bills and owes Phil $500 for tax services. Phil should
A. Use William's check as collateral for a $100 loan to tide him over until William pays him.
B. Refuse to give William the check until William pays him the $500.
C. Get William's written authorization to endorse the check, cash the check, and reduce the amount William owes him to $400.
D. Turn the check directly over to William.

53. Which of the following statements with respect to executing a Power-of-Attorney is false?
A. The IRS will accept a Power-of-Attorney other than Form 2848 provided such document satisfies the requirements of Reg. 601.504(a).
B. In the case of any matter concerning a joint return in which both husband and wife are not to be represented by the same recognized representative(s), the Power-of-Attorney must be executed by the spouse who is to be represented.

C. In the case of a corporation, a Power-of-Attorney may be executed only by the officer or employee who signs the return.
D. In the case of a partnership, a Power-of-Attorney must be executed by all partners, or if executed in the name of the partnership, by the partner or partners duly authorized to act for the partnership. The partner or partners must certify that they have such authority.

54. The filing of a Power-of-Attorney does not authorize the recognized representative to sign a tax return on behalf of the taxpayer unless such act is
    A. Permitted under the Internal Revenue Code and the regulations thereunder.
    B. Specifically authorized in the Power-of-Attorney.
    C. Neither permitted under the Internal Revenue Code and the pertinent regulations nor specifically authorized in the Power-of-Attorney.
    D. Both permitted under the Internal Revenue Code and the regulations there under and specifically authorized in the Power-of-Attorney.

55. Regarding a Tax Information Authorization, Form 8821, which of the following statements is true?
    A. The appointee can advocate the taxpayer's position.
    B. The appointee can execute waivers.
    C. The appointee can represent the taxpayer by correspondence.
    D. None of the answers are correct.

56. Which of the following would not allow the IRS to disclose the results of an examination of your 2005 1040 to the return preparer of the 2005 return?
    A. You submit a Power-of-Attorney, Form 2848, with the IRS authorizing representation by your return preparer for income tax matters for tax years 2003, 2004, and 2005.
    B. You submit a tax information authorization, Form 8821, with the IRS for your return preparer for income tax matters for the tax year 2005.
    C. You checked the Yes box in the third party designee area of the 2005 tax return and entered "Preparer" after the return preparer's name in the designee space.
    D. Your return preparer is also your legal guardian and submits a Form 56, Notice Concerning Fiduciary Relationship.

57. With regard to the declaration of the representative on a Power-of-Attorney, all of the following statements are true, except:
    A. A fiduciary is required to show his/her relationship.
    B. An attorney must indicate the state in which (s)he is admitted to practice.
    C. A CPA must include the state in which (s)he is licensed to practice.
    D. A full-time employee must show his/her title.

58. A Power-of-Attorney must contain all of the following information except the
    A. Type of tax involved.
    B. Specific year(s)/period(s) involved.
    C. Identification number of the representative (i.e., Social Security number and/or employer identification number).
    D. Name and mailing address of the recognized representative(s).

59. Which of the following is false regarding the execution of a Power-of-Attorney?
    A. In the case of a partnership (that is not dissolved), the Power-of-Attorney must be executed by the partner or partners duly authorized to act for the partnership. The partner or partners must certify that they have such authority.
    B. If a joint return is involved in which both the husband and wife are to be represented by the same representative(s), either the husband or the wife alone can execute the Power-of-Attorney.
    C. If a corporation is involved, the Power-of-Attorney must be executed by an officer of the corporation having authority to legally bind the corporation. The officer must certify that (s)he has such authority.
    D. If a dissolved partnership is involved, each of the former living partners must execute a Power-of-Attorney.

60. All of the following statements regarding changes to powers of attorney are true except
    A. A recognized representative may withdraw from representation in a matter in which a Power-of-Attorney has been filed.
    B. A taxpayer may revoke a Power-of-Attorney without authorizing a new representative.
    C. If specifically authorized on the Power-of-Attorney, a recognized representative may delegate authority to another recognized representative.
    D. After a substitution of a representative is made, both the old representative and the newly recognized representatives will be considered the taxpayer's representative.

61. Nancy, who is enrolled to practice before the IRS, has been granted Power-of-Attorney to represent Lee in a matter before the IRS. Nancy wants to delegate that authority to another representative. Regarding this substitution of authority, which of the following statements is false?
    A. The Power-of-Attorney, whether it is IRS Form 2848, Power-of-Attorney and Declaration of Representative, or a non-IRS Power-of-Attorney, must specifically provide that Nancy can substitute her authority.
    B. The new representative must be an individual who is recognized to practice before the IRS.
    C. The new representative must file a written declaration in accordance with the regulations with the appropriate IRS offices.
    D. Nancy need only file a signed statement (notice of substitution or delegation) with the appropriate IRS offices.

62. A properly executed Power-of-Attorney must contain all of the following except
    A. Identification number of the taxpayer (i.e., Social Security number or employer identification number).
    B. The specific year(s) and period(s) involved.
    C. Name of the preparer of the return for the year(s) and period(s) involved.
    D. Signature of the appointed representative.

63. Judith wants to revoke a Power-of-Attorney that she previously executed and does not want to name a new representative. In order to do this, what is Judith's most appropriate action?
    A. Judith must call the IRS toll free number, verify that she is Judith, and inform them she wants to revoke the current Power-of-Attorney that is on file.
    B. Judith must send a letter to her nearest IRS Center informing them that she wants to revoke the current Power-of-Attorney that is on file.
    C. Judith must send a copy of the previously executed Power-of-Attorney to the IRS (with an original signature) and write "REVOKE" across the top of the Power-of-Attorney.
    D. Judith must send a new Power-of-Attorney to the IRS office(s) where the prior power was originally filed and name herself as the representative.

64. A Centralized Authorization File (CAF) number may be issued to which of the following?
    A. An attorney licensed by the state of Texas who represents taxpayers before the IRS solely at IRS offices in Texas.
    B. An attorney licensed by the state of Texas who files powers of attorney at the Austin Service Center.
    C. A financial advisor named as a designee in a tax information authorization.
    D. All of the answers are correct.

65. Which of the following is false with respect to the IRS's Centralized Authorization File (CAF)?
    A. The issuance of a CAF number indicates that a person is either recognized or authorized to practice before the IRS under the provisions of Treasury Department Circular 230.
    B. A Power-of-Attorney will not be rejected based on the absence of a CAF number.
    C. Information recorded onto the CAF system enables IRS personnel who do not have a copy of the actual Power-of-Attorney or tax information authorization to verify the authority of the taxpayer's representative.
    D. If a representative wants his/her non-IRS Power-of-Attorney entered into the CAF, the representative should attach it to a completed "transmittal" Form 2848 and submit it to the IRS.

66. What is the purpose of the Centralized Authorization File (CAF) number?
    A. Before the PTIN, this was the number a preparer would use to sign an electronically filed return.

    B. The CAF number is another means of tracing enrolled agents.
    C. Use of the CAF number allows the IRS to verify an individual's authority to practice before the IRS.
    D. None of the answers are correct.

67. With regard to the Centralized Authorization File (CAF) number on powers of attorney, which of the following is true?
    A. Powers of attorney that relate to specific tax periods, or to any other Federal tax matter such as application for an employee identification number, will be entered onto the CAF system.
    B. A CAF number is an indication of authority to practice before the IRS.
    C. The fact that a Power-of-Attorney cannot be entered onto the CAF system affects its validity.
    D. A Power-of-Attorney that does not include a CAF number will not be rejected.

68. Which of the following statements with respect to the IRS's Centralized Authorization File (CAF) is false?
    A. The issuance of a CAF number does not indicate that a person is recognized or authorized to practice before the IRS.
    B. Information from both powers of attorney and tax information authorizations is recorded onto the CAF system.
    C. A tax information authorization or Power-of-Attorney will be rejected based on the absence of a CAF number.
    D. Only documents that concern a matter relating to a specific tax period that ends no later than 3 years after the date a Power-of-Attorney is received by the IRS will be recorded onto the CAF system.

69. Receipt of a Centralized Authorization File (CAF) number indicates which, if any, of the following with respect to the recipient?
    A. Recognition or authorization to represent taxpayers before the IRS.
    B. Certification that an enrolled agent is in an "active" status according to the Office of Director of Practice records.
    C. Receipt by the IRS of certification from a state that an attorney or a CPA has completed continuing professional education requirements and possesses a current license.
    D. None of the answers are correct.

70. You have a durable Power-of-Attorney--not a Form 2848--that contains all information required for validity under the Conference and Practice Requirements. In order to have the IRS enter this durable Power-of-Attorney onto the Centralized Authorization File, you must submit
    A. The durable Power-of-Attorney and Form 8821, Tax Information Authorization.
    B. The durable Power-of-Attorney and your Social Security number.
    C. The durable Power-of-Attorney and a completed Form 2848.

D. The durable Power-of-Attorney and Form 8821, Tax Information Authorization AND the durable Power-of-Attorney and your Social Security number.

71. All of the following statements concerning the IRS's Centralized Authorization File (CAF) number are true except
    A. The CAF number entitles the person to whom it is assigned to practice before any office of the IRS except a regional appeals office.
    B. The CAF allows IRS personnel to identify representatives and the scope of their authority and will automatically direct copies of notices and correspondence to the person authorized by the taxpayer.
    C. A CAF number is a unique number that will be assigned to any person who files with the IRS a Power-of-Attorney and a written declaration that (s)he is currently qualified to practice before the IRS and is authorized to represent the particular party on whose behalf (s)he acts.
    D. A CAF number is a unique number that will be assigned to any person who files with the IRS a tax information authorization.

72. Which of the following is not a proper execution of a Power-of-Attorney or tax information authorization?
    A. For a corporation, by an officer having authority to bind the corporation.
    B. For a deceased taxpayer, by the executor or administrator.
    C. For a taxpayer with a court-appointed guardian, by the one appointed.
    D. For a partnership, by any partner.

73. A Power-of-Attorney or tax information authorization should contain all of the following information except
    A. The taxpayer's intent as to the scope of authority of the representative.
    B. The divisions of the IRS that are involved in the matter covered by the Power-of-Attorney.
    C. The type of tax involved.
    D. The year(s) or period(s).

74. With regard to powers of attorney, which of the following statements is false?
    A. Form 2848, Power-of-Attorney and Declaration of Representative, can be used to appoint an unenrolled return preparer as a taxpayer's representative before revenue agents and examining officers of the Examination Division of the IRS.
    B. A taxpayer's representative can receive and endorse the taxpayer's check related to income tax from the U.S. Treasury if so authorized on the taxpayer's Power-of-Attorney, Form 2848.
    C. A document other than Form 2848 can be used to appoint a Power-of-Attorney if it contains the information required by the IRS.
    D. A taxpayer can execute a durable Power-of-Attorney, which specifies that the appointment of the attorney-in-fact will not end due to the incapacity or incompetency of the taxpayer.

75. If a Power-of-Attorney specifically authorizes the substitution of a recognized representative, which document need not be submitted to the IRS?
    A. A written declaration of representative executed by the new representative.
    B. A notice of substitution filed by the original representative.
    C. The original Power-of-Attorney.
    D. A notarized letter from the taxpayer advising the IRS that the authorization to substitute remains valid.

76. With regard to Centralized Authorization File (CAF) numbers, which of the following statements is true?
    A. The CAF number is entered into the IRS database, which allows the IRS to send copies of notices to the representative.
    B. A CAF number copy of notices indicates that an individual is either recognized or authorized to practice before the IRS.
    C. A CAF number is assigned only to enrolled agents, CPAs, and attorneys.
    D. A Power-of-Attorney submitted without a CAF number will be rejected based on the absence of a CAF number.

77. With regard to Centralized Authorization File (CAF) numbers, which of the following statements is false?
    A. The issuance of a CAF number does not indicate that a person is either recognized or authorized to practice before the IRS.
    B. The purpose of the CAF number is to facilitate the processing of a Power-of-Attorney or a tax information authorization submitted by a recognized representative or designee.
    C. A recognized representative or a designee should include the same CAF number on every Power-of-Attorney or tax information authorization filed.
    D. A tax information authorization or Power-of-Attorney that does not include a CAF number will be rejected based on the absence of that number.

78. A Power-of-Attorney is required in all of the following circumstances, except.
    A. To furnish information at the request of the IRS.
    B. To authorize the extension of the statute of limitations.
    C. To execute a closing agreement under Sec. 7121.
    D. To receive a refund check.

79. Tax return information is typically confidential; disclosure of return information is permitted to all of the following parties EXCEPT:
    A. Congressional committees.
    B. Relatives of the taxpayer.
    C. A person designated by the taxpayer.
    D. State tax officials.

80. Margaret Smith is a CPA who is representing John & Mary Jones before the Wage and Investment Division of the IRS. The Service is questioning John & Mary on contributions that were listed on page 2 of their 2004 Form 1040. While reviewing the documentation provided by John & Mary, Margaret discovers contributions that were made to a non-qualified organization. What is the appropriate action for Margaret to take?
    A. Margaret must advise John & Mary on how to keep the omission from being discovered by the IRS.
    B. Margaret must notify the IRS that she is no longer representing John & Mary by withdrawing her Form 2848.
    C. Margaret must advise John & Mary promptly of the omission and the consequences provided by the Internal Revenue Code and Regulations for such omission.
    D. Margaret must immediately advise the IRS examiner of the non-qualified contributions.

81. Judith wants to revoke a Power-of-Attorney that she previously executed and does not want to name a new representative. In order to do this, what is Judith's most appropriate action?
    A. Judith must call the IRS toll free number, verify that she is Judith and inform them she wants to revoke the current Power-of-Attorney that is on file.
    B. Judith must send a letter to her nearest IRS Center informing them that she wants to revoke the current Power-of-Attorney that is on file.
    C. Judith must send a copy of the previously executed Power-of-Attorney to the IRS (with an original signature) and write "REVOKE" across the top of the Power-of-Attorney.
    D. Judith must send a new Power-of-Attorney to the IRS office(s) where the prior power was originally filed and name herself as the representative.

82. Which of the following is correct regarding a refund check?
    A. Form 2848, Power-of-Attorney, may be used to authorize cashing of a refund check.
    B. Form 2848, Power-of-Attorney, may be used to authorize receipt a refund check.
    C. Form 8821, Tax Information Authorization must be signed before a refund check may be applied to a fee for electronic filing.
    D. Both Form 2848 and Form 8821 must be used to authorize cashing a refund check.

83. Who is authorized to practice before the IRS if they hold Power-of-Attorney?
    A. Any person considered an enrolled agent under Circular 230, who is not currently under suspension or disbarment from practice before the IRS who files a written declaration that he or she is currently qualified as an enrolled agent and is authorized to represent the particular party on whose behalf he or she acts.

B. Any attorney who is not currently under suspension or disbarment from practice before the IRS who files a written declaration that he or she is currently qualified as an attorney and is authorized to represent the particular party on whose behalf he or she acts.
C. Both A and B.
D. Neither A or B.

84. Janet is not an enrolled agent, CPA, attorney, or enrolled actuary. In 1999, the president of Widgets-R-Us engaged Janet to prepare the company's 1998 Form 1120-S. Janet prepared the 1998 income tax return for Widgets-R-Us and signed it as the preparer. This is the only return Janet prepared for Widgets-R-Us. In December 2000, the IRS began an examination of Widgets-R-Us' 1997 and 1998 Federal income tax returns. Janet has a Power-of-Attorney to represent Widgets-R-Us for 1997 and 1998. Under Circular 230, Janet is permitted to represent Widgets- R-Us during the examination with regard to its:
A. 1997 Form 1120-S only.
B. 1998 Form 1120-S only.
C. 1997 and 1998 Forms 1120-S.
D. None of the above.

85. For taxpayers that want someone to represent them in their absence at an examination or at an appeal within the IRS, all of the following statements are **correct** except:
A. The taxpayer must furnish that representative with written authorization on Form 2848, Power-of-Attorney and Declaration of Representative, or any other properly written authorization.
B. The representative can be an attorney, certified public accountant, or an enrolled agent.
C. The representative can be anyone who helped the taxpayer prepares the return.
D. Even if the taxpayer appointed a representative, the taxpayer may attend the examination or appeals conference and may act on his or her own behalf.

86. With regard to the declaration of the representative on a power or attorney, all of the following statements are true, except:
A. A fiduciary is required to show his/her relationship.
B. An attorney must indicate the State in which he/she is admitted to practice.
C. A CPA must include the State in which he/she is licensed to practice.
D. A full time employee must show his/her title.

3.06   UNIT 3: ANSWERS

1. **(B) Correct**
   Form 2848, Power-of-Attorney and Declaration of Representative, is a legal document used to authorize an individual to represent a taxpayer before the IRS and authorize the IRS to release confidential tax information to an individual for the account matters(s) specified. Form 2848 (Power-of-Attorney and Declaration of Representative) can only be granted to an individual eligible to practice before the Internal Revenue Service (e.g. Attorney, CPA or Enrolled Agent). Merely passing the EA Exam does not mean that a candidate has the authority to represent someone. After a person has passed both the exam and a background check, the Director of the office of responsibility will issue a certificate of enrolled which will allow such person to practice before the IRS.

2. **(A) Correct**
   The representative named under a Power-of-Attorney is not permitted to sign the taxpayer's personal income tax return unless both of the following exist:
   (a) The signature is permitted under the Internal Revenue Code and the related regulations.
   (b) The taxpayer *specifically* authorizes the representative's signature through the Power-of-Attorney.

3. **(B) Correct**
   Any representative, other than an unenrolled preparer, can perform the following acts on behalf of the taxpayer:
   (i) Represent taxpayer before any office of the IRS.
   (ii) Record the interview.
   (iii) Sign an offer or a waiver of restriction on assessment or collection of a tax deficiency, or a waiver of notice of disallowance of claim for credit or refund.
   (iv) Sign a consent to extend the statutory time period for assessment or collection of a tax.
   (v) Sign a closing agreement.
   (vi) Receive, but not endorse or cash, a refund check drawn on the U.S. Treasury. The taxpayer must specifically *initial* Form 2848 showing the name of the individual designated to receive the refund check.

4. **(B) Correct**
   Any notice or other written communication required or permitted to be given to a taxpayer in any matter before the IRS may be given to the representative as well as the taxpayer. The representative alone may not receive the notice or other written communication.

5. **(B) Correct**
   Form 2848 (Power-of-Attorney and Declaration of Representative) can only be granted to an individual eligible to practice before the Internal Revenue Service. This includes unenrolled agents.

6. **(B) Correct**
   Form 8821, Tax Information Authorization, only authorizes an appointee to receive certain confidential tax information. Form 2848, Power-of-Attorney and Declaration of Representative, is used to authorize an individual to represent a taxpayer before the IRS.

7. **(A) Correct**
   Any representative, other than an unenrolled preparer, can perform the following acts on behalf of the taxpayer:
   (i) Represent taxpayer before any office of the IRS.
   (ii) Record the interview.
   (iii) Sign an offer or a waiver of restriction on assessment or collection of a tax deficiency, or a waiver of notice of disallowance of claim for credit or refund.
   (iv) Sign a consent to extend the statutory time period for assessment or collection of a tax.
   (v) Sign a closing agreement.
   (vi) Receive, but not endorse or cash, a refund check drawn on the U.S. Treasury. The taxpayer must specifically *initial* Form 2848 showing the name of the individual designated to receive the refund check.

8. **(A) Correct**
   A Power-of-Attorney or a tax information authorization is not required in cases docketed in the Tax Court. The representative of a taxpayer must be admitted to practice before the Tax Court. When the taxpayer petition to Tax Court is signed by a representative admitted to practice before the Tax Court, that representative will be recognized as representing that party.

9. **(B) Correct**
   An enrolled agent who is an income tax return preparer may receive but not endorse or cash, a refund check drawn on the U.S. Treasury. The taxpayer must specifically *initial* Form 2848 showing the name of the individual designated to receive the refund check.

10. **(B) Correct**
    An Attorney, CPA, and Enrolled Agent may receive but not endorse or cash, a refund check drawn on the U.S. Treasury. The taxpayer must specifically *initial* Form 2848 showing the name of the individual designated to receive the refund check.

11. **(B) Correct**
    The filing of Form 2848 will not revoke any Form 8821 that is in effect, and vice versa.

12. **(A) Correct**
    Entry onto the Centralized Authorization File (CAF) system enables IRS employees who do not have access to the actual Power-of-Attorney or tax information authorization to:
    a) Determine whether a recognized representative or appointee is authorized to discuss specific confidential tax information;
    b) Determine the extent to which a recognized representative or appointee has been authorized to represent a taxpayer; and
    c) Send copies of notices and other IRS communications to the person (individual or other entity) designated on the form.

13. **(B) Correct**
    Form 8821 authorizes any individual, corporation, firm, organization, or partnership a taxpayer designates, to inspect and/or receive your confidential information in any office of the IRS for the type of tax and the years or periods taxpayers list on Form 8821. An unenrolled preparer is not a qualified representative.

14. **(B) Correct**
    Form 8821 authorizes any individual, corporation, firm, organization, or partnership a taxpayer designates, to inspect and/or receive your confidential information in any office of the IRS for the type of tax and the years or periods taxpayers list on Form 8821. Form 8821 is not used to grant authority for representation, but for authorizing tax information. Form 2848 is used when a taxpayer wants to authorize another to represent the taxpayer at a conference with the IRS or prepare and file a written response to the IRS.

15. **(A) Correct**
    Form 2848 (Power-of-Attorney and Declaration of Representative) is used when a taxpayer wants to authorize another to represent the taxpayer at a conference with the IRS or prepare and file a written response to the IRS.

16. **(B) Correct**
    A newly filed Power-of-Attorney concerning the same matter will revoke a previously filed Power-of-Attorney. However, the new Power-of-Attorney will not revoke the prior Power-of-Attorney if it specifically states it does not revoke such prior Power-of-Attorney and either of the following is attached to the new Power-of-Attorney:
    (a) A copy of the unrevoked prior Power-of-Attorney, or
    (b) A statement signed by the taxpayer listing the name and address of each representative authorized under the prior unrevoked Power-of-Attorney.

17. **(B) Correct**
A recognized representative can substitute or delegate authority under the Power-of-Attorney to another recognized representative *only if* the act is specifically authorized under the Power-of-Attorney. After a substitution has been made, *only* the newly recognized representative will be recognized as the taxpayer's representative. If a delegation of power has been made, <u>*both*</u> the original and the delegated representative will be recognized by the IRS to represent the taxpayer.

18. **(B) Correct**
A tax representative (an Attorney, CPA, and Enrolled Agent) may receive but <u>not</u> endorse or cash, a refund check drawn on the U.S. Treasury. The taxpayer must specifically *initial* Form 2848 showing the name of the individual designated to receive the refund check.

19. **(A) Correct**
<u>Unenrolled</u> agents are only permitted to represent or advocate a position before the IRS on matters related to the specific returns they prepared. Thus, John can represent the Mr. and Mrs. Black concerning their 1999 return only.

20. **(A) Correct**
The IRS will accept a copy of a Power-of-Attorney that is submitted by facsimile transmission (fax).

21. **(B) Correct**
Any representative, other than an unenrolled preparer, <u>can</u> Sign an offer or a waiver of restriction on assessment or collection of a tax deficiency, or a waiver of notice of disallowance of claim for credit or refund.

22. **(B) Correct**
A newly filed Power-of-Attorney concerning the same matter will revoke a previously filed Power-of-Attorney. However, the new Power-of-Attorney will not revoke the prior Power-of-Attorney if it specifically states it does not revoke such prior Power-of-Attorney and either of the following is attached to the new Power-of-Attorney:
    (a) A copy of the unrevoked prior Power-of-Attorney, or
    (b) A statement signed by the taxpayer listing the name and address of each representative authorized under the prior unrevoked Power-of-Attorney.

23. **(A) Correct**
A tax representative (an Attorney, CPA, and Enrolled Agent) may receive but <u>not</u> endorse or cash, a refund check drawn on the U.S. Treasury. The taxpayer must specifically *initial* Form 2848 showing the name of the individual designated to receive the refund check.

24. **(A) Correct**
    The Centralized Authorization File (CAF) is an electronic database containing tax practitioner records. The CAF contains:
    (1) Minimal taxpayer information (name and Taxpayer Information Number). Taxpayer's address and phone information are <u>not</u> recorded on the CAF.
    (2) Third party name, address, telephone number, fax number, types of authorization levels, and CAF status information such as revocations, deletions, suspension, disbarment, and undeliverable.
    (3) A summary of the types of tax form and tax period(s).

25. **(A) Correct**
    CAF examiners do not verify the credentials or practice status of the party listed as a representative on Form 2848. The Office of Professional Responsibility determines credentials and practice status.

26. **(B) Correct**
    A newly filed Power-of-Attorney concerning the same matter will revoke a previously filed Power-of-Attorney. However, the new Power-of-Attorney will not revoke the prior Power-of-Attorney if it specifically states it does not revoke such prior Power-of-Attorney and either of the following is attached to the new Power-of-Attorney:
    (a) A copy of the unrevoked prior Power-of-Attorney, or
    (b) A statement signed by the taxpayer listing the name and address of each representative authorized under the prior unrevoked Power-of-Attorney.

27. **(B) Correct**
    Any preparer who endorses or otherwise negotiates any check made to a taxpayer shall pay a penalty of <u>$500</u> with respect to each such check. The penalty does not apply with respect to deposit by a bank of the full amount of the check in the taxpayer's account for the benefit of the taxpayer. Jim is not a Bank and therefore has violated the prohibition against endorsing or otherwise negotiating a refund check of a return he prepared.

28. **(A) Correct**
    The Centralized Authorization File (CAF) is an electronic database containing tax practitioner records. A CAF number is assigned to a tax practitioner when a Form 2848 or Form 8821 is filed. This number represents a file that contains information regarding the type of authorization that taxpayers have given representatives for the various modules within their accounts.

29. **(B) Correct**
    A tax representative (an Attorney, CPA, and Enrolled Agent) may receive but <u>not</u> endorse or cash, a refund check drawn on the U.S. Treasury. The taxpayer must

specifically *initial* Form 2848 showing the name of the individual designated to receive the refund check.

30. **(A) Correct**
Form 2848, Power-of-Attorney and Declaration of Representative, is a legal document used to authorize an individual to represent a taxpayer before the IRS and authorize the IRS to release confidential tax information to an individual for the account matters(s) specified. Form 2848 (Power-of-Attorney and Declaration of Representative) can only be granted to an individual eligible to practice before the Internal Revenue Service (e.g. Attorney, CPA or Enrolled Agent).

31. **(A) Correct**
A recognized representative can substitute or delegate authority under the Power-of-Attorney to another recognized representative *only if* the act is specifically authorized under the Power-of-Attorney. After a substitution has been made, *only* the newly recognized representative will be recognized as the taxpayer's representative. If a delegation of power has been made, *both* the original and the delegated representative will be recognized by the IRS to represent the taxpayer.

32. **(A) Correct**
A properly executed Power-of-Attorney can be used in connection with more than one particular type of tax.

33. **(A) Correct**
A tax information authorization is not required of a taxpayer's representative at a conference that is also attended by the taxpayer.

34. **(B) Correct**
Form 2848, Power-of-Attorney and Declaration of Representative, is a legal document used to authorize an individual to represent a taxpayer before the IRS and authorize the IRS to release confidential tax information to an individual for the account matters(s) specified. Form 2848 (Power-of-Attorney and Declaration of Representative) can only be granted to an individual eligible to practice before the Internal Revenue Service (e.g. Attorney, CPA or Enrolled Agent).

35. **(B) Correct**
Any representative, other than an unenrolled preparer, can perform the following acts requiring Power-of-Attorney, on behalf of the taxpayer:
    (1) Represent taxpayer before any office of the IRS.
    (2) Record the interview.
    (3) Sign an offer or a waiver of restriction on assessment or collection of a tax deficiency, or a waiver of notice of disallowance of claim for credit or refund.
    (4) Sign a consent to extend the statutory time period for assessment or collection of a tax.

(5) Sign a closing agreement.
  (6) Receive, <u>but not</u> endorse or cash, a refund check drawn on the U.S. Treasury. The taxpayer must specifically *initial* Form 2848 showing the name of the individual designated to receive the refund check.

36. **(B) Correct**
A properly executed Power-of-Attorney can be used in connection with more than one particular type of tax matter or more than one taxable year. The Power-of-Attorney must clearly express the taxpayer's intention as to the scope of the authority of the representative and must also clearly specify the tax matter(s) to which the authority relates.

37. **(A) Correct**
A recognized representative can substitute or delegate authority under the Power-of-Attorney to another recognized representative *only if* the act is specifically authorized under the Power-of-Attorney. After a substitution has been made, *only* the newly recognized representative will be recognized as the taxpayer's representative. If a delegation of power has been made, <u>both</u> the original and the delegated representative will be recognized by the IRS to represent the taxpayer.

38. **(A) Correct**
If the taxpayer does not have a copy of the Power-of-Attorney needing to be revoked or withdrawn, he or she must send a statement to the office of the IRS where the taxpayer originally filed the Power-of-Attorney.
The statement of revocation or withdrawal must:
  (1) Indicate that the authority of the Power-of-Attorney is revoke.
  (2) List the tax matters and periods.
  (3) Be signed and dated by the taxpayer or representative.

39. **(D) Correct**
Request for disclosure of confidential tax return information is done by using Form 8821.

40. **(D) Correct**
Any representative, other than an unenrolled preparer, can perform the following acts requiring Power-of-Attorney, on behalf of the taxpayer:
  (1) Represent taxpayer before any office of the IRS.
  (2) Record the interview.
  (3) Sign an offer or a waiver of restriction on assessment or collection of a tax deficiency, or a waiver of notice of disallowance of claim for credit or refund.
  (4) Sign a consent to extend the statutory time period for assessment or collection of a tax.
  (5) Sign a closing agreement.

(6) Receive, but not endorse or cash, a refund check drawn on the U.S. Treasury. The taxpayer must specifically *initial* Form 2848 showing the name of the individual designated to receive the refund check.

41. **(B) Correct**
The IRS will accept a copy of a Power-of-Attorney that is submitted by facsimile transmission (fax). A taxpayer's signature on a Power-of-Attorney does not have to be notarized or witnessed. A Power-of-Attorney is generally terminated if the taxpayer becomes incapacitated or incompetent. The Power-of-Attorney can continue, however, in the case of taxpayer's incapacity or incompetency if the taxpayer authorizes this on Form 2848, or if the taxpayer's *non-IRS durable Power-of-Attorney* meets all the requirements for acceptance by the IRS.

42. **(C) Correct**
The taxpayer must also attach (to the non-IRS Power-of-Attorney) a signed and dated statement made by the representative. This statement is referred to as the *Declaration of Representative* and is contained in *Part II* of Form 2848. The statement should read:
   1) I am not currently under suspension or disbarment from practice before the Internal Revenue Service or other practice of my profession by any other authority,
   2) I am aware of the regulations contained in Treasury Department Circular No. 230 (31 CFR, Part 10) concerning the practice of attorneys, certified public accountants, enrolled agents, enrolled actuaries, and others,
   3) I am authorized to represent the taxpayer(s) identified in the Power-of-Attorney; and
   4) I am authorized to practice before the Internal Revenue Service as an individual described in 26 CFR 601.502(b).

43. **(B) Correct**
A tax representative (an Attorney, CPA, and Enrolled Agent) may receive but not endorse or cash, a refund check drawn on the U.S. Treasury. The taxpayer must specifically *initial* Form 2848 showing the name of the individual designated to receive the refund check.

44. **(D) Correct**
See Answer #42.

45. **(B) Correct**
See Answer #42.

46. **(B) Correct**
Taxpayers have the right to represent themselves or have someone else represent them before the IRS in connection with a Federal tax matter. If a taxpayer wants someone to

represent him/her before the IRS, the taxpayer must file Form 2848 (Power-of-Attorney and Declaration of Representative) with the IRS office where he/she wants the representative to act. The representative must be a person authorized to practice before the IRS. The taxpayer's signature on Form 2848 allows the individual named to *represent* the taxpayer before the IRS and to *receive* tax information.

47. **(C) Correct**
Any person considered an enrolled agent under Circular 230 or an attorney who is not currently under suspension or disbarment from practice before the IRS who files a written declaration that he or she is currently qualified as an enrolled agent or an attorney and is authorized to represent the particular party on whose behalf (s)he acts.

48. **(B) Correct**
Any representative, other than an unenrolled preparer, can perform the following acts requiring Power-of-Attorney, on behalf of the taxpayer:
    (1) Represent taxpayer before any office of the IRS.
    (2) Record the interview.
    (3) Sign an offer or a waiver of restriction on assessment or collection of a tax deficiency, or a waiver of notice of disallowance of claim for credit or refund.
    (4) Sign a consent to extend the statutory time period for assessment or collection of a tax.
    (5) Sign a closing agreement.
    (6) Receive, but not endorse or cash, a refund check drawn on the U.S. Treasury. The taxpayer must specifically *initial* Form 2848 showing the name of the individual designated to receive the refund check.

49. **(D) Correct**
If a taxpayer wishes to revoke an existing Power-of-Attorney and he/she does not want to name a new representative, or if a representative wants to withdraw from a representation, the taxpayer must send a copy of the previously executed Power-of-Attorney to the IRS. The copy of the Power-of-Attorney must have a current signature (under the original signature on line 9) of the taxpayer if the taxpayer is *revoking* or of the representative if the representative is *withdrawing*. Taxpayer must write "REVOKE" across the top of Form 2848. One can revoke a Power-of-Attorney for which a Form 2848 was not filed by writing a letter to that effect and sending it, along with a copy of the original Power-of-Attorney, to each office of the IRS where you originally filed it. A new Power-of-Attorney revokes a prior Power-of-Attorney if it is granted by the taxpayer to another recognized representative with respect to the same matter, unless the new Power-of-Attorney states otherwise and another condition is met.

50. **(D) Correct**
See Answer #48.

51. **(A) Correct**
The taxpayer may list any tax years or periods that have already ended as of the date of signing the Power-of-Attorney. However, the taxpayer may include on a Power-of-Attorney only future tax periods that end no later than 3 years after the date the Power-of-Attorney is received by the IRS. The 3 future periods are determined starting after December 31 of the year the Power-of-Attorney is received by the IRS. However, one should avoid general references such as all years or all periods.

52. **(D) Correct**
A tax representative (an Attorney, CPA, and Enrolled Agent) may receive but <u>not</u> endorse or cash, a refund check drawn on the U.S. Treasury. The taxpayer must specifically *initial* Form 2848 showing the name of the individual designated to receive the refund check.

53. **(C) Correct**
The IRS will accept a *non-IRS Power-of-Attorney*, but a completed transmittal Form 2848 must be attached in order for the Power-of-Attorney to be entered on the *Centralized Authorization File* (CAF) system. A Form 2848 and Form 8821 for a jointly filed authorization will be processed, if after researching each tax year(s), it is determined the tax-year(s) are filed jointly. The year(s) that are not filed jointly will be processed separately, as though each spouse filed a separate Form 2848 or 8821, and will be recorded to their individual taxpayer account. This includes future years covered by the forms. In the case of any matter concerning a joint return in which both husband and wife are not to be represented by the same recognized representative(s), the Power-of-Attorney must be executed by the spouse who is to be represented. In the case of a partnership, a Power-of-Attorney must be executed by all partners, or if executed in the name of the partnership, by the partner or partners duly authorized to act for the partnership. The partner or partners must certify that they have such authority.

54. **(D) Correct**
The representative named under a Power-of-Attorney is not permitted to sign the taxpayer's personal income tax return unless both of the following exist:
   (a) The signature is permitted under the Internal Revenue Code and the related regulations.
   (b) The taxpayer *specifically* authorizes the representative's signature through the Power-of-Attorney.

55. **(D) Correct**
Form 8821 authorizes any individual, corporation, firm, organization, or partnership a taxpayer designates, to inspect and/or receive your confidential information in any office of the IRS for the type of tax and the years or periods taxpayers list on Form 8821.

56. **(C) Correct**
    The *Checkbox election* is made directly on the tax form. Checkbox authority:
    a) Does not allow a designee to represent the taxpayer.
    b) Is not recorded on the CAF.
    c) Is recorded directly to the taxpayers account.
    d) Mirrors Form 8821 authority.
    e) Allows the designee to provide or receive information on any issue in connection with the tax period covered by the return on which the designation was made for a period not to exceed one year.
    f) Allows the designee to receive written account information/transcripts upon request for a period not to exceed one year.
    g) Is available on Forms 720, 941, 941PR, 941SS, 1040, 1041, 1120, 2290 and CT-1
    h) Can co-exist with a Power-of-Attorney for the same tax period.

    A representative must file Form 8821, tax information authorization, to receive or inspect confidential tax information on behalf of the taxpayer, unless the representative has filed Form 2848 to perform those specific acts. A legal guardian who files Form 56, Notice Concerning Fiduciary Relationship, is allowed to receive confidential information. Designating a person to prepare a tax return is not sufficient authorization for that person to receive confidential information from the IRS regarding that particular income tax return.

57. **(A) Correct**
    A person who prepares an income tax return or claim for refund for an estate or a trust, but only if such person is a fiduciary or is an officer, general partner, or employee of the fiduciary, is not considered a tax preparer and therefore cannot be a representative under the Power-of-Attorney requirements.

58. **(C) Correct**
    A Power-of-Attorney or tax information authorization should contain the following information:
    (a) Type of tax involved.
    (b) Specific year(s)/period(s) involved.
    (c) Name and mailing address of the recognized representative(s).
    (d) The taxpayer's intent as to the scope of authority of the representative.

    Identification number of the representative, like SSNs or EIN is *not* required on the Power-of-Attorney.

59. **(B) Correct**
    In the case of any matter concerning a joint return in which both husband and wife are not to be represented by the same recognized representative(s), the Power-of-Attorney must be executed by the spouse who is to be represented. In the case of a partnership, a Power-of-Attorney must be executed by all partners, or if executed in the name of the partnership, by the partner or partners duly authorized to act for the partnership. The partner or partners must certify that they have such authority. If a dissolved partnership

is involved, each of the former living partners must execute a Power-of-Attorney. If a corporation is involved, the Power-of-Attorney must be executed by an officer of the corporation having authority to legally bind the corporation. The officer must certify that (s)he has such authority.

60. **(D) Correct**
A recognized representative can substitute or delegate authority under the Power-of-Attorney to another recognized representative *only if* the act is specifically authorized under the Power-of-Attorney. After a substitution has been made, *only* the newly recognized representative will be recognized as the taxpayer's representative.
If a delegation of power has been made, <u>both</u> the original and the delegated representative will be recognized by the IRS to represent the taxpayer. If a taxpayer wishes to revoke an existing Power-of-Attorney and he or she does not want to name a new representative, or if a representative wants to withdraw from a representation, the taxpayer must send a copy of the previously executed Power-of-Attorney to the IRS.
If the taxpayer does not have a copy of the Power-of-Attorney needing to be revoked or withdrawn, he or she must send a statement to the office of the IRS where the taxpayer originally filed the Power-of-Attorney.

61. **(D) Correct**
See Answer #60

62. **(C) Correct**
A Power-of-Attorney must contain all of the following information:
    (a) Type of tax involved.
    (b) Specific year(s)/period(s) involved.
    (c) Name and mailing address of the recognized representative(s).
Identification number of the representative, like SSNs or EIN is <u>not</u> required on the Power-of-Attorney.

63. **(C) Correct**
The copy of the Power-of-Attorney must have a current signature (under the original signature on line 9) of the taxpayer if the taxpayer is *revoking* or of the representative if the representative is *withdrawing*. Taxpayer must write "<u>REVOKE</u>" across the top of Form 2848.

64. **(D) Correct**
The Centralized Authorization File (CAF) is an electronic database containing tax practitioner records. A CAF number is assigned to a tax practitioner when a Form 2848 or Form 8821 is filed. All of these individuals would therefore be included in CAF.

65. **(A) Correct**
Information recorded onto the CAF system enables IRS personnel who do not have a copy of the actual Power-of-Attorney or tax information authorization to verify the

authority of the taxpayer's representative. If a representative wants his/her non-IRS Power-of-Attorney entered into the CAF, the representative should attach it to a completed "transmittal" Form 2848 and submit it to the IRS. A Power-of-Attorney will not be rejected based on the absence of a CAF number.

66. **(C) Correct**
See Answer #65

67. **(D) Correct**
A Power-of-Attorney that <u>does not</u> include a CAF number will <u>not be</u> rejected.

68. **(C) Correct**
A Power-of-Attorney will not be rejected based on the absence of a CAF number. A CAF number is assigned to a tax practitioner when a Form 2848 or Form 8821 is filed. The CAF database accepts up to 3 future years.

69. **(D) Correct**
See answers #s 64, 65, 67, and 68

70. **(C) Correct**
The IRS will accept a *non-IRS Power-of-Attorney*, but a completed transmittal Form 2848 must be attached in order for the Power-of-Attorney to be entered on the *Centralized Authorization File* (CAF) system.

71. **(A) Correct**
A CAF number is a unique number that will be assigned to any person who files with the IRS a Power-of-Attorney and a written declaration that (s)he is currently qualified to practice before the IRS and is authorized to represent the particular party on whose behalf (s)he acts. A CAF number will be assigned to any person who files with the IRS a tax information authorization.
Entry onto the Centralized Authorization File (CAF) system enables IRS employees who do not have access to the actual Power-of-Attorney or tax information authorization to:
    a) Determine whether a recognized representative or appointee is authorized to discuss specific confidential tax information;
    b) Determine the extent to which a recognized representative or appointee has been authorized to represent a taxpayer; and
    c) Send copies of notices and other IRS communications to the person (individual or other entity) designated on the form.

72. **(D) Correct**
In the case of a partnership, a Power-of-Attorney must be executed by <u>all</u> partners, or if executed in the name of the partnership, by the partner or partners duly authorized to act for the partnership. The partner or partners must certify that they have such authority. If a dissolved partnership is involved, each of the former living partners must

execute a Power-of-Attorney. If a corporation is involved, the Power-of-Attorney must be executed by an officer of the corporation having authority to legally bind the corporation. The officer must certify that (s)he has such authority.

73. **(B) Correct**
A Power-of-Attorney or tax information authorization should contain the following information:
    (a) Type of tax involved.
    (b) Specific year(s)/period(s) involved.
    (c) Name and mailing address of the recognized representative(s).
    (d) The taxpayer's intent as to the scope of authority of the representative.
Identification number of the representative, like SSNs or EIN is not required on the Power-of-Attorney.

74. **(B) Correct**
Form 2848, Power-of-Attorney and Declaration of Representative, can be used to appoint an unenrolled return preparer as a taxpayer's representative before revenue agents and examining officers of the Examination Division of the IRS. A document other than Form 2848 can be used to appoint a Power-of-Attorney if it contains the information required by the IRS. A taxpayer can execute a durable Power-of-Attorney, which specifies that the appointment of the attorney-in-fact will not end due to the incapacity or incompetency of the taxpayer. A tax representative (an Attorney, CPA, and Enrolled Agent) may receive but <u>not</u> endorse or cash, a refund check drawn on the U.S. Treasury. The taxpayer must specifically *initial* Form 2848 showing the name of the individual designated to receive the refund check.

75. **(D) Correct**
To make a substitution or delegation, the representative must file the following items with the IRS office(s) where the Power-of-Attorney was filed:
1. A written notice of substitution or delegation signed by the recognized representative.
2. A written declaration of representative made by the new representative.
3. A copy of the Power-of-Attorney that specifically authorizes the substitution or delegation.

76. **(A) Correct**
Entry onto the Centralized Authorization File (CAF) system enables IRS employees who do not have access to the actual Power-of-Attorney or tax information authorization to:
    a) Determine whether a recognized representative or appointee is authorized to discuss specific confidential tax information;
    b) Determine the extent to which a recognized representative or appointee has been authorized to represent a taxpayer; and

c) Send copies of notices and other IRS communications to the person (individual or other entity) designated on the form.

77. **(D) Correct**
    - The issuance of a CAF number <u>does not</u> indicate that a person is either recognized or authorized to practice before the IRS.
    - The purpose of the CAF number is to facilitate the processing of a Power-of-Attorney or a tax information authorization submitted by a recognized representative or designee.
    - A recognized representative or a designee should include the same CAF number on every Power-of-Attorney or tax information authorization filed.

78. **(A) Correct**
    Any representative, other than an unenrolled preparer, can perform the following acts requiring Power-of-Attorney, on behalf of the taxpayer:
    (1) Represent taxpayer before any office of the IRS.
    (2) Record the interview.
    (3) Sign an offer or a waiver of restriction on assessment or collection of a tax deficiency, or a waiver of notice of disallowance of claim for credit or refund.
    (4) Sign a consent to extend the statutory time period for assessment or collection of a tax.
    (5) Execute a closing agreement under Sec. 7121.
    (6) Receive, <u>but not</u> endorse or cash, a refund check drawn on the U.S. Treasury. The taxpayer must specifically *initial* Form 2848 showing the name of the individual designated to receive the refund check.
    (7) Authorize the extension of the statute of limitations.

79. **(B) Correct**
    Disclosure of return information is permitted to congressional committees, a person designated by the taxpayer, and State tax officials. Disclosure is not permitted to relatives of the taxpayer.

80. **(C) Correct**
    A practitioner who knows that his or her client has not complied with the revenue laws or has made an error or omission in any return, document, affidavit, or other required paper, has the responsibility to advise the client promptly of the noncompliance, error, or omission, and the consequences of the noncompliance, error, or omission.

81. **(C) Correct**
    The copy of the Power-of-Attorney must have a current signature (under the original signature on line 9) of the taxpayer if the taxpayer is *revoking* or of the representative if the representative is *withdrawing*. Taxpayer must write "<u>REVOKE</u>" across the top of Form 2848. One can revoke a Power-of-Attorney for which a Form 2848 was not filed by

writing a letter to that effect and sending it, along with a copy of the original Power-of-Attorney, to each office of the IRS where you originally filed it.

82. **(B) Correct**
A tax representative (an Attorney, CPA, and Enrolled Agent) may receive but <u>not</u> endorse or cash, a refund check drawn on the U.S. Treasury. The taxpayer must specifically *initial* Form 2848 showing the name of the individual designated to receive the refund check.

83. **(C) Correct**
The following are authorized to practice before the IRS if they hold Power-of-Attorney?
- Any person considered an enrolled agent under Circular 230, who is not currently under suspension or disbarment from practice before the IRS who files a written declaration that he or she is currently qualified as an enrolled agent and is authorized to represent the particular party on whose behalf he or she acts.
- Any attorney who is not currently under suspension or disbarment from practice before the IRS who files a written declaration that he or she is currently qualified as an attorney and is authorized to represent the particular party on whose behalf he or she acts.

84. **(B) Correct**
Unenrolled return preparers are limited to representation of a taxpayer before revenue agents and examining officers of the Examination Division in the offices of District Director with respect to the tax liability of the taxpayer for the taxable year or period covered by a return prepared by the unenrolled return preparer. Since Widgets-R-Us engaged Janet to prepare the company's 1998 Form 1120-S, she can only represent Widgets- R-Us during the examination with regard to its 1998 Form 1120-S.

85. **(C) Correct**
For taxpayers that want someone to represent them in their absence at an examination or at an appeal within the IRS, the taxpayer must furnish that representative with written authorization on Form 2848, Power-of-Attorney and Declaration of Representative, or any other properly written authorization. The representative can be an attorney, certified public accountant, or an enrolled agent. Even if the taxpayer appointed a representative, the taxpayer may attend the examination or appeals conference and may act on his or her own behalf.

86. **(A) Correct**
Within the power of attorney, the representative must declare the following:
(1) I am not currently under suspension or disbarment from practice before the Internal Revenue Service;

(2) I am aware of regulations contained in Circular 230 (31 CFR, Part 10), as amended, concerning the practice of attorneys, certified public accountants, enrolled agents, enrolled actuaries, and others;

(3) I am authorized to represent the taxpayer(s) identified in Part I for the tax matter(s) specified there; and

(4) I am one of the following:

    (a) **Attorney**—a member in good standing of the bar of the highest court of the jurisdiction (state) shown below.

    (b) **Certified Public Accountant**—duly qualified to practice as a certified public accountant in the jurisdiction (state) shown below.

    (c) **Enrolled Agent**—enrolled as an agent under the requirements of Circular 230.

    (d) **Officer**—a bona fide officer of the taxpayer's organization.

    (e) **Full-Time Employee**—a full-time employee of the taxpayer.

    (f) **Family Member**—a member of the taxpayer's immediate family (for example, spouse, parent, child, brother, or sister).

    (g) **Enrolled Actuary**—enrolled as an actuary by the Joint Board for the Enrollment of Actuaries under 29 U.S.C. 1242

    (h) **Unenrolled Return Preparer**—the authority to practice before the Internal Revenue Service is limited by Circular 230, section. One must have prepared the return in question and the return must be under examination by the IRS.

    (i) **Student Attorney**—student who receives permission to practice before the IRS by virtue of their status as a law student under section 10.7(d) of Circular 230.

    (j) **Student CPA**—student who receives permission to practice before the IRS by virtue of their status as a CPA student under section 10.7(d) of Circular 230.

    (k) **Enrolled Retirement Plan Agent**—enrolled as a retirement plan agent under the requirements of Circular 230.

UNIT 4: COLLECTION PROCESS

Unit 4 Contents:
4.01 NOTICE OF UNDERREPORTED INCOME - CP-2000
4.02 THE COLLECTION PROCESS
4.03 AUTOMATED COLLECTION SYSTEM (ACS):
4.04 THE FEDERAL TAX LIEN
4.05 LEVY
4.06 BANKRUPTCY
4.07 INNOCENT SPOUSE RELIEF (INJURED SPOUSE)
4.08 INSTALLMENT AGREEMENT
4.09 OFFERS IN COMPROMISE
4.10 PERIOD FOR COLLECTION AFTER ASSESSMENT
4.11 TAXPAYER ADVOCATE SERVICE (TAS)
4.12 UNIT 4: QUESTIONS
4.13 UNIT 4: ANSWERS

4.01 NOTICE OF UNDERREPORTED INCOME — CP-2000

The IRS compares the information reported on forms W-2, 1098, 1099, etc., with income and deductions reported on income tax returns. If a taxpayer forgot to report any income, payments, credits, or overstated certain deductions on an income tax return, a taxpayer may receive a Notice CP-2000. The notice number CP-2000 appears on page 1 in the upper right-hand corner. It also shows a phone number that a taxpayer can call if the taxpayer needs assistance after he or she has responded and is not satisfied with the outcome. The notice informs a taxpayer of the proposed changes to income, payments, credits, or deductions; and the amount due to IRS, or refund due to a taxpayer. It is normally a five to six page letter. The size of the notice varies according to the number of issues identified in a taxpayer notice. The first page of the CP-2000 is called the "Summary Page". It provides a brief summary of the notice and instructions on what a taxpayer should do to determine if the taxpayer agrees or disagrees with the proposed changes.

A response page is also included to indicate whether the taxpayer agrees or disagrees with the proposed changes. It also has an area to authorize someone other than the taxpayer to discuss and give information to the IRS pertaining to the proposed changes. The taxpayer must respond within 30 days of the date of the notice or 60 days if he or she lives outside the United States.

4.02 THE COLLECTION PROCESS

Reg. Sec 301.6303-1 states that the district director or the director of the regional service center shall, after making assessment of tax, give notice to each person liable for the unpaid tax, stating the amount and demanding payment. Therefore, the collection process begins at the IRS service center where notices are generated requesting payment.

If a tax return is selected for examination, the IRS will send a notice of deficiency against a taxpayer. The notice of deficiency must be sent within 3 years of the filing date of the return. The 3-year time limit for making an assessment may be extended within that period by an agreement in writing signed by both the IRS and the taxpayer.

This letter is the IRS's notice of its intention to assess unpaid tax. Within 90 days (150 days if mailed to a taxpayer outside the United States) after the IRS mails the deficiency notice, the taxpayer may petition the Tax Court to re-determine the deficiency. The 10-year collections period begins to run only after the IRS has made a formal assessment, either by Form 23C (Assessment Certificate) or at the end of a deficiency proceeding in Tax Court.

The initial notice and demand is typically followed by two or three computer-generated billing notices issued by an IRS Submission Processing. The notice cycle then shifts to the branch of the IRS that implements collection action for issuance of the formal notice of intent to levy. Most balance due amounts are forwarded to the Automated Collection System (ACS) branch of the IRS.

When resolving tax problems with the IRS, taxpayers:
- (a) May be entitled to a reimbursement for fees charged by their banks if the IRS has erroneously levied their account.
- (b) Should first request assistance from IRS collection employees or their managers before seeking assistance from the problem resolution officer.
- (c) May request assistance from the IRS on Form 911, Application for Assistance Order to Relieve Hardship If there is a significant hardship because of the collection of the tax liability.

4.03   AUTOMATED COLLECTION SYSTEM (ACS):

ACS is a computerized system that maintains balance-due accounts and return delinquency investigations. ACS usually matches taxpayer identification numbers to bank accounts and wage sources and may serve levies on these banks or sources after appropriate procedures have been followed. If ACS ultimately is unable to collect an outstanding tax liability, the account is sent to the IRS territory in which the taxpayer resides. Upon receipt by the field office, the account is typically assigned to an IRS revenue officer, who is responsible for the collection of that account. The revenue officer determines the appropriate mode of collection, which may include administrative collection enforcement through the use of the federal tax lien or levy or through the commencement of a judicial tax collection proceeding.

4.04   THE FEDERAL TAX LIEN

The federal tax lien is the backbone of the federal tax collection process. A federal tax lien gives the IRS legal claim to the property subject to the lien as security or payment for the tax debt. Elements of a federal tax lien are:

(1) Assessment.
(2) Notice and demand.
(3) Failure to pay.

Thus, for a lien to arise the tax must be assessed, the IRS must make notice and demand on the taxpayer, and the taxpayer must fail to pay within 10 days after notice and demand (Code Sec. 6331).

A lien attaches to all of the taxpayer's property and rights to property owned on or acquired after the date of assessment (the lien filing date) (Code Sec.6321). The federal tax lien is an encumbrance on property. However, the lien itself does not result in the direct collection of any tax liability. A filed notice of tax lien can be withdrawn if withdrawal will speed collecting the tax. The law also requires the IRS to notify the taxpayer in writing within 5 business days after the filing of a lien.

Three (3) devices are available to the IRS to enforce the federal tax lien:
(a) Administrative levy.
(b) Administrative seizure.
(c) Judicial collection remedies.

The taxpayer may appeal the implementation of enforced collection or seek to enter an installment payment arrangement or make an offer in compromise with the IRS. Appeal rights also exist for liens, levies defaulted installment agreements and rejected offers in compromise. If administrative resolution is not possible, relief may be obtained by filing a bankruptcy petition.

➢ Releasing a Lien:

The will issue a Release of the Notice of Federal Tax Lien:
1) Within 30 days after the taxpayer satisfies the tax due (including interest and other additions) by paying the debt or by having it adjusted, or
2) Within 30 days after IRS accepts a bond that the taxpayer submits, guaranteeing payment of the debt.

The taxpayer must pay all fees that a state or other jurisdiction charges to file and release the lien. These fees will be added to the balance amount owed. It is a public notice to the taxpayer's creditors that the government has a claim against all of the taxpayer's real, personal, and/or business property, including property that was acquired after the lien came into existence. A taxpayer can sue the federal government for damages if the IRS knowingly or negligently fails to release a Notice of Federal Tax Lien when a release is warranted.

4.05   LEVY

Under Code Section 6331(b), the term "levy" includes the power of distraint and seizure by any means. The IRS may levy upon (seize) a taxpayer's property and rights to property if a taxpayer fails to pay a tax liability. *A Levy* is a legal seizure (taking) of property to satisfy a tax debt.

The first step in the levy process is to provide a taxpayer with a written *Notice and Demand* for payment. A notice and demand is a notice which states that the tax has been assessed and demands that payment be made. If the taxpayer fails to pay the tax within 10 days after receipt of the "Notice and Demand," the IRS may seize a taxpayer's property, but no sooner than 30 days after sending the taxpayer a second notice, called a *Final Notice of Intent to Levy*. The two notices, however, may be sent at the same time. In addition, the IRS is required to send the taxpayer a pre-levy Collection Due Process Hearing Notice (pre-levy CDP notice) at least 30 days prior to levying.

If the IRS levies a taxpayer's bank account, the bank is required to hold the funds the taxpayer has on deposit, up to the amount the taxpayer owes, for 21 days. Levies can be made on property that is the taxpayer's but is held by third parties. The IRS will release a levy if the IRS determines the levy is creating an economic hardship for the taxpayer.
Jeopardy levies may occur when the IRS waives the 10-day notice and demand period and/or the 30-day Final Notice (Notice of Intent to Levy) period because a delay would endanger the collection of tax.

> ➤ **Pre-levy CDP Notice:**

This notice preceding the levy is a brief statement written in simple and nontechnical terms. It includes a description of:
   (1) The statutory provisions relating to the levy and sale of property.
   (2) The procedures applicable to the levy and sale of property.
   (3) The administrative appeals available to the taxpayer with respect to the levy and sale and the procedures relating to those appeals.
   (4) The alternatives available to taxpayers that could prevent levy on the property (including installment agreements).
   (5) The statutory provisions relating to redemption of property and the release of liens on property.
   (6) The procedures applicable to the redemption of property and the release of a lien on property.

The notice of intent to levy must:
   (a) Be given in person.
   (b) Be left at the dwelling or usual place of business of the taxpayer, or
   (c) Be sent by registered or certified mail to the taxpayer's last known address.

➤ Prohibited Levy:

No levy may be made on the property:
1. Of any person on a day when that person is required to appear in response to a summons issued by the Secretary of the Treasury for the purpose of collecting any underpayment of tax.
2. If the estimated amount of the expenses that would be incurred with respect to the levy and sale of the property exceeds its fair market value at the time of the levy.
3. During the consideration or pendency of an offer in compromise or an installment agreement (Code Sec. 6331(k)).

➤ Continuous Levy Provisions:

IRS levies extend only to property held by the taxpayer or a third party at the time of the levy. Property received after notice of levy can be reached only by a *subsequent* levy. However, a levy on wages and salary (including fees, bonuses and commissions) remains viable until the tax liability covered by the levy is satisfied or becomes unenforceable because of a lapse of time. This type of levy must be promptly released when the liability out of which it arose is satisfied or becomes unenforceable due to lapse of time, and the IRS must promptly notify the person upon whom the levy was made (usually the employer) that it has been released. These continuous levy provisions apply to salary or wages earned but not yet paid at the time of levy and salary or wages earned and becoming payable (or paid in the form of an advance) after the date of the levy until the levy is released.

➤ Property Exempt from Levy:

The following items are exempt from levy:
1) Wearing apparel and such school books
2) Fuel, provisions, furniture, and personal effects
3) Books and tools necessary for the trade, business, or profession
4) Unemployment benefits
5) Undelivered mail
6) Annuity or pension payments under the Railroad Retirement Act
7) Workmen's compensation
8) Judgments for support of minor children
9) Minimum exemption for wages, salary, and other income
10) Certain service-connected disability payments
11) Certain public assistance payments
12) Assistance under job training partnership act
13) Residences and businesses are not exempt from levy. However, special rules apply for seizures of residences and businesses. Any real property used as a residence by the taxpayer, or any real property of the taxpayer (other than property that is rented) used by any other individual as a residence, is exempt from levy if the amount of the tax liability does not exceed $5,000.
14) The principal residence of the taxpayer cannot be levied unless the IRS obtains a court order from a district court judge or magistrate.

15) Tangible personal or real property (other than real property which is rented) used in the trade or business of an individual taxpayer cannot be levied unless the IRS determines that collection is in jeopardy or unless the District Director approves the levy in writing. The IRS must obtain a court order to seize personal property on private premises (Code Sec. 6334).

➤ Release of levy

The IRS will release a levy on property if:
  (1) The liability for which the levy was made is satisfied or becomes unenforceable through lapse of time.
  (2) Release of the levy will facilitate collection of the tax liability.
  (3) The taxpayer has entered into an installment payment agreement (unless the agreement prohibits releasing the levy),
  (4) A determination has been made that the levy is causing an economic hardship due to the financial condition of the taxpayer.
  (5) The fair market value of the property exceeds the tax liability and release of the levy on the property could be made without hindering the collection of the liability (Code Sec. 6343(a)(1)).

The IRS will notify the party in possession of the levied property that the release has been authorized. The release of the levy may be faxed. The IRS will generally respond to a request within 10 business days.

Request for release of levy - A taxpayer may request a release of levy in writing or by telephone from the district director for the IRS district in which the levy was made. The IRS will respond to the request within 30 days. If a sale is scheduled before the expiration of the 30 day period and the request is made at least 5 days before the sale, the IRS will respond to the request before the sale and, if necessary, postpone the sale in order to make the determination. The IRS has the discretion to proceed with a scheduled sale if the request is not made at least 5 days prior to the sale. The release of levy rules do not apply to perishable goods (Reg. Sec. 301.6343-1(c)).

➤ Sale of seized property

Notice of sale - After seizure of the property, the district director give notice of sale in writing to the owner. The notice will:
  (a) Specify the property to be sold, time, place, manner, and conditions of the sale
  (b) Expressly state that only the right, title, and interest of the delinquent taxpayer in and to such property is to be offered for sale.
  (c) The notice shall also be published in some newspaper published in the county wherein the seizure is made or in a newspaper generally circulated in that county.

Before the sale of property, the IRS will compute a minimum bid price. If the minimum is not offered at the sale, the IRS may buy the property. The taxpayer may request a re-computation if (s)he is in disagreement with the minimum price the IRS has determined it will accept for the property. After the sale, proceeds are applied first to the expenses of the levy and sale. A taxpayer has the right to an administrative review of a seizure action when the IRS has taken personal property that is necessary to the maintenance of the taxpayer's business.

Time and place of sale - The time of sale may not be less than 10 days or more than 40 days from the time of giving public notice (If the IRS seizes property that is not perishable, the IRS will wait at least 10 days after seizure before conducting the sale). The place of sale must be within the county in which the property is seized, except that if it appears to the district director under whose supervision the seizure was made that substantially higher bids may be obtained for the property if the sale is held at a place outside such county, he may order that the sale be held in such other place. The sale must be held at the time and place stated in the notice of sale.

Sale of Perishable Goods - When a district director determines that seized property cannot be kept without great expense or that it is liable to perish or become greatly reduced in price or value by keeping, the director is required to appraise the value of the property and return it to the owner if the owner

Redemption of Levied Property before Sale - A person whose real or personal property has been levied upon has the right to redeem the property before sale by paying the amount due, plus expenses of the proceeding. The amount due is the full amount of taxes, penalties, and interest, plus expenses related to the seizure and anticipated sale.

Redemption of Levied Property After Sale - After a tax sale has taken place, personal property may not be redemed. Real property that has been sold may be redeemed at any time within 180 days after the sale by paying the amount that the purchaser paid, plus interest at the rate of 20% per year on that amount. The date of the sale does not count in calculating the 180 day time period.

4.06 BANKRUPTCY

Bankruptcy proceedings begin with the filing of a petition in bankruptcy court, and that filing creates the bankruptcy estate. The bankruptcy estate generally consists of all of the assets of the person or entity filing the bankruptcy petition. The bankruptcy estate is treated as a separate taxable entity if the bankruptcy petition is filed by an individual under chapter 7 or 11 of the Bankruptcy Code. Generally, when a debt owed to another person or entity is canceled, the amount canceled or forgiven is considered income that is taxed to the person owing the debt. If a debt is canceled under a bankruptcy proceeding, the amount canceled is not income. However, the canceled debt reduces other tax benefits to which the debtor would otherwise be entitled.

The estate in a chapter 7 case is represented by a trustee. The trustee is appointed under the Bankruptcy Code to administer the estate and liquidate any nonexempt assets of the estate. In chapter 11, the debtor often remains in control of the assets as a "debtor-in-possession" and acts as the bankruptcy trustee. If a husband and wife file a joint bankruptcy petition and their bankruptcy estates are jointly administered, their estates must be treated as two separate entities for tax purposes. Two separate tax returns must be filed (if they separately meet the filing requirements).

Filing a petition in bankruptcy under Title 11 of the United States Code automatically stays assessment and collection of a tax. The stay remains in effect until the bankruptcy court discharges liability for the tax or lifts the stay. A taxpayer's appeal to the IRS regarding the IRS's filing of a Notice of Federal Tax Lien may succeed if the taxpayer is in bankruptcy and subject to the automatic stay provisions when the lien is filed. This usually happens if the taxpayer believes the IRS filed a Notice of Federal Tax Lien in error.

For all bankruptcy cases filed after October 16, 2005, the Bankruptcy Code provides that if the debtor does not file a tax return that becomes due after the commencement of the bankruptcy case, or obtain an extension for filing the return before the due date, the taxing authority may request that the court either dismiss the case or convert the case to a case under another chapter of the Bankruptcy Code. If the debtor does not file the required return or obtain an extension within 90 days after the request is made, the bankruptcy court must dismiss or convert the case.

4.07   INNOCENT SPOUSE RELIEF (INJURED SPOUSE)

When a taxpayer files a joint income tax return, the law makes both the taxpayer and the spouse responsible for the entire tax liability. This is called 'joint and several liability'. Joint and several liability applies not only to the tax liability shown on the return but also to any additional tax liability the IRS determines to be due, even if the additional tax is due to income, deductions, or credits of spouse or former spouse. The taxpayer remains jointly and severally liable for the taxes, and the IRS still can collect from the taxpayer even if he or she later divorces and the divorce decree states that the former spouse will be solely responsible for the tax.

In some cases, a spouse (or former spouse) will be relieved of the tax, interest, and penalties on a joint tax return. Three types of relief are available to married persons who filed joint returns:
   (1) Innocent spouse relief.
   (2) Separation of liability relief.
   (3) Equitable relief.

Married persons who did not file joint returns, but who live in community property states, may also qualify for relief.

Innocent Spouse Relief – A taxpayer must meet all of the following conditions to qualify for innocent spouse relief.
   1. Taxpayer filed a joint return.
   2. There is an understated tax on the return that is due to erroneous items of spouse (or former spouse).

3. Taxpayer can show that when he or she signed the joint return and did not know, and had no reason to know, that the understated tax existed (or the extent to which the understated tax existed).
4. Taking into account all the facts and circumstances, it would be unfair to hold the taxpayer liable for the understated tax.

Separation of Liability Relief - Under this type of relief, the understated tax (plus interest and penalties) on the joint return is allocated between the taxpayer and the spouse (or former spouse). The understated tax allocated to the taxpayer is generally the amount he or she is responsible for.

This type of relief is available only for unpaid liabilities resulting from the understated tax. Refunds are not allowed.

To request separation of liability relief, one must have filed a joint return and meet either of the following requirements at the time he or she files Form 8857:
- No longer married to or are legally separated from the spouse with regard to the joint return for which one is requesting relief. (Under this rule, one is no longer married if one is widowed.)
- Not a member of the same household as the spouse with regard to the joint return at any time during the 12-month period ending on the date one files Form 8857.

Equitable Relief - Unlike innocent spouse relief or separation of liability relief, one can get equitable relief from an understated tax or an underpaid tax. An underpaid tax is an amount of tax properly reported on the return but not paid. For example, a joint 2005 return shows that taxpayer and spouse owed $5,000. The taxpayer pays $2,000 with the return. The taxpayer has an underpaid tax of $3,000. If one is granted relief for an underpaid tax, he or she is eligible for a refund of separate payments that made after July 22, 1998. However, one is not eligible for refunds of payments made with the joint return, joint payments, or payments that the spouse (or former spouse) made. For example, withholding tax and estimated tax payments cannot be refunded because they are considered made with the joint return.

Installment Agreements vs. Offers in Compromise

Installment agreements and *offers in compromise* are two of the most common ways for taxpayers to resolve their outstanding tax liabilities. An installment agreement is an agreement between the IRS and a taxpayer that allows the taxpayer to pay assessed tax liabilities over time. An offer in compromise is different in that if it is accepted by the IRS, it allows a taxpayer to pay a specified amount to settle assessed tax liabilities, plus penalties and interest, for less than the amount owed. Installment agreements are entered into with the understanding that the tax liability, plus penalties and interest, will be paid in full. An installment agreement, unlike an offer in compromise, does not reduce the balance due. On the contrary, an installment agreement actually has the effect of increasing the total amount due, because penalties and interest continue to accrue during the duration of the agreement, until the balance is paid in full.

4.08 INSTALLMENT AGREEMENT

An Installment Agreement allows taxpayers to pay their full debt in smaller, more manageable amounts. Installment agreements generally require equal monthly payments. The amount of installment payments and the number taxpayers make will be based on the amount owed and the ability to pay that amount within the time the IRS can legally collect payment. Once an installment payment plan has been approved, the IRS <u>will</u> continue to charge the taxpayer's account with interest on the taxpayer's unpaid balance of penalties and interest. Installment payments may be paid by electronic transfers from the taxpayer's bank account. While the taxpayer is making installment payments, the IRS may require the taxpayer to provide financial information on his/her financial condition to determine any change in his/her ability to pay. The IRS may file a Notice of Federal Tax Lien to secure the government's interest until the taxpayer makes the final payment. Failure to pay an installment can result in the termination of the agreement. Installment payments may be paid by payroll deductions from the taxpayer's employer.

Requesting an Installment Agreement:
Before requesting an installment agreement, the taxpayer (or practitioner) should have a complete understanding of the taxpayer's case, especially the amount of the unpaid liability and the tax years and/or periods for which the liability is owed. This information can be found in IRS *collection notices* that the taxpayer may have received, or by obtaining the taxpayer's transcripts of account from the IRS. The transcripts of account will give the most complete picture of the taxpayer's case. The taxpayer must be in compliance with current tax filing and payment requirements. The IRS will not consider granting an installment agreement unless all returns have been filed for the last 6 years (and the IRS may require the filing of delinquent returns for earlier years as well). The taxpayer must also be current with estimated tax payments or have adequate withholding (IRM 5.1.11).

Extensions of Time to Pay:
If a taxpayer is able to pay a tax liability in full, but needs some additional time to obtain the funds, a short term extension of time to pay a tax liability may be available as an alternative to an installment agreement. For taxpayers whose cases are in the notice stage or are being handled by the IRS Automated Collection System (ACS), the IRS can generally authorize an extension of time to pay delinquent liabilities in full, without requiring taxpayers to submit collection information statements.

Termination of an Installment Agreement:
The IRS may terminate an installment agreement without notice if the IRS believes that collection of the underlying tax is in jeopardy. Additionally, the IRS may terminate an installment agreement if:
    (a) Information that was provided to the IRS in connection with either the granting of the installment agreement or a request for a financial update was inaccurate or incomplete in any material respect.
    (b) The taxpayer fails to pay an installment payment when due.

(c) The taxpayer fails to pay another tax liability when due (including under other TINs for the same taxpayer).
(d) The taxpayer fails to provide a financial condition update when requested.
(e) The taxpayer refuses to pay a modified payment amount based upon updated financial information.

Unless the collection of tax is in jeopardy, the IRS must notify the taxpayer in writing at least 30 days prior to altering, modifying or terminating an installment agreement. The notice must describe the reason for the proposed modification or termination of the agreement.

Types of Installment Agreements:
There are 4 types of installment agreements.
   (a) Guaranteed installment agreements.
   (b) Streamlined installment agreements.
   (c) In-business trust-fund express agreements.
   (d) Installment agreements requiring financial analysis.

(a) *Guaranteed installment agreements* - A guaranteed installment agreement is available for the payment of tax liabilities of $10,000 or less, exclusive of interest, penalties, additions to tax, and any other additional amounts, provided that the liability can be paid within 3 years and certain conditions are met. Taxpayers seeking a guaranteed installment agreement are not required to submit a Collection Information Statement or otherwise disclose information about their ability to pay their outstanding tax liabilities.

(b) *Streamlined installment agreements* - A "streamlined" installment agreement is generally available for unpaid liabilities of up to $25,000, including assessed tax, penalties and interest, provided that the balance due will be paid in full within 5 years. No financial statement is required for a streamlined installment agreement.

(c) *In-business trust-fund express agreements* - An in-business trust fund express installment agreement is available to business taxpayers with employment tax liabilities (i.e., trust fund liabilities) that do not exceed $10,000 and can be paid within 2 years or before the expiration of the collection statute of limitations, whichever is earlier. No financial statement is required, and the IRS does not make a determination regarding asserting the Trust Fund Recovery.

(d) *Installment agreements requiring financial analysis* – This type of agreement is for taxpayers who do not qualify for a guaranteed, streamlined, or in-business trust fund express installment agreement, typically because their total tax liabilities exceed $25,000. The IRS requires these taxpayers to submit a collection information statement, detailing their income, expenses and assets (Code Sec. 6159).

Penalties or Additions to Tax:
No interest is imposed on most penalties, additional amounts, and additions to tax if the amount is paid within 21 days from the date the IRS issues a notice and demand for payment. If the amount is not paid within the 21-day period, interest accrues from the date of the notice and demand to the date of payment. If the total of tax, interest, and penalties equals or exceeds $100,000, the tax must be paid within 10 business days. Interest will continue to accrue if the tax is not paid within 21 calendar days (or where applicable, 10 business days).

When income tax return is examined by the IRS and the taxpayer agrees with the proposed changes, the taxpayer has several ways by which he or she may settle the account and pay any additional tax that is due. If a taxpayer pays when he or she signs the agreement, the interest is generally figured *from the due date of the return to the date of his payment*. If the taxpayer does not pay the additional tax when he or she signs the agreement, he or she will receive a bill and the interest on the additional tax is generally figured *from the due date of the return to the billing date* (Code Sec. 6601).

4.09 OFFERS IN COMPROMISE

The Commissioner of the IRS has the authority to compromise all taxes (including any interest, penalty, or addition to the tax) arising under the revenue laws of the United States, except those relating to alcohol, tobacco, and firearms. Submission of an offer in compromise will usually extend the statute of limitations on collection of an account. Taxpayers have a right by law to submit an offer in compromise on their unpaid tax liability. With an offer in compromise, the taxpayer may be allowed to pay less than the full amount owed and the Collection actions, such as levy, may be delayed. A rejected offer in compromise may also be appealed.

> **Definition:**

An offer in compromise (OIC) is an agreement between a taxpayer and the IRS that settles the taxpayer's tax liabilities for less than the full amount owed. If the liabilities can be fully paid through an installment agreement or other means, the taxpayer will in most cases not be eligible for an OIC. In most cases, the IRS will not accept an offer unless the amount offered by the taxpayer is equal to or greater than the reasonable collection potential (the RCP). The RCP is how the IRS measures the taxpayer's ability to pay. The RCP includes the value that can be realized from the taxpayer's assets, such as real property, automobiles, bank accounts, and other property. In addition to property, the RCP also includes anticipated future income, less certain amounts allowed for basic living expenses.

The IRS may accept an OIC based on three grounds:
(a) **Doubt as to liability** - This ground is only met when genuine doubt exists that the IRS has correctly determined the amount owed.

(b) ***Doubt that the amount owed is collectible*** - This means that doubt exists in any case where the taxpayer's assets and income are less than the full amount of the tax liability. The doubt as to the liability for the amount owed must be supported by the evidence.

(c) ***Effective tax administration*** - An offer may be accepted based on effective tax administration when there is no doubt that the full amount owed can be collected, but requiring payment in full would either create an economic hardship or would be unfair and inequitable because of exceptional circumstances.

➤ Lump sum installment:

Taxpayers may choose to pay the offer amount in a *lump sum* or in *installment payments*. A lump sum offer is defined as an offer payable in 5 or fewer installments. If a taxpayer submits a lump sum offer, the taxpayer must include with the Form 656 a nonrefundable payment equal to 20% of the offer amount. This payment is required in addition to the $150 application fee. The 20% amount will be applied to the taxpayer's tax liability and the taxpayer has a right to specify the particular tax liabilities to which the periodic payments will be applied.

➤ Periodic payment offer:

Periodic payment offer is payable in 6 or more installments. When submitting a periodic payment offer, the taxpayer must include the first proposed installment payment along with the Form 656. This payment is required in addition to the $150 application fee. This amount is nonrefundable. While the IRS is evaluating a periodic payment offer, the taxpayer must continue to make the installment payments provided for under the terms of the offer. These amounts are also nonrefundable. These amounts are applied to the tax liabilities and the taxpayer has a right to specify the particular tax liabilities to which the periodic payments will be applied.

➤ Statutory Time:

Ordinarily, the statutory time within which the IRS may engage in collection activities is suspended during the period that the OIC is under consideration and is further suspended if the OIC is rejected by the IRS and the taxpayer appeals the rejection to the IRS Office of Appeals within 30 days from the date of the notice of rejection.

➤ Accepted OIC:

If the IRS accepts the taxpayer's offer in compromise (OIC), the IRS expects that the taxpayer will have no further delinquencies and will fully comply with the tax laws. If the taxpayer does not abide by all the terms and conditions of the OIC, the IRS may determine that the OIC is in default. To avoid a default, the taxpayer must timely file all tax returns and timely pay all taxes for 5 years or until the offered amount is paid in full, whichever period is longer. When an OIC is declared to be in default, the agreement is no longer in effect and the IRS may then collect the amounts originally owed, plus interest and penalties.

> **Rejected and Returned OIC:**

If the IRS rejects an OIC, then the taxpayer will be notified by mail. The letter will explain the reason that the IRS rejected the offer and will provide detailed instructions on how the taxpayer may appeal the decision to the IRS Office of Appeals. The appeal must be made within 30 days from the date of the letter. An OIC is returned to the taxpayer rather than rejected, in cases where the taxpayer has:
   (a) Not submitted necessary information.
   (b) Filed for bankruptcy.
   (c) Failed to include a required application fee or nonrefundable payment with the offer.
   (d) Failed to file tax returns or pay current tax liabilities while the offer is under consideration.

A return is different from a rejection because there is no right to appeal the IRS's decision to return the offer.

4.10 PERIOD FOR COLLECTION AFTER ASSESSMENT

Code Section 6502 provides that the IRS generally has 10 years from the date of assessment to collect a tax liability by levy or by court proceeding. The 10-year limitations period may be extended by execution of a written agreement with the IRS. If collection is not begun within the limitations period, the IRS generally will be unable to collect the tax. However, where a bond has been given to secure collection of a tax, suit may be maintained on such bond, even though the statute of limitations has expired on the assessment and collection of the tax.

If a timely court proceeding has commenced for the collection of the tax, then the period during which the tax may be collected is extended until the liability for tax (or a judgment against the taxpayer) is satisfied or becomes unenforceable.

Effective after 1999, the 10-year limitations period on collections may not be extended if there has not been a levy on any of the taxpayer's property. If the taxpayer entered into an installment agreement with the IRS, however, the 10-year limitations period may be extended for the period that the limitations period was extended under the original terms of the installment agreement plus 90 days. If, in any request made on or before December 31, 1999, a taxpayer agreed to extend the 10-year period of limitations on collections, the extension will expire on the latest of:
   (1) The last day of the original 10-year limitations period,
   (2) December 31, 2002, or
   (3) In the case of an extension in connection with an installment agreement, the 90th day after the extension.

The date of the assessment is the date the summary record is signed by the assessment officer. The date on which a levy on property or rights to property is made is the date on which the notice of seizure is given (Reg. Sec. 301.6502-1).

Code Sec. 6503 provides for the suspension of the collection period in several situations. The more common situations are:
- (i) Issuance of a statutory notice of deficiency.
- (ii) Assets of the taxpayer in control or custody of a court.
- (iii) Taxpayer is outside of the United States for a continuous period of 6 months.
- (iv) An extension exists for the payment of an estate tax.
- (v) A wrongful seizure of property or a wrongful lien on property.
- (vi) Taxpayer's bankruptcy automatically stays assessment or collection.

Each time an extension is requested, the IRS must notify the taxpayer that the taxpayer may refuse to extend the period of limitations or may limit the extension to particular issues or to a particular period of time. Form 872-A (Special Consent to Extend Time to Assess Tax) extends the assessment period indefinitely.

4.11 TAXPAYER ADVOCATE SERVICE (TAS)

The Taxpayer Advocate Service is an independent organization within the IRS whose employees assist taxpayers who are experiencing economic harm, who are seeking help in resolving tax problems that have not been resolved through normal channels, or who believe that an IRS system or procedure is not working as it should. Taxpayers may be eligible for assistance if:
- (a) They are experiencing economic harm or significant cost (including fees for professional representation),
- (b) They have experienced a delay of more than 30 days to resolve their tax issue, or
- (c) They have not received a response or resolution to the problem by the date that was promised by the IRS.

TAS also identifies systemic problems that exist within the IRS and propose changes in the administrative practices while identify potential legislative changes which may be appropriate to mitigate such problems. These observations and proposals are presented to Congress each year in the National Taxpayer Advocate's *Annual Report to Congress.* The Problem Resolution program is under the authority of the National Taxpayer Advocate.

Functions of TAS:
The functions of the Taxpayer Advocate Office are:
- a) To assist taxpayers in resolving problems with the IRS.
- b) To identify areas in which taxpayers have problems dealing with the IRS.
- c) To the extent possible, to propose changes in the IRS's administrative practices that would mitigate such problems.
- d) To identify possible law changes that might also mitigate such problems.

Responsibilities of TAS:

The National Taxpayer Advocate is responsible for:
1) Monitoring the coverage and geographical allocation of local offices of taxpayer advocates.
2) Developing guidelines for IRS officers and employees outlining the criteria for referral of taxpayer inquiries to local offices of taxpayer advocates.
3) Ensuring that local telephone numbers for each local office of taxpayer advocate are published and available to taxpayers served by the office.
4) In conjunction with the Commissioner, developing career paths for local taxpayer advocates choosing to make a career in the Office of Taxpayer Advocate.

The National Taxpayer Advocate also appoints local taxpayer advocates, with at least one in each state, and evaluates and makes personnel decisions with respect to taxpayer advocate employees.

IRS's Problem Resolution Program - A taxpayer may obtain written advice from the IRS through the IRS's problem resolution program. The taxpayer may make inquiries and seek answers to complaints and problems to the problem resolution officer in his or her district. Through the problem resolution program, a taxpayer may file an application for a taxpayer assistance order (TAO). A TAO may be issued by the National Taxpayer Advocate (who is in charge of the nationwide management of the problem resolution program), or a designee of the Taxpayer Advocate, if it is determined that the taxpayer is suffering or will suffer a significant hardship because of the manner in which the IRS is enforcing the tax laws.

The Taxpayer Advocate Service will also attempt to assist the taxpayer in cases in which the taxpayer has not received a response or resolution to a problem or inquiry by the date given by the IRS, or in instances in which a system or procedure did not operate as intended or did not resolve the problem. TAO cannot be used to circumvent provisions of the Code, even if application of the Code will result in significant hardship to the taxpayer. Accordingly, if a taxpayer files a claim for refund after the period of limitations has expired, a TAO cannot be issued, even though the taxpayer may be suffering a significant hardship (Code Sec. 7803).

4.12   UNIT 4: QUESTIONS

TRUE/FALSE QUESTIONS:
Please select either (A) for True or (B) for False

1. Filing a petition in bankruptcy under Title 11 of the United States Code automatically stays assessment and collection of a tax. The stay remains in effect until the bankruptcy court discharges liability for the tax or lifts the stay.
    A. TRUE.
    B. FALSE.

2. Generally, the IRS has the authority to collect outstanding federal taxes for not more than three years from the date of assessment.
    A. TRUE.
    B. FALSE.

3. Bankruptcy proceedings will always result in the discharge of federal tax liabilities.
    A. TRUE.
    B. FALSE.

4. A levy is a legal claim against your property used as a security for the tax debt; whereas, a lien is a legal seizure of your property to satisfy a tax debt.
    A. TRUE.
    B. FALSE.

5. A taxpayer's appeal to the IRS regarding the IRS's filing of a Notice of Federal Tax Lien may succeed if the taxpayer is in bankruptcy and subject to the automatic stay provisions when the lien is filed.
    A. TRUE.
    B. FALSE.

6. Unemployment, job training benefits, and workers' compensation are exempt from levy by the IRS.
    A. TRUE.
    B. FALSE.

7. A federal tax lien gives the IRS legal claim to the property subject to the lien as security or payment for the tax debt.
    A. TRUE.
    B. FALSE.

8. A levy is the taking of property to satisfy a tax liability.
    A. TRUE.
    B. FALSE.

9. According to Section 6334, unemployment benefits are the only property exempt from levy by federal law.
   A. TRUE.
   B. FALSE.

10. Once served, a levy on salary or wages continues for 90 days or until satisfaction of the tax liability.
    A. TRUE.
    B. FALSE.

11. A levy may be sent to a taxpayer by mail or left at the taxpayer's home or workplace.
    A. TRUE.
    B. FALSE.

12. Bankruptcy proceedings will always permanently stop the IRS from enforcement action.
    A. TRUE.
    B. FALSE.

13. A Notice of Federal Tax Lien does not attach to property acquired after the lien filing date.
    A. TRUE.
    B. FALSE.

14. The IRS may use a levy to legally seize your property to satisfy a tax debt.
    A. TRUE.
    B. FALSE.

15. A federal tax lien gives the IRS a legal claim to your property as security for payment of your tax debt.
    A. TRUE.
    B. FALSE.

MULTIPLE CHOICE QUESTIONS:
Please select the most appropriate answer.

16. The collection process begins
    A. At the IRS service center where notices are generated requesting payment.
    B. In an IRS automated collection branch when telephone contact is made with the taxpayer.
    C. Only after the problem resolution officer has acted upon the taxpayer's claim.
    D. With the filing of a Notice of Federal Tax Lien.

17. The initial action required in the collection process is
    A. The filing of a Notice of Levy.
    B. An assessment.
    C. The receipt of the fourth notice by certified mail.
    D. A notification of a pending examination audit.

18. With regard to the statute of limitations, all of the following statements apply to requests to extend the statute, effective date prior to December 31, 2002. All of the statements are true except
    A. If tax has been assessed within the 3-year limitation period, the IRS generally has 10 years following the assessment to begin a proceeding to collect the tax by levy or in a court proceeding.
    B. Form 872-A, Special Consent to Extend Time to Assess Tax, extends the assessment period indefinitely.
    C. The 10-year collection period may not be extended after it has expired, even if there has been a levy on any part of the taxpayer's property prior to the expiration and the extension is agreed to in writing before the levy is released.
    D. Each time an extension is requested, the IRS must notify the taxpayer that the taxpayer may refuse to extend the period of limitations or may limit the extension to particular issues or to a particular period of time.

19. When dealing with IRS employees, you have certain rights. Which of the following most accurately reflects those rights?
    A. A right of appeal is available for most collection actions.
    B. A right of representation is only available in audit matters; it is not available for collection matters.
    C. A case may not be transferred to a different IRS office, even if your authorized representative is located in an area different from your residence.
    D. If you disagree with the IRS employee who handles your case, you must first have the employee's permission before requesting a meeting with the manager.

20. With regard to an installment agreement with the IRS to pay a federal tax debt, which of the following statements is false?
    A. Once an installment payment plan has been approved, the IRS will not continue to charge the taxpayer's account with interest on the taxpayer's unpaid balance of penalties and interest.
    B. Installment payments may be paid by electronic transfers from the taxpayer's bank account.
    C. While the taxpayer is making installment payments, the IRS may require the taxpayer to provide financial information on his/her financial condition to determine any change in his/her ability to pay.
    D. The IRS may file a Notice of Federal Tax Lien to secure the government's interest until the taxpayer makes the final payment.

21. Mr. and Mrs. Johnson's 2003 individual tax return was selected for audit by the IRS in December 2004. The audit was completed on May 3, 2005, and the Johnsons agreed to an increase in tax of $5,800. The actual assessment was made on June 8, 2005. The IRS Collection Division has until what date to collect the tax due (disregarding weekends and holidays)?
    A. April 15, 2007.
    B. May 3, 2008.
    C. June 15, 2008.
    D. June 8, 2015.

22. Which of the following may the IRS settle by accepting an Offer in Compromise for less than the full amount of the balance due?
    A. A tax deficiency, but not penalties and accrued interest.
    B. A tax deficiency plus penalties, but not accrued interest.
    C. A tax deficiency plus accrued interest, but not penalties.
    D. A tax deficiency plus penalties and accrued interest.

23. Late payments by a taxpayer on an installment agreement to pay a tax liability will
    A. Necessitate payment by certified check.
    B. Extend the statute of limitations.
    C. Generate a Notice of Intent to Levy.
    D. Generate a 30-day notice as to the cessation of the agreement.

24. Which of the following statements is false with respect to taxpayers' offers in compromise on unpaid tax liabilities?
    A. A compromise may be made only when doubt exists as to the liability for the amount owed.
    B. The Commissioner of Internal Revenue has the authority to compromise all taxes (including any interest, penalty, or addition to the tax) arising under the revenue laws of the United States, except those relating to alcohol, tobacco, and firearms.
    C. Submission of an offer in compromise will usually extend the statute of limitations on collection of an account.
    D. Taxpayers have a right by law to submit an offer in compromise on their unpaid tax liability.

25. Madonna received a Notice of Tax Due and Demand for Payment in the amount of $30,000 as a result of an examination of her 2003 Form 1040. She is not able to pay the entire amount at this time and would like to set up an installment agreement. Which of the following statements are not true regarding setting up an installment agreement?
    A. Madonna must wait for a Notice of Federal Tax Lien to be filed before she can request an installment agreement.
    B. Madonna may have to fill out a Collection Information Statement.
    C. Madonna will be charged a user fee to set up an installment agreement.

D. Madonna must file all of her returns that are due to be eligible for an installment agreement.

26. Generally, how long does the IRS have to collect outstanding federal taxes?
    A. 10 years from the due date of the return.
    B. 10 years from the date the return is filed.
    C. 10 years from the date of the notice of deficiency.
    D. 10 years from the date of assessment.

27. Sam timely filed his U.S. individual income tax return for calendar year 1993 without any extensions. The return showed a balance of income taxes due in the amount of $55,000. Sam has not paid his IRS liability, nor has he entered into any installment agreement extending the statute of limitations or submitted any offer in compromise. The statute of limitations for collection of Sam's tax liability expires on which of the following dates?
    A. April 15, 1997.
    B. April 15, 2003.
    C. December 31, 2003.
    D. April 15, 2004.

28. After assessment, as a general rule, the IRS has the authority to collect outstanding federal taxes for which of the following?
    A. Three years.
    B. Five years.
    C. Ten years.
    D. Twenty years.

29. Which of the following may the IRS settle by accepting an Offer in Compromise for less than the full amount of the balance due?
    A. There is doubt as to whether or not the assessed tax is correct.
    B. There is doubt as to the collectability.
    C. Both A and B as stated above.
    D. A tax deficiency plus accrued interest, but not penalties.

30. Which of the following statements with respect to taxpayers' offers in compromise on unpaid tax liabilities is true?
    A. A taxpayer does not have the right to submit an offer in compromise on his/her tax bill but is given the opportunity in order to increase voluntary compliance with the tax laws.
    B. Doubt as to the liability for the amount owed must be supported by evidence, and the amount acceptable under the offer in compromise will depend on the degree of doubt found in the particular case.
    C. Submission of an offer in compromise automatically suspends the collection of an account.

D. If the offer in compromise is made on the grounds that doubt exists as to the taxpayer's ability to make full payment on the amount owed, the amount offered must give sufficient consideration only to the taxpayer's present earning capacity.

31. Which of the following is true with respect to an offer in compromise?
    A. The taxpayer may be allowed to pay less than the full amount owed.
    B. Collection actions, such as levy, may be delayed.
    C. A rejected offer may be appealed.
    D. All of the answers are correct.

32. The installment agreement is one of the acceptable methods of paying off a tax debt to the United States Treasury. Financial information on a "Collection Information Statement" may be required as a condition of the installment agreement. Generally, an installment agreement will be accepted without this statement if the dollar amount is
    A. $20,000 or less if it is a joint return.
    B. $25,000 or more.
    C. At least $15,000 for the current year, but less than $20,000 for all years.
    D. $10,000 or less.

33. The IRS may accept an Offer in Compromise to settle unpaid tax accounts for less than the full amount due. A Collection Information Statement (financial statement) is not required with the offer when the reason for the offer is
    A. Doubt as to liability.
    B. Doubt as to collectability.
    C. To promote effective tax administration.
    D. Economic hardship.

34. Which of the following statements with respect to resolving tax problems involving the collection process is false?
    A. You may be entitled to a reimbursement for fees charged by your bank if the IRS has erroneously levied your account.
    B. You should first request assistance from IRS collection employees or their managers before seeking assistance from the problem resolution officer.
    C. If you suffer a significant hardship because of the collection of the tax liability, you may request assistance from the IRS on Form 911, Application for Assistance Order to Relieve Hardship.
    D. IRS collection division managers have the authority to issue a Taxpayer Assistance Order if a taxpayer is about to suffer a significant hardship because of the collection of the tax liability.

35. If the taxpayer cannot resolve a collection problem through discussions with the revenue officer or his/her manager, the taxpayer should contact
    A. An IRS taxpayer service representative.
    B. The IRS district problem resolution officer.

C. The IRS district director.
D. The IRS regional appeals office.

36. With regard to the IRS filing a Notice of Federal Tax Lien, which of the following statements is not a requirement?
    A. The IRS must assess the tax.
    B. The IRS must send the taxpayer a notice and demand for payment.
    C. The IRS must give individual notices to all of the taxpayer's creditors.
    D. The taxpayer must neglect or refuse to pay the tax or otherwise neglect or refuse to resolve his/her tax liability problems.

37. Which of the following statements regarding a Notice of Federal Tax Lien is true?
    A. It is a public notice to the taxpayer's creditors that the government has a claim against all of the taxpayer's property, not including property that is acquired after the lien came into existence.
    B. All fees charged by the state or other jurisdiction for both filing and releasing the lien will be added to the balance the taxpayer owes.
    C. The IRS will issue a Release of the Notice of Federal Tax Lien within 10 days after acceptance of a bond guaranteeing payment of the liability.
    D. A taxpayer cannot sue the federal government for damages if the IRS negligently fails to release a Notice of Federal Tax Lien when a release is warranted.

38. A tax lien is a legal claim to property as security or payment for a tax debt. Select the best answer regarding the filing of a Notice of Federal Tax Lien
    A. May be filed simultaneously with a Notice and Demand for Payment.
    B. May be filed when a tax deficiency resulting from an audit is agreed to.
    C. May not be filed when an installment agreement is in effect and payments are being made.
    D. May be filed after a tax liability is assessed, billed, and the debt is not paid within 10 days of notification.

39. When levies are attached, the IRS has the authority to take property to satisfy a tax debt. The IRS may levy all of the following except
    A. Accounts receivable.
    B. Workers' compensation.
    C. Rental income.
    D. Commissions.

40. Once a notice of federal tax lien has been filed, all of the following are true except
    A. The lien applies to all of the taxpayer's real and personal property and to all of his/her rights to property until the tax is paid or the lien is removed.
    B. The IRS will issue a release of the notice of federal tax lien within 15 business days after the taxpayer satisfies the tax due (including interest and other additions) by

paying the debt, by having it adjusted, or if the IRS accepts a bond that the taxpayer submits, by guaranteeing a payment of the debt.
C. By law, a filed notice of tax lien can be withdrawn if withdrawal will speed collecting the tax.
D. The law requires the IRS to notify the taxpayer in writing within 5 business days after the filing of a lien.

41. With regard to seizure of property in satisfaction of a tax liability, all of the following are true except
    A. Any real property used as a residence by the taxpayer may not be seized to satisfy a levy of $5,000 or less.
    B. The taxpayer's principal residence may not be seized without the written approval of a U.S. district court judge or magistrate.
    C. Before the sale of property, the IRS will compute a minimum bid price. If the minimum is not offered at the sale, the IRS may buy the property.
    D. If the proceeds of a sale by the IRS are less than the total of the tax bill and the expenses of the levy and sale, the taxpayer will not have to pay the balance.

42. Mr. Alomar's income tax return was examined by the IRS, and he agreed with the proposed changes. He has several ways by which he may settle his account and pay any additional tax that is due. Which of the following statements with respect to this situation is false?
    A. If he pays when he signs the agreement, the interest is generally figured from the due date of the return to the date of his payment.
    B. If he does not pay the additional tax when he signs the agreement, he will receive a bill. The interest on the additional tax is generally figured from the due date of the return to the billing date.
    C. If the bill is delayed, he will not be billed for additional interest for more than 60 days from the date he signed the agreement.
    D. If he pays the amount due within 21 days of the billing date, he will not have to pay more interest or penalties.

43. Mr. Smith's 2003 income tax return, which he filed on May 3, 2004, was examined by the IRS. Smith did not have an extension of time to file. On October 20, 2005, he signed a report agreeing to a deficiency of $10,000. He received a notice and demand showing additional tax, interest, and penalties. The notice was dated November 7, 2005. If Mr. Smith paid the bill on November 12, 2005, which of the following reflects the date interest started accruing and the date it stopped?

	Interest Started	Interest Ended
A.	4/16/04	11/7/05
B.	4/16/04	11/12/05
C.	5/3/04	11/7/05
D.	10/20/05	11/12/05

44. With regard to the levy method used by the IRS to collect tax that has not been paid voluntarily, which of the following statements is false?
   A. The IRS cannot levy any state income tax refund checks and apply the state refund to a federal tax debt.
   B. If the IRS levies a taxpayer's bank account, the bank is required to hold the funds the taxpayer has on deposit, up to the amount the taxpayer owes, for 21 days.
   C. Levies can be made on property that is the taxpayer's but is held by third parties.
   D. The IRS will release a levy if the IRS determines the levy is creating an economic hardship for the taxpayer.

45. Which of the following statements in respect to IRS seizure and sale of a taxpayer's property to satisfy his/her federal tax bill is false?
   A. A taxpayer does not have the right to redeem any property seized once the IRS has sold it.
   B. Unless the property is perishable and must be sold immediately, the IRS will wait at least 10 days after seizure before conducting the sale.
   C. Before the date of sale, the IRS may release the property to the taxpayer if (s)he pays the amount equal to the amount of the government's interest in the property.
   D. The taxpayer may request a re-computation if (s)he is in disagreement with the minimum price the IRS has determined it will accept for the property.

46. Which of the following best describes a levy when it relates to a tax debt?
   A. A levy is not a legal seizure of property.
   B. A levy on salary or wages will end when the time expires for legally collecting the tax.
   C. A levy can only be released by the filing of a lien.
   D. A levy does not apply to wearing apparel and school books.

47. If the IRS must seize (levy) a taxpayer's property, the taxpayer has the right by federal law to keep all of the following except
   A. A limited amount of personal belongings, furniture, and business or professional books and tools.
   B. Unemployment and job training benefits and workers' compensation.
   C. Salary or wages that have been included in a judgment for court-ordered child support payments.
   D. The taxpayer's primary residence if the collection of tax is in jeopardy.

48. Which of the following statements with respect to IRS seizure and sale of a taxpayer's property to satisfy the taxpayer's tax bill is false?
   A. A seizure may not be made on any property if the estimated cost of the seizure and sale exceeds the fair market value of the property to be seized.
   B. A taxpayer has the right to an administrative review of a seizure action when the IRS has taken personal property that is necessary to the maintenance of the taxpayer's business.

C. The IRS must wait 30 days after seizure before conducting a sale.
D. After the sale, proceeds are applied first to the expenses of the levy and sale.

49. With respect to the IRS's seizures and sales of personal property to satisfy a federal tax debt, which of the following statements is false?
    A. After the notice of sale has been given to the taxpayer, the IRS must wait 10 days before conducting the sale unless the property is perishable and must be sold immediately.
    B. After the sale, the IRS uses the proceeds first to satisfy the tax debt.
    C. If real estate was sold, the taxpayer, or anyone with an interest in the property, may redeem it at any time within 180 days after the sale by paying the purchaser the amount paid for the property plus a certain percentage of interest.
    D. Before the date of sale, the IRS computes a "minimum bid price," which is the lowest amount the IRS will accept for the sale of that property to protect the taxpayer's interest in that property.

50. All of the following statements with regard to interest and penalties on agreed cases are true except
    A. Jan agreed to the proposed changes. She signed the agreement form and paid the additional tax. Jan will pay interest on the additional tax. Interest is figured from the due date of the return to the date she paid the additional tax. Joseph agreed to the proposed changes. He signed the agreement form, but he did not pay the additional tax.
    B. Joseph received a bill that included the interest. He paid the bill of $5,500 11 days after the billing date. He will not have to pay more interest or penalties.
    C. Jody agreed to the proposed changes. She signed the agreement form, but she did not pay the additional tax of $2,700. On June 5, 2005, Jody received a bill dated June 2, 2005 that included the interest. She paid the bill on June 21, 2005. Jody will owe additional interest.
    D. Jane agreed to the proposed changes. She signed the agreement form on May 18, 2005, but she did not pay the bill until October 3, 2005. Jane will owe additional interest.

51. Which of the following statements with respect to a levy is false?
    A. A levy can be made on property in the hands of third parties or in the taxpayer's possession.
    B. Generally, court authorization is not required before levy action is taken.
    C. A Final Notice of Intent to Levy is not enforceable unless this notice is given to the taxpayer in person.
    D. The IRS must release a levy if the fair market value of the property exceeds the levy and its release would not hinder the collection of tax.

52. Jeopardy levies may occur when the IRS waives the 10-day notice and demand period and/or the 30-day Final Notice (Notice of Intent to Levy) period because
    A. The taxpayer has filed for bankruptcy protection.
    B. The seized property is perishable in nature.
    C. The IRS is working in conjunction with the Drug Enforcement Administration.
    D. A delay would endanger the collection of tax.

53. A taxpayer's primary residence may not be seized and sold by the IRS unless the collection of the tax is in jeopardy or approval has been secured from
    A. The involved revenue officer's immediate supervisor.
    B. The IRS chief of collections.
    C. The IRS district director or assistant district director.
    D. The IRS regional commissioner or assistant regional commissioner.

54. Which of the following statements is false in respect to a Notice of Federal Tax Lien?
    A. It is a public notice to the taxpayer's creditors that the government has a claim against all of the taxpayer's real, personal, and/or business property, including property that was acquired after the lien came into existence.
    B. All fees charged by the state or other jurisdiction for both filing and releasing the lien will be added to the balance you owe.
    C. The IRS will issue a Release of the Notice of Federal Tax Lien within 30 days after acceptance of a bond guaranteeing payment of the liability.
    D. A taxpayer cannot sue the federal government for damages if the IRS knowingly or negligently fails to release a Notice of Federal Tax Lien when a release is warranted.

55. Which of the following statements with respect to resolving tax problems involving the collection process is false?
    A. A taxpayer may be entitled to a reimbursement for fees charged by his/her bank if the IRS has erroneously levied his/her account.
    B. A taxpayer should first request assistance from IRS collection employees or their managers before seeking assistance from the problem resolution officer.
    C. If a taxpayer suffers a significant hardship because of the collection of the tax liability, (s)he may request assistance from the IRS on Form 911, Application for Assistance Order to Relieve Hardship.
    D. While a taxpayer is making installment payments, interest will continue to accrue only on the tax liability due.

56. During the period of an installment agreement
    A. All payments must be made timely, and interest and penalties must continue to accrue.
    B. Timely payments suspend the accrual of interest and penalties.
    C. Payments can be made only by certified check.
    D. A release of Notice of Federal Tax Lien is filed.

57. If the IRS seizes property that is not perishable, the IRS will
    A. Request sealed bids for the property.
    B. Advertise the sale for 90 days before the sale.
    C. Conduct the sale after the property has been held 60 days.
    D. Wait at least 10 days after seizure before conducting the sale.

58. With regard to an installment agreement with the IRS to pay a federal tax debt, which of the following statements is false?
    A. Failure to pay an installment can result in the termination of the agreement.
    B. Installment payments may be paid by payroll deductions from the taxpayer's employer.
    C. While the taxpayer is making installment payments, the IRS may require the taxpayer to provide financial information on his/her financial condition to determine any change in his/her ability to pay.
    D. Installment plans are set up so that tax liability due will be paid off in four equal installments.

4.13   UNIT 4: ANSWERS

1. **(A) Correct**
   Filing a petition in bankruptcy under Title 11 of the United States Code automatically stays assessment and collection of a tax. The stay remains in effect until the bankruptcy court discharges liability for the tax or lifts the stay.

2. **(B) Correct**
   Code Section 6502 provides that the IRS generally has 10 years from the date of assessment to collect a tax liability by levy or by court proceeding. The 10-year limitations period may be extended by execution of a written agreement with the IRS.

3. **(B) Correct**
   For all bankruptcy cases filed after October 16, 2005, the Bankruptcy Code provides that if the debtor does not file a tax return that becomes due after the commencement of the bankruptcy case, or obtain an extension for filing the return before the due date, the taxing authority may request that the court either dismiss the case or convert the case to a case under another chapter of the Bankruptcy Code. If the debtor does not file the required return or obtain an extension within 90 days after the request is made, the bankruptcy court must dismiss or convert the case.

4. **(B) Correct**
   A *Lien* is a legal claim against property used as a security for the tax debt; whereas, a *Levy* is a legal seizure (taking) of property to satisfy a tax debt.

5. **(A) Correct**
   A taxpayer's appeal to the IRS regarding the IRS's filing of a Notice of Federal Tax Lien may succeed if the taxpayer is in bankruptcy and subject to the automatic stay provisions when the lien is filed. This usually happens if the taxpayer believes the IRS filed a Notice of Federal Tax Lien in error.

6. **(A) Correct**
   The following items are exempt from levy:
   (a) Wearing apparel and such school books
   (b) Fuel, provisions, furniture, and personal effects
   (c) Books and tools necessary for the trade, business, or profession
   (d) Unemployment benefits
   (e) Undelivered mail
   (f) Annuity or pension payments under the Railroad Retirement Act
   (g) Workmen's compensation
   (h) Judgments for support of minor children
   (i) Minimum exemption for wages, salary, and other income

(j) Certain service-connected disability payments
(k) Certain public assistance payments
(l) Assistance under job training partnership act
(m) Residences in small deficiency cases - If the amount of the levy does not exceed $5,000, any real property used as a residence by the taxpayer or any real property used as a residence by the taxpayer.

7. **(A) Correct**
The federal tax lien is the backbone of the federal tax collection process. A federal tax lien gives the IRS legal claim to the property subject to the lien as security or payment for the tax debt.
Elements of a federal tax lien are:
(1) Assessment.
(2) Notice and demand.
(3) Failure to pay.

8. **(A) Correct**
A <u>Levy</u> is a legal seizure (taking) of property to satisfy a tax debt.

9. **(B) Correct**
See Answer #6

10. **(B) Correct**
Levy on wages and salary (including fees, bonuses and commissions) remains viable until the tax liability covered by the levy is satisfied or becomes unenforceable because of a lapse of time. This type of levy must be promptly released when the liability out of which it arose is satisfied or becomes unenforceable due to lapse of time, and the IRS must promptly notify the person upon whom the levy was made (usually the employer) that it has been released. These continuous levy provisions apply to salary or wages earned but not yet paid at the time of levy and salary or wages earned and becoming payable (or paid in the form of an advance) after the date of the levy until the levy is released.

11. **(A) Correct**
The notice of intent to levy must:
(a) Be given in person.
(b) Be left at the dwelling or usual place of business of the taxpayer, or
(c) Be sent by registered or certified mail to the taxpayer's last known address.

12. **(B) Correct**
Filing a petition in bankruptcy under Title 11 of the United States Code automatically stays assessment and collection of a tax. The stay remains in effect until the bankruptcy court discharges liability for the tax or lifts the stay. A taxpayer's appeal to the IRS regarding the IRS's filing of a Notice of Federal Tax Lien may succeed if the taxpayer is in

bankruptcy and subject to the automatic stay provisions when the lien is filed. This usually happens if the taxpayer believes the IRS filed a Notice of Federal Tax Lien in error.

13. **(B) Correct**
A lien attaches to all of the taxpayer's property and rights to property owned on or acquired after the date of assessment (the lien filing date) (Code Sec.6321).

14. **(A) Correct**
The IRS may levy upon (seize) a taxpayer's property and rights to property if a taxpayer fails to pay a tax liability. *A Levy* is a legal seizure (taking) of property to satisfy a tax debt.

15. **(A) Correct**
The federal tax lien is the backbone of the federal tax collection process. A federal tax lien gives the IRS legal claim to the property subject to the lien as security or payment for the tax debt.

16. **(A) Correct**
Reg. 301.6303-1 states that the district director or the director of the regional service center shall, after making assessment of tax, give notice to each person liable for the unpaid tax, stating the amount and demanding payment. Therefore, the collection process begins at the IRS service center where notices are generated requesting payment.

17. **(B) Correct**
Elements of a federal tax lien are:
   (1) Assessment.
   (2) Notice and demand.
   (3) Failure to pay.
Thus, for a lien to arise the tax must be assessed, the IRS must make notice and demand on the taxpayer, and the taxpayer must fail to pay within 10 days after notice and demand (Code Sec. 6331).

18. **(C) Correct**
Code Section 6502 provides that the IRS generally has 10 years from the date of assessment to collect a tax liability by levy or by court proceeding. The 10-year limitations period may be extended by execution of a written agreement with the IRS. If collection is not begun within the limitations period, the IRS generally will be unable to collect the tax. Each time an extension is requested, the IRS must notify the taxpayer that the taxpayer may refuse to extend the period of limitations or may limit the extension to particular issues or to a particular period of time. Form 872-A (Special Consent to Extend Time to Assess Tax) extends the assessment period indefinitely.

19. **(A) Correct**
    If a taxpayer disagrees with the IRS about the amount of tax liability or certain collection actions, he or she has the right to ask the Appeals Office to review the case. The taxpayer may also ask a court to review the case. This (right of appeals) is one of the most important rights during the collection process.

20. **(A) Correct**
    An Installment Agreement allows taxpayers to pay their full debt in smaller, more manageable amounts. Installment agreements generally require equal monthly payments. The amount of installment payments and the number taxpayers make will be based on the amount owed and the ability to pay that amount within the time the IRS can legally collect payment. Once an installment payment plan has been approved, the IRS will continue to charge the taxpayer's account with interest on the taxpayer's unpaid balance of penalties and interest. Installment payments may be paid by electronic transfers from the taxpayer's bank account. While the taxpayer is making installment payments, the IRS may require the taxpayer to provide financial information on his/her financial condition to determine any change in his/her ability to pay. The IRS may file a Notice of Federal Tax Lien to secure the government's interest until the taxpayer makes the final payment.

21. **(D) Correct**
    Code Section 6502 provides that the IRS generally has 10 years from the date of assessment to collect a tax liability by levy or by court proceeding. Thus, 10 years from June 8, 2005 will end the statutory limitation on June 8, 2015.

22. **(D) Correct**
    If the IRS accepts the taxpayer's offer in compromise (OIC), the IRS expects that the taxpayer will have no further delinquencies and will fully comply with the tax laws. If the taxpayer does not abide by all the terms and conditions of the OIC, the IRS may determine that the OIC is in default. To avoid a default, the taxpayer must timely file all tax returns and timely pay all taxes for 5 years or until the offered amount is paid in full, whichever period is longer. When an OIC is declared to be in default, the agreement is no longer in effect and the IRS may then collect the amounts originally owed, plus interest and penalties.

23. **(D) Correct**
    Unless the collection of tax is in jeopardy, the IRS must notify the taxpayer in writing at least 30 days prior to altering, modifying or terminating an installment agreement. The notice must describe the reason for the proposed modification or termination of the agreement (Code Sec. 6159(b)(5)).

24. **(A) Correct**
    The Commissioner of the IRS has the authority to compromise all taxes (including any interest, penalty, or addition to the tax) arising under the revenue laws of the United

States, except those relating to alcohol, tobacco, and firearms. Submission of an offer in compromise will usually extend the statute of limitations on collection of an account. Taxpayers have a right by law to submit an offer in compromise on their unpaid tax liability.

25. **(A) Correct**

    Before requesting an installment agreement, the taxpayer (or practitioner) should have a complete understanding of the taxpayer's case, especially the amount of the unpaid liability and the tax years and/or periods for which the liability is owed. This information can be found in IRS collection notices that the taxpayer may have received, or by obtaining the taxpayer's transcripts of account from the IRS.

26. **(D) Correct**

    Code Section 6502 provides that the IRS generally has 10 years from the date of assessment to collect a tax liability by levy or by court proceeding.

27. **(D) Correct**

    Code Section 6502 provides that the IRS generally has 10 years from the date of assessment to collect a tax liability by levy or by court proceeding. Sam's 1993 tax return was due on April 15, 1994. Thus, 10 years from April 15, 1994 will end the statutory limitation on April 15, 2004.

28. **(C) Correct**

    Code Section 6502 provides that the IRS generally has 10 years from the date of assessment to collect a tax liability by levy or by court proceeding.

29. **(C) Correct**

    The IRS may accept an OIC based on three grounds:
    - (a) *Doubt as to liability* - This ground is only met when genuine doubt exists that the IRS has correctly determined the amount owed.
    - (b) *Doubt that the amount owed is collectible* - This means that doubt exists in any case where the taxpayer's assets and income are less than the full amount of the tax liability.
    - (c) *Effective tax administration* - An offer may be accepted based on effective tax administration when there is no doubt that the full amount owed can be collected, but requiring payment in full would either create an economic hardship or would be unfair and inequitable because of exceptional circumstances.

30. **(B) Correct**

    Doubt as to the liability for the amount owed must be supported by evidence, and the amount acceptable under the offer in compromise will depend on the degree of doubt found in the particular case. The doubt as to the liability for the amount owed must be supported by the evidence.

31. **(D) Correct**

The Commissioner of the IRS has the authority to compromise all taxes (including any interest, penalty, or addition to the tax) arising under the revenue laws of the United States, except those relating to alcohol, tobacco, and firearms. Submission of an offer in compromise will usually extend the statute of limitations on collection of an account. Taxpayers have a right by law to submit an offer in compromise on their unpaid tax liability. With an offer in compromise, the taxpayer may be allowed to pay less than the full amount owed and the Collection actions, such as levy, may be delayed. A rejected offer in compromise may also be appealed.

32. **(D) Correct**

A guaranteed installment agreement is available for the payment of tax liabilities of $10,000 or less, exclusive of interest, penalties, additions to tax, and any other additional amounts, provided that the liability can be paid within 3 years and certain conditions are met. Taxpayers seeking a guaranteed installment agreement are not required to submit a Collection Information Statement or otherwise disclose information about their ability to pay their outstanding tax liabilities.

33. **(A) Correct**

The IRS may accept an OIC based on three grounds:
   (a) *Doubt as to liability* - This ground is only met when genuine doubt exists that the IRS has correctly determined the amount owed.
   (b) *Doubt that the amount owed is collectible* - This means that doubt exists in any case where the taxpayer's assets and income are less than the full amount of the tax liability. The doubt as to the liability for the amount owed must be supported by the evidence.

   (c) *Effective tax administration* - An offer may be accepted based on effective tax administration when there is no doubt that the full amount owed can be collected, but requiring payment in full would either create an economic hardship or would be unfair and inequitable because of exceptional circumstances.

34. **(D) Correct**

When resolving tax problems with the IRS, taxpayers:
   (a) May be entitled to a reimbursement for fees charged by their banks if the IRS has erroneously levied their account.
   (b) Should first request assistance from IRS collection employees or their managers before seeking assistance from the problem resolution officer.
   (c) May request assistance from the IRS on Form 911, Application for Assistance Order to Relieve Hardship If there is a significant hardship because of the collection of the tax liability.

35. **(B) Correct**

    The Taxpayer Advocate Service will also attempt to assist the taxpayer in cases in which the taxpayer has not received a response or resolution to a problem or inquiry by the date given by the IRS, or in instances in which a system or procedure did not operate as intended or did not resolve the problem. TAO cannot be used to circumvent provisions of the Code, even if application of the Code will result in significant hardship to the taxpayer. Accordingly, if a taxpayer files a claim for refund after the period of limitations has expired, a TAO cannot be issued, even though the taxpayer may be suffering a significant hardship (Code Sec. 7803).

36. **(C) Correct**

    Elements of a federal tax lien are:
    (1) Assessment.
    (2) Notice and demand.
    (3) Failure to pay.

    Thus, for a lien to arise the tax must be assessed, the IRS must make notice and demand on the taxpayer, and the taxpayer must fail to pay within 10 days after notice and demand (Code Sec. 6331).

37. **(B) Correct**

    The will issue a Release of the Notice of Federal Tax Lien:
    1) Within 30 days after the taxpayer satisfies the tax due (including interest and other additions) by paying the debt or by having it adjusted, or
    2) Within 30 days after IRS accepts a bond that the taxpayer submits, guaranteeing payment of the debt.

    In addition, the taxpayer must pay all fees that a state or other jurisdiction charges to file and release the lien. These fees will be added to the amount owed.

38. **(D) Correct**

    Thus, for a lien to arise the tax must be assessed, the IRS must make notice and demand on the taxpayer, and the taxpayer must fail to pay within 10 days after notice and demand (Code Sec. 6331).

39. **(B) Correct**

    The following items are exempt from levy:
    (a) Wearing apparel and such school books
    (b) Fuel, provisions, furniture, and personal effects
    (c) Books and tools necessary for the trade, business, or profession
    (d) Unemployment benefits
    (e) Undelivered mail
    (f) Annuity or pension payments under the Railroad Retirement Act
    (g) Workmen's compensation
    (h) Judgments for support of minor children
    (i) Minimum exemption for wages, salary, and other income

(j) Certain service-connected disability payments
(k) Certain public assistance payments
(l) Assistance under job training partnership act
(m) Residences in small deficiency cases - If the amount of the levy does not exceed $5,000, any real property used as a residence by the taxpayer or any real property used as a residence by the taxpayer.

40. **(B) Correct**
A lien attaches to all of the taxpayer's property and rights to property owned on or acquired after the date of assessment (the lien filing date) (Code Sec.6321). The federal tax lien is an encumbrance on property. However, the lien itself does not result in the direct collection of any tax liability. A filed notice of tax lien can be withdrawn if withdrawal will speed collecting the tax. The law also requires the IRS to notify the taxpayer in writing within 5 business days after the filing of a lien.

41. **(D) Correct**
Before the sale of property, the IRS will compute a minimum bid price. If the minimum is not offered at the sale, the IRS may buy the property.
Residences in small deficiency cases are exempt from levy - If the amount of the levy does not exceed $5,000, any real property used as a residence by the taxpayer or any real property used as a residence by the taxpayer. The IRS must get a court order to seize most taxpayers' residences.

42. **(C) Correct**
No interest is imposed on most penalties, additional amounts, and additions to tax if the amount is paid within 21 days from the date the IRS issues a notice and demand for payment. If the amount is not paid within the 21-day period, interest accrues from the date of the notice and demand to the date of payment. If the total of tax, interest, and penalties equals or exceeds $100,000, the tax must be paid within 10 business days. Interest will continue to accrue if the tax is not paid within 21 calendar days (or where applicable, 10 business days).
When income tax return is examined by the IRS and the taxpayer agrees with the proposed changes, the taxpayer has several ways by which he or she may settle the account and pay any additional tax that is due. If a taxpayer pays when he or she signs the agreement, the interest is generally figured *from the due date of the return to the date of his payment*. If the taxpayer does not pay the additional tax when he or she signs the agreement, he or she will receive a bill and the interest on the additional tax is generally figured *from the due date of the return to the billing date* (Code Sec. 6601)

43. **(A) Correct**
When income tax return is examined by the IRS and the taxpayer agrees with the proposed changes, the taxpayer has several ways by which he or she may settle the account and pay any additional tax that is due. If a taxpayer pays when he or she signs the agreement, the interest is generally figured *from the due date of the return to the*

date of his payment. If the taxpayer does not pay the additional tax when he or she signs the agreement, he or she will receive a bill and the interest on the additional tax is generally figured *from the due date of the return to the billing date* (Code Sec. 6601). In this case Mr. Smith did not pay the additional tax when he signed the agreement. Therefore interest will start accruing on 4/16/04 (due date of the return) through 11/7/05 (billing date).

44. **(A) Correct**
If the IRS levies a taxpayer's bank account, the bank is required to hold the funds the taxpayer has on deposit, up to the amount the taxpayer owes, for 21 days. Levies can be made on property that is the taxpayer's but is held by third parties. The IRS will release a levy if the IRS determines the levy is creating an economic hardship for the taxpayer.

45. **(A) Correct**
Before the sale of property, the IRS will compute a minimum bid price. If the minimum is not offered at the sale, the IRS may buy the property. The taxpayer may request a re-computation if (s)he is in disagreement with the minimum price the IRS has determined it will accept for the property. The time of sale may not be less than 10 days or more than 40 days from the time of giving public notice. The place of sale must be within the county in which the property is seized, except that if it appears to the district director under whose supervision the seizure was made that substantially higher bids may be obtained for the property if the sale is held at a place outside such county, he may order that the sale be held in such other place. The sale must be held at the time and place stated in the notice of sale. A person whose real or personal property has been levied upon has the right to redeem the property before sale by paying the amount due, plus expenses of the proceeding. The amount due is the full amount of taxes, penalties, and interest, plus expenses related to the seizure and anticipated sale.

46. **(B) Correct**
IRS levies extend only to property held by the taxpayer or a third party at the time of the levy. Property received after notice of levy can be reached only by a *subsequent* levy. However, a levy on wages and salary (including fees, bonuses and commissions) remains viable until the tax liability covered by the levy is satisfied or becomes unenforceable because of a lapse of time. This type of levy must be promptly released when the liability out of which it arose is satisfied or becomes unenforceable due to lapse of time, and the IRS must promptly notify the person upon whom the levy was made (usually the employer) that it has been released. These continuous levy provisions apply to salary or wages earned but not yet paid at the time of levy and salary or wages earned and becoming payable (or paid in the form of an advance) after the date of the levy until the levy is released.

47. **(D) Correct**
    The following items are exempt from levy:
    1) Wearing apparel and such school books
    2) Fuel, provisions, furniture, and personal effects
    3) Books and tools necessary for the trade, business, or profession
    4) Unemployment benefits
    5) Undelivered mail
    6) Annuity or pension payments under the Railroad Retirement Act
    7) Workmen's compensation
    8) Judgments for support of minor children
    9) Minimum exemption for wages, salary, and other income
    10) Certain service-connected disability payments
    11) Certain public assistance payments
    12) Assistance under job training partnership act
    13) Residences exempt in small deficiency cases and principal residences and certain business assets exempt <u>in absence of certain approval or jeopardy</u>.
        a) Residences in small deficiency cases - If the amount of the levy does not exceed $5,000, any real property used as a residence by the taxpayer or any real property used as a residence by the taxpayer.
        b) Principal residence in other deficiency cases - The IRS must get a court order to seize most taxpayers' residences.

48. **(C) Correct**
    The IRS will release a levy on property if:
    (1) The liability for which the levy was made is satisfied or becomes unenforceable through lapse of time.
    (2) Release of the levy will facilitate collection of the tax liability.
    (3) The taxpayer has entered into an installment payment agreement (unless the agreement prohibits releasing the levy).
    (4) A determination has been made that the levy is causing an economic hardship due to the financial condition of the taxpayer.
    (5) The fair market value of the property exceeds the tax liability and release of the levy on the property could be made without hindering the collection of the liability (Code Sec. 6343(a)(1)).

    After the notice of sale has been given to the taxpayer, the IRS must wait 10 days before conducting the sale unless the property is perishable and must be sold immediately. Before the sale of property, the IRS will compute a minimum bid price. If the minimum is not offered at the sale, the IRS may buy the property. The taxpayer may request a re-computation if (s)he is in disagreement with the minimum price the IRS has determined it will accept for the property. After the sale, proceeds are applied first to the expenses of the levy and sale. A taxpayer has the right to an administrative review of a seizure action when the IRS has taken personal property that is necessary to the maintenance of the taxpayer's business. After the notice of sale has been given to the taxpayer, the IRS must wait 10 days before conducting the sale unless the property is perishable and must be sold immediately.

49. **(B) Correct**
Before the sale of property, the IRS will compute a minimum bid price. If the minimum is not offered at the sale, the IRS may buy the property. The taxpayer may request a re-computation if (s)he is in disagreement with the minimum price the IRS has determined it will accept for the property. After the sale, proceeds are applied first to the expenses of the levy and sale. A taxpayer has the right to an administrative review of a seizure action when the IRS has taken personal property that is necessary to the maintenance of the taxpayer's business. After the notice of sale has been given to the taxpayer, the IRS must wait 10 days before conducting the sale unless the property is perishable and must be sold immediately. After a tax sale has taken place, personal property may not be redeemed. Real property that has been sold may be redeemed at any time within 180 days after the sale by paying the amount that the purchaser paid, plus interest at the rate of 20% per year on that amount. The date of the sale does not count in calculating the 180 day time period.

50. **(C) Correct**
No interest is imposed on most penalties, additional amounts, and additions to tax if the amount is paid within 21 days from the date the IRS issues a notice and demand for payment. If the amount is not paid within the 21-day period, interest accrues from the date of the notice and demand to the date of payment. If the total of tax, interest, and penalties equals or exceeds $100,000, the tax must be paid within 10 business days. Interest will continue to accrue if the tax is not paid within 21 calendar days (or where applicable, 10 business days).
When income tax return is examined by the IRS and the taxpayer agrees with the proposed changes, the taxpayer has several ways by which he or she may settle the account and pay any additional tax that is due. If a taxpayer pays when he or she signs the agreement, the interest is generally figured *from the due date of the return to the date of his payment*. If the taxpayer does not pay the additional tax when he or she signs the agreement, he or she will receive a bill and the interest on the additional tax is generally figured *from the due date of the return to the billing date* (Code Sec. 6601).

51. **(C) Correct**
A levy can be made on property in the hands of third parties or in the taxpayer's possession. Generally, court authorization is not required before levy action is taken. The IRS must release a levy if the fair market value of the property exceeds the levy and its release would not hinder the collection of tax.

52. **(D) Correct**
Jeopardy levies may occur when the IRS waives the 10-day notice and demand period and/or the 30-day Final Notice (Notice of Intent to Levy) period because a delay would endanger the collection of tax.

53. **(C) Correct**
    Tangible personal or real property (other than real property which is rented) used in the trade or business of an individual taxpayer cannot be levied unless the IRS determines that collection is in jeopardy or unless the District Director approves the levy in writing. The IRS must obtain a court order to seize personal property on private premises (Code Sec. 6334).

54. **(D) Correct**
    The will issue a Release of the Notice of Federal Tax Lien:
    1) Within 30 days after the taxpayer satisfies the tax due (including interest and other additions) by paying the debt or by having it adjusted, or
    2) Within 30 days after IRS accepts a bond that the taxpayer submits, guaranteeing payment of the debt.
    The taxpayer must pay all fees that a state or other jurisdiction charges to file and release the lien. These fees will be added to the balance amount owed. It is a public notice to the taxpayer's creditors that the government has a claim against all of the taxpayer's real, personal, and/or business property, including property that was acquired after the lien came into existence. A taxpayer <u>can</u> sue the federal government for damages if the IRS knowingly or negligently fails to release a Notice of Federal Tax Lien when a release is warranted.

55. **(D) Correct**
    When resolving tax problems with the IRS, taxpayers:
    (a) May be entitled to a reimbursement for fees charged by their banks if the IRS has erroneously levied their account.
    (b) Should first request assistance from IRS collection employees or their managers before seeking assistance from the problem resolution officer.
    (c) May request assistance from the IRS on Form 911, Application for Assistance Order to Relieve Hardship If there is a significant hardship because of the collection of the tax liability.

56. **(A) Correct**
    An installment agreement, unlike an offer in compromise, does not reduce the balance due. On the contrary, an installment agreement actually has the effect of increasing the total amount due, because penalties and interest continue to accrue during the duration of the agreement, until the balance is paid in full.

57. **(D) Correct**
    The time of sale may not be less than 10 days or more than 40 days from the time of giving public notice (If the IRS seizes property that is not perishable, the IRS will wait at least 10 days after seizure before conducting the sale). The place of sale must be within the county in which the property is seized, except that if it appears to the district director under whose supervision the seizure was made that substantially higher bids may be obtained for the property if the sale is held at a place outside such county, he

may order that the sale be held in such other place. The sale must be held at the time and place stated in the notice of sale.

58. **(D) Correct**

An Installment Agreement allows taxpayers to pay their full debt in smaller, more manageable amounts. Installment agreements generally require equal monthly payments. The amount of installment payments and the number taxpayers make will be based on the amount owed and the ability to pay that amount within the time the IRS can legally collect payment. Once an installment payment plan has been approved, the IRS will continue to charge the taxpayer's account with interest on the taxpayer's unpaid balance of penalties and interest. Installment payments may be paid by electronic transfers from the taxpayer's bank account. While the taxpayer is making installment payments, the IRS may require the taxpayer to provide financial information on his/her financial condition to determine any change in his/her ability to pay. The IRS may file a Notice of Federal Tax Lien to secure the government's interest until the taxpayer makes the final payment. Failure to pay an installment can result in the termination of the agreement. Installment payments may be paid by payroll deductions from the taxpayer's employer.

UNIT 5: EXAMINATION OF RETURNS AND APPEALS PROCESS

Unit 4 Contents:
- 5.01 EXAMINATION OF RETURNS
- 5.02 APPEALS PROCESS
- 5.03 REFUNDS AND CREDIT
- 5.04 UNIT 5: QUESTIONS
- 5.05 UNIT 5: ANSWERS

5.01   EXAMINATION OF RETURNS

Processing of Returns

When tax returns are filed in the office of the district director of the IRS or the office of the director of a regional service center, they are first checked for:
- (i) Form.
- (ii) Execution.
- (iii) Mathematical accuracy.

Mathematical errors are corrected and a correction notice of any such error is sent to the taxpayer. Notice and demand is made for the payment of any additional tax or refund is made of any overpayment. Returns are classified for examination at regional service centers. Certain individual income tax returns with potential unallowable items are delivered to Examination Divisions at regional service centers for correction by *correspondence*. Otherwise, returns with the highest examination potential are delivered to district Examination Divisions based on workload capacities. Those most in need of examination are selected for office or field examination.

Selection of Returns for Audit

The IRS audits only a small percentage of the returns filed each year, particularly those filed by individuals. Deciding which returns to audit is largely within the IRS's discretion. The IRS may not initiate an examination solely to harass a taxpayer or solely to obtain evidence for a criminal prosecution. Also, members of the executive branch of the federal government cannot directly or indirectly request the IRS to conduct or terminate an audit of any particular person (Code Sec. 7217).

The IRS selects returns for examination by several methods. It uses computer programs to identify returns that may have incorrect amounts. These programs may be based on:
- (1) Matching programs that use information returns, such as Forms 1099 and W-2, or Form 8300 (Report of Cash Payments Over $10,000 Received in a Trade or Business).
- (2) Studies of past examinations.
- (3) Certain issues identified by compliance projects.

Many returns are selected through the use of a computer program called the *Discriminant Function System* (DIF). This program scores each return that is filed for potential error based upon past IRS audit experience. The returns receiving high scores are made available for examination. (DIF) also identifies returns that have special features or characteristics, or that require special handling. These include individual returns with:
- (i) Unallowable items.
- (ii) Tax shelters.
- (iii) Form 8283 (Non-Cash Charitable Contributions).
- (iv) A refund of $2 million or more.
- (v) Corporate returns with partnership issues (IRM 4.1.3.2).

Other returns are selected at random under current national or regional studies, such as the National Research Program (NRP). The IRS also often develops programs that target specific areas of taxpayer noncompliance such as the Non-filers Program and the Withholding Compliance Program.

The IRS also uses information from outside sources such as newspapers, public records, and individuals.

Examination of Returns

There are two types of examination:
1) Office examination.
2) Field examination.

A taxpayer may represent him or herself at an examination or may be represented or accompanied by an attorney, a CPA, a person enrolled to practice before the IRS, or the preparer.

Restrictions on IRS Examinations

Only one inspection of a taxpayer's books may be made for any tax year unless the IRS notifies the taxpayer that an additional inspection is necessary. The notification must be in writing. A second examination is permitted with the taxpayer's consent. As long as an investigation is continuing, the IRS can look at the same books or records on more than one occasion.

Contacts by the IRS that are not an examination include:
- (i) Contact with the taxpayer to correct mathematical or clerical errors.
- (ii) Contact to verify or adjust a discrepancy between the taxpayer's tax return and information return.
- (iii) Adjustments of an unallowable item through a service center correction program,
- (iv) Contact to verify a discrepancy between the income tax return and the books and records of an employee plan or an exempt organization.
- (v) Contact to evaluate the taxpayer's data processing and accounting systems to see if the taxpayer may limit its retention of machine-sensible records.

Generally, a taxpayer cannot get an injunction to block an investigation by the IRS. The taxpayer's remedy is to claim that the second inspection is illegal at a hearing to enforce the summons. If the same items were examined in either of the previous 2 years and the examination resulted in no change to the tax liability, the IRS might suspend but not cancel an audit in order to avoid repetitive examinations of the same items. The IRS tries to avoid repeat examinations of the same items, but sometimes this happens. If a tax return was examined for the same items in either of the 2 previous years and no change was proposed to tax liability, the taxpayer should contact the IRS as soon as possible to see if the examination should be discontinued.

1. Office Examination

Examination at Divisions at regional service centers:
Individual income tax returns identified as containing unallowable items are examined by Examination Divisions at *regional service centers*. Correspondence examination methods are used here. If the taxpayer requests an interview to discuss the proposed adjustments, the case is transferred to the taxpayer's district office. If the taxpayer does not agree to the proposed adjustments, regular appeals procedures will commence.

Examinations at district office:
Some tax returns are examined at *district offices* by office examination techniques. These returns include some business returns, as well as some individual income tax returns. Office examinations are conducted primarily by the interview method. Examinations are conducted by correspondence only when warranted by the nature of the questionable items and by the convenience and characteristics of the taxpayer. In a correspondence examination, the taxpayer is asked to explain or send supporting evidence by mail, while in an office interview examination, the taxpayer is asked to appear at the district director's office for an interview and must bring certain records in support of the return. During the interview examination, the taxpayer has the right to point out to the examining officer any amounts included in the return which are not taxable, or any deductions which the taxpayer failed to claim on the return. If it develops that a field examination is necessary, the examiner may conduct such examination.

2. Field Examination

Certain returns are examined by field examination which involves an examination of the taxpayer's books and records on the taxpayer's premises. An examiner will check the entire return filed by the taxpayer and will examine all books, papers, records, and memoranda dealing with matters required to be included in the return.

Conclusion

At the conclusion of an office or field examination, the taxpayer is given an opportunity to agree with the findings of the examining officer. If the taxpayer does not agree, the examining officer will inform the taxpayer of the taxpayer's appeal rights. If the taxpayer does agree with the proposed changes, the examining officer will invite the taxpayer to execute either Form 870

(Waiver of Restrictions on Assessment and Collection of Deficiency in Tax and Acceptance of Over-assessment). When the taxpayer agrees with the proposed changes but does not offer to pay any deficiency or additional tax which may be due, the examining officer will also invite payment (by check or money order), together with any applicable interest or penalty.

The taxpayer's acceptance of an agreed over-assessment does not prevent the taxpayer from filing a claim and bringing a suit for the additional tax, nor does it preclude the Government from maintaining suit to recover an erroneous refund.

Transfer of Returns between Districts

Generally, a taxpayer's return is examined in the area where he or she lives. But if the return can be examined more quickly and conveniently in another area, such as where books and records are located, the taxpayer can ask to have the case transferred to that area. When request is received to transfer taxpayer returns to another district for examination, the district director having jurisdiction may transfer the case, together with pertinent records to the district director of such other district. The IRS will determine the time and place of the examination. In determining whether a transfer should be made, circumstances such as the following will be considered:
  (1) Change of the taxpayer's domicile, either before or during examination.
  (2) Discovery that taxpayer's books and records are kept in another district.
  (3) Change of domicile of an executor or administrator to another district before or during examination.
  (4) The effective administration of the tax laws (26 CFR 601.105(k)).

The place of examination <u>will not</u> be considered solely for the convenience of the taxpayer's representative. However, the place of examination <u>may be</u> considered for the convenience of the IRS.

Mathematical or Clerical Errors

Within 60 days after the notice of additional tax due is sent to the taxpayer, the taxpayer may request an abatement (reduction) of an assessment based on mathematical or clerical errors. If the taxpayer requests an abatement, the IRS must abate the additional tax and cannot reassess it except in accordance with the deficiency procedures. During the 60-day period, the IRS is prohibited from collecting the deficiency by levy or a proceeding in court. Supplying an omitted schedule is treated as a request for abatement.

Mathematical or clerical errors include:
  1) Errors in addition, subtraction, multiplication or division.
  2) Incorrect use of a tax table.
  3) Entries on a return that are inconsistent with other entries on the return.
  4) Omission of information that is required to substantiate an entry on the return.
  5) Deductions or credits that exceed the statutorily prescribed limits, whether as a specified monetary amount, percentage, ratio or fraction.

6) on a return claiming the earned income credit:
    (i) An omission of a required taxpayer identification number.
    (ii) A claim that relies on net earnings from self-employment on which self-employment tax has not been paid.
    (iii) An omission of required information from a taxpayer who previously made an improper claim for the credit.
    (iv) A noncustodial parent's use of a child to qualify for the credit.
7) Omissions concerning the dependent care credit and personal exemptions.
8) Omission of a child's correct identification number on a return that claims a credit for that child.
9) Omission of a dependent's correct identification number on a return that claims a Hope scholarship or lifetime learning credit for the dependent's nondeductible higher-education expenses.
10) Claiming the dependent care credit, the child credit, the earned income credit, or the 2008 recovery refund credit, when the computation of the credit on the return reflects an individual's age as being different from the age based on the individual's taxpayer identification number that is required to be shown on the return.
11) An omission of a correct social security number for the taxpayer, or for at least one of the spouses on a joint return, when the return claims the making work pay credit or the government retiree credit.
12) An omission of any increase in tax caused by the recapture of the national first-time homebuyer credit.
13) An entry on a return claiming the national first-time homebuyer credit if:
    (i) The IRS obtains information from the person issuing a taxpayer identification number (TIN) for a taxpayer who purchases a home after November 6, 2009 that indicates that neither the taxpayer nor the taxpayer's spouse was at least 18 years old on the date of the purchase.
    (ii) Information on at least one of the taxpayer's returns for the preceding two tax years is inconsistent with the taxpayer's eligibility for the credit.
    (iii) The taxpayer fails to attach to the return a properly executed copy of the settlement statement used to complete the purchase.
14) Any underpayment caused by the failure of a partner in an electing large partnership to treat an item on his return in a manner consistent with the treatment of the item on the partnership's return.
15) Failure to complete and file the forms needed to claim the low-income housing credit.

An entry on a return that is inconsistent with other entries on the return is treated as a mathematical error only where it is apparent which of the inconsistent entries is correct and which is incorrect. Therefore, when a taxpayer files a Form 1040 that reports income in a different amount from the Form W-2 that is attached to the return, the IRS will not treat the inconsistency as a mathematical error and must send a deficiency notice to the taxpayer (Code Sec. 6213).

IRS Contact of Third-Parties

The IRS must give the taxpayer reasonable notice before contacting other persons about the taxpayer's tax matters. A written consent from the taxpayer is not required. The taxpayer must be given reasonable notice in advance that, in examining or collecting tax liability, the IRS may contact third parties such as neighbors, banks, employers, or employees. The IRS must also give the taxpayer notice of specific contacts by providing a record of persons contacted on both a periodic basis and upon the taxpayer's request. This provision <u>does not</u> apply:
- (a) To any pending criminal investigation,
- (b) When providing notice would jeopardize collection of any tax liability,
- (c) Where providing notice may result in reprisal against any person, or
- (d) When taxpayer authorizes the contact.

Abatement of Interest

The IRS may abate (reduce) the amount of interest owed if the interest is due to an unreasonable error or delay by an IRS officer or employee in performing a ministerial or managerial. Only the amount of interest on income, estate, gift, generation-skipping, and certain excise taxes can be reduced. The amount of interest will not be reduced if the taxpayer contributed significantly to the error or delay. Also, the interest will be reduced only if the error or delay happened after the IRS contacted the taxpayer in writing about the deficiency or payment on which the interest is based. An audit notification letter is such a contact. The IRS cannot reduce the amount of interest due to a general administrative decision, such as a decision on how to organize the processing of tax returns. A refund or abatement of interest, penalties, or additions to tax caused by certain IRS errors or delays, or certain erroneous written advice from the IRS is completed on form 843.

Ministerial Act - This is a procedural or mechanical act, not involving the exercise of judgment or discretion, during the processing of a case after all prerequisites (for example, conferences and review by supervisors) have taken place. A decision concerning the proper application of federal tax law (or other federal or state law) is not a ministerial act. For example, an examination of a tax return reveals tax due for which a notice of deficiency (90-day letter) will be issued. After the taxpayer and the IRS discuss the issues, the notice is prepared and reviewed. After the review process, issuing the notice of deficiency is a ministerial act. If there is an unreasonable delay in sending the notice of deficiency to the taxpayer, the IRS can reduce the interest resulting from the delay.

Ministerial act is also an administrative act during the processing of a case that involves the loss of records or the exercise of judgment or discretion concerning the management of personnel. A decision concerning the proper application of federal tax law (or other federal or state law) is not a managerial act. For example, a revenue agent is examining your tax return. During the middle of the examination, the agent is sent to an extended training course. The agent's supervisor decides not to reassign the case, so the work is unreasonably delayed until the agent returns. Interest from the unreasonable delay can be abated since both the decision to send the agent to the training class and not to reassign the case is a managerial act (Publication 556).

5.02 APPEALS PROCESS

Taxpayers who wish to contest tax liabilities or determinations proposed against them by the IRS may use an administrative appeals procedure. The <u>Appeals Division</u> of the IRS administers that procedure. Appeals operate offices and sub offices throughout the country. *Ex parte* communications between any Appeals employee and other IRS employees are prohibited if these communications appear to compromise independence. When the IRS determines that a taxpayer has a tax liability, the taxpayer may file an appeal, petition the Tax Court or pay the tax and file a refund claim. An administrative appeal does not preclude a Tax Court petition or a refund claim. The main advantage of an appeal is that the taxpayer has a chance to resolve the case without the expense of litigation.

The IRS maintains an Appeals Office, separate and independent of the district offices. The Appeals Office is the <u>only level</u> of administrative appeal within the IRS. A taxpayer who disagrees with an examination can request a conference with Appeals Office personnel. These conferences are held in an informal manner by correspondence, by telephone or at a personal conference (Reg. Sec. 601.016(c)).

There are some restrictions on the jurisdiction of the Appeals office. Appeals cannot handle some types of cases that are docketed in the Tax Court. Appeals officers cannot decide cases on alcohol, tobacco, firearms or wagering taxes or cases involving a conscientious objection to paying tax.

At or before the initial in-person interview with the taxpayer relating to the determination of any tax, the IRS must provide the taxpayer with an explanation of the audit process and the taxpayer's rights under the process (Code Sec. 7521). Taxpayer's rights are contained in Publication 1.

Initiating an Appeal

If the examination of a taxpayer's return by the IRS results in a disagreement over whether the taxpayer owes additional income tax, the IRS must issue a formal letter called a notice of deficiency before the taxpayer can appeal his/her case to the Tax Court. Before issuing a notice of deficiency, the IRS sends a preliminary notice advising the taxpayer of his right to appeal (<u>the 30-day letter</u>). A taxpayer may initiate an appeal within 30 days after receiving notice from the IRS of the right to appeal if the taxpayer does not agree with the proposed changes from an examination. The 30-day letter must identify the amount of the tax, interest, and penalties included in the notice. It must also describe why the IRS believes these amounts are due. If the taxpayer makes the request for an appeal and protests the IRS findings, the case is referred to Appeals. To appeal the IRS's findings in field examination cases, the taxpayer must file a written protest if the proposed additional liability exceeds $10,000 for any tax period. A written protest is required for all penalties that have already been assessed. If the proposed adjustments in a field examination case exceed $2,500 but do not exceed $10,000, the taxpayer must file a <u>brief written statement</u> of the issues.

The taxpayer does not have to make a written protest to appeal the following:
   a) Field examinations resulting in adjustments of $2,500.

b) Office examinations.
c) Correspondence audits.

A written protest should include the following:
1) A statement that the taxpayer wishes to appeal the findings of the IRS to the Appeals office.
2) The taxpayer's name, address and daytime telephone number.
3) A copy of the letter showing the proposed changes and findings that the taxpayer does not agree with or the date and symbols from the letter.
4) A list of the changes that the taxpayer does not agree with and why.
5) The tax periods involved.
6) A statement of facts supporting the taxpayer's position.
7) A statement of the law or other authorities that are relied upon (Reg. Sec. 601.105(c)).

Written protests which taxpayers are required to file with the District Director to bring unagreed tax cases before the Appellate Division may now be certified as true under the penalties of perjury. Formerly such written protests had to be filed under oath (Rev. Proc. 61-36). A representative qualified to practice before the IRS can prepare or sign a formal written protest on behalf of a client to request an appeals conference. In any case in which the taxpayer's representative is unable or unwilling to declare of his/her own knowledge that the facts in a claim, written argument, brief, or recitation of facts are TRUE and correct, the IRS may request the taxpayer to make such a declaration under penalty of perjury.

A written protest would be required when the total amount of the proposed change in tax for the period is over $25,000, regardless of whether the examination was a field, office or correspondence audit. When the total amount of the change, including interest and penalties, is $25,000 or less, the taxpayer could request Appeals consideration by filing a Small Case Request. The taxpayer would indicate the disagreed adjustments and provide his reasons for the disagreement. The taxpayer could also provide any other information he believes is pertinent (Reg. Sec. 601.106(a)(1)(iii)).

The taxpayer is not automatically entitled to an administrative appeal. Appeals may refuse to consider a case if it receives the request for an appeal:
(i) Within 120 days before the limitations period for assessment expires in non-estate tax cases, or
(ii) Within 180 days before the limitations period expires in estate tax cases

Taxpayers must file a written protest in the following cases.
(a) All employee plan and exempt organization cases without regard to the dollar amount at issue.
(b) All partnership and S corporation cases without regard to the dollar amount at issue.
(c) All other cases, unless taxpayer qualifies for the small case request procedure, or other special appeal procedures such as requesting Appeals consideration of liens, levies, seizures, or installment agreements (Publication 556).

Appeals Case Settlement

Any settlement between a taxpayer and an Appeals officer is reviewed by a superior. Generally, the reviewing officer approves the settlement. If the settlement is disapproved as being too favorable to the taxpayer, the taxpayer has a right to a conference with the reviewing officer. A settlement reached with an Appeals officer is not binding upon the IRS until it has been approved by the officer's superior.

The IRS and the taxpayer enter into one of five types of settlement agreements:
- (a) A waiver of restrictions on assessment.
- (b) A special waiver of restrictions on assessment.
- (c) A closing agreement.
- (d) A collateral agreement.
- (e) A compromise agreement.

The waiver of Restrictions on Assessment - is used when a mutual-concession settlement is not involved. However, it may be used in a mutual-concession settlement if the taxes involved in the mutual concessions are not material.

The Special Waiver of Restrictions on Assessment - is used when material mutual concessions are made. It offers the taxpayer greater finality because it contains a pledge by the IRS against reopening the case absent fraud, malfeasance, concealment or misrepresentation. A case may also be reopened for an important mistake in mathematical calculation.

Closing Agreements – If either party desires greater finality in a settlement agreement, the IRS or the taxpayer may request entry into a closing agreement in addition to the execution of a Form 870 (Waiver of Restrictions on Assessment and Collection of Deficiency in Tax and Acceptance of Over-assessment) and Form 870-AD (Offer to Waive Restrictions on Assessment and Collection of Tax Deficiency and to Accept Over-assessment). A closing agreement sets out the terms of the settlement and provides that those terms are binding on both parties. An Appeals officer may request a closing agreement in:
- (i) Split-issue settlements.
- (ii) Whipsaw cases.
- (iii) Settlements that affect later years
- (iv) To protect the interests of the government.

Collateral Agreements - Collateral agreements are used primarily in related cases in which the IRS desires consistent treatment of issues. For example, the IRS may request a collateral agreement from a beneficiary who will receive assets from an estate. The agreement obligates the beneficiary to use the same valuation for income tax purposes as was used for estate tax purposes. Two important distinctions between collateral agreements and closing agreements are that collateral agreements do not bind the IRS, only the taxpayer, and that they are administrative devices not provided by the Code. Taxpayers seeking greater finality should enter into closing agreements.

Compromise Agreements - The IRS may compromise any civil or criminal case by allowing the taxpayer to pay an amount less than the amount actually owed. The liability may be compromised upon any of the following three grounds:
   (i) Doubt as to liability.
   (ii) Doubt as to collectibility.
   (iii) The necessity to promote effective tax administration.

Appeals offices have limited authority to enter into compromise agreements. They may accept offers of compromise in civil cases involving liabilities of under $100,000 and may reject compromise offers of any amount

Mediation

If the taxpayer and Appeals cannot agree on a settlement, a mediation procedure may be used. This procedure attempts to resolve issues in cases while they are in the jurisdiction of Appeals. It may be used only after Appeals settlement discussions are unsuccessful and when the issues not being mediated are resolved. Mediation is available for both legal and factual issues.

Mediation is not available for:
   (i) An issue designated for litigation or docketed in any court.
   (ii) Collection cases.
   (iii) Issues for which mediation would not be consistent with sound tax administration, such as issues governed by closing agreements or controlling Supreme Court precedent.
   (iv) Frivolous issues.
   (v) Cases in which the taxpayer did not act in good faith during settlement negotiations (IRM 8.7.9).

Deficiency Notice

Once any appeal process within the IRS is complete, the IRS may issue a statutory notice of deficiency. Once the IRS issues a deficiency notice, the taxpayer has 90 days to file a Tax Court petition. If the taxpayer does not file a petition, the IRS will <u>assess</u> the taxes. This statutory Notice of Deficiency is also known as a <u>90-day letter</u> because the taxpayer generally has 90 days (150 days if mailed when the taxpayer is outside the United States) from the date of the letter to file a petition with the United States Tax Court. After a deficiency notice is mailed to the taxpayer and the taxpayer files a timely Tax Court petition, the IRS <u>cannot</u> determine an additional deficiency for the same tax unless:
   (i) There is fraud.
   (ii) Mathematical or clerical errors have been made.
   (iii) The IRS makes a termination or jeopardy assessment.

A notice of deficiency is not an assessment. If the taxpayer consents, the IRS can withdraw any notice of deficiency. However, after the notice is withdrawn, the taxpayer cannot file a petition with the Tax Court based on the withdrawn notice, and the IRS may later issue a notice of deficiency greater or less than the amount in the withdrawn deficiency.

Requirements for a Deficiency Notice:
Deficiency notices:
   (1) Must describe the *basis for* and identify the *amount* of the tax due, interest, and penalties included in the notice.
   (2) Must inform the taxpayer of his right to contact a local office of the taxpayer advocate and the location and the phone number of the appropriate office.
   (3) Must contain the date determined by the IRS to be the last day that the taxpayer can file a petition with the Tax Court.
   (4) Must provide information about the tax code provision under which any interest is computed and computation of the interest (Code Sec. 6631).

The IRS can issue a notice of deficiency at any time after the return is filed and before the period for assessing tax expires. The IRS can send a notice of deficiency to the taxpayer by certified or registered mail. Once the IRS delivers a properly addressed notice of deficiency to the Postal Service, there is a strong presumption that the notice was properly delivered. The mailing date of the notice starts the running of the 90-day period for filing a Tax Court petition regarding the deficiency. The notice must be mailed to the taxpayer's <u>last known address</u>. A taxpayer's last known address is the address that appears on the taxpayer's most recently filed federal tax return. However, if the taxpayer gives the IRS clear and concise notification of a different address, that address is the taxpayer's last known address (Code Sec. 6751).

A taxpayer can challenge the validity of a deficiency notice in a U.S. district court or the Court of Federal Claims. Filing a Tax Court petition waives any challenge to the validity of the notice, except for challenges based on jurisdiction.

Rescinding Deficiency Notices:
The IRS can rescind notices with the consent of the taxpayer. Once rescinded, the notice is treated as though it were never issued. The taxpayer and the IRS are returned to the positions they had before the notice was issued. However, the statute of limitations on assessment and collection is suspended for the period during which the rescinded notice was outstanding. The taxpayer has no right to appeal to the Tax Court. The IRS may issue a second notice containing a deficiency greater than the one in the rescinded notice.
The IRS will not rescind a notice of deficiency if:
   (1) The assessment period will expire in 90 days or less, unless the taxpayer agrees to extend the assessment period.
   (2) The taxpayer has filed a Tax Court petition.
   (3) The period for filing a Tax Court petition has expired and the taxpayer has not filed a petition.
   (4) The taxpayer signed a special consent to extend the time for assessment of tax on Form 872-A before the deficiency notice was issued (Code Sec. 6212).

Appeals to the Courts

If a taxpayer and the IRS still disagree after the appeals conference, the taxpayer may be entitled to take his/her case to:
   (1) The United States Tax Court.
   (2) The United States Court of Federal Claims.
   (3) The United States District Court.

These courts are independent of the IRS.

A case petitioned to the United States Tax Court will normally be considered for settlement by an Appeals Office before the Tax Court hears the case.

If a taxpayer unreasonably fails to pursue the IRS' appeals system, or if the case is intended primarily to cause a delay or the taxpayer position is frivolous or groundless, the Tax Court may impose a penalty of up to $25,000.

The Government cannot ask the taxpayer to waive his/her right to sue the United States or a Government officer or employee for any action taken in connection with the tax laws. However, the taxpayer's right to sue can be waived if:
   (i) The taxpayer knowingly and voluntarily waives that right.
   (ii) The request to waive that right is made in writing to the taxpayer's attorney or other federally authorized practitioner.
   (iii) The request is made in person and the taxpayer's attorney or other representative is present.

Burden of Proof

For court proceedings resulting from examinations started after July 22, 1998, the IRS generally has the burden of proof for any factual issue if the taxpayer met the following requirements:
   (a) Introduced credible evidence relating to the issue.
   (b) Complied with all substantiation requirements of the Internal Revenue Code.
   (c) Maintained all records required by the Internal Revenue Code.
   (d) Cooperated with all reasonable requests by the IRS for information regarding the preparation and related tax treatment of any item reported on the tax return.
   (e) Had a net worth of $7 million or less and not more than 500 employees at the time the tax liability is contested in any court proceeding if the tax return is for a corporation, partnership, or trust.

5.03 REFUNDS AND CREDIT

Limitations on Refunds and Credit

Code Section 6511 states that a claim for refund or credit for an overpayment must be filed within 3 years from the time the <u>return was filed</u> or within 2 years from the time the <u>tax was paid</u>, whichever occurs later. The amount that may be refunded or credited is limited by similar time periods. The IRS can extend the time for filing a refund claim or determining the allowable amount of a refund claim for a taxpayer affected by a presidentially declared disaster. The limitation periods for recovering a refund do not run during any period in which an individual cannot manage his financial affairs for medical reasons.

Other Statutory Limitations on Special Refunds or Credits:

(1) Claim relating to bad debts or securities (stocks and bonds) losses have statutory period of 7 years from return due date.
(2) Claims for overpayment of self-employment tax based on Tax Court determination of employment status have a statutory period on or before the last day of the second year after the calendar year in which the determination becomes final.
(3) Claims relating to amounts included in income that are later recaptured have one year after the date on which the recaptured amount is paid by the taxpayer.
(4) Claims relating to foreign tax credit have 10 years from due date of return for tax year in which foreign taxes are paid or accrued.
(5) Claims relating to net operating loss (NOL) or capital loss carry-backs have 3 years after due date of return (including extensions) for tax year of loss.

If a taxpayer is filing a claim for credit or refund based on contested income tax issues considered in previously examined returns and <u>does not</u> want to appeal within the IRS but wants go straight to court, (s)he should pay all of the additional tax and then file a claim request in writing that the claim be immediately rejected. When a taxpayer promptly receives a notice of claim disallowance, a taxpayer may bring a suit to the appropriate United States District Court or Court of Federal Claims against the IRS after 6 months from the date of filing the claim or before the expiration of 2 years from the date of mailing by certified mail or registered mail by the Secretary to the taxpayer of a notice of the disallowance of the part of the claim to which the suit or proceeding relates (Code Sec. 6532).

Extending the Tax Assessment Period

Assessment statutes of limitations generally limit the time the IRS has to make tax assessments to within 3 years after a return is due or filed, whichever is later. The Service cannot assess additional tax after the time for assessment has expired under any statute of limitations

The IRS is legally prohibited from making a refund or credit for a claim if the taxpayer files it after the filing period has expired under the statute of limitations. Also, if the taxpayer disagrees with the return examination findings, The IRS cannot provide the taxpayer with an

administrative appeal within the IRS unless sufficient time remains on the statute of limitations. Because of these restrictions, the Service identifies tax returns under examination for which the statutory period for assessment is about to expire and requests that the taxpayer extend the assessment statute of limitations. This additional time allows the taxpayer to:
- (a) Provide further documentation to support your position.
- (b) Request an appeal if you do not agree with the examiner's findings.
- (c) Claim a tax refund or credit.

The extended assessment statute allows the IRS time to properly complete the examination of the tax return and to make any additional assessment or reduction in the previously assessed tax liability that is required. Generally, the Revenue Agent must advise the taxpayer that he/she has a right to refuse to extend the statute of limitations, and if he/she does agree to an extension, the agreement can be restricted as to particular issues on the tax return.

Limit on Amount of Refund

If a taxpayer files a claim for refund within 3 years after filing the return, the credit or refund cannot be more than the part of the tax paid within the 3 years (plus the length of any extension of time granted for filing your return) before the claim was filed.

EXAMPLE 1:
John made estimated tax payments of $1,000 and got an automatic extension of time from April 15, 2003, to August 15, 2003, to file his 2002 income tax return. When he filed his return on that date, he paid an additional $200 tax. Three years later, on August 15, 2006, he filed an amended return and claimed a refund of $700. Because he filed within 3 years after filing your return, he could get a refund of any tax paid after April 15, 2003.

EXAMPLE 2:
The situation is the same as in Example 1, except that John filed his return on October 31, 2003, 2½ months after the extension period ended. He paid an additional $200 on that date. Three years later, on October 27, 2006, he filed an amended return and claim a refund of $700. Although John filed his claim within 3 years from the date he filed his original return, the refund is limited to $200. The estimated tax of $1,000 was paid before the 3 years plus the 4-month extension period.

Claim filed after the 3-year period - If a taxpayer files a claim after the 3-year period, but within 2 years from the time he/she paid the tax, the credit or refund cannot be more than the tax you paid within the 2 years immediately before you filed the claim

EXAMPLE:
Mary filed her 2002 tax return on April 15, 2003. She paid $500 in tax. On November 2, 2004, after an examination of your 2002 return, she had to pay $200 in additional tax. On May 2, 2006, she filed a claim for a refund of $300. Her refund will be limited to the $200 she paid during the 2 years immediately before you filed your claim.

Explanation of Any Claim for Refund Disallowance

The IRS must explain to the taxpayer the specific reasons why a claim for refund is disallowed or partially disallowed. Claims for refund are disallowed based on a preliminary review or on further examination. Some of the reasons a claim may be disallowed include the following:
  (i) It was filed late.
  (ii) It was based solely on the unconstitutionality of the revenue acts.
  (iii) It was waived as part of a settlement.
  (iv) It covered a tax year or issues which were part of a closing agreement or an offer in compromise.
  (v) It was related to a return closed by a final court order.

Reduced Refund

Tax refund may be reduced by:
  (a) An additional tax liability.
  (b) Amounts owed for past-due child support.
  (c) Debts owed to another federal agency.
  (d) Past-due legally enforceable state income tax obligations.

For the above mentioned reductions, a taxpayer cannot use the appeal and refund procedures. However, the taxpayer may be able to take action against the other agency.

State Income Tax Obligations:

Federal tax overpayments can be used to offset past-due, legally enforceable state income tax obligations. For the offset procedure to apply, the federal income tax return must show an address in the state that requests the offset. In addition, the state must first:
  (i) Notify the taxpayer by certified mail with return receipt that the state plans to ask for an offset against federal income tax overpayment.
  (ii) Give the taxpayer at least 60 days to show that some or all of the state income tax is not past due or not legally enforceable.
  (iii) Consider any evidence from the taxpayer in determining that income tax is past due and legally enforceable.
  (iv) Satisfy any other requirements to ensure that there is a valid past-due, legally enforceable state income tax obligation.
  (v) Show that all reasonable efforts to obtain payment have been made before requesting the offset.

  NOTE: A Past-due, legally enforceable state income tax obligation is an debt
   1) Established by a court decision or administrative hearing and no longer subject to judicial review, or
   2) That is assessed, uncollected, can no longer be re-determined, and is less than 10 years overdue.

Offset Priorities:
(1) Overpayments are offset in the following order.
(2) Federal income tax owed.
(3) Past-due child support.
(4) Past-due, legally enforceable debt owed to a federal agency.
(5) Past-due, legally enforceable state income tax debt.
(6) Future federal income tax liability.

If more than one state agency requests an offset for separate debts, the offsets apply against overpayment in the order in which the debts accrued. In addition, state income tax includes any local income tax administered by the chief tax administration agency of a state. The Tax Court cannot decide the validity or merits of the credits or offsets (for example, collection of delinquent child support or student loan payments) made that reduce or eliminate a refund to which you were otherwise entitled.

Injured Spouse Exception:
When a joint return is filed and the refund is used to pay one spouse's past-due child support, spousal support, or a federal debt, the other spouse can be considered an injured spouse. An injured spouse can get a refund for his or her share of the overpayment that would otherwise be used to pay the past-due amount.

One is considered an injured spouse if:
1) He/she is not legally obligated to pay the past-due amount and
2) He/she meets any of the following conditions:
    (i) Made and reported tax payments (such as federal income tax withheld from wages or estimated tax payments).
    (ii) Had earned income (such as wages, salaries, or self-employment income) and claimed the earned income credit or the additional child tax credit.
    (iii) Claimed a refundable credit, such as the health coverage tax credit or the refundable credit for prior year minimum tax.

If one is an injured spouse, he/she can obtain the portion of the joint refund by completing Form 8379 (Request for Innocent Spouse Relief).

5.04 UNIT 5: QUESTIONS

TRUE/FALSE QUESTIONS
Please select either (A) for True or (B) for False

1. You can request your tax return examination be moved to another IRS area if your books and records are located in the other area.
   A. TRUE
   B. FALSE

2. Only one level of appeal exists within the IRS. All appeals are made to the appeals office.
   A. TRUE
   B. FALSE

3. If the examination of a taxpayer's return by the IRS results in a disagreement over whether the taxpayer owes additional income tax, the IRS must issue a formal letter called a notice of deficiency before the taxpayer can appeal his/her case to the Tax Court.
   A. TRUE
   B. FALSE

4. If you do not agree with the proposed changes from an examination, you must go directly to Appeals within 15 days.
   A. TRUE
   B. FALSE

5. If the proposed increase or decrease in tax resulting from an IRS examination, conducted at the taxpayer's place of business, exceeds $2,500 but is not more than $10,000, the taxpayer or the taxpayer's representative must provide a brief written statement explaining the disputed issues within 30 days of the issuance of the 30-day letter.
   A. TRUE
   B. FALSE

6. Mr. Vincent's income tax return was examined by an IRS tax auditor in an IRS office. The tax auditor proposed an additional tax liability of $12,000. Mr. Vincent does not agree with the auditor's findings and wishes to schedule a conference with an IRS regional appeals office. Vincent must file a written protest of the auditor's findings to obtain an appeals conference.
   A. TRUE
   B. FALSE

7. If the IRS selects a return for audit and the taxpayer responds that they have been audited within the prior five years, the IRS will discontinue the examination.
   A. TRUE
   B. FALSE

8. Jack and Jill's joint return was selected for examination in 2004. There was no change to the one issue examined---medical expense. In 2005, they received a notice that their return was selected for examination and the issues were exemptions and contributions. Because they received a no-change in 2004, they should contact the IRS to see if the examination should be discontinued in 2005.
   A. TRUE
   B. FALSE

9. The taxpayer must file a claim for a credit or refund within 3 years from the date (s)he filed his/her original return or 2 years from the date (s)he paid the tax, whichever is later.
   A. TRUE
   B. FALSE

10. Richard's 2001 and 2003 returns were examined for charitable contributions and employee business expenses. Both examinations resulted in no change to the return as filed. Richard has been notified that his 2004 return has been selected for examination for claimed business bad debts. Since Richard has two prior no change audits, upon notifying the IRS, the examination should be discontinued.
    A. TRUE
    B. FALSE

11. Lamar's income tax returns for 2001 and 2003 were examined by the IRS. Both examinations covered Schedule C income and expenses and resulted in no change in income tax. On September 15, 2005, he received notice that his income tax return for 2004 will be examined as part of the IRS Taxpayer Compliance Measurement Program. Lamar should contact the IRS immediately to exclude his income tax return from examination under the repetitive audit procedures.
    A. TRUE
    B. FALSE

12. In any case in which a recognized representative is unable or unwilling to declare his/her own knowledge that the facts are TRUE and correct, the IRS may require the taxpayer to make such a declaration under penalty of perjury.
    A. TRUE
    B. FALSE

13. A written protest should contain the taxpayer's name and address, the years involved, and a schedule of the changes with which (s)he disagrees. It should state the facts supporting the taxpayer's position and the law or authority on which (s)he relied. (S)he does not need to declare as TRUE, under penalties of perjury, the facts given in the protest because (s)he signed the original tax return under penalties of perjury.
    A. TRUE
    B. FALSE

14. In any case in which the taxpayer's representative is unable or unwilling to declare of his/her own knowledge that the facts in a claim, written argument, brief, or recitation of facts are TRUE and correct, the IRS may request the taxpayer to make such a declaration under penalty of perjury.
    A. TRUE
    B. FALSE

15. Ruth's 2003 and 2004 returns were examined for investment expenses. Both examinations resulted in no change to the return as filed. Ruth was notified that her 2005 return was selected for examination for investment expenses. Since Ruth has two prior no change audits, she should notify the IRS to see if the examination should be discontinued.
    A. TRUE
    B. FALSE

16. A representative qualified to practice before the IRS <u>cannot</u> prepare or sign a formal written protest on behalf of a client to request an appeals conference.
    A. TRUE
    B. FALSE

17. In the process of examining or collecting your tax liability, the IRS may contact third parties. The IRS must give the taxpayer reasonable notice before making any inquiries of third parties such as neighbors, banks, employers, and other employees. This notification must include the specific names of those it intends to contact.
    A. TRUE
    B. FALSE

18. The IRS has selected Ada's 2002 tax return for examination. The only item of inquiry in the IRS contact letter was for verification of charitable contributions. Ada's tax return for 2000 was also examined to verify her charitable contributions, and no change was proposed to her tax liability. If Ada advises the IRS representative that no change resulted in her tax return for 2000, the examination of her tax return for 2002 might be discontinued.
    A. TRUE
    B. FALSE

19. During February 2005, Arnold's tax return for 2003 was selected for an IRS examination in Los Angeles, California. This is where Arnold lived, maintained his business in 2003, and had his accountant prepare his tax return. Late in 2004, Arnold moved to Biloxi, Mississippi, and took his books and records with him. Arnold can request to have his case transferred to Biloxi, Mississippi.
    A. TRUE
    B. FALSE

20. Generally, a return is examined in the IRS district where the taxpayer lives. But if the return can be examined more quickly and conveniently in another district, such as where the books and records are located, the taxpayer can ask to have the case transferred.
    A. TRUE
    B. FALSE

21. If a taxpayer agrees with proposed audit changes and signs an agreement form at the conclusion of the audit, no interest will be charged on any balance due.
    A. TRUE
    B. FALSE

22. Ned's individual income tax return was under IRS examination. Five months before the expiration of the statute of limitations, the Revenue Agent wanted Ned to agree to extend the statute of limitations. Generally, the Revenue Agent must advise Ned that he has a right to refuse to extend the statute of limitations, and if he does agree to an extension, the agreement can be restricted as to particular issues on the tax return.
    A. TRUE
    B. FALSE

23. A taxpayer can appeal to a court only after an unsuccessful appeal before an IRS Appeals Officer.
    A. TRUE
    B. FALSE

24. Before you take your case to the Tax Court, the IRS must send you a notice of deficiency. Then you have 60 days to file a petition with the Tax Court.
    A. TRUE
    B. FALSE

25. A Statutory Notice of Deficiency is also known as a 90-day letter because the taxpayer generally has 90 days from the date of the letter to file a petition with the United States Tax Court.
    A. TRUE
    B. FALSE

26. If, after a Collection Due Process hearing with the Office of Appeals to discuss an IRS levy or lien, you do not agree with the Appeals determination, you have 30 days from the date of the determination to bring suit to contest the determination.
   A. TRUE
   B. FALSE

27. If a taxpayer does not respond to a 30-day letter or if (s)he does not reach an agreement with an appeals officer, (s)he will receive a statutory notice of deficiency. A statutory notice of deficiency allows a taxpayer 90 days (150 days if mailed when the taxpayer is outside the United States) from the date of this notice to file a petition with the Tax Court.
   A. TRUE
   B. FALSE

28. If a taxpayer is filing a claim for credit or refund based on contested income tax issues considered in previously examined returns and does not want to appeal within the IRS, (s)he should request in writing that the claim be immediately rejected.
   A. TRUE
   B. FALSE

29. If the IRS disallows or rejects your timely filed claim for a refund or does not act on your claim within 6 months after you file it, you can only take your claim to Appeals.
   A. TRUE
   B. FALSE

30. Peter did not want to use the administrative appeal process within the IRS to contest income tax issues considered in the audit of his return. He filed a claim for refund and requested that the claim be immediately rejected. The IRS promptly sent him a notice of claim disallowance. Peter has 2 years from the date of the notice of disallowance to file a refund suit in a United States district court or in the United States Court of Federal Claims.
   A. TRUE
   B. FALSE

31. A Statutory Notice of Deficiency is also known as a 90-day letter because the taxpayer generally has 90 days from the date of the letter to file a petition with the United States Tax Court.
   A. TRUE
   B. FALSE

32. Frank Beck did not agree with the proposed changes resulting from an IRS examination. He did not respond to the 30-day letter that was issued by the IRS. The IRS will send Frank a 60-day letter, also known as a statutory notice of deficiency.
   A. TRUE

B. FALSE

33. If a taxpayer is filing a claim for credit or refund based on contested income tax issues considered in previously examined returns and wants to appeal within the IRS, (s)he should request in writing that the claim be immediately rejected.
    A. TRUE
    B. FALSE

34. If a proposed increase or decrease in tax, including penalties, or refund, determined by the IRS, from an examination conducted at the taxpayer's place of business, exceeds $2,500 but is not more than $25,000, a brief written statement has to be provided to obtain an appeals office conference.
    A. TRUE
    B. FALSE

35. Joseph received a bill from the IRS for additional tax due of $1,000 plus accrued interest of $150. If Joseph pays the $1,000 tax in full, this will stop the accrual of any additional interest.
    A. TRUE
    B. FALSE

36. Dave operates a retail business as a sole proprietorship with stores in several locations in the Toledo, Ohio area. The books and records for all of the stores are maintained at the main store near his residence. Dave's tax returns have always been prepared by his longtime accountant in Toledo. Dave has been notified that his 2005 1040 has been selected for an examination. Dave's brother-in-law in Detroit, Michigan, a district away, has just passed the enrolled agent's examination, and Dave's wife would like him to handle the examination. The IRS will likely approve a transfer to the Detroit office, provided a properly executed Form 2848 is submitted with the request.
    A. TRUE
    B. FALSE

37. The IRS may abate (reduce) the amount of interest you owe if the interest is due to an unreasonable error or delay by an IRS officer or employee in performing a ministerial or managerial act.
    A. TRUE
    B. FALSE

38. The IRS may not contact third parties such as neighbors, banks, or employers without the taxpayer's written consent.
    A. TRUE
    B. FALSE

39. Joseph received a bill from the IRS for additional tax due of $2,000, plus accrued interest of $300. If Joseph pays the $2,000 tax in full, this will stop the accrual of any additional interest.
   A. TRUE
   B. FALSE

MULTIPLE CHOICE QUESTIONS:
Please select the most appropriate answer.

40. Before the initial in-person interview between the IRS and the taxpayer to determine or collect any taxes, a taxpayer should receive which one of the following publications from the IRS?
    A. Publication 586A, The Collection Process (Income Tax Accounts), or Publication 594, The Collection Process (Employment Tax Accounts).
    B. Publication 5, Appeal Rights and Preparation of Protests for Unagreed Cases.
    C. Form 2848, Power of Attorney and Declaration of Representative.
    D. Publication 1, Your Rights as a Taxpayer.

41. All of the following reasons are acceptable for transferring an examination from one IRS district to another except
    A. The place of examination is solely for the convenience of the taxpayer's representative (books and records are located at his/her client's office which is located within the current IRS district).
    B. Books and records are located in another district.
    C. The place of examination is for the convenience of the IRS.
    D. The taxpayer's residence has changed since the return was filed.

42. The IRS has begun an examination of Mark's 2009 income tax return. The IRS would like to ask Mark's neighbors questions with respect to that examination. There is no pending criminal investigation into the matter, and there is no evidence that such contact will result in reprisals against the neighbors or jeopardize collection of the tax liability. Before the IRS contacts the neighbors, the IRS must
    A. Provide Mark with reasonable notice of the contact.
    B. Make an assessment of Mark's tax liability.
    C. Ask the court for a third-party record-keeper subpoena.
    D. Mail Mark a statutory notice of deficiency.

43. Marty timely filed his Federal income tax return for 2001. It was selected for examination. During the course of the examination, the Revenue Agent first assigned to the case retired. A second Revenue Agent proposed adjustments to the tax return which Marty believed were erroneous. The second Revenue Agent was assigned to an extended training assignment. Before going on training, Marty and the second Revenue

Agent orally agreed that the statute of limitations could be extended to December 31, 2005. Which of the following statements is applicable in order for the IRS to protect its rights?

A. An assessment of income taxes must be made before December 31, 2005.
B. A Statutory Notice of Deficiency must be mailed on or before December 31, 2005.
C. A Statutory Notice of Deficiency must be mailed on or before April 15, 2005.
D. The assessment of tax can be made at any time.

44. Caroline received an audit notification letter scheduling an appointment for July 1, 2004 for the examination of her tax year 2002 Form 1040 return. The week before the scheduled appointment, she received a telephone call from the IRS office canceling the appointment. She was told that she would be contacted at a later date to reschedule the appointment. She was not contacted until July 1, 2005, when she was advised of a new appointment date. Errors identified in the examination resulted in her owing additional tax of $4,000 plus accrued interest of $600. Caroline does not believe that she should have to pay interest for the period that she was waiting for her appointment to be rescheduled. How should she proceed?

A. Pay the tax and interest and deduct the interest on her 2005 return, the year paid.
B. Immediately request an Appeals conference to contest the interest.
C. Request an abatement of the interest by filing a Form 843 with the IRS service center where she filed her 2002 return.
D. Immediately petition the Tax Court to contest the interest.

45. Which of the following statements with respect to the preparation of a case for appeal before an IRS appeals office is false?

A. The appeals office is the only level of appeal within the IRS.
B. A written protest or brief statement of disputed issues is required in a situation in which the proposed increase in tax determined by examination is $2,300.
C. An S corporation must submit a written protest.
D. A written protest must contain a statement stating the law or other authority on which the taxpayer is relying.

46. Mr. Garcia's individual income tax return was examined, and the IRS issued a statutory notice of deficiency. Mr. Garcia wishes to contest the liability by bypassing the IRS's appeals system and taking his case straight to court. Mr. Garcia should

A. Contact the IRS problem resolution officer.
B. Pay the tax and petition the U.S. Tax Court.
C. Not pay the tax and file a written protest requesting immediate consideration by the U.S. Court of Federal Claims.
D. Pay the tax, file a claim for refund requesting that the claim be immediately rejected so he may file a refund suit in district court.

47. Under what circumstances may the examination of a tax return be transferred to another district?

A. The taxpayer has moved and now resides in another district.
B. The books and records are located in another district.
C. The taxpayer requests a transfer to another district.
D. All of the answers are correct.

48. Read the following statements regarding the IRS's appeals system:
    (1) Because people sometimes disagree on tax matters, the IRS has an administrative appeals process.
    (2) Most differences can be settled within this system without expensive and time-consuming court trials.
    (3) A taxpayer cannot appeal his/her case based only on moral, religious, political, constitutional, conscientious, or similar grounds.
    (4) If a taxpayer does not want to appeal his/her case within the IRS, (s)he can take the case directly to court.

    Select the best answer from the following options:
    A. 1 and 2 are TRUE; 3 and 4 are FALSE
    B. 1, 2, and 3 are TRUE; 4 is FALSE
    C. All are TRUE
    D. All are FALSE

49. With respect to preparation of a case for IRS appeals, the following statements are TRUE except
    A. A brief written statement of the disputed issue(s) is not required if the increase or decrease in tax, including penalties, or refund, determined by examination is more than $2,500 but not more than $10,000.
    B. If the proposed increase or decrease in tax, including penalties or claimed refund is more than $25,000, the taxpayer must submit a written protest of the disputed issues, including a statement of facts supporting the taxpayer's position on all disputed issues.
    C. A declaration that the statement of facts is TRUE under penalties of perjury must be added and signed by the taxpayer.
    D. If a representative submits the protest for the taxpayer, (s)he must submit a declaration stating that (s)he submitted the protest and accompanying documents and whether (s)he knows personally that the statement of facts in the protest and accompanying documents are TRUE and correct.

50. Sam is the sole shareholder in an S corporation. The S corporation was examined and the IRS proposed a $20,000 deficiency. What must Sam do to request an appeals conference?
    A. File a formal written protest.
    B. Pay the deficiency.
    C. Hire a federally authorized tax practitioner to represent the S corporation.
    D. Nothing because he is eligible for the small case procedure.

51. Peter's return was examined, and the result was additional tax of $16,000 due to unreported lottery winnings. Peter has received a letter notifying him of his right to appeal the proposed changes within 30 days. Which of the following should Peter do in preparing his appeal?
    A. Call the examiner and request a conference.
    B. Provide a brief written statement of the disputed issues.
    C. Submit a written protest within the time limit specified.
    D. Submit a written protest explaining additional expenses not previously claimed.

52. Which of the following statements concerning the preparation of a case for appeal before an IRS appeals office is false?
    A. A written protest is required if the proposed increase in tax is more than $10,000.
    B. A written protest is not required for refunds.
    C. Partnerships must submit written protests.
    D. A protest prepared by a representative must declare whether (s)he knows personally that the statement of facts in the protest and the accompanying documents is TRUE and correct.

53. At the conclusion of an audit, the taxpayer can appeal the tax decision to a local appeals office. Which statement regarding appeal procedures is false?
    A. If the total amount for any tax period is not more than $25,000, a formal written protest is not required.
    B. A taxpayer may represent himself at an appeals conference.
    C. Written protests do not require a signature.
    D. All partnership and S corporation cases require formal written protests.

54. D's tax return for 2003 was examined by the IRS for contributions and medical expenses. The examination resulted in "no change" to his tax liability. He received notification of an examination for the same items for his 2005 tax return. What action should he take?
    A. Notify the IRS of the prior year's examination as soon as possible.
    B. Do not respond to the audit notification.
    C. Set up an appointment for the current examination and do not discuss the prior examination.
    D. Call the IRS Problem Resolution Office.

55. On April 21, 2005, Vern, a calendar-year taxpayer, filed his 2000 through 2004 income tax returns. His tax was paid through withholding. The following was shown on the tax returns:

    | 2000 | amount owed | $300 |
    | 2001 | refund | $500 |
    | 2002 | refund | $400 |

2003	refund	$100
2004	amount owed	$200

What is the amount of refund due or tax owed by Vern?
A. $0
B. $500 refund.
C. $300 refund.
D. $400 tax owed.

56. Which of the following statements concerning the procedure for a written protest submitted by a representative to obtain an appeals office conference is false?
    A. A written protest is required when the tax due, including penalties, is more than $10,000.
    B. A written protest must contain the tax years involved and a statement that the taxpayer wants to appeal to the appeals office.
    C. A written protest must contain a statement of facts for each disputed issue and a statement of law or other authority relied upon for each issue.
    D. A written protest must contain a declaration under penalties of perjury, signed by the taxpayer, that the statement of facts is TRUE and correct.

57. Wesley timely filed his tax year 2002 Form 1040 tax return on April 15, 2003 and paid the $2,000 tax as shown on the return at the time of filing. The return was subsequently examined and Wesley signed an agreement form for the proposed changes on October 31, 2004. He paid the additional tax due of $10,000 on December 31, 2004. In 2005, Wesley located missing records which he believes would make $5,000 of the additional assessment erroneous. Which of the following statements accurately states the date by which Wesley must file a claim for refund?
    A. October 31, 2006, two years from signing the agreement form.
    B. April 15, 2006, three years from the due date of the original return.
    C. December 31, 2006, two years from when the additional tax was paid.
    D. No claim for refund can be filed since an examination agreement form was signed.

58. The examination of Greta's tax return for 2003 resulted in adjustments creating a tax liability in the amount of $30,000. Greta does not believe she owes anything. A Notice of Proposed Income Tax Deficiency is issued to Greta, who wants to appeal the Revenue Agent's adjustments to the IRS Office of Appeals. Greta must file a written protest letter no later than which of the following periods?
    A. 10 days.
    B. 30 days.
    C. 90 days.
    D. None of the answers are correct.

59. A claim for refund must be filed
    A. No later than 3 years after you filed your original return.

B. No later than 2 years from the date you paid the tax.
C. No later than 3 years after you filed your original return or no later than 2 years from the date you paid the tax, whichever is later.
D. 4 years after making estimated payments.

60. Barry's individual income tax return for 2004 was examined by the IRS, which resulted in a tax assessment in the amount of $10,000. Thereafter, Barry discovered papers which he believed would show that the IRS determination was erroneous. Barry can claim a refund of income taxes as follows:
    A. Take a credit for the amount on his 2005 return.
    B. File Form 1045, Application for Tentative Refund.
    C. File an amended return within three years from the date he filed his original return for 2004 or two years from the date he paid the tax, whichever is later.
    D. Immediately sue for a refund in court.

61. Charlie had income tax withheld from his wages during 2002 in the amount of $5,000. Charlie filed an automatic extension of time to file his tax return for that year to August 16, 2003, together with making an additional payment in the amount of $2,000 with the extension. Charlie filed his tax return on November 15, 2003, and paid the balance shown to be due on the return of $1,000 on that date. Charlie discovered an error in his return on November 1, 2006. On that same date he filed a claim for refund in the amount of $6,000. Assuming the grounds set forth in the claim are proper, what refund can Charlie recover for 2002?
    A. $6,000
    B. $2,000
    C. $1,000
    D. $0

62. The Statutory Notice of Deficiency is also known as
    A. A 30-day letter because the taxpayer generally has 30 days from the date of the letter to file a petition with the Tax Court.
    B. A 90-day letter because the taxpayer generally has 90 days from the date of the letter to file a petition with the Tax Court.
    C. An Information Document Request (IDR) because the taxpayer is asked for information to support its position regarding its liability for tax.
    D. A notice and demand because the taxpayer is put on notice that the tax liability is due and owing.

63. Which of the following statements relating to the statutory notice of deficiency is false?
    A. If a taxpayer receives a notice of deficiency and sends money to the IRS without written instructions, the IRS will treat it as a payment, and the taxpayer will not be able to petition the Tax Court.
    B. A notice of deficiency is not an assessment.

C. If the taxpayer consents, the IRS can withdraw any notice of deficiency. However, after the notice is withdrawn, the taxpayer cannot file a petition with the Tax Court based on the withdrawn notice, and the IRS may later issue a notice of deficiency greater or less than the amount in the withdrawn deficiency.
D. The notice of deficiency provides the taxpayer 90 days (150 days if the taxpayer lives outside the United States) to either agree to the deficiency or file a petition with the Tax Court for a redetermination of the deficiency.

64. Gina disagreed with the results of an IRS examination of her tax return. She pursued the appeals procedures and disagreed with the appeals officer. If she wishes to appeal further, Gina may
   A. Request a conference with a new appeals officer in a different district.
   B. Wait for a notice of deficiency, fail to pay the tax, and petition the district court.
   C. Wait for a notice of deficiency, fail to pay the tax, and petition the Tax Court.
   D. Submit a revised written protest that outlines the issues and authority for the position taken.

65. A disagreement with the IRS can be taken to the United States Tax Court if
   A. It pertains to income tax.
   B. A statutory notice of deficiency has been issued.
   C. A petition is filed within 90 days from the date a statutory notice of deficiency is mailed (150 days if it is addressed to the taxpayer outside the United States).
   D. All of the answers are correct.

66. Anna's 2005 individual tax return was examined, and the IRS proposed changes resulting in additional tax. Anna wishes to bypass the IRS's appeal system and file a refund suit in the U.S. Court of Federal Claims on contested income tax issues. Your advice to Anna should be that she
   A. Request that her return be reexamined.
   B. Pay all of the additional tax and file another 1040 tax return.
   C. Pay all of the additional tax and then file a claim for refund and request in writing that the claim be immediately rejected.
   D. File a claim for refund and do nothing else.

67. Julie, who lives in Washington, D.C., operated a business without books and records. Her business income and expenses were reported on Schedule C. Julie's tax return for 2003 was examined and substantial adjustments were proposed. Julie disagreed with the adjustments and wants to take her case directly to Tax Court. A Statutory Notice of Deficiency was issued to Julie by the IRS Area Director. Julie can file a petition for a small tax case before the U.S. Tax Court during which of the following periods beginning from the date of the issuance of the notice?
   A. 30 days.
   B. 90 days.
   C. 150 days.

D. None of the answers are correct.

68. After the issuance of a Statutory Notice of Deficiency, failure to timely file a petition with Tax Court will result in which of the following?
   A. The IRS will issue a 30-day letter.
   B. The IRS will assess the tax it says the taxpayer owes.
   C. The IRS will issue a 90-day letter.
   D. You will be required to post a deposit before being allowed to request an extension for time to file a petition.

69. Which of the following statements with respect to court petitions and court appeals is TRUE?
   A. A taxpayer may petition the United States Tax Court for a judicial determination of his/her tax liability within a specified period (generally 90 days) after receiving a notice of deficiency or paying the tax.
   B. Both the taxpayer and the government may appeal decisions of the Tax Court or district court to the appropriate circuit court of appeals.
   C. Decisions of the courts of appeals and some decisions of other federal courts cannot be reviewed by the United States Supreme Court.
   D. If a taxpayer's claim for refund is denied by the IRS or if no decision is made by the IRS in 6 months, the taxpayer may petition either the U.S. Court of Federal Claims or the U.S. circuit court of appeals having jurisdiction over the taxpayer.

70. In the process of preparing Orlo Corporation's 2003 return, Dave, an enrolled agent, provided to Orlo Corporation calculations he had prepared computing basis of property that was sold and reported on the 1120 Form 4797. Later, when Orlo Corporation's 2003 return was examined by the IRS, Orlo Corporation refused to provide the IRS with the calculations, claiming that this was a privileged communication between Orlo Corporation and its federally authorized practitioner. Which of the following statements is TRUE?
   A. Orlo Corporation does not have to provide the calculations to the IRS because they are privileged under the Federal Tax Practitioner privilege rules.
   B. Orlo Corporation must provide the calculations to the IRS because privilege does not apply to a determination with respect to an item that will be presented to the government on an original return.
   C. Orlo Corporation must provide the calculations to the IRS because the Federal Tax Practitioner privilege does not apply to documents written by Dave because he is not a CPA.
   D. Orlo Corporation does not have to provide the calculations to the IRS if they believe this transaction might be construed as a tax shelter.

71. All of the following should be contained in a written protest letter except
   A. A statement that the taxpayer wants to appeal the findings of the examiner to the appeals office.

B. The date and symbols from the letter showing the proposed adjustments and findings being protested.
C. Tax periods or years involved.
D. A statement indicating whether the examination was originally handled through correspondence, by a tax auditor, or by an IRS agent.

72. Mr. K, who lives in Dallas, Texas, received a letter from the IRS stating that the result of a recent field examination is a tax deficiency of $15,000. The examination was handled at Mr. K's place of business by a revenue agent. The letter also states that Mr. K has a right to file a protest if he does not agree with the proposal. Generally, how many days does K have to file a written protest?
    A. 15 days.
    B. 30 days.
    C. 60 days.
    D. 90 days.

73. In response to a preliminary (30-day) letter, a written statement discussing the facts and legal arguments must accompany a written request for an appeals conference in which of the following cases?
    A. A $2,000 tax increase was proposed.
    B. The tax return examination was made in an IRS office by a tax auditor.
    C. The tax return examination was made by correspondence.
    D. A disallowance of a $3,000 refund claim was proposed.

74. If your tax return was examined for the same items in either of the 2 previous years and no change was proposed to your tax liability
    A. You may ignore the examination notice.
    B. You should call the Taxpayer Advocate Office and file a complaint.
    C. You should call the IRS as soon as possible to see if the examination should be discontinued.
    D. You should write a letter to the Service Center and complain that the Revenue Agents are harassing you.

XXXXXXXXXXXXXXXXXXXXXXXXXXXXXXXXXXXXXXXXXXXXXXXXXXXXXXXXXXXXXXXXX
5.05   UNIT 5: ANSWERS
XXXXXXXXXXXXXXXXXXXXXXXXXXXXXXXXXXXXXXXXXXXXXXXXXXXXXXXXXXXXXXXXX

1. **(A) Correct**
   Generally, a taxpayer's return is examined in the area where he or she lives. But if the return can be examined more quickly and conveniently in another area, such as where books and records are located, the taxpayer can ask to have the case transferred to that area. When request is received to transfer taxpayer returns to another district for examination, the district director having jurisdiction may transfer the case, together with pertinent records to the district director of such other district. The IRS will determine the time and place of the examination. In determining whether a transfer should be made, circumstances such as the following will be considered:
   (1) Change of the taxpayer's domicile, either before or during examination.
   (2) Discovery that taxpayer's books and records are kept in another district.
   (3) Change of domicile of an executor or administrator to another district before or during examination.
   (4) The effective administration of the tax laws (26 CFR 601.105(k)).

2. **(A) Correct**
   The IRS maintains an Appeals Office, separate and independent of the district offices. The Appeals Office is the only level of administrative appeal within the IRS. A taxpayer who disagrees with an examination can request a conference with Appeals Office personnel. These conferences are held in an informal manner by correspondence, by telephone or at a personal conference (Reg. Sec. 601.016(c)).

3. **(A) Correct**
   If the examination of a taxpayer's return by the IRS results in a disagreement over whether the taxpayer owes additional income tax, the IRS must issue a formal letter called a notice of deficiency before the taxpayer can appeal his/her case to the Tax Court. Before issuing a notice of deficiency, the IRS sends a preliminary notice advising the taxpayer of his right to appeal (the 30-day letter).

4. **(B) Correct**
   A taxpayer may initiate an appeal within 30 days after receiving notice from the IRS of the right to appeal if the taxpayer does not agree with the proposed changes from an examination. The 30-day letter must identify the amount of the tax, interest, and penalties included in the notice. It must also describe why the IRS believes these amounts are due.

5. **(A) Correct**
   To appeal the IRS's findings in field examination cases, the taxpayer must file a written protest if the proposed additional liability exceeds $10,000 for any tax period. A written

protest is required for all penalties that have already been assessed. If the proposed adjustments in a field examination case exceed $2,500 but do not exceed $10,000, the taxpayer must file a brief written statement of the issues.

The taxpayer does not have to make a written protest to appeal the following:
    a) Field examinations resulting in adjustments of $2,500.
    b) Office examinations.
    c) Correspondence audits.

6. **(B) Correct**
The taxpayer does not have to make a written protest to appeal the following:
    a) Field examinations resulting in adjustments of $2,500.
    b) Office examinations.
    c) Correspondence audits.

7. **(B) Correct**
Generally, a taxpayer cannot get an injunction to block an investigation by the IRS. The taxpayer's remedy is to claim that the second inspection is illegal at a hearing to enforce the summons. If the same items were examined in either of the previous 2 years and the examination resulted in no change to the tax liability, the IRS might suspend <u>but not</u> cancel an audit in order to avoid repetitive examinations of the same items.

8. **(B) Correct**
Generally, a taxpayer cannot get an injunction to block an investigation by the IRS. The taxpayer's remedy is to claim that the second inspection is illegal at a hearing to enforce the summons. If the same items were examined in either of the previous 2 years and the examination resulted in no change to the tax liability, the IRS might suspend <u>but not</u> cancel an audit in order to avoid repetitive examinations of the same items. As long as an investigation is continuing, the IRS can look at the same books or records on more than one occasion.

9. **(A) Correct**
Code Section 6511 states that a claim for refund or credit for an overpayment must be filed within 3 years from the time the <u>return was filed</u> or within 2 years from the time the <u>tax was paid</u>, whichever occurs later.

10. **(B) Correct**
See Answer # 8

11. **(B) Correct**
See Answer # 8

12. **(A) Correct**

    Written protests which taxpayers are required to file with the District Director to bring unagreed tax cases before the Appellate Division may now be certified as true under the penalties of perjury. Formerly such written protests had to be filed under oath (Rev. Proc. 61-36). In any case in which the taxpayer's representative is unable or unwilling to declare of his/her own knowledge that the facts in a claim, written argument, brief, or recitation of facts are TRUE and correct, the IRS may request the taxpayer to make such a declaration under penalty of perjury.

13. **(B) Correct**

    A written protest should include the following:
    1) A statement that the taxpayer wishes to appeal the findings of the IRS to the Appeals office.
    2) The taxpayer's name, address and daytime telephone number.
    3) A copy of the letter showing the proposed changes and findings that the taxpayer does not agree with or the date and symbols from the letter.
    4) A list of the changes that the taxpayer does not agree with and why.
    5) The tax periods involved.
    6) A statement of facts supporting the taxpayer's position.
    7) A statement of the law or other authorities that are relied upon (Reg. Sec. 601.105(c)).
    8) Written protests which taxpayers are required to file with the District Director to bring unagreed tax cases before the Appellate Division may now be certified as true under the penalties of perjury. Formerly such written protests had to be filed under oath (Rev. Proc. 61-36).

14. **(A) Correct**

    Written protests which taxpayers are required to file with the District Director to bring unagreed tax cases before the Appellate Division may now be certified as true under the penalties of perjury. Formerly such written protests had to be filed under oath (Rev. Proc. 61-36). In any case in which the taxpayer's representative is unable or unwilling to declare of his/her own knowledge that the facts in a claim, written argument, brief, or recitation of facts are TRUE and correct, the IRS may request the taxpayer to make such a declaration under penalty of perjury.

15. **(A) Correct**

    Generally, a taxpayer cannot get an injunction to block an investigation by the IRS. The taxpayer's remedy is to claim that the second inspection is illegal at a hearing to enforce the summons. If the same items were examined in either of the previous 2 years and the examination resulted in no change to the tax liability, the IRS might suspend but not cancel an audit in order to avoid repetitive examinations of the same items. Since the audit is related to a tax return on its 3rd year, Ruth should notify the IRS to see if the examination should be discontinued.

16. **(B) Correct**
    A representative qualified to practice before the IRS can prepare or sign a formal written protest on behalf of a client to request an appeals conference. In any case in which the taxpayer's representative is unable or unwilling to declare of his/her own knowledge that the facts in a claim, written argument, brief, or recitation of facts are TRUE and correct, the IRS may request the taxpayer to make such a declaration under penalty of perjury.

17. **(A) Correct**
    The IRS must give the taxpayer reasonable notice before contacting other persons about the taxpayer's tax matters. The taxpayer must be given reasonable notice in advance that, in examining or collecting your tax liability, the IRS may contact third parties such as neighbors, banks, employers, or employees. The IRS must also give the taxpayer notice of specific contacts by providing a record of persons contacted on both a periodic basis and upon the taxpayer's request. This provision does not apply:
    (a) To any pending criminal investigation,
    (b) When providing notice would jeopardize collection of any tax liability,
    (c) Where providing notice may result in reprisal against any person, or
    (d) When you authorized the contact.

18. **(A) Correct**
    Generally, a taxpayer cannot get an injunction to block an investigation by the IRS. The taxpayer's remedy is to claim that the second inspection is illegal at a hearing to enforce the summons. If the same items were examined in either of the previous 2 years and the examination resulted in no change to the tax liability, the IRS might suspend <u>but not</u> cancel an audit in order to avoid repetitive examinations of the same items. As long as an investigation is continuing, the IRS can look at the same books or records on more than one occasion.

19. **(A) Correct**
    Generally, a taxpayer's return is examined in the area where he or she lives. But if the return can be examined more quickly and conveniently in another area, such as where books and records are located, the taxpayer can ask to have the case transferred to that area. When request is received to transfer taxpayer returns to another district for examination, the district director having jurisdiction may transfer the case, together with pertinent records to the district director of such other district. The IRS will determine the time and place of the examination. In determining whether a transfer should be made, circumstances such as the following will be considered:
    (1) Change of the taxpayer's domicile, either before or during examination.
    (2) Discovery that taxpayer's books and records are kept in another district.
    (3) Change of domicile of an executor or administrator to another district before or during examination.
    (4) The effective administration of the tax laws (26 CFR 601.105(k)).

20. **(A) Correct**

See Answer # 19

21. **(B) Correct**

At the conclusion of an office or field examination, the taxpayer is given an opportunity to agree with the findings of the examining officer. If the taxpayer does not agree, the examining officer will inform the taxpayer of the taxpayer's appeal rights. If the taxpayer does agree with the proposed changes, the examining officer will invite the taxpayer to execute either Form 870 (Waiver of Restrictions on Assessment and Collection of Deficiency in Tax and Acceptance of Over-assessment). When the taxpayer agrees with the proposed changes but does not offer to pay any deficiency or additional tax which may be due, the examining officer will also invite payment (by check or money order), together with any applicable interest or penalty.

22. **(A) Correct**

The extended assessment statute allows the IRS time to properly complete the examination of the tax return and to make any additional assessment or reduction in the previously assessed tax liability that is required. Generally, the Revenue Agent must advise the taxpayer that he/she has a right to refuse to extend the statute of limitations, and if he/she does agree to an extension, the agreement can be restricted as to particular issues on the tax return.

23. **(B) Correct**

A taxpayer may elect to bypass the IRS appeals system and take a case directly to the U.S. Tax Court, the U.S. Court of Federal Claims, or a U.S. district court.

24. **(B) Correct**

Once any appeal process within the IRS is complete, the IRS may issue a statutory notice of deficiency. Once the IRS issues a deficiency notice, the taxpayer has 90 days to file a Tax Court petition. If the taxpayer does not file a petition, the IRS will assess the taxes.

25. **(A) Correct**

Once any appeal process within the IRS is complete, the IRS may issue a statutory notice of deficiency. Once the IRS issues a deficiency notice, the taxpayer has 90 days to file a Tax Court petition. If the taxpayer does not file a petition, the IRS will assess the taxes. This statutory Notice of Deficiency is also known as a 90-day letter because the taxpayer generally has 90 days from the date of the letter to file a petition with the United States Tax Court.

26. **(A) Correct**

If the examination of a taxpayer's return by the IRS results in a disagreement over whether the taxpayer owes additional income tax, the IRS must issue a formal letter called a notice of deficiency before the taxpayer can appeal his/her case to the Tax Court. Before issuing a notice of deficiency, the IRS sends a preliminary notice advising the taxpayer of his right to appeal (the 30-day letter). A taxpayer may initiate an appeal within 30 days after receiving notice from the IRS of the right to appeal if the taxpayer does not agree with the proposed changes from an examination. The 30-day letter must identify the amount of the tax, interest, and penalties included in the notice. It must also describe why the IRS believes these amounts are due.

27. **(A) Correct**
    Once the IRS issues a deficiency notice, the taxpayer has 90 days to file a Tax Court petition. If the taxpayer does not file a petition, the IRS will assess the taxes. This statutory Notice of Deficiency is also known as a 90-day letter because the taxpayer generally has 90 days (150 days if mailed when the taxpayer is outside the United States) from the date of the letter to file a petition with the United States Tax Court.

28. **(A) Correct**
    If a taxpayer is filing a claim for credit or refund based on contested income tax issues considered in previously examined returns and does not want to appeal within the IRS, (s)he should request in writing that the claim be immediately rejected.

29. **(B) Correct**
    If a taxpayer is filing a claim for credit or refund based on contested income tax issues considered in previously examined returns and does not want to appeal within the IRS, (s)he should request in writing that the claim be immediately rejected. When a taxpayer promptly receives a notice of claim disallowance, A taxpayer may bring a suit to the appropriate District Court or Court of Federal Claims against the IRS after 6 months from the date of filing the claim or before the expiration of 2 years from the date of mailing by certified mail or registered mail by the Secretary to the taxpayer of a notice of the disallowance of the part of the claim to which the suit or proceeding relates (Code Sec. 6532).

30. **(B) Correct**
    If a taxpayer is filing a claim for credit or refund based on contested income tax issues considered in previously examined returns and does not want to appeal within the IRS, (s)he should request in writing that the claim be immediately rejected. When a taxpayer promptly receives a notice of claim disallowance, A taxpayer may bring a suit to the appropriate District Court or Court of Federal Claims against the IRS after 6 months from the date of filing the claim or before the expiration of 2 years from the date of mailing by certified mail or registered mail by the Secretary to the taxpayer of a notice of the disallowance of the part of the claim to which the suit or proceeding relates (Code Sec. 6532).

31. **(A) Correct**
    Once the IRS issues a deficiency notice, the taxpayer has 90 days to file a Tax Court petition. If the taxpayer does not file a petition, the IRS will assess the taxes. This statutory Notice of Deficiency is also known as a 90-day letter because the taxpayer

generally has 90 days (150 days if mailed when the taxpayer is outside the United States) from the date of the letter to file a petition with the United States Tax Court.

32. **(B) Correct**
See answer # 31

33. **(B) Correct**
If a taxpayer is filing a claim for credit or refund based on contested income tax issues considered in previously examined returns and <u>does not</u> want to appeal within the IRS, (s)he should request in writing that the claim be immediately rejected.

34. **(B) Correct**
To appeal the IRS's findings in field examination cases, the taxpayer must file a written protest if the proposed additional liability exceeds $10,000 for any tax period. A written protest is required for all penalties that have already been assessed. If the proposed adjustments in a field examination case exceed $2,500 but do not exceed $10,000, the taxpayer must file a brief written statement of the issues.
The taxpayer does not have to make a written protest to appeal the following:
    a) Field examinations resulting in adjustments of $2,500.
    b) Office examinations.
    c) Correspondence audits.

35. **(B) Correct**
If you think that you will owe additional tax at the end of the examination, you can stop the further accrual of interest by sending money to the IRS to cover all or part of the amount you think you will owe. Interest on part or all of any amount you owe will stop accruing on the date the IRS receives your money. You can send an amount either in the form of a deposit in the nature of a cash bond or as a payment of tax. Both a deposit and a payment stop any further accrual of interest. However, making a deposit or payment will stop the accrual of interest on only the amount you sent. Because of compounding rules, interest will continue to accrue on accrued interest, even though you have paid the underlying tax.

36. **(B) Correct**
Generally, a taxpayer's return is examined in the area where he or she lives. But if the return can be examined more quickly and conveniently in another area, such as where books and records are located, the taxpayer can ask to have the case transferred to that area. When request is received to transfer taxpayer returns to another district for examination, the district director having jurisdiction may transfer the case, together with pertinent records to the district director of such other district. The IRS will determine the time and place of the examination. In determining whether a transfer should be made, circumstances such as the following will be considered:
    (1) Change of the taxpayer's domicile, either before or during examination.
    (2) Discovery that taxpayer's books and records are kept in another district.

(3) Change of domicile of an executor or administrator to another district before or during examination.
(4) The effective administration of the tax laws (26 CFR 601.105(k)).

Merely passing the EA exam does not make Dave's brother-in-law in Detroit an executor or administrator to another district before or during examination and none of the other criteria above have been met.

37. **(A) Correct**
The IRS may abate (reduce) the amount of interest owed if the interest is due to an unreasonable error or delay by an IRS officer or employee in performing a ministerial or managerial. Only the amount of interest on income, estate, gift, generation-skipping, and certain excise taxes can be reduced. The amount of interest will not be reduced if the taxpayer contributed significantly to the error or delay. Also, the interest will be reduced only if the error or delay happened after the IRS contacted the taxpayer in writing about the deficiency or payment on which the interest is based. An audit notification letter is such a contact. The IRS cannot reduce the amount of interest due to a general administrative decision, such as a decision on how to organize the processing of tax returns.

38. **(B) Correct**
The IRS must give the taxpayer reasonable notice before contacting other persons about the taxpayer's tax matters. A written consent from the taxpayer is not required. The taxpayer must be given reasonable notice in advance that, in examining or collecting your tax liability, the IRS may contact third parties such as neighbors, banks, employers, or employees. The IRS must also give the taxpayer notice of specific contacts by providing a record of persons contacted on both a periodic basis and upon the taxpayer's request. This provision <u>does not</u> apply:
    (a) To any pending criminal investigation,
    (b) When providing notice would jeopardize collection of any tax liability,
    (c) Where providing notice may result in reprisal against any person, or
    (d) When you authorized the contact.

39. **(B) Correct**
No interest is imposed on most penalties, additional amounts, and additions to tax if the amount is paid within 21 days from the date the IRS issues a notice and demand for payment. If the amount is not paid within the 21-day period, interest accrues from the date of the notice and demand to the date of payment. If the total of tax, interest, and penalties equals or exceeds $100,000, the tax must be paid within 10 business days. Interest will continue to accrue if the tax is not paid within 21 calendar days (or where applicable, 10 business days). When income tax return is examined by the IRS and the taxpayer agrees with the proposed changes, the taxpayer has several ways by which he or she may settle the account and pay any additional tax that is due. If a taxpayer pays when he or she signs the agreement, the interest is generally figured *from the due date*

of the return to the date of his payment. If the taxpayer does not pay the additional tax when he or she signs the agreement, he or she will receive a bill and the interest on the additional tax is generally figured *from the due date of the return to the billing date* (Code Sec. 6601).

40. **(D) Correct**
At or before the initial in-person interview with the taxpayer relating to the determination of any tax, the IRS must provide the taxpayer with an explanation of the audit process and the taxpayer's rights under the process (Code Sec. 7521). Taxpayer's rights are contained in Publication 1 (Your Rights as a Taxpayer).

41. **(A) Correct**
The IRS will determine the time and place of the examination. In determining whether a transfer should be made, circumstances such as the following will be considered:
   (1) Change of the taxpayer's domicile, either before or during examination.
   (2) Discovery that taxpayer's books and records are kept in another district.
   (3) Change of domicile of an executor or administrator to another district before or during examination.
   (4) The effective administration of the tax laws (26 CFR 601.105(k)).
The place of examination will not be considered solely for the convenience of the taxpayer's representative. However, the place of examination may be considered for the convenience of the IRS.

42. **(A) Correct**
The IRS must give the taxpayer reasonable notice before contacting other persons about the taxpayer's tax matters. The taxpayer must be given reasonable notice in advance that, in examining or collecting your tax liability, the IRS may contact third parties such as neighbors, banks, employers, or employees. The IRS must also give the taxpayer notice of specific contacts by providing a record of persons contacted on both a periodic basis and upon the taxpayer's request. This provision does not apply:
   (a) To any pending criminal investigation,
   (b) When providing notice would jeopardize collection of any tax liability,
   (c) Where providing notice may result in reprisal against any person, or
   (d) When you authorized the contact.

43. **(C) Correct**
Statutory Notices of Deficiency must be mailed within the statute of limitations period. Because the agreement between Marty and the second Revenue Agent, to extend the statute of limitations to December 31, 2005, was oral rather than written, the IRS will fall on the default statutory deadline. The 2001 tax returns were due on April 15, 2002. Therefore, the IRS must mail the Notice by April 15, 2005.

44. (C) Correct

The IRS may abate (reduce) the amount of interest owed if the interest is due to an unreasonable error or delay by an IRS officer or employee in performing a ministerial or managerial. Only the amount of interest on income, estate, gift, generation-skipping, and certain excise taxes can be reduced. The amount of interest will not be reduced if the taxpayer contributed significantly to the error or delay. Also, the interest will be reduced only if the error or delay happened after the IRS contacted the taxpayer in writing about the deficiency or payment on which the interest is based. An audit notification letter is such a contact. The IRS cannot reduce the amount of interest due to a general administrative decision, such as a decision on how to organize the processing of tax returns. A refund or abatement of interest, penalties, or additions to tax caused by certain IRS errors or delays, or certain erroneous written advice from the IRS is completed on form 843.

45. (B) Correct

Taxpayers must file a written protest in the following cases.

(a) All employee plan and exempt organization cases without regard to the dollar amount at issue.
(b) All partnership and S corporation cases without regard to the dollar amount at issue.
(c) All other cases, unless taxpayer qualifies for the small case request procedure, or other special appeal procedures such as requesting Appeals consideration of liens, levies, seizures, or installment agreements (Publication 556).

A written protest should include the following:

(1) A statement that the taxpayer wishes to appeal the findings of the IRS to the Appeals office.
(2) The taxpayer's name, address and daytime telephone number.
(3) A copy of the letter showing the proposed changes and findings that the taxpayer does not agree with or the date and symbols from the letter.
(4) A list of the changes that the taxpayer does not agree with and why.
(5) The tax periods involved.
(6) A statement of facts supporting the taxpayer's position.
(7) A statement of the law or other authorities that are relied upon (Reg. Sec. 601.105(c)).

46. (D) Correct

If a taxpayer is filing a claim for credit or refund based on contested income tax issues considered in previously examined returns and <u>does not</u> want to appeal within the IRS but go straight to court, (s)he should request in writing that the claim be immediately rejected. When a taxpayer promptly receives a notice of claim disallowance, A taxpayer may bring a suit to the appropriate United States District Court or Court of Federal Claims against the IRS after 6 months from the date of filing the claim or before the expiration of 2 years from the date of mailing by certified mail or registered mail by the

Secretary to the taxpayer of a notice of the disallowance of the part of the claim to which the suit or proceeding relates (Code Sec. 6532).

47. **(D) Correct**

The IRS will determine the time and place of the examination. In determining whether a transfer should be made, circumstances such as the following will be considered:
   (1) Change of the taxpayer's domicile, either before or during examination.
   (2) Discovery that taxpayer's books and records are kept in another district.
   (3) Change of domicile of an executor or administrator to another district before or during examination.
   (4) The effective administration of the tax laws (26 CFR 601.105(k)).

The place of examination <u>will not</u> be considered solely for the convenience of the taxpayer's representative. However, the place of examination <u>may be</u> considered for the convenience of the IRS.

48. **(C) Correct**

Because people sometimes disagree on tax matters, the IRS has an administrative appeals process. Most differences can be settled within this system without expensive and time-consuming court trials. A taxpayer cannot appeal his/her case based only on moral, religious, political, constitutional, conscientious, or similar grounds. If a taxpayer does not want to appeal his/her case within the IRS, (s)he can take the case directly to court.

49. **(A) Correct**

A <u>brief</u> written statement of the disputed issue(s) <u>is required</u> if the increase or decrease in tax, including penalties, or refund, determined by examination is more than $2,500 but not more than $10,000. If the proposed increase or decrease in tax, including penalties or claimed refund is more than $25,000, the taxpayer must submit a written protest of the disputed issues, including a statement of facts supporting the taxpayer's position on all disputed issues. A declaration that the statement of facts is TRUE under penalties of perjury must be added and signed by the taxpayer. If a representative submits the protest for the taxpayer, (s)he must submit a declaration stating that (s)he submitted the protest and accompanying documents and whether (s)he knows personally that the statement of facts in the protest and accompanying documents are TRUE and correct.

50. **(A) Correct**

Taxpayers must file a written protest in the following cases.
   (a) All employee plan and exempt organization cases without regard to the dollar amount at issue.
   (b) All partnership and S corporation cases without regard to the dollar amount at issue.

(c) All other cases, unless taxpayer qualifies for the small case request procedure, or other special appeal procedures such as requesting Appeals consideration of liens, levies, seizures, or installment agreements (Publication 556).

51. **(C) Correct**
If the proposed increase or decrease in tax, including penalties or claimed refund is more than $25,000, the taxpayer must submit a written protest of the disputed issues, including a statement of facts supporting the taxpayer's position on all disputed issues.

52. **(B) Correct**
See Answer # 45

53. **(C) Correct**
See Answer # 45

54. **(A) Correct**
Generally, a taxpayer cannot get an injunction to block an investigation by the IRS. The taxpayer's remedy is to claim that the second inspection is illegal at a hearing to enforce the summons. If the same items were examined in either of the previous 2 years and the examination resulted in no change to the tax liability, the IRS might suspend but not cancel an audit in order to avoid repetitive examinations of the same items. The IRS tries to avoid repeat examinations of the same items, but sometimes this happens. If a tax return was examined for the same items in either of the 2 previous years and no change was proposed to your tax liability, the taxpayer should contact the IRS as soon as possible to see if the examination should be discontinued.

55. **(A) Correct**
Code Section 6511 states that a claim for refund or credit for an overpayment must be filed within 3 years from the time the return was filed or within 2 years from the time the tax was paid, whichever occurs later. In this case the "2 years from the time the tax was paid" condition does not apply because no tax was paid. Thus, based on the 3 years from the time the return was filed, the $500 refund for the 2001 return is lost because it is outside the 3-year statutory limit. The refunds of $500 for the 2002 and 2003 tax years (within the 3-year limit) will be offset by the tax liability of $500 for the 2000 and 2004 returns. The IRS has a statutory limit of 10 years on tax liability and therefore the 2000 liability of $300 is included in the calculation.

56. **(D) Correct**
See Answer # 45

57. **(C) Correct**
Code Section 6511 states that a claim for refund or credit for an overpayment must be filed within 3 years from the time the return was filed or within 2 years from the time the tax was paid, whichever occurs later. He paid the additional tax due of $10,000 on

December 31, 2004 later. Wesley must file a claim for refund by December 31, 2006, two years from when the additional tax was paid.

58. **(C) Correct**
Once the IRS issues a deficiency notice, the taxpayer has 90 days to file a Tax Court petition. If the taxpayer does not file a petition, the IRS will assess the taxes. This statutory Notice of Deficiency is also known as a <u>90-day letter</u> because the taxpayer generally has 90 days (150 days if mailed when the taxpayer is outside the United States) from the date of the letter to file a petition with the United States Tax Court.

59. **(C) Correct**
Code Section 6511 states that a claim for refund or credit for an overpayment must be filed within 3 years from the time the <u>return was filed</u> or within 2 years from the time the <u>tax was paid</u>, whichever occurs later.

60. **(C) Correct**
See answer # 59

61. **(C) Correct**
If a taxpayer files a claim for refund within 3 years after filing the return, the credit or refund cannot be more than the part of the tax paid within the 3 years (plus the length of any extension of time granted for filing your return) before the claim was filed. If a taxpayer files a claim after the 3-year period, but within 2 years from the time he/she paid the tax, the credit or refund cannot be more than the tax you paid within the 2 years immediately before you filed the claim. Therefore, the $5,000 withholding and the $2,000 Charlie paid with the extension do not fall within 3-year statutory limit for claim of refund. Nevertheless, the $1,000 balance paid with the return is within the 3-year statutory limit for claim of refund.

62. **(B) Correct**
This statutory Notice of Deficiency is also known as a <u>90-day letter</u> because the taxpayer generally has 90 days (150 days if mailed when the taxpayer is outside the United States) from the date of the letter to file a petition with the United States Tax Court.

63. **(A) Correct**
A notice of deficiency is not an assessment. If the taxpayer consents, the IRS can withdraw any notice of deficiency. However, after the notice is withdrawn, the taxpayer cannot file a petition with the Tax Court based on the withdrawn notice, and the IRS may later issue a notice of deficiency greater or less than the amount in the withdrawn deficiency. This statutory Notice of Deficiency is also known as a <u>90-day letter</u> because the taxpayer generally has 90 days (150 days if mailed when the taxpayer is outside the United States) from the date of the letter to file a petition with the United States Tax Court.

64. **(C) Correct**
If a taxpayer is filing a claim for credit or refund based on contested income tax issues considered in previously examined returns and does not want to appeal within the IRS but wants go straight to court, (s)he should request in writing that the claim be immediately rejected. When a taxpayer promptly receives a notice of claim disallowance, A taxpayer may bring a suit to the appropriate United States District Court or Court of Federal Claims against the IRS after 6 months from the date of filing the claim or before the expiration of 2 years from the date of mailing by certified mail or registered mail by the Secretary to the taxpayer of a notice of the disallowance of the part of the claim to which the suit or proceeding relates (Code Sec. 6532).

65. **(D) Correct**
A disagreement with the IRS can be taken to the United States Tax Court if it pertains to income tax, if a statutory notice of deficiency has been issued, and if a petition is filed within 90 days from the date a statutory notice of deficiency is mailed (150 days if it is addressed to the taxpayer outside the United States).

66. **(C) Correct**
If a taxpayer is filing a claim for credit or refund based on contested income tax issues considered in previously examined returns and does not want to appeal within the IRS but wants go straight to court, (s)he should pay all of the additional tax and then file a claim request in writing that the claim be immediately rejected.

67. **(B) Correct**
A notice of deficiency is not an assessment. If the taxpayer consents, the IRS can withdraw any notice of deficiency. However, after the notice is withdrawn, the taxpayer cannot file a petition with the Tax Court based on the withdrawn notice, and the IRS may later issue a notice of deficiency greater or less than the amount in the withdrawn deficiency. This statutory Notice of Deficiency is also known as a 90-day letter because the taxpayer generally has 90 days (150 days if mailed when the taxpayer is outside the United States) from the date of the letter to file a petition with the United States Tax Court.

68. **(B) Correct**
Once any appeal process within the IRS is complete, the IRS may issue a statutory notice of deficiency. Once the IRS issues a deficiency notice, the taxpayer has 90 days to file a Tax Court petition. If the taxpayer does not file a petition, the IRS will assess the taxes.

69. **(B) Correct**
Both the taxpayer and the government may appeal decisions of the Tax Court or district court to the appropriate circuit court of appeals. Decisions of the courts of appeals and some decisions of other federal courts can be reviewed by the United States Supreme Court. When a taxpayer promptly receives a notice of claim disallowance, a taxpayer may bring a suit to the appropriate United States District Court or Court of Federal

Claims against the IRS <u>after</u> 6 months from the date of filing the claim or <u>before</u> the expiration of 2 years from the date of mailing by certified mail or registered mail by the Secretary to the taxpayer of a notice of the disallowance of the part of the claim to which the suit or proceeding relates (Code Sec. 6532).

70. **(B) Correct**

    For court proceedings resulting from examinations started after July 22, 1998, the IRS generally has the burden of proof for any factual issue if the taxpayer met the following requirements:
    (a) Introduced credible evidence relating to the issue.
    (b) Complied with all substantiation requirements of the Internal Revenue Code.
    (c) Maintained all records required by the Internal Revenue Code.
    (d) Cooperated with all reasonable requests by the IRS for information regarding the preparation and related tax treatment of any item reported on the tax return.
    (e) Had a net worth of $7 million or less and not more than 500 employees at the time the tax liability is contested in any court proceeding if the tax return is for a corporation, partnership, or trust.

    Therefore, Orlo Corporation must provide the calculations to the IRS because privilege does not apply to a determination with respect to an item that will be presented to the government on an original return.

71. **(D) Correct**

    Taxpayers must file a written protest in the following cases.
    (a) All employee plan and exempt organization cases without regard to the dollar amount at issue.
    (b) All partnership and S corporation cases without regard to the dollar amount at issue.
    (c) All other cases, unless taxpayer qualifies for the small case request procedure, or other special appeal procedures such as requesting Appeals consideration of liens, levies, seizures, or installment agreements (Publication 556).

    A written protest should include the following:
    (1) A statement that the taxpayer wishes to appeal the findings of the IRS to the Appeals office.
    (2) The taxpayer's name, address and daytime telephone number.
    (3) A copy of the letter showing the proposed changes and findings that the taxpayer does not agree with or the date and symbols from the letter.
    (4) A list of the changes that the taxpayer does not agree with and why.
    (5) The tax periods involved.
    (6) A statement of facts supporting the taxpayer's position.
    (7) A statement of the law or other authorities that are relied upon (Reg. Sec. 601.105(c)).

72. **(B) Correct**
If the examination of a taxpayer's return by the IRS results in a disagreement over whether the taxpayer owes additional income tax, the IRS must issue a formal letter called a notice of deficiency before the taxpayer can appeal his/her case to the Tax Court. Before issuing a notice of deficiency, the IRS sends a preliminary notice advising the taxpayer of his right to appeal (<u>the 30-day letter</u>). A taxpayer may initiate an appeal within 30 days after receiving notice from the IRS of the right to appeal if the taxpayer does not agree with the proposed changes from an examination. The 30-day letter must identify the amount of the tax, interest, and penalties included in the notice. It must also describe why the IRS believes these amounts are due. If the taxpayer makes the request for an appeal and protests the IRS findings, the case is referred to Appeals. To appeal the IRS's findings in field examination cases, the taxpayer must file a written protest if the proposed additional liability exceeds $10,000 for any tax period. A written protest is required for all penalties that have already been assessed. If the proposed adjustments in a field examination case exceed $2,500 but do not exceed $10,000, the taxpayer must file a <u>brief written statement</u> of the issues.

73. **(D) Correct**
See answer # 72

74. **(C) Correct**
Generally, a taxpayer cannot get an injunction to block an investigation by the IRS. The taxpayer's remedy is to claim that the second inspection is illegal at a hearing to enforce the summons. If the same items were examined in either of the previous 2 years and the examination resulted in no change to the tax liability, the IRS might suspend <u>but not</u> cancel an audit in order to avoid repetitive examinations of the same items. The IRS tries to avoid repeat examinations of the same items, but sometimes this happens. If a tax return was examined for the same items in either of the 2 previous years and no change was proposed to your tax liability, the taxpayer should contact the IRS as soon as possible to see if the examination should be discontinued.

UNIT 6: FEDERAL TAX AUTHORITY

Unit 6 Contents:
- 6.01 SOURCES OF TAX LAW
- 6.02 STATUTORY SOURCES
- 6.03 ADMINISTRATIVE SOURCES
- 6.04 JUDICIAL SOURCES
- 6.05 UNIT 6: QUESTIONS
- 6.06 UNIT 6: ANSWERS

6.01 SOURCES OF TAX LAW

There are 3 primary sources of tax law:
(1) Statutory (Legislative branch)
(2) Administrative rulings (Executive branch)
(3) Judicial decisions (Judicial Branch)

Statutory sources include:
a) U.S. Constitution
b) Tax Treaties
c) Internal Revenue Code

Administrative sources include:
a) Treasury Regulations
b) Revenue Rulings
c) Revenue procedures
d) Letter Rulings
e) Other IRS Pronouncements

Judicial sources include:
a) Supreme Court
b) Court of appeals
c) U.S. Court of Federal Claims
d) District Courts
e) Tax Court

NOTE: In general, the IRS may exercise executive, judicial, and legislative power.

6.02   STATUTORY SOURCES

U.S. Constitution
The U.S. Constitution is the supreme source of all federal tax laws. Congress makes the laws, or *statutes*.

Tax Treaties
Tax treaties are agreements between countries in regard to treatment of tax items. The main objectives for entering into a treaty often involve:
    (i) Preventing double taxation.
    (ii) Eliminating tax evasion.
    (iii) Encouraging cross-border trade efficiency.

Internal Revenue Code
Statutes are organized by subject matter into the U.S. Code. These statutes are organized alphabetically and assigned title numbers. Title 26 of the U.S.C. is the Internal Revenue Code. All courts are bound by the Code section.

The hierarchy of the U.S.C. is as follows:
Subtitles→Chapters→Subchapters→Parts→Sections→Subsections

Subtitles are assigned capital letters. Current subtitles are from A to K.

Subtitles:	Tax Law Covered
A	Income Taxes.
B	Estate and Gift Taxes.
C	Employment Taxes.
D	Miscellaneous Excise Taxes.
E	Alcohol, Tobacco and Certain Other Excise Taxes.
F	Procedure and Administration.
G	The Joint Committee on Taxation.
H	Financing of Presidential Campaigns.
I	Trust Fund Code Coal Industry Health Benefits.
J	Coal Industry Health Benefits
K	Group Health Plan Portability, Access, and Renewability Requirements.

Each subtitle contains of non-repeating *chapter* numbers used in ascending order through the Internal Revenue Code. A subtitle may contain numerous chapters. These chapter numbers narrowly defines the area of tax law outlined on the subtitle.

Example:
Title 26: Internal Revenue Code
- Subtitle A: Income Taxes
  - Chapter 1: Normal Taxes and Surtaxes

The chapters are further divided into subchapters with a group of provisions that relates to a specific area of the tax law. Subchapters <u>may</u> sometimes be divided into parts, which may further be divided into subparts. These parts provide a grouping of provisions that address the same issue. Letters are used to indicate subchapters.

Example:
Title 26: Internal Revenue Code
- Subtitle A: Income Taxes
  - Chapter 1: Normal Taxes and Surtaxes
    - Subchapter B: Computation of Taxable Income
      - Part VI: Itemized Deductions for Individuals and Corporations

Sections are the most important division of the Internal Revenue Code. Each section is used once within the code. Sections may contain *subsections, paragraphs, subparagraphs, and clauses*. Sections are denoted by numbers (1, 2, 3, etc.), Subsections by lowercase letters (a, b, c, etc), Paragraphs by numbers (1, 2, 3, etc.), subpapragraphs by capital letters (A, B, C, etc.), and clauses by lower roman numerals (I, ii, iii, etc).

Example:
Title 26: Internal Revenue Code
- Subtitle A: Income Taxes
  - Chapter 1: Normal Taxes and Surtaxes
    - Subchapter B: Computation of Taxable Income
      - Part VI: Itemized Deductions for Individuals and Corporations
        - Section 162: Trade or business expenses
          - Subsection (e): Denial of deduction for certain lobbying and political expenditures
            - Paragraph (2) Exception for local legislation
              - Sub-paragraph (B)
                - Clause (ii)

6.03　ADMINISTRATIVE SOURCES

Treasury Regulations

Treasury Regulations are the tax regulations issued by the IRS, a bureau of the U.S. Department of the Treasury. These Treasury Regulations are the Treasury Department's official interpretations of the Internal Revenue Code (IRC) and are published in the Federal Register in the form of Treasury Decisions (TDs). Treasury Decisions are issued in a proposed form 30 days before they are published in final form in order to allow comments from interested parties. This is done through public hearings and allows the IRS to make any relevant changes. When an agency like the IRS decides to adopt any specific regulations, the regulations must be consistent with standards established in the legislation that created the agency.

The three categories of Regulations are:
   (1) Legislative
   (2) Interpretative
   (3) Procedural
   (1) **Legislative Regulations** - are those for which the IRS is specifically authorized by the IRC to prescribe the operating rules. They provide the details of the meaning and rules for that particular Code section. Generally, legislative regulations have the force and effect of law.
   (2) **Interpretative Regulations** – These regulations explain the IRS's position on the various sections of the IRC. Although interpretative regulations do not have the force and effect of law, the courts customarily accord them substantial weight.
   (3) **Procedural Regulations** - are considered to be directive rather than mandatory and, thus, do not have the force and effect of law.

Interpretative regulations are issued under the general authority of Internal Revenue Section 7805(a). Legislative regulations are issued under the authority of the specific Internal Revenue Code section to which they relate. Treasury Regulations are binding on any court of law.

Proposed Regulations – Before and during public hearings, Treasury Decisions are referred to as Proposed Regulations and they do not have the effects of the law. After changes have been made to the Treasury Decisions, they are published in their final form. Final Regulations are combined with the approved Treasury Decisions and results into a full set of IRS Regulations. After the combination has taken place, the Treasury Decision title is dropped and the pronounced is then referred to as Regulation.

Temporary Regulations – The IRS sometimes issues Temporary Regulations in reaction to a congressional of judicial change in the tax law or interpretation. They are issued to provide guidance for the public and IRS employees until final regulations are issued. Temporary Regulations do not undergo the public hearing process and have the full effect of the law, just like the Final Regulations. Temporary Regulations expire after 3 years from the date of issuance (Code Sec. 7805).

Final Regulations - have the full effect of the law and supersede temporary regulations.

Revenue Rulings
Revenue Rulings are official public administrative rulings by the IRS. They are published conclusions as to the application of the law. A revenue ruling can be relied upon as precedent

by all taxpayers. A taxpayer may seek advice from the IRS as to the proper tax treatment of a transaction. This is called a private letter ruling. A private letter ruling binds only the IRS and the requesting taxpayer. Thus, a private ruling may not be cited or relied upon for precedent. The IRS does have the option of redacting the text of a private ruling and issuing it as a revenue ruling, which become binding on all taxpayers and the IRS.

Revenue rulings are published both in the Internal Revenue Bulletin and in the Federal Register. The numbering system for revenue rulings corresponds to the year in which they are issued. For example, Rev. Rul. 99-14 was the 14th revenue ruling issued in 1999.

Revenue Rulings are part of second tier authorities and generally do not prevail over legislative regulations, the Internal Revenue Code, Court Cases and Treaties, thus, they do not have the force and effect of regulations. A taxpayer can appeal adverse return examination decisions based on revenue rulings.

Revenue Procedures

A revenue procedure is an official statement of a procedure that affects the rights or duties of taxpayers under the law, while a revenue ruling is the conclusion of the IRS on how the law is applied to a specific set of facts. Generally, a revenue ruling states the IRS position, whereas a revenue procedure provides return filing or other instructions concerning the IRS position.

    A. For example, a revenue ruling holds that taxpayers may deduct certain automobile expenses, and a revenue procedure provides that taxpayers entitled to deduct these automobile expenses may compute them by applying certain mileage rates in lieu of determining actual operating expenses. Revenue rulings and revenue procedures are alike in that both are issued only by the National Office and both are for the information and guidance of taxpayers. Taxpayers <u>can</u> appeal adverse return examination decisions based on revenue rulings and revenue procedures to the courts.

Letter Rulings

Letter Rulings include:
- (a) Private letter rulings
- (b) Technical Advice Memorandum
- (c) Determination Letters

(a) **Private Letter Rulings** – PLRs are written decisions by the National office of the IRS in response to taxpayer requests for guidance. A private letter ruling binds only the IRS and the requesting taxpayer. Thus, a private ruling may not be cited or relied upon for precedent. The IRS does have the option of redacting the text of a private ruling and issuing it as a revenue ruling, which becomes binding on all taxpayers and the IRS. Some private letter rulings are ultimately published as a public Revenue ruling and become binding on the IRS for all taxpayers. The IRS does not publish its reply, but sends it only to the taxpayer that submitted the request.

(b) **Technical Advice Memorandum** - A technical advice memorandum (TAM) is guidance furnished by the Office of Chief Counsel upon the request of an IRS director or an area director, appeals, in response to technical or procedural questions that develop during a proceeding. A request for a TAM generally stems from an examination of a taxpayer's return, a consideration of a taxpayer's claim for a refund or credit, or any other matter involving a specific taxpayer under the jurisdiction of the territory manager or the area director, appeals. Technical Advice Memoranda are issued only on closed transactions and provide the interpretation of proper application of tax laws, tax treaties, regulations, revenue rulings or other precedents. The advice rendered represents a final determination of the position of the IRS, but only with respect to the specific issue in the specific case in which the advice is issued. Technical Advice Memoranda are generally made public after all information has been removed that could identify the taxpayer whose circumstances triggered a specific memorandum.

(c) **Determination Letters** – Is similar to a private letter ruling except that it is issued by the office of the local IRS district director, rather than the National office of the IRS. Determination Letters usually relate to completed transactions that normally lead to the issuance of a private letter ruling. They deal with issues are transactions that are not so controversial. An example would be determining whether or not a retirement or pension plan put in place by an employer meets all the criteria established by the IRS for the structure and function of retirement plans. Determination Letters are not published in any official IRS publication.

Numbering System:
The IRS assigns a nine-digit document number to each written determination in Letter Rulings for identification purposes:
   (i) The first four digits indicate the year in which the ruling was issued.
   (ii) The next two numbers indicate the week.
   (iii) The last three indicate the number of the ruling for the week.

Example:
Ltr. Rul. 200952010

Where:
2009 - The year the Ruling was issued
52 – The week on the year the Ruling was issued.
010 – This is the 10th Ruling that was issued that week.

NOTE: Before 2000, two digits instead of four digits were used to signify the year, e.g., 9915017

IRS Pronouncements
These include:
   (a) Acquiescence and non-acquiescence

(b) Internal Revenue Bulletin
(c) Chief Council Memoranda
(d) Announcements and Notices
(e) Miscellaneous IRS Publications

Acquiescence and non-acquiescence – *Acquiescence* means that the court decision will be followed in similar situations even thought the decision was adverse to (ruled against) the IRS. *Non-acquiescence* – means that the IRS disagrees with the adverse decision in the case and will follow the decision only for the sake of that particular taxpayer whose case resulted in the adverse ruling. Acquiescence and non-acquiescence is not issued if the IRS prevails in a court case. The issuance of acquiescence does not mean that the IRS agrees with the adverse decision, but only that it will not pursue the matter in a similar and subsequent case. The IRS issues acquiescence and non-acquiescence as *Actions on Decision* (AOD). These AODs are initially published in the Internal Revenue Bulletins and thereafter, in the Cumulative Bulletin. AODs are public documents and usually include:

(i) The <u>issue</u> decided against the IRS.
(ii) The pertinent <u>facts</u>.
(iii) A discussion of the <u>reasoning</u> (conclusion) supporting the acquiescence or non-acquiescence decision.

The Commissioner of Internal Revenue will publicly announce acquiescence or nonacquiescence to the adverse regular decisions of all other courts except the U.S. Supreme Court. The Commissioner of Internal Revenue may at any time revise a non-acquiescence to a decision in a prior case. Similarly, an acquiescence may be withdrawn at any time with retroactive effect if the purpose is to correct a mistake in the application of tax law.

Internal Revenue Bulletin - The Internal Revenue Bulletin (IRB) is the authoritative instrument for announcing official rulings and procedures of the IRS and for publishing Treasury Decisions, Executive Orders, Tax Conventions, legislation, court decisions, and other items of general interest.

Chief Council Memoranda – The IRS does not publish these documents, but they are available through commercial publishers like RIA and CCH. A *Technical Memorandum* (TM) is generated for the purpose of a Proposed Regulation, while a *General Counsel's Memorandum* (GCM) is generated for the purpose of Revenue Rulings and Private Letter Rulings.

Announcements and Notices – These are published in the weekly *Internal Revenue Bulletin* and are related to items of general importance to the taxpayers. *Announcements* are public pronouncements that have immediate or short-term value such as approaching deadline for making an election. Notices contain guidance involving substantive interpretations of the code or other provisions of the law that usually have long-tem application.

IRS Publications – These are general and specialized documents that help the taxpayer meet their tax obligations but are not reliable as a source of tax law. Publications are available in both electronic and print formats. The most common publication is Publication 17 related to the Federal Income Tax.

6.04   JUDICIAL SOURCES

Taxpayers that do not agree with an IRS examination conclusion may take their cases to any of the following courts:
   (i)   U.S. Tax Court
   (ii) U.S. Court of Federal Claims
   (iii) U.S. District Court

Tax Court

The U.S. Tax Court is a trial court that hears only Federal tax cases. Tax Court is established by IRC Section 7441 rather than the U.S. Constitution. Taxpayers cannot request jury trial before the tax court. If a particular case involves an unusual, important, or new issue, more than one judge or the entire Tax Court consisting of 19 judges may hear the case in an **en banc** sitting of the court. En banc is a decision by all judges if the court instead of single judge or a selected set of judges. A dictum is a court's statement of opinion on a legal point not necessary for the decision of the case. Dictum is not controlling but may be persuasive to another court deciding the issue at hand. The Tax Court's jurisdiction covers income, estate, gift, excise, and private foundation taxes, but has no jurisdiction over employment taxes.

For a case to be heard in the Tax Court, the taxpayer must petition the Tax Court within 90 days of the IRS mailing of the notice of deficiency and demand for payment of the disputed amount. The taxpayer does not need to pay the disputed tax liability before the case is heard.

The Tax Court issues two kinds of decisions:
(1) *Regular Decision* – Involves a new or unusual point of law, as determined by the Chief Judge.
(2) *Memorandum Decision* – Decision concerns only the application of existing law or interpretation of facts.

Tax Court decisions may be appealed in Courts of Appeals in different geographical regions or circuits. Under the **Golsen rule**, the Tax Court will follow the Courts of Appeals that has direct jurisdiction over the taxpayer in question. If the Court of Appeals that has the Jurisdiction over the taxpayer has not ruled on the matter, the Tax Court will decide the case on the basis of its own interpretation of the matter. This *Golsen rule* means that the Tax Court may reach opposite decisions based on identical facts for taxpayers differentiated solely by geographical areas in which they live in.

When the tax court reaches its decision, it usually does not compute the tax that is due to the IRS or the refund that is due to the taxpayer (known as the *155 rule*). The computation is left to be determined by the IRS and the taxpayer. However, the court will compute the tax only if there is no agreement reached between the IRS and the taxpayer. The Tax Court examines the entire tax return while the District Courts examine a specific issue.

The Tax Court will issue either a regular report or a memorandum decision depending upon the issues involved and the relative value of the decision being made.

Small Case Division – The Tax Court has a small cases division that is similar to a Small Claims Court. The Small Case division hears cases if the amount of disputed deficiency, including penalties, or claim of overpayment <u>does not</u> exceed $50,000. The taxpayer may be represented by an attorney or may represent himself (*pro se*). Written briefs or formal oral arguments are <u>not</u> required in the Small cases Court. Issues brought before the small cases Court are fact-based. E.g. the taxpayer has documented proof of claiming a particular credit that was denied by the IRS.

Small Cases decisions, also known as Summary Motions are not published by the government by are available through commercial publishers like RIA and CCH. Small Cases Decisions cannot be used as precedents when dealing with the IRS.

The decision of the Small Cases Judge is <u>final and may not be appealed</u> by the taxpayer or the IRS.

Section 7491 (Burden of Proof) - In 1998, Congress adopted a new statutory provision that shifts the burden of proof in federal income tax cases to the IRS. This provision is effective for court proceedings arising in connection with examinations commenced after July 22, 1998.

The burden of proof in a Tax Court case is usually on the taxpayer, with the following *exception* as provided by Code Section 7491:
- Where the taxpayer introduces credible evidence relevant to ascertaining the taxpayer's liability, the burden of proof in court proceedings shifts to the IRS with respect to factual issues related to income, estate, gift, and generation-skipping transfer taxes.

  To be eligible, the taxpayer must prove that he or she has
  (i) Complied with present-law substantiation requirements, whether generally or specifically imposed.
  (ii) Complied with present-law recordkeeping requirements.
  (iii) Cooperated with reasonable IRS requests for meetings, interviews, witnesses, documents, and information.

- Where the taxpayer-petitioner is a partnership, corporation, or trust, the taxpayer must show that its net worth does not exceed $7 million and that it does not have more than 500 employees.

District Courts

District Courts hear cases involving legal issues based on the entire U.S. Code (USC), rather than just the Internal Revenue Code (IRC). A taxpayer who disagrees with the IRS may take the case to the District Court **only** after paying the disputed tax liability. In a District Court tax case, the taxpayer will more likely be suing the IRS for a refund of the disputed tax liability.

In the District Court, cases are heard before one judge rather than by a panel of judges and a taxpayer <u>can</u> request a jury trial.

Court of Federal Claims

This court deals with cases concerning all monetary claims (tax refunds) against the Federal government. Before a tax case can be heard in the Court of Federal Claims, the taxpayer must pay all disputed tax liability and then sue the government for a refund. Appeal made to a U.S. district court or the U.S. Court of Federal Claims must be brought within 2 years of the date of the formal notice from the IRS.

Court of Federal Claims is a national court that must follow the decisions of the Federal District Court of Appeals, but is not bound by the geographical Circuit Courts of Appeals that have ruled on similar cases. The IRS does not publish decisions by U.S. district courts or the U.S. Court of Federal Claims. To find these decisions, one must look to publications issued by commercial printing houses like CCH or RIA.

Court of Appeals

Court of Appeals will generally hear only cases that involve a question of the law. Congress has created 13 Courts of Appeals, 11 of which are organized in geographical circuits. A Court of Appeals usually carries precedence because each circuit is independent from each other and must follow only the decision of the U.S. Supreme Court.

Supreme Court

This is the highest appellate court in the nation, i.e., the final level of appeal and the sovereign legal authority. The Supreme Court meets and hears cases only in Washington, D.C. The Supreme Court has 9 justices sitting on the panel. The Supreme Court does not conduct jury trials. Cases are not heard automatically at the Supreme Court. Permission to have a case heard must be requested by a **writ of Certiorari**. A *writ of certiorari* generally means an order by a higher court directing a lower court, tribunal, or public authority to send the record in a given case for review. The Supreme Court is not obligated to hear any case, but does it at its own discretion. If the Supreme Court decides to hear the case, then a *writ of certiorari* is granted. In denying a petition for certiorari, it does not mean that the Supreme Court is upholding or confirming a lower court's decision. It is neither a reversal nor agreement with the lower court. It means that the Supreme Court simply does not find the case to be interesting or important enough. For federal tax purposes, the most common type of case that the U.S. Supreme Court hears is one in which a federal tax statute is ruled to be invalid.

6.05   UNIT 6: QUESTIONS

TRUE/FALSE QUESTIONS
Please select either (A) for True or (B) for False

1. Generally, the Tax Court hears cases before any tax has been assessed and paid; however, if you pay the tax after the notice of deficiency has been issued, you **cannot** petition the Tax Court for review.
   A. TRUE
   B. FALSE

2. When a taxpayer and the IRS do not reach agreement on proposed audit changes, the taxpayer may take the case to the Tax Court. If the case is handled under the small tax case procedures, the decision is final and cannot be appealed.
   A. TRUE
   B. FALSE

3. For court proceedings resulting from examinations started after July 1998, the IRS has the burden of proof for any factual issue. Therefore, taxpayers are no longer required to maintain records to substantiate items claimed on tax returns.
   A. TRUE
   B. FALSE

4. Karl had his 1999 income tax return examined resulting in adjustments. Karl has administratively appealed the adjustments. Some of them were sustained, resulting in an income tax deficiency in the amount of $45,000. Karl now wants to appeal his case to the U.S. Tax Court. He will handle the case himself since he cannot afford a lawyer. Karl is entitled to invoke the Small Tax Case procedure.
   A. TRUE
   B. FALSE

5. Brittany's 2003 return was selected for an examination. Information was requested to support claimed business expenses. Brittany failed to provide the IRS with any of the requested information because she felt the examination was an unwarranted invasion of her privacy. The IRS issued a Notice of Deficiency and Brittany filed a petition with the Tax Court. Since the examination was started after July 22, 1998, the IRS will have the burden of proof in the Tax Court Proceedings.
   A. TRUE
   B. FALSE

6. If you disagree with IRS after the Appeals conference, you can take your case to the United States Tax Court, the United States District Court, or the United States Court of Federal Claims.

A. TRUE
   B. FALSE

7. Before you take your case to the Tax Court, the IRS must send you a notice of deficiency. Then you have 60 days to file a petition with the Tax Court.
   A. TRUE
   B. FALSE

8. In a small tax case ($50,000 or less for any tax year or period), you can present your case to the Tax Court for a decision that is final and that you cannot appeal.
   A. TRUE
   B. FALSE

9. A taxpayer can appeal to a court only after an unsuccessful appeal before an IRS Appeals Officer.
   A. TRUE
   B. FALSE

10. Kevin and Keith are partners in a body shop business. Both of them had their individual returns examined and both disagreed with the IRS. Kevin decided to take his case to IRS Appeals. After the conference he and the IRS still disagreed. Keith decided to bypass IRS Appeals. After satisfying certain procedural and jurisdictional requirements, both Kevin and Keith can take their cases to the following courts: United States Tax Court, the United States Court of Federal Claims, or the United States District Court.
    A. TRUE
    B. FALSE

11. Johnny disagreed with the IRS examiner and her supervisor regarding his income tax case. His appeal rights were explained to him and he wanted to go to Tax Court. Johnny must receive a notice of deficiency before he can go to Tax Court.
    A. TRUE
    B. FALSE

MULTIPLE CHOICE QUESTIONS:
Please select the most appropriate answer.

12. Which of the following is not one of the three classes of Treasury Regulations?
    A. Temporary.
    B. Judicial.
    C. Final.
    D. Proposed.

13. With regard to Treasury Regulations, which of the following statements is false?
    A. Notices of proposed rulemaking are required for proposed regulations and are published in the Federal Register so that interested parties have an opportunity to participate in the rule-making process.
    B. Until final regulations are issued, temporary regulations have the same force and effect of law as final regulations.
    C. Legislative regulations are those for which the IRS is specifically authorized by the Internal Revenue Code to provide the details of the meaning and rules for particular Code sections.
    D. Interpretative regulations, which explain the IRS's position on the various sections of the Code, are not accorded great weight by the courts.

14. Which of the following is false with respect to classes of regulations?
    A. Temporary regulations are issued to provide guidance for the public and IRS employees until final regulations are issued.
    B. Public hearings are not held on temporary regulations.
    C. Proposed regulations have the same force and effect of law as temporary regulations.
    D. Public hearings are held on proposed regulations if written requests are made.

15. Which of the following statements with respect to regulations is false?
    A. All regulations are written by the Office of the Chief Counsel, IRS, and approved by the Secretary of Treasury.
    B. Public hearings are not held on temporary regulations.
    C. Although IRS employees are bound by the regulations, the courts are not.
    D. Public hearings are not held on proposed regulations.

16. With regard to revenue rulings and revenue procedures, which of the following statements is false?
    A. A revenue ruling is a published official interpretation of tax law by the IRS that sets forth the conclusion of the IRS on how the tax law is applied to an entire set of facts.
    B. Revenue rulings have the force and effect of Treasury Regulations.
    C. A revenue procedure is a published official statement of procedure that either affects the rights or duties of taxpayers or other members of the public under the Internal Revenue Code and related statutes and regulations or, if not necessarily affecting the rights and duties of the public, should be a matter of public knowledge.
    D. Revenue procedures are directive and not mandatory so that a taxpayer has no vested right to the benefit of the procedures when the IRS deviates from its internal rules.

17. Which of the following statements with respect to revenue rulings and revenue procedures is false?

A. Revenue procedures are official statements of procedures that either affect the rights or duties of taxpayers or other members of the public or should be a matter of public knowledge.
B. The purpose of revenue rulings is to promote uniform application of the tax laws.
C. Taxpayers cannot appeal adverse return examination decisions based on revenue rulings and revenue procedures to the courts.
D. IRS employees must follow revenue rulings and revenue procedures.

18. Which of the following statements best describes the applicability of a constitutionally valid Internal Revenue Code section on the various courts?
    A. Only the Supreme Court is not bound to follow the Code section. All other courts are bound to the Code section.
    B. Only the Tax Court is bound to the Code section. All other courts may waiver from the Code section.
    C. Only district claims, and appellate courts are bound by the Code section. The Supreme and Tax Courts may waiver from it.
    D. All courts are bound by the Code section.

19. Which of the following statements is false?
    A. The Tax Court will issue either a regular report or a memorandum decision depending upon the issues involved and the relative value of the decision being made.
    B. The Commissioner of Internal Revenue may issue a public acquiescence or nonacquiescence on district court or Court of Federal Claims cases.
    C. Interpretative regulations are issued under the general authority of Internal Revenue Sec. 7805(a), and legislative regulations are issued under the authority of the specific Internal Revenue Code section to which they relate.
    D. The government prints the regular and memorandum Tax Court decisions in bound volumes.

20. With regard to terminology relating to court decisions, which of the following statements is false?
    A. Decision, the court's formal answer to the principal issue in litigation, is legally binding and is enforceable by the authority of the court.
    B. Dictum, a court's statement of opinion on a legal point not necessary for the decision of the case, is not controlling but may be persuasive to another court deciding the issue dealt with by the dictum.
    C. Acquiescence by the Commissioner of IRS on adverse regular Tax Court decisions generally means the IRS will follow the Court's decision in cases involving similar facts.
    D. A writ of certiorari is a petition issued by the lower appellate court to the Supreme Court to hear a case that is not subject to obligatory review by the Supreme Court.

21. Which of the following statements with respect to court decisions is false?
    A. Petition to the Supreme Court to hear a case that is not subject to obligatory review is by writ of certiorari.
    B. Decisions of the courts other than the Supreme Court are binding on the Commissioner of Internal Revenue only for the particular taxpayer and for the years litigated.
    C. The citator contains case histories and recent case developments, such as appeals, writs of certiorari, and related cases.
    D. The denial of a writ of certiorari is the equivalent of a disagreement.

22. The Commissioner of Internal Revenue will not publicly announce acquiescence or nonacquiescence to the adverse regular decisions of which of the following courts?
    A. United States Tax Court.
    B. United States district court.
    C. United States Supreme Court.
    D. United States Court of Federal Claims.

23. To research whether the IRS has announced an opinion on a Tax Court decision, refer to which of the following references for the original announcement?
    A. Circular 230.
    B. Federal Register.
    C. Internal Revenue Bulletin.
    D. Tax Court Reports.

24. Which of the following statements regarding the Commissioner of Internal Revenue's position on court decisions is false?
    A. The decisions of the courts, other than the Supreme Court, are binding on the commissioner only for the particular taxpayer and for the years litigated.
    B. The commissioner may decide to acquiesce to an adverse regular Tax Court decision.
    C. The commissioner cannot withdraw acquiescence and substitute nonacquiescence.
    D. The acquiescence program is not intended as a substitute for a ruling or regulation program.

25. Which of the following statements is false with respect to court decisions?
    A. Acquiescence by the Commissioner of Internal Revenue to regular Tax Court adverse decisions generally means that the IRS will follow the Tax Court decision in cases involving similar facts.
    B. Petition to the Supreme Court to hear a case is by writ of certiorari, which is initially requested by the appealing party and is issued by the Supreme Court to the lower appellate court, requesting the record of a case for review.
    C. A memorandum decision issued by the Tax Court is thought to be of little value as a precedent because the issue has been decided many times.

D. Dictum is the court's formal answer to the principal issue in litigation. It is legally binding and is enforceable by the authority of the courts.

26. With regard to revenue rulings and revenue procedures, which of the following statements is false?
    A. Revenue rulings do not have the force and effect of regulations.
    B. A taxpayer cannot appeal adverse return examination decisions based on revenue rulings.
    C. A revenue procedure is an official statement of procedure published in the Internal Revenue Bulletin.
    D. Revenue rulings are published conclusions as to the application of the law.

27. Which of the following statements regarding Treasury Regulations is false?
    A. Regulations are binding on all courts except the U.S. Supreme Court.
    B. Interpretative regulations are issued under the general mandate of Sec. 7805(a).
    C. Some Code sections specifically authorize regulations to provide the details of the meaning and rules for that particular Code section. These are called legislative regulations.
    D. Temporary regulations are issued to provide guidance for the public and IRS employees until final regulations are issued.

28. Which of the following statements relating to Treasury Regulations is false?
    A. Temporary regulations are issued to provide guidance for the public and IRS employees until final regulations are issued.
    B. Public hearings are always held on temporary regulations.
    C. Final regulations supersede temporary regulations.
    D. Proposed regulations are issued to solicit public written comments.

29. Which of the following is a false statement regarding court cases, revenue rulings, and revenue procedures?
    A. U.S. Supreme Court decisions on federal tax matters are published in Internal Revenue Bulletins.
    B. Announcements concerning the IRS's acquiescence or nonacquiescence in Tax Court decisions (other than memorandum decisions) that are adverse to the government's position are published in Internal Revenue Bulletins.
    C. The IRS does not publish decisions by United States district courts or the United States Court of Federal Claims. To find these decisions, one must look to publications issued by commercial printing houses.
    D. The denial of a writ of certiorari by the U.S. Supreme Court is the equivalent of a reversal or disagreement.

30. The maximum amount of deficiency per tax year or tax period that may be heard by the Small Tax Case Division of the U.S. Tax Court is
    A. $2,500

B. $10,000
C. $50,000
D. $75,000

31. Disputes involving what areas of taxation may **not** be resolved in the United States Tax Court?
    A. Income tax
    B. Gift tax
    C. Employment tax
    D. Estate tax

32. Which of the following statements is false with respect to the United States Tax Court?
    A. It has jurisdiction over all federal taxes.
    B. It is authorized by the Internal Revenue Code, but is entirely separate from the IRS.
    C. Its regular decisions are printed in bound volumes by the government.
    D. It is based in Washington.

33. Nick wants his income tax case to be handled under the Tax Court's "small tax case procedure." All of the following statements regarding the "small tax case procedure" are true except
    A. The amount in the case must be $50,000 or less for court proceedings begun after July 22, 1998.
    B. The amount must be paid before going to Tax Court.
    C. The Tax Court must approve the request that the case be handled under the small tax case procedure.
    D. The decision is final and cannot be appealed.

34. Within 6 months from the date he filed it, Y received a formal notice from the IRS by certified mail disallowing his $10,000 tax refund claim. What is Y's appeal?
    A. File a protest and request that the matter be referred to the IRS appeals office.
    B. File suit in his U.S. district court or the U.S. Court of Federal Claims no later than 2 years after the date of the notice.
    C. File a petition with the U.S. Tax Court.
    D. File a petition with the U.S. Tax Court and ask that it be handled under the "small tax case procedure."

35. All of the following statements concerning court appeals and court petitions are true except
    A. Both the taxpayer and the government may appeal decisions of the Tax Court or a district court to the appropriate circuit court of appeals.
    B. The decisions of courts of appeal and some decisions of other federal courts may be reviewed by the U.S. Supreme Court.
    C. For federal tax purposes, the most common type of case that the U.S. Supreme Court hears is one in which a federal tax statute is ruled to be invalid.

D. If a taxpayer's claim for refund is denied by the IRS or if no decision is made in 6 months, the taxpayer may petition either the U.S. Court of Federal Claims or the U.S. Circuit Court of Appeals.

36. The petition for the U.S. Supreme Court to issue a writ of certiorari is a formal request for review. The granting of a writ of certiorari is
    A. Subsequent to an informal request for review.
    B. Discretionary.
    C. Allowed in criminal cases only.
    D. Not permitted after a decision by a U.S. court of appeals.

37. Which of the following statements best describes how regulatory agencies of the U.S. government such as the IRS are restricted in the adoption of specific regulations?
    A. Regulations must be consistent with standards established in the legislation that created the agency.
    B. The agencies must first conduct a study showing that the benefits of a proposed regulation exceed its costs.
    C. Businesses subject to the regulation must be given notice 1 year before the regulation will be put into effect.
    D. The President of the United States must sign the regulation before it becomes effective.

38. In general, the IRS may exercise
    A. Judicial power only.
    B. Executive power only.
    C. Both judicial and executive power, but not legislative power.
    D. Executive, judicial, and legislative power.

39. Kevin Blue had his 2004 tax return examined by the IRS. Kevin did not agree with the results and was informed by the examiner that he could appeal the findings to the Appeals Division. Kevin decided he would rather have his case heard in Tax Court and bypass the Appeals Division. What must Kevin do?
    A. When Kevin receives the proposed adjustments (30-day letter), he must file a petition with the United States Tax Court.
    B. Kevin should file a petition with the United States Tax Court immediately after he advises the examiner that he wants to go to Tax Court.
    C. Kevin must wait to receive the Statutory Notice of Deficiency (90-day) letter before he can petition the United States Tax Court.
    D. Kevin must pay the tax before he can file a petition with the United States Tax Court.

40. If you don't agree with the IRS examination conclusion you may take your case to which of the following:
    A. United States Tax Court

B. United States Court of Federal Claims
   C. United States District Court
   D. All of the above

41. The "Small Tax Case" procedures in the Tax Court allow resolution of cases under a set of rules that are simpler than the normal Tax Court procedures. A case may be designated a "Small Tax Case" in the Tax Court, if the amount of tax at issue for each tax year or period is not more than:
   A. $50,000.
   B. $100,000.
   C. $125,000.
   D. $150,000.

42. The IRS has the burden of proof for any factual issue in a court proceeding if the taxpayer has:
   A. Provided credible evidence relating to the issue in a court proceeding.
   B. Complied with all substantiation requirements and maintained all required records.
   C. Cooperated with all reasonable requests by the IRS for information regarding the preparation and related tax treatment of any item reported on the return.
   D. All of the above.

43. Harry claimed gambling losses on his income tax return. The return was examined by the IRS and the losses were disallowed. Harry pursued an appeal before the IRS Appeals Office, which sustained the Revenue Agent's adjustment. Harry now wants to take his case to a judge. In which of the following courts can Harry file a tax action?
   A. United States Court of Federal Claims.
   B. United States District Court.
   C. United States Tax Court.
   D. All of the above.

44. Louie is the sole shareholder of a perfume manufacturing corporation. The corporation's tax return was examined, resulting in disagreed adjustments which were appealed and sustained at the IRS Appeals Office. Louie still believes that the adjustments are erroneous and wants a judge to hear his reasons. The corporation timely files a petition in the U.S. Tax Court contesting the adjustments. At the beginning of the trial, the attorney for the corporation files a motion requesting the judge to order that the IRS has the burden to prove that its adjustments are not erroneous. Which of the following criteria must be satisfied before the burden of proof shifts to the IRS?
   A. The corporation must have maintained all records required and complied with all substantiation requirements under the Internal Revenue Code.
   B. The corporation must have cooperated with all reasonable requests by the revenue agent for information regarding the items being questioned on its return.
   C. The corporation had a net worth of $7,000,000 or less at the time the petition was filed in the Tax Court.

D. All of the above.

45. Which statement is **not** correct concerning the small tax case procedure of the Tax Court?
    A. The disputed tax must be $50,000 or less for any one year or period ($10,000 or less for court proceedings beginning on or before July 22, 1998).
    B. The decision is final.
    C. No appeal is available for cases decided under this procedure.
    D. The tax must have been assessed and paid before the Tax Court proceedings

46. To which court may a taxpayer petition, without first paying the disputed tax, regarding a disagreement with the IRS?
    A. District Court.
    B. Court of Federal Claims.
    C. Tax Court.
    D. All of the above.

47. To research whether the IRS has announced an opinion on a Tax Court decision, refer to which of the following references for the original announcement:
    A. Circular 230.
    B. Federal Register.
    C. Internal Revenue Bulletin.
    D. Tax Court Reports.

48. A disagreement with the IRS can be taken to the United States Tax Court if:
    A. It pertains to income tax.
    B. A statutory notice of deficiency has been issued.
    C. A petition is filed within 90 days from the date a statutory notice of deficiency is mailed (150 days if it is addressed to the taxpayer outside the United States).
    D. All of the above.

49. Nicholas wants his income tax case to be handled under the Tax Court's "small tax case procedure." All of the following statements regarding the "small tax case procedure" are correct except:
    A. The amount in the case must be $10,000 or less for any one-tax year for court proceedings begun on or before July 22, 1998; or $50,000 or less for court proceedings begun after July 22, 1998.
    B. The amount must be paid before going to Tax Court.
    C. The Tax Court must approve the request that the case be handled under the small tax case procedure.
    D. The decision is final and cannot be appealed.

XXXXXXXXXXXXXXXXXXXXXXXXXXXXXXXXXXXXXXXXXXXXXXXXXXXXXXXXXXXXXXXX
6.06   UNIT 6: ANSWERS
XXXXXXXXXXXXXXXXXXXXXXXXXXXXXXXXXXXXXXXXXXXXXXXXXXXXXXXXXXXXXXXX

1. **(B) Correct**
   For a case to be heard, the taxpayer must petition the Tax Court within 90 days of the IRS mailing of the notice and demand for payment of the disputed amount. The taxpayer <u>does not</u> need to pay the disputed tax liability before the case is heard.

2. **(A) Correct**
   The Tax Court has a small cases division that is similar to a Small Claims Court. The decision of the Small Cases Judge is <u>final and may not be appealed</u> by the taxpayer or the IRS.

3. **(B) Correct**
   In 1998 Congress adopted a new statutory provision that shifts the burden of proof in federal income tax cases to the IRS. This provision is effective for court proceedings arising in connection with examinations commenced after July 22, 1998. The burden of proof in a Tax Court case is always on the taxpayer, with the following exception as provided by Code Sec. 7491:
   - Where the taxpayer introduces credible evidence relevant to ascertaining the taxpayer's liability, the burden of proof in court proceedings shifts so that the IRS has the burden of proof with respect to factual issues related to income, estate, gift, and generation-skipping transfer taxes.

   To be eligible, the taxpayer must prove that he or she has
   (i)   Complied with present-law substantiation requirements, whether generally or specifically imposed.
   (ii) Complied with present-law recordkeeping requirements.
   (iii) Cooperated with reasonable IRS requests for meetings, interviews, witnesses, documents, and information.

4. **(A) Correct**
   The Small Case division hears cases if the amount of disputed deficiency, including penalties, or claim of overpayment <u>does not exceed $50,000.</u> The taxpayer may be represented by an attorney or may represent himself (*pro se*).

5. **(B) Correct**
   Where the taxpayer introduces credible evidence relevant to ascertaining the taxpayer's liability, the burden of proof in court proceedings shifts so that the IRS has the burden of proof with respect to factual issues related to income, estate, gift, and generation-skipping transfer taxes.

6. **(A) Correct**
   Where the taxpayer introduces credible evidence relevant to ascertaining the taxpayer's liability, the burden of proof in court proceedings shifts so that the IRS has the burden of proof with respect to factual issues related to income, estate, gift, and generation-skipping transfer taxes. Since Brittany failed to provide the IRS with any of the requested information, the burden of proof in the court proceedings does not shift to the IRS.

7. **(B) Correct**
   For a case to be heard, the taxpayer must petition the Tax Court within 90 days of the IRS mailing of the notice and demand for payment of the disputed amount. The taxpayer <u>does not</u> need to pay the disputed tax liability before the case is heard.

8. **(A) Correct**
   The Small Case division hears cases if the amount of disputed deficiency, including penalties, or claim of overpayment <u>does not exceed $50,000.</u> The decision of the Small Cases Judge is <u>final and may not be appealed</u> by the taxpayer or the IRS.

9. **(B) Correct**
   A taxpayer can appeal to a court directly without going through the IRS appeal process.

10. **(A) Correct**
    After satisfying certain procedural and jurisdictional requirements, a taxpayer has the freedom to bypass IRS Appeals. Both Kevin and Keith can take their cases to the following courts: United States Tax Court, the United States Court of Federal Claims, or the United States District Court.

11. **(A) Correct**
    For a case to be heard, the taxpayer must petition the Tax Court within 90 days of the IRS mailing of the notice and demand for payment of the disputed amount.

12. **(B) Correct**
    The 3 classes of Treasury Regulations are:
    (a) Temporary regulations
    (b) Proposed regulations
    (c) Final regulations

13. **(D) Correct**
    Interpretative regulations explain the IRS's position on the various sections of the IRC. Although interpretative regulations do not have the force and effect of law, the courts customarily accord them substantial weight.

14. **(C) Correct**
    Before and during public hearings, Treasury Decisions are referred to as Proposed Regulations and they do <u>not</u> have the effects of the law. Temporary Regulations do not

undergo the public hearing process and have the full effect of the law, just like the Final Regulations.

15. **(D) Correct**

    Public hearings <u>are</u> held on proposed regulations.

16. **(B) Correct**

    Public administrative rulings are part of second tier authorities and generally do not prevail over legislative regulations, the Internal Revenue Code, Court Cases and Treaties. However, they hold higher weight than tier 3 authorities such as legislative history and private letter rulings.

17. **(C) Correct**

    Taxpayers <u>can</u> appeal adverse return examination decisions based on revenue rulings and revenue procedures to the courts.

18. **(D) Correct**

    Statutes are organized by subject matter into the United States Code. These statutes are organized alphabetically and assigned title numbers. Title 26 of the U.S.C. is the Internal Revenue Code. All courts are bound by the Code section.

19. **(D) Correct**

    Interpretative regulations are issued under the general authority of Internal Revenue Section 7805(a), and legislative regulations are issued under the authority of the specific Internal Revenue Code section to which they relate. The Tax Court will issue either a regular report or a memorandum decision depending upon the issues involved and the relative value of the decision being made.

20. **(D) Correct**

    A *writ of certiorari* generally means an order by a higher court directing a lower court, tribunal, or public authority to send the record in a given case for review. If the Supreme Court decides to hear the case, then a *writ of certiorari* is granted. In denying a petition for certiorari, it does not mean that the Supreme Court is upholding or confirming a lower court's decision. It means that the Supreme Court simply does not find the case to be interesting or important enough. The Supreme Court is not obligated to hear any case, but does it at its own discretion.

21. **(D) Correct**

    Acquiescence means that the court decision will be followed in similar situations even thought the decision was adverse to (ruled against) the IRS. *Non-acquiescence* – means that the IRS disagrees with the adverse decision in the case and will follow the decision only for the sake of that particular taxpayer whose case resulted in the adverse ruling. Acquiescence and non-acquiescence is not issued if the IRS prevails in a court case. The issuance of acquiescence does not mean that the IRS agrees with the adverse decision, but only that it will not pursue the matter in a similar and subsequent case.

22. **(C) Correct**
The Commissioner of Internal Revenue will publicly announce acquiescence or nonacquiescence to the adverse regular decisions of all other courts except the United States Supreme Court.

23. **(C) Correct**
The Internal Revenue Bulletin (IRB) is the authoritative instrument for announcing official rulings and procedures of the IRS and for publishing Treasury Decisions, Executive Orders, Tax Conventions, legislation, court decisions, and other items of general interest.

24. **(C) Correct**
The Commissioner of Internal Revenue may at any time revise a non-acquiescence to a decision in a prior case. Similarly, an acquiescence may be withdrawn at any time with retroactive effect if the purpose is to correct a mistake in the application of tax law.

25. **(D) Correct**
A dictum is a court's statement of opinion on a legal point not necessary for the decision of the case. Dictum is not controlling but may be persuasive to another court deciding the issue at hand.

26. **(B) Correct**
Revenue Rulings are official public administrative rulings by the IRS. They are published conclusions as to the application of the law. A revenue ruling can be relied upon as precedent by all taxpayers. A taxpayer may seek advice from the IRS as to the proper tax treatment of a transaction. This is called a private letter ruling. A private letter ruling binds only the IRS and the requesting taxpayer. Thus, a private ruling may not be cited or relied upon for precedent. The IRS does have the option of redacting the text of a private ruling and issuing it as a revenue ruling, which become binding on all taxpayers and the IRS. Revenue rulings are published both in the Internal Revenue Bulletin and in the Federal Register. Revenue Rulings are part of 2nd tier authorities and generally do not prevail over legislative regulations, the Internal Revenue Code, Court Cases and Treaties, thus, they do not have the force and effect of regulations. A taxpayer can appeal adverse return examination decisions based on revenue rulings.

27. **(A) Correct**
Legislative regulations - are those for which the IRS is specifically authorized by the IRC to prescribe the operating rules. They provide the details of the meaning and rules for that particular Code section. Generally, legislative regulations have the force and effect of law.

Interpretative regulations – These regulations explain the IRS's position on the various sections of the IRC. Although interpretative regulations do not have the force and effect of law, the courts customarily accord them substantial weight.
Procedural regulations - are considered to be directive rather than mandatory and, thus, do not have the force and effect of law.

Interpretative regulations are issued under the general authority of Internal Revenue Section 7805(a). Legislative regulations are issued under the authority of the specific Internal Revenue Code section to which they relate. Treasury Regulations are binding on any court of law.

28. **(B) Correct**
The IRS sometimes issues Temporary Regulations in reaction to a congressional of judicial change in the tax law or interpretation. They are issued to provide guidance for the public and IRS employees until final regulations are issued. Temporary Regulations do not undergo the public hearing process and have the full effect of the law, just like the Final Regulations. Temporary Regulations expire after 3 years from the date of issuance (Code Sec. 7805).

29. **(D) Correct**
If the Supreme Court decides to hear the case, then a *writ of certiorari* is granted. In denying a petition for certiorari, it does not mean that the Supreme Court is upholding or confirming a lower court's decision. It is neither a reversal nor agreement with the lower court. It means that the Supreme Court simply does not find the case to be interesting or important enough.

30. **(C) Correct**
The Tax Court has a small cases division that is similar to a Small Claims Court. The Small Case division hears cases if the amount of disputed deficiency, including penalties, or claim of overpayment does not exceed $50,000.

31. **(C) Correct**
The Tax Court's jurisdiction covers income, estate, gift, excise, and private foundation taxes, but has no jurisdiction over employment taxes.

32. **(A) Correct**
Please see answer #31

33. **(B) Correct**
For a case to be heard, the taxpayer must petition the Tax Court within 90 days of the IRS mailing of the notice and demand for payment of the disputed amount. The taxpayer does not need to pay the disputed tax liability before the case is heard.

34. **(B) Correct**

    Before a tax case can be heard in the U.S. district court or Court of Federal Claims, the taxpayer must pay all disputed tax liability and then sue the government for a refund. Appeal made to a U.S. district court or the U.S. Court of Federal Claims must be brought within 2 years of the date of the formal notice from the IRS.

35. **(D) Correct**

    Appeal made to a U.S. district court or the U.S. Court of Federal Claims must be brought within 2 years of the date of the formal notice from the IRS.

36. **(B) Correct**

    The Supreme Court is not obligated to hear any case, but does it at its own discretion. If the Supreme Court decides to hear the case, then a *writ of certiorari* is granted. In denying a petition for certiorari, it does not mean that the Supreme Court is upholding or confirming a lower court's decision. It is neither a reversal nor agreement with the lower court.

37. **(A) Correct**

    When an agency like the IRS decides to adopt any specific regulations, the regulations must be consistent with standards established in the legislation that created the agency.

38. **(D) Correct**

    In general, the IRS may exercise executive, judicial, and legislative power.

39. **(C) Correct**

    For a case to be heard, the taxpayer must petition the Tax Court within 90 days of the IRS mailing of the notice and demand for payment of the disputed amount. The taxpayer does not need to pay the disputed tax liability before the case is heard.

40. **(D) Correct**

    Taxpayers that do not agree with an IRS examination conclusion may take their cases to any of the following courts:
    - (i) U.S. Tax Court
    - (ii) U.S. Court of Federal Claims
    - (iii) U.S. District Court

41. **(A) Correct**

    The Tax Court has a small cases division that is similar to a Small Claims Court. The Small Case division hears cases if the amount of disputed deficiency, including penalties, or claim of overpayment does not exceed $50,000.

42. **(D) Correct**

    The burden of proof in a Tax Court case is always on the taxpayer, with the following exception as provided by Code Sec. 7491:

- Where the taxpayer introduces credible evidence relevant to ascertaining the taxpayer's liability, the burden of proof in court proceedings shifts so that the IRS has the burden of proof with respect to factual issues related to income, estate, gift, and generation-skipping transfer taxes. To be eligible, the taxpayer must prove that he or she has
    (i) Complied with present-law substantiation requirements, whether generally or specifically imposed.
    (ii) Complied with present-law recordkeeping requirements.
    (iii) Cooperated with reasonable IRS requests for meetings, interviews, witnesses, documents, and information.

43. **(D) Correct**
    Taxpayers that do not agree with an IRS examination conclusion may take their cases to any of the following courts:
    (i) U.S. Tax Court
    (ii) U.S. Court of Federal Claims
    (iii) U.S. District Court

44. **(D) Correct**
    In 1998, Congress adopted a new statutory provision that shifts the burden of proof in federal income tax cases to the IRS. This provision is effective for court proceedings arising in connection with examinations commenced after July 22, 1998.

    The burden of proof in a Tax Court case is usually on the taxpayer, with the following *exception* as provided by Code Section 7491:
    - Where the taxpayer introduces credible evidence relevant to ascertaining the taxpayer's liability, the burden of proof in court proceedings shifts to the IRS with respect to factual issues related to income, estate, gift, and generation-skipping transfer taxes. To be eligible, the taxpayer must prove that he or she has
        (i) Complied with present-law substantiation requirements, whether generally or specifically imposed.
        (ii) Complied with present-law recordkeeping requirements.
        (iii) Cooperated with reasonable IRS requests for meetings, interviews, witnesses, documents, and information.

    - Where the taxpayer-petitioner is a partnership, corporation, or trust, the taxpayer must show that its net worth does not exceed $7 million and that it does not have more than 500 employees.

45. **(D) Correct**
    For a case to be heard in the Tax Court, the taxpayer must petition the Tax Court within 90 days of the IRS mailing of the notice and demand for payment of the disputed amount. The taxpayer <u>does not</u> need to pay the disputed tax liability before the case is heard. The Small Case division hears cases if the amount of disputed deficiency,

including penalties, or claim of overpayment <u>does not</u> exceed $50,000. The decision of the Small Cases Judge is <u>final and may not be appealed</u> by the taxpayer or the IRS.

46. **(C) Correct**
The taxpayer <u>does not</u> need to pay the disputed tax liability before the case is heard in the Tax Court.

47. **(C) Correct**
The Internal Revenue Bulletin (IRB) is the authoritative instrument for announcing official rulings and procedures of the IRS and for publishing Treasury Decisions, Executive Orders, Tax Conventions, Legislation, Court Decisions, and other items of general interest.

48. **(D) Correct**
For a case to be heard in the Tax Court, the taxpayer must petition the Tax Court within 90 days of the IRS mailing of the notice of deficiency and demand for payment of the disputed amount. The taxpayer <u>does not</u> need to pay the disputed tax liability before the case is heard.

49. **(B) Correct**
See answer # 48

UNIT 7: ELECTRONIC FILING AND RECORD-KEEPING

Unit 7 Contents:
7.01   AUTHORIZED IRS E-FILE PROVIDER
7.02   E-FILE APPLICATION AND PARTICIPATION
7.03   SUITABILITY CHECK
7.04   RALS AND FEE RESTRICTIONS
7.05   RESPONSIBILITIES OF E-FILE PROVIDERS
7.06   ADVERTISING STANDARDS
7.07   SANCTIONS
7.08   E-FILE PROVIDER PENALTIES
7.09   RECORD-KEEPING
7.10   BASIC RECORDS
7.11   SPECIFIC RECORDS
7.12   HOW LONG TO KEEP RECORDS
7.13   BOOKKEEPING SYSTEM
7.14   UNIT 7: QUESTIONS
7.15   UNIT 7: ANSWERS

7.01   AUTHORIZED IRS *E-FILE* PROVIDER

The procedures governing participation in the IRS *e-file* Program are included in Publication 3112.

A participant in IRS *e-file* is referred to as an "Authorized IRS *e-file* Provider." There are 5 categories of Authorized IRS *e-file* Providers:
  1) Electronic Return Originator.
  2) Intermediate Service Provider.
  3) Software Developer.
  4) Transmitter.
  5) Reporting Agent.

These 5 categories of Authorized IRS *e-file* Providers are not mutually exclusive. For example, an ERO can at the same time be a Transmitter, Software Developer, or Intermediate Service Provider depending on the function(s) performed.

An Authorized IRS *e-file* Provider (Provider) is a business or organization authorized by the IRS to participate in IRS *e-file*. It may be a sole proprietorship, partnership, corporation, or other entity. The firm submits an *e-file* application, meets the eligibility criteria, and must pass a suitability check before the IRS assigns an Electronic Filing Identification Number (EFIN). Applicants accepted for participation in IRS *e-file* are Authorized IRS *e-file* Providers.

Advantages of Using The IRS *E-file* System
  (1) Returns are processed faster and with fewer errors. This means quicker refunds and less

contact with the IRS.
(2) Provides proof of receipt within 48 hours of sending returns to the IRS.
(3) Individual and business clients can *e-file* balance due returns and schedule an electronic funds transfer (EFT) from their account for any date.
(4) Taxpayers can delay out of pocket expenses by paying their individual income tax with a credit card.
(5) Provides good return on investment by saving money on costs of printing, mailing, and document storage.
(6) Helps to keep client information more organized, centralized, and readily available when needed.

7.02   E-FILE APPLICATION AND PARTICIPATION

The IRS *e-file* Application is available at the IRS Web site *IRS.gov* via e-services. Each individual who is a Principal or Responsible Official must register for e-services on the IRS Web site prior to submitting the IRS *e-file* Application to the IRS. When completing the IRS *e-file* Application the applicant provides basic information about the business and its Principals and at least one Responsible Official. The roles of Principal and Responsible Official are not mutually exclusive; a Principal may also serve as the Responsible Official.

Responsible Official - A Responsible Official is:
(a) An individual with authority over the IRS *e-file* operation of the office(s) of the Authorized IRS *e-file* Provider.
(b) The first point of contact with the Service.
(c) Has authority to sign revised IRS *e-file* applications.
(d) Is responsible for ensuring that the Authorized IRS *e-file* Provider adheres to the provisions of this revenue procedure and the publications and notices governing the IRS *e-file* Program.

Principal - The Principal for a business or organization includes the following:
(1) Sole Proprietorship - The sole proprietor is the Principal for a sole proprietorship.
(2) Partnership - Each partner who has a 5 percent or more interest in a partnership is a Principal. If no partner has at least a 5 percent or more interest in the partnership, the Principal is an individual authorized to act for the partnership in legal and/or tax matters.
(3) Corporation - The President, Vice-President, Secretary, and Treasurer are each a Principal of the corporation.
(4) Other - The Principal for an entity that is not a sole proprietorship, partnership, or corporation is an individual authorized to act for the entity in legal and/or tax matters.

Principal or Responsible Official must:
(1) Be a United States citizen or an alien lawfully admitted for permanent residence.
(2) Be 21 years of age as of the date of application.
(3) Meet applicable state and local licensing and/or bonding requirements for the

preparation and collection of tax returns.
(4) Answer several personal questions and sign the Terms of Agreement (TOA) using a PIN, selected during initial registration for e-services.
(5) Submit additional information such as fingerprint cards or evidence of professional status. In lieu of fingerprints, Principals and Responsible Officials may choose to submit evidence that they are one of the following:
- (i) Attorney
- (ii) CPA
- (iii) Enrolled Agent
- (iv) Office of a publicly held Corporation
- (v) Banking official (Bonded and fingerprinted within the last 2 years)

7.03   SUITABILITY CHECK

The IRS conducts a suitability check on the applicant and on all Principals and Responsible Officials listed on e-file applications to determine the applicant's suitability to be an Authorized IRS *e-file* Provider. IRS does not complete suitability checks on:
- (a) Applicants applying only as a Software Developer.
- (b) Contacts
- (c) Delegated Users

Circular 230 Practitioners, including attorneys, certified public accountants and enrolled agents eligible to practice before the IRS, who submit an IRS *e-file* Application to get access to the e-services incentive products are subject to suitability checks.

Suitability checks may include the following:
- (i) A criminal background check.
- (ii) A credit history check.
- (iii) A tax compliance check to ensure that all required returns are filed and paid, and to identify assessed penalties.
- (iv) A check for prior non-compliance with IRS *e-file* requirements.

Contacts - Contact persons should be available on a daily basis for the IRS to contact them for general questions during testing and the processing year. Contacts may be a Principal or Responsible Official. They may also be persons distinct from the Principals and Responsible Officials but if they are, they do not have access to private information that is only available to Principals and Responsible Officials.

Delegated Users - Delegated Users are individuals authorized by the Provider to use one or more of the e-services products even though they are not a Principal or Responsible Official. A Principal or Responsible Official appoints an individual as a Delegated User on the IRS *e-file* Application available on the IRS Web site. A Delegated User should be an employee, partner, or other member of the Firm/Organization or have a business relationship with the

Firm/Organization. Principals and Responsible Officials are responsible for the actions of all Delegated Users on the firm's application. A Principal or Responsible Official may authorize a Delegated User with any or all the following authorities:
  a) Viewing, updating, signing, and submitting IRS *e-file* Applications
  b) Accessing e-services incentive products (Disclosure Authorization, Electronic
  c) Account Resolution and Transcript Delivery System)
  d) Transmitting Forms 990, 1120, and 1120-POL through the Internet (Internet
  e) Transmitter)
  f) Requesting a new password (Security Manager)
  g) Viewing Software Developer information

Denial to Participate in IRS *E-file*

An applicant may be denied participation in IRS *e-file* for a variety of reasons that include:
  1) An indictment or conviction of any criminal offense under the laws of the United States or of a state or other political subdivision, or an active IRS criminal investigation.
  2) Failure to file timely and accurate Federal, state, or local tax returns.
  3) Failure to timely pay any Federal, state, or local tax liability.
  4) Assessment of penalties.
  5) Suspension or disbarment from practice before the IRS or before a state or local tax agency.
  6) Disreputable conduct or other facts that may adversely impact IRS e-file.
  7) Misrepresentation on an IRS e-file Application.
  8) Unethical practices in return preparation.
  9) Assessment against the applicant of a penalty under Section 6695(g) (Relates to the due diligence requirements for Earned Income Tax Credit claims on individual income tax returns).
  10) Stockpiling returns prior to official acceptance to participate in IRS e-file.
  11) Knowingly and directly or indirectly employing or accepting assistance from any firm, organization, or individual denied participation in IRS e-file, or suspended or expelled from participating in IRS e-file. This includes any individual whose actions resulted in the denial, suspension, or expulsion of a firm from IRS e-file.
  12) Knowingly and directly or indirectly accepting employment as an associate, correspondent, or as a subagent from, or sharing fees with, any firm, organization, or individual denied participation in IRS e-file, or suspended or expelled from participating in IRS e-file. This includes any individual whose actions resulted in denial, suspension, or expulsion of a firm from IRS e-file.
  13) Enjoined from filing returns by a Federal or State court injunction or prohibited from filing returns by any Federal or State legal action that prohibits them from participation. A type of such legal action is a Federal Executive Order such as Executive Order 13224 (September 23, 2001), which involves prohibitions directed at terrorist individuals and organizations.

Acceptance to Participate in IRS *e-file*
After an applicant passes the suitability check and the IRS completes processing the application, the IRS:
    (1) Notifies the applicant of acceptance to participate in IRS *e-file*
    (2) Assigns Electronic Identification <u>Filing</u> Numbers (EFINs) to all Providers
    (3) Assigns Electronic Identification <u>Transmission</u> Numbers (ETINs) to Transmitters, Software Providers, and Online Providers.

- The IRS assigns EFINs with prefix codes 10, 21, 32, 44, and 53 to Online Providers.
- All Providers must include their identification numbers with the electronic return data of all returns it transmits to the IRS.
- Transmitters and Software Developers must complete testing before acceptance.
- Authorized IRS *e-file* Providers do not have to reapply each year as long as they continue to e-file returns. However, if a Provider does not e-file returns for two consecutive years, the IRS will notify the Provider of removal from the IRS active Provider list. The IRS may reactivate a Provider if the Provider replies within sixty days and requests reactivation. Otherwise, the Provider will have to complete and submit a new application.
- If the IRS <u>suspends</u> a Provider from participation in IRS *e-file*, the Provider may re-apply to participate in IRS e-file only after the suspension period is completed. Providers <u>expelled or revoked</u> from participation in IRS *e-file* usually may not reapply.
- Providers must update their application information within 30 days of the date of any changes to the information on their current application.

New Application
Applicants and Authorized IRS *e-file* Providers must submit a new application with fingerprint cards or other documentation for the appropriate individuals for any of the following:
    (1) They never participated in IRS *e-file*.
    (2) They were previously denied participation in IRS *e-file*.
    (3) They were previously suspended from IRS *e-file*.
    (4) They have not submitted any e-file returns for more than 2 years.
    (5) They want to originate the electronic submission of returns from an additional location.
    (6) The structure of the business has changed, requiring use of a new or different Taxpayer Identification Number (TIN).

Changes to IRS *e-file* Application
If a Provider is unable to update its IRS *e-file* Application electronically it may notify the IRS of changes to the below information by letter, using the firm's official letterhead:
    (a) All addresses
    (b) All telephone and fax numbers
    (c) E-mail addresses
    (d) Contact persons
    (e) Form types to be e-filed

(f) Transmission protocols
(g) Adding Federal/State e-file
(h) Changes to Foreign Filer information

Form 8633 (Application to Participate in the IRS Electronic Filing Program) is used to make the above-mentioned changes.

Revision of the IRS *e-file* Application

The following situations are changes that require revision of the IRS *e-file* Application:
   (i) The Authorized IRS *e-file* Provider is functioning solely as a Software Developer or Reporting Agent and intends to do business as an ERO, Intermediate Service Provider, or Transmitter.
   (ii) An additional Principal or Responsible Official is being added.
   (iii) A Principal or Responsible Official is changed.

A Principal or Responsible Official must be deleted.

7.04 RALS AND FEE RESTRICTIONS

Publication 1345 defines a Refund Anticipation Loan as money borrowed by a taxpayer that lender bases on a taxpayer's anticipated income tax refund, which may not agree with the amount determined when the IRS processes a tax return. A RAL is a contract between the taxpayer and the lender. The IRS has no involvement with refund anticipation loans. A lender may market a RAL under various commercial or financial product names.

Providers may not base their fees on a percentage of the refund amount or compute their fees using any figure from tax returns. When assisting a taxpayer in applying for a RAL or other financial product, the Provider may charge a flat fee for that assistance. The fee must be identical for all customers and must not relate to the amount of the refund or the financial product. The Provider must not accept a fee that is contingent upon the amount of the refund or a RAL or other financial product from a financial institution for any service connected with a financial product.

The IRS has no responsibility for the payment of any fees associated with the preparation of a return, the transmission of the electronic portion of a return or a RAL or other financial product.

Other Restrictions:
   (a) Any entity that is involved in the Form 1040 IRS *e-file* Program, including a financial institution that accepts direct deposits of income tax refunds, has an obligation to every taxpayer who applies for a RAL to clearly explain to the taxpayer that a RAL is in fact a loan and not a substitute for or a quicker way of receiving an income tax refund. An Authorized IRS *e-file* Provider must advise the taxpayer that if a Direct Deposit is not timely, the taxpayer may be liable to the lender for additional interest on the RAL.

(b) An Authorized IRS *e-file* Provider may assist a taxpayer in applying for a RAL.
(c) An Authorized IRS *e-file* Provider may charge a flat fee to assist a taxpayer in applying for a RAL. The fee must be identical for all of the Authorized IRS *e-file* Provider's customers and must not be related to the amount of the refund or a RAL. The Authorized IRS *e-file* Provider must not accept a fee from a financial institution for any service connected with a RAL that is contingent upon the amount of the refund or a RAL.
(d) The IRS has no responsibility for the payment of any fees associated with the preparation of a return, the transmission of the electronic portion of a return or a RAL.
(e) An Authorized IRS *e-file* Provider may disclose tax information to the lending financial institution in connection with an application for a RAL only with the taxpayer's written consent as specified in §301.7216-3(b) .
(f) An Authorized IRS *e-file* Provider that is also the return preparer and the financial institution or other lender that makes an RAL, may not be related taxpayers within the meaning of §267 or §707 .

7.05   RESPONSIBILITIES OF E-FILE PROVIDERS

A.   Electronic Return Originator (ERO)

An ERO is the Authorized IRS *e-file* Provider that originates the electronic submission of a return to the IRS. The ERO is usually the first point of contact for most taxpayers filing a return using IRS *e-file*. Although an ERO may also engage in return preparation, that activity is separate and different from the origination of the electronic submission of the return to the IRS. An ERO originates the electronic submission of a return after the taxpayer authorizes the filing of the return via IRS *e-file*. An ERO must originate the electronic submission of only returns that the ERO either <u>prepared or collected</u> from a taxpayer.

An ERO originates the electronic submission by any one of the following:
(1) Electronically sending the return to a Transmitter that will transmit the return to the IRS
(2) Directly transmitting the return to the IRS
(3) Providing a return to an Intermediate Service Provider for processing prior to transmission to the IRS

The ERO's responsibilities include:
(a) Timely originating the electronic submission of returns.
(b) Submitting any required supporting paper documents to the IRS.
(c) Providing copies to taxpayers.
(d) Retaining records and making records available to the IRS.
(e) Accepting returns only from taxpayers and Authorized IRS *e-file* Providers.
(f) Having only one EFIN for the same firm for use at one location, unless the IRS issued more than one EFIN to the firm for the same location. For this purpose, the business entity is generally the entity that reports on its return the income derived from electronic filing. The IRS may issue more than one EFIN to accommodate a high volume of returns, or as it determines appropriate.

(g) An ERO must clearly display the firm's "doing business as" name at all locations and sites including Web sites at which the ERO or a third party obtains information from taxpayers for electronic origination of returns by the ERO.
(h) Advising clients of the option to receive their return by direct deposit or paper check.
(i) Accept any Direct Deposit election to any eligible financial institution designated by the taxpayer.
(j) Not charging a fee for the electronic transmission of a tax return that is based upon a percentage of the taxpayer's refund amount.

An ERO must:
1) Advise taxpayers of the option to receive their refund by paper check or direct deposit.
2) Not charge a separate fee for a Direct Deposit.
3) Accept any Direct Deposit election to any eligible financial institution designated by the taxpayer.
4) Ensure that the taxpayer is eligible to choose Direct Deposit.
5) Caution the taxpayer that once the electronic portion of the return has been accepted for processing by the Service:
    a) the Direct Deposit election cannot be rescinded;
    b) the routing number of the financial institution cannot be changed; and
    c) the taxpayer's account number cannot be changed; and
6) Advise the taxpayer that refund information is available by calling the appropriate IRS phone number.

B. Intermediate Service Provider

An Intermediate Service Provider receives tax information from an ERO (or from a taxpayer who files electronically using a personal computer, modem, and commercial tax preparation software), processes the tax return information and either forwards the information to a Transmitter or sends the information back to the ERO (or taxpayer for Online Filing).

The Intermediate Service Provider's responsibilities include:
(1) Including its Electronic Filing Identification Number (EFIN) and the ERO's EFIN with all return information it forwards to a Transmitter.
(2) Serving as a contact point between its client EROs and the IRS, if requested.
(3) Providing the IRS with a list of each client ERO, if requested.
(4) Adhering to all applicable rules that apply to Transmitters.
(5) An Intermediate Service Provider must clearly display the firm's "doing business as" name at all locations and sites including Web sites at which the ERO or a third party obtains information from taxpayers for electronic origination of returns by the ERO.

C. Software Developer

A Software Developer develops software for the purposes of formatting electronic return information according to IRS *e-file* specifications and/or transmitting electronic return information directly to the IRS. Software Developers must pass what is referred to as either acceptance or assurance testing. If an Authorized IRS *e-file* Provider is a Software Developer that performs no other role in IRS *e-file* but that of software development, the Principals and Responsible Officials do not have to pass a suitability check during the application process.

A Software Developer's responsibilities include:
(1) Promptly correcting any software error causing returns to reject and distributing the correction.
(2) Ensuring its software creates accurate returns.
(3) Adhering to specifications provided by the IRS in publications.

D. Transmitter

A Transmitter transmits electronic tax return information directly to the IRS. A bump-up service provider that increases the transmission rate or line speed of formatted or reformatted information sent to the IRS via a public switched telephone network is also a Transmitter.

In order to transmit electronic return data directly to the IRS, Transmitters must be equipped with both computer hardware and software that make it possible. Prior to transmitting return data to the IRS, an application requesting the "Transmitter" Provider Option must be submitted, and an EFIN, an ETIN and a password received for testing. Testing that ensures the compatibility of transmission systems with the IRS systems must be completed to enable transmission of the electronic return data to the IRS.

A Transmitter's responsibilities include:
(1) Ensuring EFINs of Authorized IRS *e-file* Providers are included as required by IRS *e-file* specifications in the electronic return record of returns it transmits.
(2) Timely transmitting returns to the IRS, retrieving acknowledgment files, and sending the acknowledgment file information to the ERO, Intermediate Service Provider or taxpayer (for Online Filing).
(3) Promptly correcting any transmission error that causes an electronic transmission to be rejected.
(4) A Transmitter participating as an Online Provider must clearly display the firm's "doing business as" name at all locations and sites including Web sites at which the Transmitter or a third party obtains information from taxpayers for electronic origination of returns by the ERO.

E. Reporting Agent

A Reporting Agent is an accounting service, franchiser, bank, service bureau, or other entity that is authorized to perform one or more of the acts listed in Rev. Proc. 2007-38 on behalf of a taxpayer.

7.06 ADVERTISING STANDARDS

An Authorized IRS *e-file* Provider must comply with the advertising and solicitation provisions of Circular No. 230.

1) A Provider must adhere to all relevant Federal, state, and local consumer protection laws that relate to advertising and soliciting.
2) The Provider must not use improper or misleading advertising in relation to IRS *e-file*. For example, any claim concerning a faster refund by virtue of electronic filing must be consistent with the language in official IRS publications.
3) The Provider must clearly describe that a financial institution is advancing funds as a loan or will provide the funds for other financial products. It must be clear in the advertising that the taxpayer is borrowing against the anticipated refund or obtaining funds from a financial institution, and not obtaining the refund itself from the financial institution.
4) A Provider must not use the IRS name, "Internal Revenue Service," or "IRS" within a firm's name. However, once accepted to participate in IRS *e-file*, a firm may represent itself as an "Authorized IRS *e-file* Provider".
5) Advertising materials must not carry the FMS, IRS, or other Treasury Seals.
6) Providers must not use the IRS logo to portray any other relationship between the IRS and any Provider.
7) If an Authorized IRS *e-file* Provider uses radio, television, Internet, signage, or other methods of communication to advertise IRS *e-file*, the Provider must keep a copy and provide it to the IRS upon request, the text or, if prerecorded, the recorded advertisement. Provider must retain copies until the <u>end of the calendar year</u> following the last transmission or use.

IRS *E-file* Monitoring

IRS personnel monitor Authorized IRS *e-file* Providers through review of IRS records and during visits to Providers' offices and other locations where Providers perform IRS *e-file* activities. Monitoring may include, but is not limited to the following:

(a) Reviewing the quality of IRS *e-file* submissions for rejects and other defects.
(b) Checking adherence to signature requirements on returns.
(c) Scrutinizing advertising material.
(d) Examining records.
(e) Observing office procedures.
(f) Compliance with the tax return preparer regulations, including provisions of section 6695(g), which relates to the due diligence requirements for Earned Income Tax Credit claims on individual income tax returns.

7.07 SANCTIONS

Violations of IRS e-file requirements may result in warning or sanctioning an Authorized IRS e-file Provider. Sanctioning may be a written reprimand, suspension or expulsion from participation from IRS e-file, or other sanctions, depending on the seriousness of the <u>infraction</u>. The IRS categorizes the seriousness of infractions as Level One, Level Two, and Level Three.

Providers may appeal sanctions through the Administrative Review Process. An Authorized IRS e-file Provider is not entitled to an administrative review process for revocation.

A sanction is effective thirty days after the date of the letter informing the Provider of the sanction, or the date the reviewing offices or the Office of Appeals affirms the sanction, whichever is later. IRS can immediately suspend or expel an Authorized IRS e-file Provider without prior warning or notice.

Levels of Infraction
1) **Level One Infractions** - are violations of IRS *e-file* rules and requirements that have little or no adverse impact on the quality of electronically filed returns or on IRS *e-file*.

2) **Level Two Infractions** - are violations of IRS *e-file* rules and requirements that have an adverse impact upon the quality of electronically filed returns or on IRS *e-file*. Level Two Infractions include continued Level One Infractions after the IRS has brought the Level One Infraction to the attention of the Authorized IRS *e-file* Provider. Depending on the infractions, the IRS may either restrict participation in IRS *e-file* or suspend the Authorized IRS *e-file* Provider from participation in IRS *e-file* for a period of one year beginning with the effective date of suspension.

3) **Level Three Infractions** - are violations of IRS *e-file* rules and requirements that have a significant adverse impact on the quality of electronically filed returns or on IRS *e-file*. Level Three Infractions include continued Level Two Infractions after the IRS has brought the Level Two Infraction to the attention of the Authorized IRS *e-file* Provider. A Level Three Infraction may result in suspension from participation in IRS *e-file* for two years beginning with the effective date of the suspension year or depending on the severity of the infraction, such as fraud or criminal conduct, which may result in expulsion without the opportunity for future participation. The IRS reserves the right to suspend or expel an Authorized IRS *e-file* Provider prior to administrative review for Level Three Infractions.

ERO Record Keeping and Documentation Requirements
EROs must retain the following material until the end of the calendar year at the business address from which it originated the return or at a location that allows the ERO to readily access the material as it must be available at the time of IRS request. An ERO may retain the required records at the business address of the Responsible Official or at a location that allows the Responsible Official to readily access the material during any period of time the office is closed, as it must be available at the time of IRS request through the end of the calendar year.
- A copy of Form 8453, *U.S. Individual Income Tax Transmittal for an IRS e-file Return*, and supporting documents that are not included in the electronic records submitted to the IRS;
- Copies of Forms W-2, W-2G and 1099-R;
- A copy of signed IRS *e-file* consent to disclosure forms;

- A complete copy of the electronic portion of the return that can be readily and accurately converted into an electronic transmission that the IRS can process; and
- The acknowledgement file for IRS accepted returns.

Forms 8879 and 8878 must be available to the IRS in the same manner for 3 years from the due date of the return or the IRS received date, whichever is later.

EROs may electronically image and store all paper records they are required to retain for IRS *e-file*. The ERO must be able to reproduce all records with a high degree of legibility and readability (including the taxpayers' signatures) when displayed on a video terminal and when reproduced in hard copy.

Form 8453 (U.S. Individual Income Tax Declaration for an Internal Revenue Service e-file Return) must be signed after the return is prepared and before the electronic data portion of the return is submitted.

Returns Not Eligible for E-file
The following types of tax return cannot be filed electronically:
(1) Amended tax returns.
(2) Tax returns with fiscal-year tax periods.
(3) Prior-year tax returns.
(4) Tax returns with foreign addresses.
(5) Tax returns of a married couple filing separately in community property states.
(6) Tax returns for decedents.
(7) Tax returns with Taxpayer Identification Numbers (TIN) within the range of 900-00-0000 through 999-99-9999.

The Electronic Federal Tax Payment System (EFTPS)
The Electronic Federal Tax Payment System (EFTPS) is a tax payment system provided free by the U.S. Department of Treasury. Businesses and Individuals can pay all their federal taxes using EFTPS. Individuals can pay their quarterly 1040ES estimated taxes electronically using EFTPS, and they can make payments weekly, monthly, or quarterly. Both business and individual payments can be scheduled in advance. Enrollment is required to use EFTPS.

7.08   E-FILE PROVIDER PENALTIES

An Authorized IRS *e-file* Provider is a tax return preparer under the definition of section 7216(a) of the Code. Tax return preparers are subject to criminal penalties for unauthorized disclosure or use of tax return information. In addition, section 6713 establishes civil penalties for unauthorized disclosure or use of income tax return information by tax return preparers.

Under section 301.7701-15(d)(1), Authorized IRS *e-file* Providers are not tax return preparers for the purpose of assessing most preparer penalties as long as their services are limited to "typing, reproduction, or other mechanical assistance in the preparation of a return or claim for refund."

If an ERO, Intermediate Service Provider, Transmitter, or the product of a Software Developer alters the tax return information in a non-substantive way, this alteration will be considered to come under the "mechanical assistance" exception described in section 301.7701-15(d)(1), and will not cause an Authorized IRS *e-file* Provider to become a tax return preparer. A non-substantive change is a correction or change limited to a transposition error, misplaced entry, spelling error, or arithmetic correction.

A $500 penalty may be imposed, per I.R.C. §6695(f), on a return preparer who endorses or negotiates a refund check issued to any taxpayer other than the return preparer. The prohibition on return preparers negotiating a refund check is limited to a refund check for returns they prepared.

A preparer that is also a financial institution, but has not made a loan to the taxpayer on the basis of the taxpayer's anticipated refund may:
   a) Cash a refund check and remit all of the cash to the taxpayer.
   b) Accept a refund check for deposit in full to a taxpayer's account provided the bank does not initially endorse or negotiate the check.
   c) Endorse a refund check for deposit in full to a taxpayer's account pursuant to a written authorization of the taxpayer.

In certain situations, under section 7216(b)(2), disclosure of tax return information among Authorized IRS *e-file* Providers for the purpose of electronically filing a return is permissible. For example, an ERO may pass on tax return information to an Intermediate Service Provider and/or a Transmitter for the purpose of having an electronic return formatted and transmitted to the Service.

Payments
The Internal Revenue Service e-file Program allows taxpayers to schedule the payment for withdrawal on a future date. Scheduled payments must be effective on or before the return due date. For example, a Provider may transmit an individual income tax return in February and the taxpayer can specify that the withdrawal be made in April as long as it is on or before the return due date.

Rejected Tax Returns
If the IRS rejects the electronic portion of a taxpayer's individual income tax return for processing and the ERO cannot rectify the reason for the rejection, the ERO must:
   a) Take reasonable steps to inform the taxpayer of the rejection within 24 hours.
   b) Provide the taxpayer with the reject code(s) accompanied by an explanation and the sequence number of each reject code(s).

If the taxpayer chooses not to have the electronic portion of the return corrected and transmitted to the Service, or if the electronic portion of the return cannot be accepted for processing by the Service, the taxpayer must file a paper return by the later of:
- (i) The due date of the return, or
- (ii) 10 calendar days after the date the Service gives notification that the electronic portion of the return is rejected or that the electronic portion of the return cannot be accepted for processing.

The paper return should include an explanation of why the return is being filed after the due date.

7.09　RECORD-KEEPING

Both Publications 552 and 225 contain detailed information about record keeping guidelines for taxpayers.

Employment Taxes - If you have employees, you must keep all employment tax records for at least 4 years after the date the tax becomes due or is paid, whichever is later.

Records for Nontax Purposes - When your records are no longer needed for tax purposes, do not discard them until you check to see if you have to keep them longer for other purposes. For example, your insurance company or creditors may require you to keep them longer than the IRS does.

Copy C of Form W-2 - Keep Copy C of Form W-2 for at least 3 years after the due date for filing your income tax return. However, to help protect your social security benefits, keep Copy C until you begin receiving social security benefits, just in case there is a question about your work record and/or earnings in a particular year.

7.10　BASIC RECORDS

Basic records are the records that prove your income and expenses. The following are examples of basic records to keep for each category:

Income
- Form(s) W-2
- Form(s) 1099
- Bank statements
- Brokerage statements
- Form(s) K-1

Expenses
- Sales slips

- Invoices
- Receipts
- Canceled checks or other proof of payment
- Written communications from qualified charities

Home
- Closing statements
- Purchase and sales invoices
- Proof of payment
- Insurance records
- Receipts for improvement costs

Investments
- Brokerage statements
- Mutual fund statements
- Form(s) 1099
- Form(s) 2439

Proof of Payment

Proof of payment alone is not proof that the item claimed on your return is allowable. Taxpayers should also keep other documents that will help prove that the item is allowable.

IF payment is by	THEN the statement must show
Cash	- Amount - Payee's name - Transaction date
Check	- Check number - Amount - Payee's name - Date the check amount was posted to the account by the financial institution
Debit or credit card	- Amount charged - Payee's name - Transaction date
Electronic funds transfer	- Amount transferred - Payee's name - Date the transfer was posted to the account by the financial institution
Payroll deduction	- Amount - Payee code - Transaction date

7.11 SPECIFIC RECORDS

Alimony - If you receive or pay alimony, you should keep a copy of your written separation agreement or the divorce, separate maintenance, or support decree. If you pay alimony, you will also need to know your former spouse's social security number.

Business Use of Your Home - You should keep records that show the part of your home that you use for business and the expenses related to that use.

Casualty and Theft Losses - To deduct a casualty or theft loss, you must be able to prove that you had a casualty or theft. Your records also must be able to support the amount you claim. For a casualty loss, your records should show:
    (i) The type of casualty (car accident, fire, storm, etc.) and when it occurred,
    (ii) That the loss was a direct result of the casualty, and
    (iii) That you were the owner of the property.
For a theft loss, your records should show:
    (i) When you discovered your property was missing,
    (ii) That your property was stolen, and
    (iii) That you were the owner of the property.

Child Care Credit - You must give the name, address, and taxpayer identification number for all persons or organizations that provide care for your child or dependent. You can use Form W-10, Dependent Care Provider's Identification and Certification, or various other sources to get the information from the care provider.

Energy Incentives for Individuals - You must keep records to prove:
1) When and how you acquired the property.
2) Purchase price.
3) Deductions taken for casualty losses, such as losses resulting from fires or storms.

The following documents may show this information.
- Purchase and sales invoices.
- Manufacturer's certification statement.
- Canceled checks.
- Insurance Claims.

Gambling Winnings and Losses - You must keep an accurate diary of your winnings and losses that includes the:
- Date and type of gambling activity,
- Name and address or location of the gambling establishment,
- Names of other persons present with you at the gambling establishment, and
- Amount you won or lost.

Individual Retirement Arrangements (IRAs) - Keep copies of the following forms and records until all distributions are made from your IRA(s).

- Form 5498, IRA Contribution Information, or similar statement received for each year showing contributions you made, distributions you received, and the value of your IRA(s).
- Form 1099-R, Distribution from Pensions, Annuities, Retirement or Profit-Sharing Plans, IRAs, Insurance Contracts, etc., received for each year you received a distribution.
- Form 8606, Nondeductible IRAs, for each year you made a nondeductible contribution to your IRA or received distributions from an IRA if you ever made nondeductible contributions.

Medical and Dental Expenses - In addition to records you keep of regular medical expenses, you should keep records of transportation expenses that are primarily for and essential to medical care. You can record these expenses in a diary. You should record gas and oil expenses directly related to that transportation. If you do not want to keep records of your actual expenses, you can keep a log of the miles you drive your car for medical purposes and use the standard mileage rate. You should also keep records of any parking fees, tolls, taxi fares, and bus fares.

Taxes - Form(s) W-2 and Form(s) 1099-R show state income tax withheld from your wages and pensions. You should keep a copy of these forms to prove the amount of state withholding. If you made estimated state income tax payments, you need to keep a copy of the form or your check(s).

You also need to keep copies of your state income tax returns. If you received a refund of state income taxes, the state may send you Form 1099-G, Certain Government Payments. Keep mortgage statements, tax assessments, or other documents as records of the real estate and personal property taxes you paid.

If you deducted actual state and local general sales taxes instead of using the optional state sales tax tables, you must keep your actual receipts showing general sales taxes paid.

Sales Tax on Vehicles - If you are claiming a deduction for state or local sales taxes paid on a vehicle (new car, light truck, motor home, and motorcycle) you purchased, you need to keep your purchase contract to show how much sales tax you paid. If you bought a vehicle in a state that does not have a sales tax, such as Alaska, Delaware, Hawaii, Montana, New Hampshire, or Oregon, you can deduct fees or taxes that are a per unit fee or are based on the vehicle's sales price.

Tips - You must keep a daily record to accurately report your tips on your return. You can use Form 4070A, Employee's Daily Record of Tips, which is found in Publication 1244, Employee's Daily Record of Tips and Report to Employer, to record your tips.

7.12 HOW LONG TO KEEP RECORDS

Taxpayers must keep your records as long as they may be needed for the administration of any provision of the Internal Revenue Code. One must keep records that support an item of income or a deduction appearing on a return until the period of limitations for the return runs out. A period of limitations is the period of time after which no legal action can be brought. Generally, that means that a taxpayer must keep your records for at least 3 years from when your tax return was due or filed or within 2 years of the date the tax was paid, whichever is later.

Purchasing property with a long life, adopting the LIFO method of inventory, and changing a method of accounting are examples of business decisions that may require a person to maintain records longer than the general requirement of 3 years after the return was due or filed or 2 years after the date the tax was paid, whichever is later.

The following table contains the periods of limitations that apply to income tax returns. The years refer to the period beginning after the return was filed.

Period of Limitations

	If you.	The period is
A	Owe additional tax and (2), (3), and (4) do not apply to you	3 years
B	Do not report income that you should and it is more than 25% of the gross income shown on your return	6 years
C	File a fraudulent return	No limit
D	Do not file a return	No limit
E	File a claim for credit or refund after you filed your return	The later of 3 years or 2 years after tax was paid.
F	File a claim for a loss from worthless securities	7 years

Property - Keep records relating to property until the period of limitations expires for the year in which you <u>dispose</u> of the property in a taxable disposition. You must keep these records to figure your basis for computing gain or loss when you sell or otherwise dispose of the property. Generally, if you received property in a nontaxable exchange, your basis in that property is the same as the basis of the property you gave up. You must keep the records on the old property, as well as the new property, until the period of limitations expires for the year in which you dispose of the new property in a taxable <u>disposition</u>.

Electronic Records

When using electronic storage systems for the purpose of maintaining tax books and records, all requirements that are applicable to hard copy books and records still apply. When replacing hard copy books and records, electronic storage systems must be maintained for as long as they are material to the administration of tax law.

An electronic storage system is any system for preparing or keeping your records either by electronic imaging or by transfer to an electronic storage media. The electronic storage system must index, store, preserve, retrieve, and reproduce the electronically stored books and records in legible, readable format. Electronic storage systems are also subject to the same controls and retention guidelines as those imposed on your original hard copy books and records.

The original hard copy books and records may be destroyed **provided** that the electronic storage system has been tested to establish that the hard copy books and records are being reproduced in compliance with IRS requirements for an electronic storage system and procedures are established to ensure continued compliance with all applicable rules and regulations. You still have the responsibility of retaining any other books and records that are required to be retained.

The IRS may test your electronic storage system, including the equipment used, indexing methodology, software, and retrieval capabilities. This test is not considered an examination and the results must be shared with you. If your electronic storage system meets the requirements mentioned earlier, you will be in compliance. If not, you may be subject to penalties for non-compliance, unless you continue to maintain your original hard copy books and records in a manner that allows you and the IRS to determine your correct tax.

7.13 BOOK-KEEPING SYSTEM

Taxpayers must decide whether to use either a *single-entry* or a *double-entry* bookkeeping system. The single-entry system of bookkeeping is the simplest to maintain, but it may not be suitable for everyone. Taxpayers may find the double-entry system better because it has built-in checks and balances to assure accuracy and control. There is no specified method as long as the method used accurately reflects income and expenses.

Single-entry - A single-entry system is based on the income statement (profit or loss statement). It can be a simple and practical system if you are starting a small business. The system records the flow of income and expenses through the use of:
 (1) A daily summary of cash receipts, and
 (2) Monthly summaries of cash receipts and disbursements.

Double-entry - A double-entry bookkeeping system uses journals and ledgers. Transactions are first entered in a journal and then posted to ledger accounts. These accounts show income, expenses, assets, liabilities, and net worth. In the double-entry system, each account has a left side for debits and a right side for credits. It is self-balancing because you record every transaction as a debit entry in one account and as a credit entry in another. Under this system, the total debits must equal the total credits after posting the journal entries to the ledger accounts.

7.14   UNIT 7: QUESTIONS

TRUE/FALSE QUESTIONS
Please select either (A) for True or (B) for False

1. You should keep copy C of your W-2 for at least 7 years after you have filed your return.
   A. TRUE.
   B. FALSE.

2. If your clients keep their records on a computer, they do not have to keep all the receipts, checks, and other documents.
   A. TRUE.
   B. FALSE.

3. A checkbook can be used to keep records of both income and expenses. Taxpayers should also keep documents such as sales slips and expense receipts to support claimed income and deductions.
   A. TRUE.
   B. FALSE.

4. An Electronic Return Originator (ERO) does not have to advise its clients of the option to receive their return by direct deposit or paper check.
   A. TRUE.
   B. FALSE.

5. The tax return for a taxpayer who died within the calendar tax year may be filed electronically.
   A. TRUE.
   B. FALSE.

6. An ERO (Electronic Return Originator) may originate the electronic submission of income tax returns they prepared, but cannot electronically submit returns collected from taxpayers.
   A. TRUE.
   B. FALSE.

7. Authorized electronic filing providers may not base their fees on a percentage of the refund amount or compute their fees using any figure from tax returns. Separate fees may not be charged for direct deposits.
   A. TRUE.
   B. FALSE.

8. An ERO may not charge one fee for clients who select RALs and a different fee for those

who select direct deposits into their own accounts.
   A. TRUE.
   B. FALSE.

9. If an authorized IRS electronic filing provider uses radio, television, Internet, signage, or other methods of communication to advertise IRS electronic filing, the Provider must keep a copy and provide the text to the IRS upon request, or if prerecorded, the recorded advertisement. Copies must be maintained until the end of the calendar year following the last transmission or use.
   A. TRUE.
   B. FALSE.

10. Taxpayers can make a tax payment using EFTPS without enrolling in the system.
    A. TRUE.
    B. FALSE.

11. Margaret Bright is an enrolled agent who participates in the IRS e-file Program as an Electronic Return Originator & Transmitter. Billy Bud filed his 2005 Form 1040 electronically by the extended due date of August 15, 2006. (Billy had requested an automatic extension of time to file by August 15, 2006). On December 1, 2006 Billy realized that he did not claim a $10,000.00 contribution on his Form 1040 for 2005. Billy requested that Margaret file an amended return for 2005. Margaret is allowed to electronically file the amended return because it is prior to the end of the filing year for tax year 2005, which is December 31, 2006.
    A. TRUE.
    B. FALSE.

12. Taxpayers often elect the Direct Deposit option because it is the fastest way of receiving refunds. The Electronic Return Originator (ERO) must accept any Direct Deposit election to any eligible financial institution designated by the taxpayer.
    A. TRUE.
    B. FALSE.

13. An authorized IRS e-file Provider is not considered to be an income tax preparer as long as their services are limited to "typing, reproduction, or other mechanical assistance" in the preparation of a return. However, they are still subject to assessment of any and all return preparer penalties by the IRS.
    A. TRUE.
    B. FALSE.

14. The IRS e-file Program allows taxpayers to schedule the payment for withdrawal on a future date. Scheduled payments must be effective on or before the return due date. As an example, a Provider may transmit an individual income tax return in February and the taxpayer can specify that the withdrawal be made in April as long as it is on or

before the return due date.
- A. TRUE.
- B. FALSE.

15. Form 8453, U.S. Individual Income Tax Declaration for an IRS e-file Return, must be signed after the return is prepared and before the electronic data portion of the return is submitted.
- A. TRUE.
- B. FALSE.

16. Vivian Blake is an enrolled agent who participates in the IRS e-file Program as an Electronic Return Originator & Transmitter. Fred Birch has not filed his Form 1040 for tax years 1993 and 1994. Fred hires Vivian in March of 2006 to prepare and file the delinquent returns. Vivian will be able to electronically file the delinquent 1993 and 1994 returns after April 15, 2006 and before January 1, 2007.
- A. TRUE.
- B. FALSE.

17. Mr. Edward is an electronic return originator. Mr. Edward can charge a fee for the electronic transmission of a tax return that is based upon a percentage of the taxpayer's refund amount.
- A. TRUE.
- B. FALSE.

18. Gail files her return electronically. Her Electronic Return Originator (ERO) must notify her if her return is rejected and results in a change of more than $25 total tax.
- A. TRUE.
- B. FALSE.

19. An electronic filer using radio or television broadcasting to advertise must prerecord the broadcast and keep a copy for a period of at least 36 months from the date of the last transmission or use.
- A. TRUE.
- B. FALSE.

20. With regard to electronic filing, if the electronic portion of a taxpayer's tax return is acknowledged as rejected by the IRS for substantive reasons, the electronic return originator (ERO) must, within 24 hours of receiving the rejection, take all reasonable steps to tell the taxpayer that the taxpayer's return has not been filed.
- A. TRUE.
- B. FALSE.

21. A business operated as a sole proprietorship must use the double-entry accounting method to reflect both income and expenses for computing taxable income.

A. TRUE.
B. FALSE.

22. Federal law does not require a taxpayer to maintain any special form of records, but the records must be such that the taxpayer can prepare a complete and accurate income tax return.
    A. TRUE.
    B. FALSE.

23. Adequate records must include sufficient documents (sales slips, invoices, canceled checks, etc.) that clearly establish the income, deductions, and credits shown on the return.
    A. TRUE.
    B. FALSE.

24. Microfilm and microfiche reproductions of general books of accounts, such as cash books, journals, voucher registers, and ledgers, are accepted by the IRS for record keeping if they comply with applicable revenue procedures.
    A. TRUE.
    B. FALSE.

25. If you receive a cash gift from a relative, you should maintain a record to substantiate its receipt in order to prevent it from later being characterized as taxable income.
    A. TRUE.
    B. FALSE.

26. An accountant should furnish records or information to the IRS on first request, even if (s)he believes the information is privileged.
    A. TRUE.
    B. FALSE.

27. Employers are not required to retain withholding exemption certificates (Form W-4) filed by employees after the date of the current year's returns.
    A. TRUE.
    B. FALSE.

28. Purchasing property with a long life, adopting the LIFO method of inventory, and changing a method of accounting are all examples of business decisions that may require a person to maintain records longer than the general requirement of 3 years after the return was due or filed or 2 years after the date the tax was paid, whichever is later.
    A. TRUE.
    B. FALSE.

29. You should keep records that verify your basis in property for as long as they are needed to figure the basis of the original or replacement property.
   A. TRUE.
   B. FALSE.

30. If the electronic portion of a taxpayer's return is acknowledged as rejected by the IRS due to a substantive change, the electronic return originator (ERO) is not required to notify the taxpayer that his/her return has not been filed.
   A. TRUE.
   B. FALSE.

31. If an electronic filer charges a fee for the electronic transmission of a tax return, the fee may not be based on a percentage of the refund amount or on the amount of taxes saved.
   A. TRUE.
   B. FALSE.

32. Employers are required to keep records on employment taxes (income tax withholding, Social Security, Medicare, and federal unemployment tax) for at least 3 years after the due date of the return or after the date the tax was paid, whichever is later.
   A. TRUE.
   B. FALSE.

33. If commercially available computer software is used to summarize business expenses, the receipts and invoices need not be kept.
   A. TRUE.
   B. FALSE.

34. Todd is an ERO. He is not participating in the IRS PIN pilot. For every return he files electronically, Todd must complete, sign, and have the client sign Form 8453. He must attach each client's Forms W-2 to the Form 8453 and submit these documents to the IRS. He does not need to keep a copy of Form 8453.
   A. TRUE.
   B. FALSE.

35. On March 23, year 2, Geri prepared a year 1 individual tax return for Candy. The return shows a refund of $2,600. Geri can file Candy's return electronically.
   A. TRUE.
   B. FALSE.

36. The taxpayer should keep a copy of Form W-2 for two years.
   A. TRUE.
   B. FALSE.

MULTIPLE CHOICE QUESTIONS:
Please select the most appropriate answer.

37. George knew that he had a substantial refund for the current tax year because he had worked at a high salary early in the year with extra withholding. He was unemployed the rest of the year. He wanted to file the return electronically with direct deposit to expedite the refund. The Fix Tax Co. stated that its fee would be 10% of the refund for preparation and filing, with no additional charge for direct deposit. The No Tax Co. stated that its fee would be $35 regardless of the refund amount but that it charged a $10 fee for direct deposit request. Which of the following is true?
    A. George cannot electronically file because he is not employed at the end of the year.
    B. The Fix Tax Co. may charge a percentage of the refund because it does not charge for direct deposit.
    C. The No Tax Co. may charge the $10 direct deposit fee because its $35 filing and preparation fee is a flat fee.
    D. Neither the Fix Tax Co. nor the No Tax Co. is in compliance with electronic filing fee restrictions.

38. With regard to effective record keeping, which of the following statements is false?
    A. Records should show how much of an individual's earnings are subject to self-employment tax.
    B. A canceled check always proves payment and establishes a tax deduction.
    C. The invoice, paid receipt, or canceled check that supports an item of expense should be retained.
    D. Records should identify the source of income in order to determine if an income item is taxable or nontaxable.

39. Employers are required to keep records on employment taxes (income tax withholding, Social Security, Medicare, and federal unemployment tax) for
    A. An indefinite time.
    B. The statutory period for assessment of the employees' taxes.
    C. At least 4 years after the date the tax becomes due or is paid, whichever is later.
    D. At least 3 years after the due date of the return or 2 years after the date the tax was paid, whichever is later.

40. Which of the following is not a specific record required to be kept for income tax withholding?
    A. Each employee's date of birth.
    B. The fair market value and date of each payment of noncash compensation made to a retail commission salesperson if no income tax was withheld.
    C. The total amount and date of each wage payment and the period of time the payment covers.
    D. For accident or health plans, information about the amount of each payment.

41. How long should you keep your records?
    A. 3 years if you owe additional tax.
    B. 7 years if you file a claim for a loss from worthless securities.
    C. No limit if you do not file a return.
    D. All of the answers are correct.

42. Nancy, a calendar year taxpayer, filed her federal income tax return for tax year 2003, which was due on April 15, 2004, on May 1, 2004. Nancy did not request, and therefore did not receive, an extension of time to file her 2003 Federal Income Tax return. Nancy paid the amount due as shown on the 2003 return on June 30, 2004. Based on these facts, the last day for the IRS to assess additional tax with respect to Nancy's 2003 return is:
    A. June 20, 2006.
    B. April 15, 2007.
    C. May 1, 2007.
    D. June 20, 2007.

43. Which of the following statements with respect to effective record keeping is false?
    A. Records should identify the source of income in order to determine if an income item is taxable or nontaxable.
    B. If an individual cannot provide a canceled check to prove payment of an expense item, (s)he may be able to prove it with certain financial account statements.
    C. Records that support the basis of property should be kept until the statute of limitations expires for the year that the property was acquired.
    D. Records should show how much of an individual's earnings are subject to self-employment tax.

44. Leslie Oak, an enrolled agent, prepared the 2005 tax return for Ms. Barbara Smith. The Form 1040 tax return of Ms. Smith contained capital gains and losses (Schedule D), wages (Form W-2) and Rental Income (Schedule E). Ms. Smith signed a Form 8453, U.S. Individual Income Tax Declaration for an IRS e-file Return, which allowed Leslie to electronically file Mr. Smith's tax return. Based upon the information in the 2005 tax return of Ms. Smith, which statement below best describes the documents that Leslie Oak is required to maintain for Ms. Smith's 2005 electronically filed tax return?
    A. Leslie Oak must retain two signed copies of Form 8453.
    B. Leslie Oak does not have to retain any of the documents used in preparation of Ms. Smith's return. Leslie should secure from Ms. Smith a list of all the documents used in preparation of the return and that they were all returned to Ms. Smith (Form 8454, Return of Documents Used in Preparation of Electronically Filed Returns).
    C. Leslie Oak must retain a copy of the signed Form 8453 and paper copies of all Forms W-2.
    D. Leslie Oak must only retain one copy of the signed Form 8453.

45. You must keep your records as long as they may be needed for the administration of any provision of the Internal Revenue Code. Generally, this means you must keep records that support items shown on your return until the period of limitations for that return runs out. The period of limitations is the period of time in which you can amend your return to claim a credit or refund, or the IRS can assess additional tax. Which statement listed below is incorrect?
   A. If no other provisions apply, the statute of limitations is 3 years after the return was filed.
   B. If more than 25% of gross income has been omitted from the tax return, the statute of limitations is 6 years after the return was filed, unless the omitted amount was disclosed in the return or in a statement attached to the return, in a manner adequate to apprise the IRS of the nature and amount of the omission.
   C. If a fraudulent return is filed, the statute of limitations is 7 years.
   D. If a tax return is not filed at all, there is no statute of limitations.

46. Bethany timely filed her 2002 1040 tax return and paid the $2,000 tax as shown on the return at the time of filing. The return was subsequently examined and Bethany signed an agreement form for the proposed changes on August 20, 2004. She paid the additional tax due of $5,000 on September 30, 2004. In 2005, Tiffany located missing records, which she believes would make $3,000 of the additional assessment erroneous. Which of the following statements accurately states the date by which Bethany must file a claim for refund to get the $3,000 back?
   A. August 20, 2006, two years from signing the agreement form.
   B. April 15, 2006, three years from the due date of the original return.
   C. September 30, 2006, two years from when the additional tax was paid.
   D. No claim for refund can be filed since an examination agreement form was signed.

47. Samantha Sharp, an enrolled agent, prepares and electronically files Form 1040 tax returns. Samantha prepared the 2004 tax return for Tom, her client. Tom elects to use Form 8453 as his method of signing the return. On March 1, Samantha electronically filed Tom's tax return, which was a refund return. On March 3, Samantha received acknowledgement from the IRS that Tom's return had been accepted. On March 10, Tom received his refund. By what date must Samantha mail the executed Form 8453 to the IRS?
   A. By March 13 (within 3 business days after Tom receives his refund).
   B. By March 5 (within 5 business days after the return was electronically filed).
   C. By March 6 (within 3 business days after the return is acknowledged as accepted by the IRS).
   D. By March 31 (all Forms 8453 signed during the month must be sent to the IRS by the last day of the month).

48. Which of the following electronic return originators (EROs) can accept returns from someone other than directly from the individual taxpayer?

A. Electronic return preparers.
B. Service bureaus.
C. Electronic return collectors.
D. Drop-off collection points.

49. Some returns are not eligible for the IRS electronic filing program. Which item listed below is generally eligible to be filed through the IRS electronic filing program?
    A. Form 1040 returns.
    B. Tax returns for prior years.
    C. Fiscal year tax periods.
    D. Amended tax returns.

50. Michael Young, an Authorized IRS e-file Provider, prepared and electronically transmitted the Form 1040 return of Vivian Blue to the IRS. The IRS notified Michael that the electronic portion of Vivian's return was rejected for processing. Which statement listed below best explains what Michael must do?
    A. Michael must advise the taxpayer that the return may never be filed electronically. Vivian must return to the office, sign a paper copy of Form 1040, and mail it to the Service.
    B. If Michael cannot correct the error with the information in his possession, he must take reasonable steps to inform the taxpayer of the rejection within 24 hours and provide the taxpayer with the reject code(s) accompanied by an explanation.
    C. Michael must mail a paper copy of the return to the IRS with the original Form 8453 that Vivian signed.
    D. If Michael cannot correct the error with the information in his possession, he must take reasonable steps to inform the taxpayer of the rejection by the return due date or within 1 week, whichever date is earlier.

51. Which fee arrangement described below is permissible for an electronic return originator (ERO)?
    A. Fees based on AGI from the tax return.
    B. Fees based on % of refund.
    C. Separate fees for direct deposits.
    D. None of the answers are correct.

52. If a taxpayer's return is rejected by the IRS and the ERO cannot fix the problem and retransmit the return in the time prescribed, the ERO must make reasonable attempts to notify the taxpayer of the reject. How long from the time the return is rejected does the ERO have to try to contact the taxpayer?
    A. 12 hours.
    B. 24 hours.
    C. 48 hours.
    D. One week.

53. Authorized electronic filing providers must notify the IRS of all changes to the information they originally submitted on Form 8633, Application to Participate in the IRS Electronic Filing Program. All revisions may be made using Form 8633, but you may update certain information by letter, using the firm's official letterhead. Which of the following revisions listed below may be submitted by letter and does not require a Form 8633.
    A. Adding an additional principal of a firm, such as a partner or a corporate officer.
    B. Making a change to the Responsible Official listed on Form 8633.
    C. Adding federal/state electronic filing to your list of services.
    D. Deleting a principal that is listed on Form 8633.

54. The contractual agreement for a Refund Anticipation Loan (RAL) is between which of the following?
    A. Taxpayer and lender.
    B. Taxpayer and electronic filing provider.
    C. Electronic filing provider and the lender.
    D. IRS and the taxpayer.

55. Which of the following statements is true regarding electronically filed returns?
    A. A return for a deceased taxpayer may be electronically filed.
    B. U.S. Individual Income Tax Return for tax year 2005 may not be electronically filed after April 15, 2006.
    C. For tax year 2005, only current year tax returns may be electronically filed.
    D. For tax year 2005, all electronically filed returns require a separate signature document to be submitted to the appropriate IRS Center.

56. A Refund Anticipation Loan (RAL) is money borrowed by a taxpayer from a lender based on the taxpayer's anticipated income tax refund. Which of the statements below is true?
    A. All parties to Refund Anticipation Loan agreements, including Electronic Return Originators (EROs), must ensure that taxpayers understand that Refund Anticipation Loans are interest bearing loans and not substitutes for a faster way of receiving a refund.
    B. The IRS has minimal involvement and responsibility for Refund Anticipation Loans.
    C. The Electronic Return Originator should advise the taxpayer that if a direct deposit is not received within the expected time frame, the IRS may be liable to the lender for additional interest on the Refund Anticipation Loan.
    D. The IRS is responsible for ensuring that Refund Anticipation Loan indicators are included in the electronic return data that is transmitted to the IRS.

57. Which of the following is an acceptable method of computation for an Electronic Return Originator fee?
    A. Fees based on time required for preparation.
    B. Fees based on AGI from the tax return.

C. Fees based on percentage of refund.
D. Flat fee identical for all customers.

58. Taxpayers often elect the direct deposit option because it is the fastest way of receiving refunds. Electronic Return Originator should advise the taxpayer of the option to receive his/her refund by direct deposit or paper check. Select the statement below that is true with respect to direct deposit.
    A. The Electronic Return Originator does not have to accept a direct deposit election to a financial institution designated by the taxpayer.
    B. Refunds may be direct deposited to credit card accounts.
    C. The Electronic Return Originator may make a separate charge of only $15 or less as a processing fee if the taxpayer elects direct deposit.
    D. The Electronic Return Originator should caution taxpayers that some financial institutions do not permit the deposit of joint refunds into individual accounts.

59. A Form 1065, U.S. Partnership Return, must be filed electronically or on magnetic media if the number of partners exceeds:
    A. 50
    B. 75
    C. 100
    D. 250

60. The IRS monitors and performs annual suitability checks on authorized IRS electronic filing providers for compliance with the revenue procedure and program requirements. Violations may result in a variety of sanctions. Which statement is true with respect to sanctions the IRS may impose on an electronic filing provider?
    A. The IRS may issue a letter of reprimand or a 1-year suspension as a sanction for a level one infraction in the electronic filing program.
    B. The IRS may impose a period of suspension that includes the remainder of the calendar year in which the suspension occurs, plus the next 2 calendar years, for a level two infraction in the electronic filing program.
    C. The IRS may suspend or expel an authorized IRS electronic filing provider prior to administrative review for a level three infraction in the electronic filing program.
    D. The IRS may not impose a sanction that is greater than a 1-year suspension from the electronic filing program.

61. Which of the following returns may be electronically filed?
    A. Tax returns with fiscal-year periods.
    B. Amended tax returns.
    C. Current-year Form 1040 with foreign address.
    D. Current-year Form 1040 with APO address.

62. Which of the following statements applies to refund application loans?
    A. A refund anticipation loan is money borrowed by the taxpayer from the U.S.

Government.
B. A refund anticipation loan indicator must be included in the electronic return data that is transmitted to the IRS.
C. If the anticipated tax refund is not received after a refund anticipation loan is made, the loan is automatically subtracted from the subsequent years' refunds until paid.
D. The Treasury Department is liable for any loss suffered by taxpayers, electronic return originators, and financial institutions resulting from reduced refunds or from direct deposits not being honored if documentation is provided that correct procedures were followed.

63. Which of the following items represents sufficient documentary evidence to substantiate expenditures for travel, entertainment, or gift expenses?
A. A canceled check written to pay a motel bill on a business trip.
B. A statement from the taxpayer's employer.
C. An account book maintained daily by the taxpayer for business meals (no meal was over $10).
D. Memos on a desk calendar.

64. John Jones, an Enrolled Agent, prepared the 2004 tax return for Mr. William Smith. The return of Mr. Smith contained a schedule "C", wages (Form W-2) and retirement income (Form 1099-R). Mr. Smith signed a Form 8453, U.S. Individual Income Tax Declaration for an IRS electronically filed return, which allowed John Jones to electronically file Mr. Smith's tax return. Based upon the information in the 2004 tax return of Mr. Smith, which statement below describes the documents that Mr. Jones is required to maintain for Mr. Smith's 2004 electronically filed tax return?
A. Mr. Jones must only maintain a paper copy of the tax return and W-2.
B. Mr. Jones must only retain one of the signed Forms 8453.
C. Mr. Jones must retain a copy of the signed Form 8453 and paper copies of Forms W-2 and 1099-R, as well as any supporting documents that are not included in the electronic return data.
D. Mr. Jones does not have to retain any of the documents used in the preparation of Mr. Smith's return. Mr. Jones should secure a signed statement from Mr. Smith that lists all the documents used in the preparation of the return and that they were all returned to Mr. Smith.

7.15 UNIT 7: ANSWERS

1. **(B) Correct**
Section 1.6001-1(e) of the Regulations provides that records should be retained for so long as the contents thereof are material in the administration of any internal revenue law. Keep Copy C of Form W-2 for at least 3 years after the due date for filing your income tax return. However, to help protect your social security benefits, keep Copy C until you begin receiving social security benefits, just in case there is a question about your work record and/or earnings in a particular year.

2. **(B) Correct**
When using electronic storage systems for the purpose of maintaining tax books and records, all requirements that are applicable to hard copy books and records still apply. When replacing hard copy books and records, electronic storage systems must be maintained for as long as they are material to the administration of tax law. An electronic storage system is any system for preparing or keeping your records either by electronic imaging or by transfer to an electronic storage media. The electronic storage system must index, store, preserve, retrieve, and reproduce the electronically stored books and records in legible, readable format. Electronic storage systems are also subject to the same controls and retention guidelines as those imposed on your original hard copy books and records.

3. **(A) Correct**
A checkbook can be used to keep records of both income and expenses. Taxpayers should also keep documents such as sales slips and expense receipts to support claimed income and deductions.

4. **(B) Correct**
The ERO's responsibilities include:
   (a) Timely originating the electronic submission of returns.
   (b) Submitting any required supporting paper documents to the IRS.
   (c) Providing copies to taxpayers.
   (d) Retaining records and making records available to the IRS.
   (e) Accepting returns only from taxpayers and Authorized IRS *e-file* Providers.
   (f) Having only one EFIN for the same firm for use at one location, unless the IRS issued more than one EFIN to the firm for the same location. For this purpose, the business entity is generally the entity that reports on its return the income derived from electronic filing. The IRS may issue more than one EFIN to accommodate a high volume of returns, or as it determines appropriate.
   (g) An ERO must clearly display the firm's "doing business as" name at all locations and sites including Web sites at which the ERO or a third party obtains information from taxpayers for electronic origination of returns by the ERO.

(h) Advising clients of the option to receive their return by direct deposit or paper check.

5. **(B) Correct**
The following types of tax return <u>cannot</u> be filed electronically:
   (1) Amended tax returns.
   (2) Tax returns with fiscal-year tax periods.
   (3) Prior-year tax returns.
   (4) Tax returns with foreign addresses.
   (5) Tax returns of a married couple filing separately in community property states.
   (6) Tax returns for decedents.
   (7) Tax returns with Taxpayer Identification Numbers (TIN) within the range of 900-00-0000 through 999-99-9999.

The tax return for a taxpayer who died within the calendar tax year is a tax return for a decedent.

6. **(B) Correct**
An ERO originates the electronic submission by any one of the following:
   (1) Electronically sending the return to a Transmitter that will transmit the return to the IRS
   (2) Directly transmitting the return to the IRS
   (3) Providing a return to an Intermediate Service Provider for processing prior to transmission to the IRS

7. **(A) Correct**
Authorized electronic filing providers are also bound by the ethical standards contained in circular 230. Authorized electronic filing providers may <u>not</u> base their fees on a percentage of the refund amount or compute their fees using any figure from tax returns. Separate fees may not be charged for direct deposits. An ERO may charge clients a flat fee for assisting those who wish to apply for a RAL. An ERO may also charge one fee for clients who select RALs and a different fee for those who select direct deposits into their own accounts. The serviced for RALs and direct deposit clients are treated as being mutually exclusive and therefore the ERO both differently.

8. **(B) Correct**
Publication 1345 defines a Refund Anticipation Loan as money borrowed by a taxpayer that lender bases on a taxpayer's anticipated income tax refund. The IRS has no involvement in RALs. A RAL is a contract between the taxpayer and the lender. A lender may market a RAL under various commercial or financial product names.

9. **(A) Correct**
If an Authorized IRS *e-file* Provider uses radio, television, Internet, signage, or other methods of communication to advertise IRS *e-file*, the Provider must keep a copy and provide it to the IRS upon request, the text or, if prerecorded, the recorded

advertisement. Provider must retain copies until the <u>end of the calendar year</u> following the last transmission or use.

10. **(B) Correct**

    The Electronic Federal Tax Payment System (EFTPS) is a tax payment system provided free by the U.S. Department of Treasury. Businesses and Individuals can pay all their federal taxes using EFTPS. Individuals can pay their quarterly 1040ES estimated taxes electronically using EFTPS, and they can make payments weekly, monthly, or quarterly. Both business and individual payments can be scheduled in advance. Enrollment is required to use EFTPS.

11. **(B) Correct**

    The following types of tax return <u>cannot</u> be filed electronically:
    (1) Amended tax returns.
    (2) Tax returns with fiscal-year tax periods.
    (3) Prior-year tax returns.
    (4) Tax returns with foreign addresses.
    (5) Tax returns of a married couple filing separately in community property states.
    (6) Tax returns for decedents.
    (7) Tax returns with Taxpayer Identification Numbers (TIN) within the range of 900-00-0000 through 999-99-9999.

    Since Billy's return is an amended return, it cannot be e-filed.

12. **(A) Correct**

    The Electronic Return Originator (ERO) must accept any Direct Deposit election to any eligible financial institution designated by the taxpayer.

13. **(B) Correct**

    Under section 301.7701-15(d)(1), Authorized IRS *e-file* Providers are not tax return preparers for the purpose of assessing most preparer penalties as long as their services are limited to "typing, reproduction, or other mechanical assistance in the preparation of a return or claim for refund."

14. **(A) Correct**

    The Internal Revenue Service e-file Program allows taxpayers to schedule the payment for withdrawal on a future date. Scheduled payments must be effective on or before the return due date. As an example, a Provider may transmit an individual income tax return in February and the taxpayer can specify that the withdrawal be made in April as long as it is on or before the return due date.

15. **(A) Correct**

    Form 8453 (U.S. Individual Income Tax Declaration for an Internal Revenue Service e-file Return) must be signed after the return is prepared and before the electronic data portion of the return is submitted.

16. **(B) Correct**

    The following types of tax return <u>cannot</u> be filed electronically:
    1. Amended tax returns.
    2. Tax returns with fiscal-year tax periods.
    3. Prior-year tax returns.
    4. Tax returns with foreign addresses.
    5. Tax returns of a married couple filing separately in community property states.
    6. Tax returns for decedents.
    7. Tax returns with Taxpayer Identification Numbers (TIN) within the range of 900-00-0000 through 999-99-9999.

    Fred Birch's Form 1040 for tax years 1993 and 1994 are Prior-year tax returns and therefore cannot be e-filed.

17. **(B) Correct**

    EROs may <u>not</u> charge a fee for the electronic transmission of a tax return that is based upon a percentage of the taxpayer's refund amount.

18. **(B) Correct**

    An ERO must take reasonable steps to inform a taxpayer of the rejection of the taxpayer's electronically filed return, regardless of the reason for the rejection or change in amount of tax.

19. **(B) Correct**

    If an Authorized IRS *e-file* Provider uses radio, television, Internet, signage, or other methods of communication to advertise IRS *e-file*, the Provider must keep a copy and provide it to the IRS upon request, the text or, if prerecorded, the recorded advertisement. Provider must retain copies until the <u>end of the calendar year</u> following the last transmission or use.

20. **(A) Correct**

    If the IRS rejects the electronic portion of a taxpayer's individual income tax return for processing and the ERO cannot rectify the reason for the rejection, the ERO must:
    a) Take reasonable steps to inform the taxpayer of the rejection within 24 hours.
    b) Provide the taxpayer with the reject code(s) accompanied by an explanation.

21. **(B) Correct**

    Taxpayers must decide whether to use either a *single-entry* or a *double-entry* bookkeeping system. The single-entry system of bookkeeping is the simplest to maintain, but it may not be suitable for everyone. Taxpayers may find the double-entry system better because it has built-in checks and balances to assure accuracy and control. There is no specified method as long as the method used accurately reflects income and expenses.

22. **(A) Correct**
    Federal law does not require a taxpayer to maintain any special form of records, but the records must be such that the taxpayer can prepare a complete and accurate income tax return.

23. **(A) Correct**
    Adequate records must include sufficient documents (sales slips, invoices, canceled checks, etc.) that clearly establish the income, deductions, and credits shown on the return.

24. **(A) Correct**
    Microfilm and microfiche reproductions of general books of accounts, such as cash books, journals, voucher registers, and ledgers, are accepted by the Internal Revenue Service for record keeping if they comply with applicable revenue procedures.

25. **(A) Correct**
    Generally, cash gifts from relatives are non-taxable; therefore when someone receives a cash gift from a relative, he/she should maintain a record to substantiate its receipt in order to prevent it from later being characterized as taxable income.

26. **(B) Correct**
    If a practitioner believes that the information is *privileged*, he/she should not furnish the records or information to the IRS.

27. **(B) Correct**
    Under Reg. Sec. 31.6001-5(a)(13), employers are required to retain records of Form W-4 for each employee. These records must be retained for at least 4 years.

28. **(A) Correct**
    You must keep your records as long as they may be needed for the administration of any provision of the Internal Revenue Code. Keep records that support an item of income or a deduction appearing on a return until the period of limitations for the return runs out. A period of limitations is the period of time after which no legal action can be brought. Generally, that means you must keep your records for at least 3 years from when your tax return was due or filed or within 2 years of the date the tax was paid, whichever is later. Purchasing property with a long life, adopting the LIFO method of inventory, and changing a method of accounting are examples of business decisions that may require a person to maintain records longer than the general requirement of 3 years after the return was due or filed or 2 years after the date the tax was paid, whichever is later.

29. **(A) Correct**
    Keep records relating to property until the period of limitations expires for the year in which you dispose of the property in a taxable disposition. You must keep these records

to figure your basis for computing gain or loss when you sell or otherwise dispose of the property. Generally, if you received property in a nontaxable exchange, your basis in that property is the same as the basis of the property you gave up. You must keep the records on the old property, as well as the new property, until the period of limitations expires for the year in which you dispose of the new property in a taxable disposition.

30. **(B) Correct**
    If the electronic portion of a taxpayer's return is acknowledged as rejected by the IRS due to a substantive change, the electronic return originator (ERO) is required to notify the taxpayer that his/her return has not been filed.

31. **(A) Correct**
    Providers may not base their fees on a percentage of the refund amount or compute their fees using any figure from tax returns.

32. **(B) Correct**
    Employers are required to keep records on employment taxes (income tax withholding, Social Security, Medicare, and federal unemployment tax) for at least 4 years after the due date of the return or after the date the tax was paid, whichever is later.

33. **(B) Correct**
    If commercially available computer software is used to summarize business expenses, the receipts and invoices need to be kept.

34. **(B) Correct**
    Rev. Proc. 98-50 states that an ERO must retain a copy of Form 8453.

35. **(B) Correct**
    The following types of tax return cannot be filed electronically:
    (1) Amended tax returns.
    (2) Tax returns with fiscal-year tax periods.
    (3) Prior-year tax returns.
    (4) Tax returns with foreign addresses.
    (5) Tax returns of a married couple filing separately in community property states.
    (6) Tax returns for decedents.
    (7) Tax returns with Taxpayer Identification Numbers (TIN) within the range of 900-00-0000 through 999-99-9999.
    Candy's year 1 individual tax return is a prior-year return and therefore cannot be e-filed.

36. **(B) Correct**
    Keep Copy C of Form W-2 for at least 3 years after the due date for filing your income tax return. However, to help protect your social security benefits, keep Copy C until you begin receiving social security benefits, just in case there is a question about your work

record and/or earnings in a particular year.

37. **(D) Correct**
Providers may <u>not</u> base their fees on a percentage of the refund amount or compute their fees using any figure from tax returns. They also must <u>not</u> charge a separate fee for a Direct Deposit. Therefore, neither the Fix Tax Co. nor the No Tax Co. is in compliance with electronic filing fee restrictions.

38. **(B) Correct**
A canceled check <u>does not</u> always prove payment and establishes a tax deduction.

39. **(C) Correct**
Employers are required to keep records on employment taxes (income tax withholding, Social Security, Medicare, and federal unemployment tax) for at least <u>4 years</u> after the due date of the return or after the date the tax was paid, whichever is later.

40. **(A) Correct**
Reg. Sec. 31.6001-5(a) requires every employer to withhold income tax on wages must keep records of all remuneration paid to the employees. Employee's date of birth is not a specific record required to be kept for income tax withholding.

41. **(D) Correct**

	If you:	The period is:
A	Owe additional tax and (2), (3), and (4) do not apply to you	3 years
B	Do not report income that you should and it is more than 25% of the gross income shown on your return	6 years
C	File a fraudulent return	No limit
D	Do not file a return	No limit
E	File a claim for credit or refund after you filed your return	The later of 3 years or 2 years after tax was paid.
F	File a claim for a loss from worthless securities	7 years

42. **(C) Correct**
A period of limitations is the period of time after which no legal action can be brought. Generally, that means you must keep your records for at least 3 years from when your tax return was due or filed or within 2 years of the date the tax was paid, whichever is later. Because Nancy filed her return on May 1, 2004, the 3-year limitation period ending on May 1, 2007 is the amount of time the IRS has to assess additional tax.

43. **(C) Correct**

Keep records relating to property until the period of limitations expires for the year in which you <u>dispose</u> of the property in a taxable disposition. You must keep these records to figure your basis for computing gain or loss when you sell or otherwise dispose of the property. Generally, if you received property in a nontaxable exchange, your basis in that property is the same as the basis of the property you gave up. You must keep the records on the old property, as well as the new property, until the period of limitations expires for the year in which you dispose of the new property in a taxable <u>disposition</u>.

44. **(C) Correct**

Under Rev. Proc. 98-50, an income tax return preparer must furnish a completed copy of any return or refund claim pertaining to tax that (s)he prepares for the taxpayer either before or at the same time as (s)he presents the return to him/her for signing. The preparer or employer of the preparer must retain a completed copy of the return for a 3-year period. A return filed in the Form 1040 IRS e-file program consists of electronically transmitted data and certain paper documents. The paper portion of the return consists of Form 8453 and other paper documents that cannot be electronically transmitted. Therefore Ms. Oak must retain a copy of Form 8453

45. **(C) Correct**

See answer # 41.

46. **(C) Correct**

Taxpayers must keep your records as long as they may be needed for the administration of any provision of the Internal Revenue Code. They must keep records that support an item of income or a deduction appearing on a return until the period of limitations for the return runs out. A period of limitations is the period of time after which no legal action can be brought. Generally, that means one must keep your records for at least 3 years from when the tax return was due or filed or within 2 years of the date the tax was paid, whichever is later. If Bethany files for a credit or refund after she files her return, then the statute of limitations is the later of 3 years or 2 years after the tax was paid. Since she paid the most recent assessment on September 30, 2004, Bethany has until September 30, 2006 to file a claim for a refund.

47. **(C) Correct**

When a taxpayer elects to use Form 8453 as the method of signing the return, the return preparer must submit Form 8453 within <u>3 business days</u> after the return is acknowledged as accepted by the IRS.

48. **(B) Correct**

In certain situations, under section 7216(b)(2), disclosure of tax return information among Authorized IRS *e-file* Providers for the purpose of electronically filing a return is permissible. For example, an ERO may pass on tax return information to an Intermediate Service Provider and/or a Transmitter for the purpose of having an electronic return formatted and transmitted to the Service.

49. **(A) Correct**
The following types of tax return <u>cannot</u> be filed electronically:
(1) Amended tax returns.
(2) Tax returns with fiscal-year tax periods.
(3) Prior-year tax returns.
(4) Tax returns with foreign addresses.
(5) Tax returns of a married couple filing separately in community property states.
(6) Tax returns for decedents.
(7) Tax returns with Taxpayer Identification Numbers (TIN) within the range of 900-00-0000 through 999-99-9999.
Form 1040 returns for the current tax-year may be e-filed through the Internal Revenue Service electronic filing program.

50. **(B) Correct**
If the IRS rejects the electronic portion of a taxpayer's individual income tax return for processing and the ERO cannot rectify the reason for the rejection, the ERO must:
a) Take reasonable steps to inform the taxpayer of the rejection within 24 hours.
b) Provide the taxpayer with the reject code(s) accompanied by an explanation and the sequence number of each reject code(s).

51. **(D) Correct**
An ERO must:
1) Advise taxpayers of the option to receive their refund by paper check or direct deposit.
2) Not charge a separate fee for a Direct Deposit.
3) Accept any Direct Deposit election to any eligible financial institution designated by the taxpayer.
4) Ensure that the taxpayer is eligible to choose Direct Deposit.
5) Caution the taxpayer that once the electronic portion of the return has been accepted for processing by the Service:
   a) the Direct Deposit election cannot be rescinded;
   b) the routing number of the financial institution cannot be changed; and
   c) the taxpayer's account number cannot be changed; and
6) Advise the taxpayer that refund information is available by calling the appropriate IRS phone number.

52. **(B) Correct**
See answer # 50.

53. **(C) Correct**
If a Provider is unable to update its IRS *e-file* Application electronically it may notify the IRS of changes to the below information by letter, using the firm's official letterhead:

(a) All addresses
(b) All telephone and fax numbers
(c) E-mail addresses
(d) Contact persons
(e) Form types to be e-filed
(f) Transmission protocols
(g) Adding Federal/State e-file
(h) Changes to Foreign Filer information

Form 8633 (Application to Participate in the IRS Electronic Filing Program) is used to make the above-mentioned changes.

54. (A) Correct

Publication 1345 defines a Refund Anticipation Loan as money borrowed by a taxpayer that lender bases on a taxpayer's anticipated income tax refund. A RAL is a contract between the taxpayer and the lender. A lender may market a RAL under various commercial or financial product names.

55. (C) Correct

The following types of tax return cannot be filed electronically:
(1) Amended tax returns.
(2) Tax returns with fiscal-year tax periods.
(3) Prior-year tax returns.
(4) Tax returns with foreign addresses.
(5) Tax returns of a married couple filing separately in community property states.
(6) Tax returns for decedents.
(7) Tax returns with Taxpayer Identification Numbers (TIN) within the range of 900-00-0000 through 999-99-9999.

Form 1040 returns for the current tax-year may be e-filed through the Internal Revenue Service electronic filing program.

56. (A) Correct

a) Any entity that is involved in the Form 1040 IRS *e-file* Program, including a financial institution that accepts direct deposits of income tax refunds, has an obligation to every taxpayer who applies for a RAL to clearly explain to the taxpayer that a RAL is in fact a loan and not a substitute for or a quicker way of receiving an income tax refund. An Authorized IRS *e-file* Provider must advise the taxpayer that if a Direct Deposit is not timely, the taxpayer may be liable to the lender for additional interest on the RAL.
b) An Authorized IRS *e-file* Provider may assist a taxpayer in applying for a RAL.
c) An Authorized IRS *e-file* Provider may charge a flat fee to assist a taxpayer in applying for a RAL. The fee must be identical for all of the Authorized IRS *e-file* Provider's customers and must not be related to the amount of the refund or a RAL. The Authorized IRS *e-file* Provider must not accept a fee from a financial institution for any service connected with a RAL that is contingent upon the

amount of the refund or a RAL.
d) The IRS has no responsibility for the payment of any fees associated with the preparation of a return, the transmission of the electronic portion of a return or a RAL.
e) An Authorized IRS *e-file* Provider may disclose tax information to the lending financial institution in connection with an application for a RAL only with the taxpayer's written consent as specified in §301.7216-3(b).
f) An Authorized IRS *e-file* Provider that is also the return preparer and the financial institution or other lender that makes an RAL, may not be related taxpayers.

57. (D) Correct

See answer #56

58. (D) Correct
The Electronic Return Originator should caution taxpayers that some financial institutions do not permit the deposit of joint refunds into individual accounts.

59. (C) Correct
A Form 1065, U.S. Partnership Return, must be filed electronically or on magnetic media if the number of partners exceeds 100.

60. (C) Correct
The IRS may suspend or expel an authorized IRS electronic filing provider prior to administrative review for a level three infraction in the electronic filing program.

61. (D) Correct
Tax returns with foreign addresses <u>cannot</u> be filed electronically. APO and FPO addresses are considered as U.S. addresses.

62. (B) Correct
A refund anticipation loan indicator must be included in the electronic return data that is transmitted to the IRS.

63. (C) Correct
An account book maintained daily by the taxpayer for business meals would meet the rules for substantiation.

64. (C) Correct
Mr. Jones must retain a copy of the signed Form 8453 and paper copies of Forms W-2 and 1099-R, as well as any supporting documents that are not included in the electronic return data.

Made in the USA
Lexington, KY
06 August 2011